The Lower Depths, Summerfolk, Children of the Sun, Barbarians, Enemies

Modern, accurate and stageable translations of five of Gorky's plays, four of which have been revived and staged by the Royal Shakespeare Company. The selection, translated by Kitty Hunter-Blair and Jeremy Brooks, is introduced by Edward Braun, Professor of Drama at Bristol University.

The Lower Depths: first staged by the Moscow Art theatre in 1902, and now recognised as 'one of this century's great seminal works' (*The Guardian*). 'This translation is . . . an excellently restrained and sober piece of work . . . it has right weight, a good balance between the earthy concrete side of the play and its spiritual content.' (*Financial Times*)

Summerfolk: First staged at the Passage Theatre, St Petersburg, 1904. Seen in the light of Chekhov's *The Cherry Orchard*, which opened in the same year, *Summerfolk* depicts a society after the disintegration of feudalism, with a new class of businessmen, intellectuals and professionals.

Children of the Sun: Completed in prison in 1905 and premièred in St Petersburg in the same year. Leading Petersburg critic Alexander Kugel wrote: 'If *Summerfolk* boxed the ears of the intelligentsia, the *Children of the Sun* spits in their face.'

Barbarians: Published and staged in 1906. Anatol Lunacharsky (later to become Minister of Culture under Lenin) said: 'The moral struggle being waged throughout Russia between industrial capitalism and the petty bourgeoisie will not be quick to subside . . . (Gorky) helps us to understand and assess the mighty phenomenon of this war between the two forms of barbarism through the direct experience of real people.'

Enemies: Apart from two early productions in distant provinces, it was not performed in Russia until 1935. 'Maxim Gorky's 65-year-old play is a real discovery, the missing link between Chekhov and the Russian Revolution . . . Gorky's *Lower Depths* may be the greater play, but *Enemies* was surely his most necessary one.' *Observer*

MAXIM GORKY was born Alexei Maximovich Peshkov in Nizhny Novgorod, 225 miles east of Moscow, in 1868. By 1878 both his parents were dead and he spent his youth as a nomadic labourer. In 1898 his collection *Stories and Sketches* was published and proved an immediate success. His plays include *The Lower Depths* (1902), *Summerfolk* (1904), *Children of the Sun* (1905), *Barbarians* and *Enemies* (1906) and *Yegor Bulichev* (1932). His other books include *Childhood* and *My Universities* and the novel *The Mother*. A socialist from his early days, he never joined the Communist Party. He offered qualified support to the Soviet state after 1918, living abroad from 1924 to 1932. In 1934 he became head of the Writers' Union but his work showed an increasing awareness that something had gone wrong with the revolution. He died in 1936.

MAXIM GORKY

Five Plays

Edited and introduced by Edward Braun

The Lower Depths
Summerfolk
Children of the Sun
Barbarians
Enemies

translated by Kitty Hunter-Blair
and Jeremy Brooks

Methuen Drama

METHUEN WORLD CLASSICS

This collection first published as a Methuen paperback original in
Great Britain in 1988 by Methuen London Ltd.
Reissued with a new cover design 1994
by Methuen Drama
an imprint of Reed Consumer Books Ltd
Michelin House, 81 Fulham Road, London SW3 6RB
and Auckland, Melbourne, Singapore and Toronto
and distributed in the United States of America
by Heinemann, a division of Reed Publishing (USA) Inc
361 Hanover Street, Portsmouth, New Hampshire, NH 03801 3959

The Lower Depths first published in this translation by
Eyre Methuen Ltd in 1973, reprinted in 1985
Reprinted in Methuen's World Dramatists in 1988
Copyright © 1973 by Kitty Hunter-Blair and Jeremy Brooks
Summerfolk first published in this translation in this edition.
Copyright © 1988 by Kitty Hunter-Blair and Jeremy Brooks
Children of the Sun first published in this translation in this edition.
Copyright © 1988 by Kitty Hunter-Blair and Jeremy Brooks
Barbarians first published in this translation in this edition.
Copyright © 1988 by Kitty Hunter-Blair and Jeremy Brooks
Enemies first published in this translation in this edition.
Reprinted in Methuen's World Dramatists in 1988
Copyright © 1988 by Kitty Hunter-Blair and Jeremy Brooks
Introduction copyright © 1988 Edward Braun

British Library Cataloguing in Publication Data

Gorkii, Maskim, *1868–1936*
Gorky, five plays.–(World dramatists).
I. Title II. Hunter-Blair, Kitty
III. Brooks, Jeremy IV. Series
891.72'3

ISBN 0-413-18110-3

The painting on the front cover is 'A Humble Caller' by Illarion Prianishnikov.

Printed and bound in Great Britain by
Cox & Wyman Ltd, Reading, Berkshire

These translations are fully protected by copyright. Any enquiries
concerning the rights for professional or amateur stage production
should be made before rehearsal to the authors' agents:
Casarotto Ramsay, National House, 60–66 Wardour Street, London W1V 3HP

Applications for the right to perform the plays in North America
should be made to the Toby Cole Agency, 234 West 44th Street, Suite 402,
Sardi Building, New York, N.Y. 10036.

Contents

Maxim Gorky: A Chronology

1868*   16 March: Born, Alexei Maximovich Peshkov, in Nizhny Novgorod (now Gorky), 225 miles east of Moscow. Mother from a family of dyers; father a joiner, later a wharf-manager.

1871   Father, aged thirty-one, dies of cholera, caught from his son.

1873   Mother leaves Alexei to be brought up by his Grandmother.

1879   Mother, aged thirty-seven, dies of consumption. Grandfather sends Alexei away to earn his own living.

1879–1884   Nomadic labourer: boot-boy, errand-boy, bird-catcher, dishwasher on Volga steamers, assistant in an ikon shop. Self-education begins.

1884   Discovers Chekhov's short stories. Arrives in Kazan, hoping to enter University, but fails to get a place. Works as a stevedore, meets students, intellectuals, workers, revolutionaries. Works in a bakery. Studies the violin, tries to fall in love, but fails at both.

1887   Death of Grandmother and Grandfather.

1887   December: tries to commit suicide, succeeds only in damaging left lung.

1888   Works in a fishery on the Caspian Sea, then as a railway night-watchman. Arrested for the first time on suspicion of subversive activities.

1889   Toys with Tolstoyism and dreams of setting up a Tolstoyan commune. Goes to Moscow, hoping to meet Tolstoy, but fails to find him at home. Shows his verse to the elderly Populist writer Korolenko, whose gentle criticism causes him to tear up his manuscripts and vow never to write again.

1891   To Tiflis. Works in railway paintshop.

1891–1892   Makes first long journey on foot through the regions of the lower Volga, the Don, the Ukraine, the Crimea and the Caucasus.

1892   September: First story, *Makar Chudra*, published in Tiflis newspaper. Now assumes the pen-name 'Maxim Gorky' ('the bitter').

1892–1894   Runs away to Nizhny Novgorod with married woman, Olga Kaminskaya. Continues to write verse and stories, gets work as a clerk. Under constant police surveillance.

1894   Leaves Olga to work on newspaper in Samara, which publishes a number of his stories.

1895   Story, *Chelkash*, published in Populist magazine *Russian Wealth*.

1896   August: Married in Samara to Ekaterina Pavlovna Volzhina, a Populist radical and proof-reader on *The Samara Gazette*. Return to Nizhny Novgorod. Contracts tuberculosis, recuperates in the Crimea, paid for by a literary fund.

1897   Birth of son, Maxim.

1898   May: Arrested 'for dissemination of socialist ideas amongst workers' in Tiflis five years earlier. Spends three weeks in prison under interrogation, then released under close surveillance. Starts to write first novel, *Foma Gordeev*. New left-wing press publishes two volumes of Gorky's *Stories and Sketches* with instant success that makes him a national celebrity. Starts to correspond with Chekhov, greatly valuing his opinion. Admires *Uncle Vanya*, which he sees performed in Nizhny Novgorod.

1899   Meets Chekhov in Yalta. First visit to St.

Petersburg. Regards himself as 'close to Marxism' and becomes literary editor of Marxist periodical *Zhizn* ('Life'). Sees *Uncle Vanya* at Moscow Art Theatre. *Foma Gordeev* published.

1900   January: Meets Tolstoy in Moscow. He calls Gorky 'a real man of the people'.

April: Meets the Moscow Art Theatre company with Chekhov in Yalta and is encouraged to write for the theatre. Soon begins work on the play, *The Lower Depths*, but has the idea for another play, *Philistines*, as well.

1901   April–May: Imprisoned in Nizhny Novgorod for taking part in student demonstration in St. Petersburg.

May: birth of daughter, Katya.

September: Completes *Philistines*.

1902   February: Elected Honorary Academician in *Belles Lettres*. Election cancelled on instructions of Tsar Nicholas II, leading to resignation in protest of Chekhov and Korolenko.

26 March: Première of *Philistines* given by Moscow Art Theatre on tour in St. Petersburg.

May–August: Gorky exiled in Arzamas.

June: Completes *The Lower Depths*.

18 December: Première of *The Lower Depths* at the Moscow Art Theatre.

1903   January: *The Lower Depths* staged at Max Reinhardt's Kleines Theater in Berlin and runs for over 500 performances. Soon afterwards: London première by Stage Society. Following meeting with Lenin's supporters in Moscow, Gorky gives considerable financial support to the Social Democratic Party.

1904   April: Reads first draft of his play, *Summerfolk*, to Moscow Art Theatre company. Following criticism of the text by Nemirovich-Danchenko, Gorky reworks it extensively then offers it to other theatres.

10 November: Première of *Summerfolk* at Passage Theatre, St. Petersburg.

1905   9 January: Gorky involved in the organisation of the workers' demonstrations which are brutally suppressed in the slaughter of 'Bloody Sunday'. Gorky drafts proclamation calling for 'a united struggle against the Autocracy' and is again arrested and imprisoned.

14 February: Released from the Peter and Paul Fortress following an international outcry. Completes his next play, *Children of the Sun*, during his imprisonment.

12 October: Première of *Children of the Sun* at Vera Komissarzhevskaya's theatre in St. Petersburg, twelve days before the first Moscow Art Theatre performance.

27 November: First meeting with Lenin in St. Petersburg.

December: Organises supplies for the Moscow armed uprising.

1906   4 January: Takes refuge in Finland, but is forced to leave after five weeks. Moves on to Berlin. Gorky is accompanied by the actress, Maria Andreeva, who is now his common-law wife though Gorky has never formally divorced.

March: *Barbarians* published and given first performance in Riga.

10 April: Arrives in New York in order to campaign against a loan to the Tsarist government and to raise funds for the Bolsheviks. Meets figures from the artistic and political spheres, including Mark Twain and H.G. Wells, but is attacked in the Hearst press for his 'immoral' relationship with Andreeva and forced out of public life.

During the Summer: Lives privately with the

Martin family, first on Staten Island and then in the Adirondacks. Completes his novel, *The Mother*, and the play, *Enemies*.

August: Daughter dies of meningitis in Nizhny Novgorod.

13 October: Gorky and Andreeva sail from New York for Italy.

2 November: Arrive on Capri, where Gorky spends the next seven years.

December: *Enemies* published in Stuttgart and St. Petersburg. Serialisation of *The Mother* starts in Appleton's Magazine, New York, followed by translations into numerous other languages.

22 February: Première of *Enemies* in Poltava, despite complete ban on the play following publication.

1907   April: The publishing house, 'Knowledge', starts serialisation of *The Mother* in Russia.

May: Attends Fifth Congress of the Russian Social Democratic Party in London. Meets Shaw and Thomas Hardy, and re-encounters H.G. Wells.

1908   January: Completes the play, *The Last Ones*, which is banned in Russia for its portrayal of the police as 'inveterate scoundrels' but performed in Tashkent in June.

June: Lenin visits Gorky on Capri.

Publication of *A Confession*, the novel in which Gorky attempts a fusion of Marxism and Christianity, to become a key text in the 'God-building' heresy of Russian Marxism.

1909   July–December: With Bogdanov and Lunacharsky sets up a school for revolutionary Russian workers on Capri. Lenin attacks 'God-builders' and refuses to have any part in the school.

1910   July: Lenin and Gorky reconciled – Lenin

visits Gorky again on Capri.

During the Summer: Completion of two further plays, *Queer People* and *Vassa Zheleznova*.

September: Première of *Queer People* at the New Dramatic Theatre, St. Petersburg.

1911 February: Première of *Vassa Zheleznova* at the Nezlobin Theatre, Moscow.

Stanislavsky visits Capri and discusses the development of his 'System' with Gorky.

1912–1913 Writes *Childhood*, the first part of his autobiographical trilogy.

1912 April: First edition of *Pravda* appears in Russia, with considerable financial assistance from Gorky. But due to the cooling of his relations with the Bolsheviks he contributes no articles to the paper.

1913 February: On the 300th anniversary of the Romanov dynasty an amnesty for political exiles guilty of no violent crimes is announced. Lenin urges Gorky to return but he remains apprehensive.

July: Completes *The Zykovs* but refuses to give the play to the Moscow Art Theatre because he objects to their apolitical staging of Dostoyevsky.

31 December: Returns with Maria Andreeva to St. Petersburg.

1914 During the Summer: Works on the second part of his autobiography, *My Apprenticeship*.

1915 December: Launches new monthly literary journal, *Letopis* ('Annals').

Opposes Russia's participation in the Great War.

1917 April: Founds and edits *New Life*, a daily newspaper which becomes the most widely read amongst the intelligentsia. In his column 'Untimely Thoughts' Gorky regularly criticises

all factions, including the Bolsheviks. After
the February Revolution in 1917 he opposes
Len-
in's plans for a further Bolshevik rising. He
himself is attacked by the Right as a Bolshevik
and pro-German, and by the Leninist Left as
a proponent of 'false unification'.

1918   July: Premières of *The Last Ones* and *The
              Zykovs* in Petrograd.
              New Life forced to cease publication. Gorky is
              reconciled with Lenin but remains critical of
              the Bolshevik regime.
              December: Elected to the Executive Commit-
              tee of the Petrograd Workers' and Soldiers'
              Soviet and to its presidium.

1918–1921   Throughout the Civil War and after, Gorky
              regularly intercedes with Lenin to protect
              intellectuals and sets up organisations to
              improve their living conditions.

1921   16 October: Is persuaded finally by Lenin to
              leave Russia for medical treatment abroad, at
              the same time distancing him from hostility
              within the Party. He recuperates at a sanator-
              ium in the Black Forest.

1922–1924   Travels about Europe. Completes *My Univer-
              sities*.

1924   21 January: Death of Lenin.
              April: Gorky settles in Sorrento.
              Continues autobiographical writings.

1926   January: Completes *The Artamanov Business*.

1927   22 October: Gorky's 35th anniversary as a
              writer is celebrated at the Communist Aca-
              demy in Moscow and he is declared to be 'a
              proletarian writer'.

1928–1932   Spends the winters in Sorrento and the sum-
              mers in Moscow, eventually returning to Rus-
              sia for good.

1930–1932   Completes his final trilogy of plays, *Somov and*

Others, Yegor Bulychov and Others, Dostigayev and Others.

1932   September: Gorky's 40th anniversary as a writer. He is awarded the Order of Lenin, the Gorky Literary Institute is founded in Moscow, and *Yegor Bulychov* is given simultaneous premières in Moscow and Leningrad, initiating the revival of his earlier plays. Nizhny Novgorod is renamed Gorky.

1933   September: Première of revised version of *Enemies* at the Pushkin Theatre, Leningrad, followed shortly by a second production in Moscow.

1934   10 May: Membership ticket No 1 of Union of Soviet Writers issued to Gorky.

1934   11 May: Death of son, Maxim.
        August–September: First All-Union Congress of Soviet Writers. Gorky elected chairman. Delivers opening and closing address.

1935   October: First performance of *Enemies* at Moscow Art Theatre.
        December: Gorky completes revision of *Vassa Zheleznova*. Over next five years it is staged by almost every major Soviet theatre.

1935–1936   Gorky is twice refused a passport to travel abroad.
        18 June: Gorky dies of a lung infection associated with his tubercular condition. Rumours of suspicious circumstances have never been clarified.

*Dates for events in Russia before 1918 are given according to the 'old style' or Julian calendar which was thirteen days behind the Gregorian calendar adopted in the West.

Introduction

In June 1898 the newly-formed Moscow Art Theatre began rehearsals for its inaugural season. In his opening address to the company Stanislavsky said:

> What we are undertaking is not a simple private affair but a social task. Never forget that we are striving to brighten the dark existence of the poor classes, to afford them minutes of happiness and aesthetic uplift, to relieve the murk that envelops them. Our aim is to create the first intelligent, moral, popular theatre, and to this end we are dedicating our lives.[1]

High-flown as these sentiments may sound, there can be no doubting the sincerity of Stanislavsky and his co-director Nemirovich-Danchenko; in the seasons that followed it was confirmed by a repertoire that featured the plays of Chekhov, Hauptmann, Ibsen and Tolstoy, all of them dramatists whose preoccupation with social problems aroused the nervous vigilance of Tsarist censorship. By this time Russia was seething with social unrest and the government, rightly fearful of the threat posed by the left-wing intelligentsia, was quick to seize on any pretext for the ruthless suppression of dissent. In this situation there were those who felt that more was required of the Art Theatre than decent liberal concern. In January 1899 the young Meyerhold, then a member of the company, wrote after a rehearsal by Stanislavsky of *Hedda Gabler*:

> Are we as actors required merely to act? Surely we should be thinking as well. We need to know *why* we are acting, *what* we are acting, and *whom* we are instructing or attacking through our performance. And to do that we need to know the psychological and social significance of the play, to establish whether a given character is positive or negative, to understand which society or section of society the author is for or against.[2]

The writer who left least doubt as to where he stood was Maxim Gorky, whose first two volumes of sketches and stories had been published the previous year and had immediately secured for him at the age of thirty a popularity shared only by Tolstoy and Chekhov amongst living Russian authors. Already imprisoned twice for his connections with known revolutionaries, Gorky was kept under constant surveillance by a regime alarmed by his unique influence over the young and by the fervour with which he championed the poor and underprivileged. An early outcome of Gorky's literary success was his friendship with Chekhov, who was eight years his senior. They met first in Yalta in spring 1898 and it was there two years later that Chekhov introduced him to the Moscow Art Theatre company when they brought their productions of *The Seagull* and *Uncle Vanya* to the Crimea. Though critical of the unrestrained emotion and expansive rhetoric of Gorky's stories, Chekhov realised that he might become the dramatist that the mood of the times demanded. Deeply respectful of Chekhov, Stanislavsky and Nemirovich-Danchenko were easily persuaded, and with their encouragement Gorky was soon considering the idea of scenes depicting 'a lodging-house, foul air, trestle-beds, a long dreary winter' and called initially 'Without Sunlight'. Before long, however, he had begun work on a second play, *Philistines*, which was completed first in September 1901, despite the interruption of a further month's imprisonment for his part in a student demonstration in Nizhny Novgorod.

Gorky was persuaded that it would be wiser to submit *Philistines* to the censor rather than wait until he had completed *The Lower Depths*, a work whose compassionate portrayal of rogues and vagabonds was precisely the kind of subject that had already gained him such notoriety. So it was *Philistines*, a play with far more overt political implications, that was staged first on 26 March 1902[3] when the Art Theatre was on tour in Petersburg. It depicts the pettiness of the Russian lower-middle class in contrast with the vigour and optimism of the 'new man' of proletarian stock. With nervousness verging on paranoia, the authorities policed the select first-night subscription audience with agents clumsily disguised as ushers in evening dress. Almost inevitably the production itself proved a decorous anti-climax, partly because of the mutilation wrought on the text by the censor, partly because of the play's own looseness of form, but perhaps above all because of the company's own apprehension of its likely impact. Stanislavsky and Nemirovich-Danchenko outdid even the censor in excising anything that might cause offence, and Nemirovich went in person up to the gallery to dissuade young spectators from demonstrating, for fear of getting Gorky banned altogether. The significance of *Philistines* was not lost on Chekhov; whilst critical of the 'conservatism of its form', he wrote:

> Gorky is the first in Russia and in the world at large to have expressed contempt and loathing for the petty bourgeoisie and he has done it at the precise moment when Russia is ready for protest.[4]

Exiled once again, this time in remote Arzamas, Gorky completed *The Lower Depths* in the summer of 1902, some eight months after *Philistines*. Again the censor demanded major surgery:

> It is absolutely essential to change the policeman Medvediev into an ordinary retired soldier, since the participation of a custodian of the law in the escapades of the inmates of a doss-house is inadmissible on the stage. The end of Act Two must be substantially shortened out of respect for the deceased woman in order to remove the indelicate conversation that follows her death. Cuts are required in the speeches of the pilgrim – in particular his remarks concerning God, the after-life, deception and so on. Finally, the various crude or indecent expressions throughout the play must be removed.[5]

In Nemirovich-Danchenko's opinion the text was passed finally (with some eighty cuts) only because the authorities were convinced that it would fail anyway. If so, it was a monumental miscalculation: the opening night in Moscow on 18 December 1902, with Stanislavsky himself playing Satin and Chekhov's wife Olga Knipper as Nastya, equalled the triumph of *The Seagull* in the same theatre four years earlier. The house was in an uproar at the final curtain and a bewildered Gorky took over fifteen calls. Although differing widely in their interpretations, the Moscow critics were unanimous in their praise of both play and production. Chekhov's response had been more qualified; after his first reading of the newly completed text he wrote to Gorky:

> It is new and without question good. Act Two is especially fine – the best, the strongest, and when I read it, above all at the end, I almost jumped with pleasure . . . You have left the most interesting characters out of Act Four (apart from the Actor) and you would do well to consider what you lose by that.[6]

Then he added admiringly, 'The Actor's death is terrifying. You hit the spectator in the face without warning'. But to others he gave the opinion that it would have been better treated as a short story and he didn't like Gorky behaving 'like a priest'.

Initially Gorky was delighted with the production, which captured totally the atmosphere of the Moscow slums and faithfully re-created the characters of the down-and-outs who had been his close comrades in his youth. But soon he had second thoughts about both the play and its reception; in particular he was concerned at the significance of the pilgrim Luka who was generally taken to be the embodiment of brotherly love, with little account taken of his hurried departure at the first sign of real trouble, or of the trail of ruin and disillusion that he leaves in his wake. In 1903 Gorky said in an interview:

> In the play there is no opposition to what Luka says. The basic question that I wanted to pose was: what is better, truth or compassion? What is more necessary? Should compassion be carried to the point where it involves deception, as in Luka's case? This is not a subjective matter, but a question of universal philosophy. Luka represents compassion to the point of deception as a means

of salvation, but there is in the play no representative of truth to oppose him. Kleshch, the Baron, Pepel are facts of life – and one needs to distinguish between facts and the truth, which are far from one and the same thing . . .[7]

Significantly, Gorky makes no mention here of Satin. Some time before, he had written: 'Satin's speech about truth is pallid. But apart from Satin there is nobody to give it to, and he is incapable of expressing it more clearly. As it stands, it sounds strange coming from him.'[8]

Although hastily banned from all other Russian theatres, *The Lower Depths* continued to run with huge success at the Moscow Art Theatre, becoming a permanent fixture in the repertoire up to the present day. In January 1903 it was staged by Richard Vallentin at Reinhardt's Kleines Theater in Berlin with Reinhardt himself as Luka, and played for over 500 performances in two years. In the same year the play was given its London première by the Stage Society, then in 1905 Lugné-Poe directed it in Paris with Eleonora Duse as Vassilissa. Since then it has been constantly in the international repertoire and has been twice filmed: by Jean Renoir in 1936 as *Les Bas-fonds* with Louis Jouvet as the Baron and Jean Gabin as Pepel, and by Kurosawa in 1957 with Toshiro Mifune as Pepel.

Gorky was always prepared to rework his plays to clarify or even modify their meaning, yet he never returned to *The Lower Depths* and it remains as it was originally written – ambiguous and inconclusive. His state of mind at that time left him with no alternative: the conflict between truth and compassion, between harsh reality and the beautiful lie was within himself. Very soon he sought to resolve this contradiction by distancing himself from the bourgeois intelligentsia and aligning himself with Lenin's Social Democratic Party. Yet whilst this commitment to Marxism informed the view of society expressed by the plays that followed, his individual characters remained, like Kleshch, the Baron and Pepel, 'facts of life', complex human beings who mostly transcend dogmatic schematisation. In this respect *The Lower Depths* is by no means a play apart: like all his work it proceeds from the man himself, reflecting his own complexity and honest doubt. About one thing Gorky was never in doubt: as Satin says 'Man! There's the truth for you! What is man? It isn't me – or you – or them . . . no! It's you and me and the old man and Mahomet . . . all rolled into one.'

Whilst *The Lower Depths* drew a powerful response from the younger, radical section of the Art Theatre's public it signified the limit of social criticism that its directors could comfortably contemplate. Apprehensive of what Gorky might come up with next, Nemirovich begged Chekhov to hasten and exercise his 'wonderful poetic talent' so as to maintain the 'balance' of the company's repertoire.[9] The play that Chekhov was working on was *The Cherry Orchard* and he finally delivered it in October 1903. It received its première in Moscow the following January, six months before Chekhov's death.

Meanwhile, Gorky had returned to an idea that had occurred to him shortly after he had completed *Philistines*. According to his wife, Ekaterina Peshkova, they had spent the summer of 1902 at a dacha outside Nizhny Novgorod and Gorky had been outraged by the piles of rusty tins and wastepaper left behind by the previous year's colony of holidaymakers: 'The summer visitor is the most useless and perhaps the most harmful individual on earth; he descends on a dacha, fouls it up with rubbish and then leaves.'[10] It was this image that helped Gorky to focus in *Summerfolk* all the scorn that he felt for the business and professional classes who were concerned only with abstract idealism and their own creature comforts whilst remaining oblivious to the suffering and injustice of the world around them. Trotsky saw them as a peculiarly Russian phenomenon. In his classic study of the period, *1905*, he wrote:

> We have a hopelessly retarded bourgeois intelligentsia born to the accompaniment of socialist imprecations, which today is suspended over an abyss of class contradictions, weighed down with feudal traditions, and caught in a web of academic prejudices, lacking initiative, lacking all influence over the masses, and devoid of all confidence in the future.[11]

Eighteen months elapsed before Gorky started work on *Summerfolk* in earnest and he completed the first draft in February 1904. In April he read it to the Moscow Art Theatre company when they were on tour in Petersburg. It was only three months after the opening of *The Cherry Orchard* in Moscow, but in terms of social development the two plays span different epochs. When we get to *Summerfolk*, it is as though Lopakhin has indeed chopped down the cherry trees in Madame Ranevskaya's orchard and built dachas down by the river. The Gaev family has disintegrated, no longer supported by unpaid serf-labour yet disabled by upbringing from keeping pace with a Russian society struggling belatedly to drag itself out of feudalism. In place of the gentry and their faithful retainers has come a new class of businessmen, intellectuals and professionals: including men from nowhere like Lopakhin himself, the son of a village shopkeeper and still self-conscious in his white waistcoat and brown boots. The town glimpsed on the horizon of Chekhov's play has grown with the advent of industry and created new opportunities for the sons and daughters of the poor and illiterate. Doctors, engineers, lawyers, writers: they have all 'got on' and now have time to relax away from the everyday struggle. They feel they have earned the right to drink a little, flirt a little, play chess with a neighbour, put on theatricals, or go for a swim. And yet for some of them, all this is not enough:

> We're the children of cooks and washerwomen and decent working people – we *should* be different! This country's never before had an educated class with direct blood ties to the people – surely this blood relationship ought to have nourished in us a burning desire to bring some light and meaning into the lives of our own people? . . . They sent us on ahead to seek out a road that would lead them to a better life, and we left them behind, went on and lost our way and created a lonely wilderness for ourselves. (Maria Lvovna, Act Four.)

For as their kind sat philosophising, three thousand factories had failed in the past three years, casting over 100,000 workers onto the streets. Widespread famine on mismanaged estates had provoked looting by peasants in the Ukraine, countered by the military with savage punitive expeditions and the mass flogging of the culprits. Student demonstrations were charged down by cavalry, and in 1903 the Minister of the Interior had been assassinated inside the Mariinsky Palace by a twenty-year-old terrorist. In the same year Lenin had manoeuvred the Bolshevik faction into a position of control in the Social Democratic Party abroad, whilst in Russia workers' committees began to infiltrate industry. In July 1903 a quarter of a million responded to the call for a general strike in mines, factories, ports, railways and oil-fields in the South. Reactionary feelings exploded in dreadful anti-Semitic pogroms in White Russia and Bessarabia which the authorities did little to control and were suspected of instigating.

Having himself kept faith with his working-class upbringing by throwing in his lot with the revolutionary movement, Gorky conceived *Summerfolk* as a withering rebuke to those who shrank from a similar commitment and who, like Sergei Bassov in the play and like the liberal Kadet Party in Russia, professed a belief in the power of good-will and evolution to transform the country.

Gorky's read-through left the Art Theatre uneasy. Whilst Stanislavsky was reluctant to condemn the play outright, Nemirovich showed no such caution. In a detailed appraisal he informed Gorky that he could see little in its favour apart from his portrayal of the poetess, Kaleria. Not only was it structurally weak, he said, but Gorky's anger had yielded an assembly of characters unworthy of artistic attention. Gorky took this criticism as proof of the political differences that lay between him and the Art Theatre and he declared himself open to other offers. At the same time, however, he recognised that the text needed further work, and it was only after three complete revisions that he handed it over to his publisher. By that time, he had promised it to Vera Komissarzhevskaya, Russia's greatest interpreter of modern dramatic roles, who had formed a new company in Petersburg committed to the staging of innovative work. With Komissarzhevskaya herself playing Varvara Mikhailovna, *Summerfolk* opened at the

Passage Theatre on 10 November 1904. Gorky had not been encouraged by the rehearsals and the first night confirmed his fears: '. . . apart from Komissarzhevskaya and Bravich (as Bassov) everyone was bad, and Maria Lvovna was fat, ridiculous and vulgar'.[12] But whatever the shortcomings of the production or, for that matter, the unresolved structural looseness of the text, they did nothing to lessen the impact on the audience. It split down the middle into furiously opposed factions. Gorky was delighted. In a letter to Leonid Andreev he wrote: 'Needless to say, I have not revised my opinion of *Summerfolk* in the light of these events. *Summerfolk* is not art, but it's certainly a shot in the bullseye, and I am happy, like a devil who has tempted the righteous to get roaring drunk.'[13] The critical response was no less noisy and no less divided. The following January Lunacharsky, the Marxist critic and Minister of Culture after 1917, wrote in the journal *Pravda*:

> As a work of art, as a truly conceived and beautifully executed overall picture of the inner life of a whole section of our society, Gorky's new play is a significant literary event that gladdens the heart. It is itself a symptom, one swallow that heralds the true spring – not the spring decreed by official calendars, but the spring that breaks the ice and covers the earth with flowers, whatever date the official calendar shows. It is a spring that is merry and joyful, but at the same time cruel, since much has to melt and burn up in the rays of midsummer . . . To judge from a number of Luka's speeches in *The Lower Depths* Gorky was in danger of turning soft. Thank goodness, this has not happened and cruelty has prevailed in him. More and more cruelty is going to be required by the people of tomorrow.[14]

The majority, opposing view was that political commitment had caused Gorky to lose all grasp of dramatic technique and depth of characterisation. The following year, in the aesthetic journal *The Golden Fleece*, the poet Alexander Blok wrote:

> . . . starting with *Summerfolk* Gorky loses his grip . . . Whenever his plays depict businessmen, scholars, intellectuals, workers, engineers, capitalists, they are devoid of

dramatic conflict, and everyone speaks in a feeble voice, barely audible from the stage, slightly more audible in the pages of a short story, and probably *highly audible* as a piece of militant political journalism.[15]

Summerfolk had received twenty-four performances by 9 January 1905 when barely a mile from the theatre hundreds of peaceful demonstrators were slaughtered by Tsarist troops on 'Bloody Sunday'. So much for Sergei Bassov's advocacy of 'benevolence and evolutionism'. Gorky immediately drafted a proclamation condemning Nicholas II as a murderer and calling for 'a united struggle against the Autocracy'. He was immediately arrested and all performances of *Summerfolk* cancelled – 'due to the illness of Madame Komissarzhevskaya', according to the posters. If so, it was a long illness, since the play was not performed again until the autumn, after which it remained in the repertoire for the remaining two years of the theatre's existence.

Gorky was imprisoned in the Peter and Paul Fortress until an international outcry forced his release on 14 February. Two days earlier, he had completed the first draft of *Children of the Sun*. Sub-titled initially a 'tragi-comedy', it had taken him just eight days to write and had to be surrendered for scrutiny before he was freed. The violence in Act Four provoked by the cholera epidemic seems to situate the action in 1892 when similar events occurred in towns on the Volga; but the images of popular insurrection that haunt Lisa's distracted mind must have been conceived with Bloody Sunday in mind. Certainly the Petersburg censor's office was in no doubt about this and recommended the total banning of the play. Curiously, when Gorky and his publisher appealed against the decision it was reversed by a superior, presumably because he feared that such a ban would risk an even greater scandal. In fact, Gorky himself claims to have written to the censor alerting him to this possibility. Against his better judgement, Gorky was persuaded by Stanislavsky and members of the company to release *Children of the Sun* to the Art Theatre. This he did only on the assurance that Nemirovich-Danchenko would be restrained from distorting the text. At

the same time, he agreed to a production at Komissarzhevskaya's theatre, with the actress playing Liza, and it was there
that the play had its première on 12 October 1905. The
interpretation of the director Arbatov and his company was
unequivocally satirical, with little sympathy for the character
of Protassov. The critics were unanimous in their condemna-
tion, and the leading Petersburg critic Alexander Kugel wrote:
'If *Summerfolk* boxed the ears of the intelligentsia, then
Children of the Sun spits in their face'.[16]

However much the events of 1905 might have hardened his
views, Gorky's initial conception of Protassov was far more
sympathetic. Originally, he had planned to write a play called
'The Astronomer' in collaboration with Leonid Andreev. It
owed its inspiration to the words of the German astronomer,
Herman Klein (1844–1914):

> When Raphael was painting his Sistine Madonna, when
> Newton was contemplating the law of gravity, when
> Spinoza was writing his *Ethics* and Goethe his *Faust*, the
> sun was at work in all of them. All of us, geniuses and mere
> mortals, strong and weak, emperors and beggars, all of us
> are children of the sun.[17]

It was this view of human potential together with the problems
involved in harnessing it to human needs that informed the
Moscow Art Theatre's reading of the play. Stanislavsky
encouraged Kachalov to play Protassov as a visionary akin to
his own portrayals of Stockmann in Ibsen's *An Enemy of the
People*, Astrov in *Uncle Vanya* and Vershinin in *Three Sisters*.
But all such subtleties were swept away by the events of the
opening night on 24 October. The previous week the Bolshevik
Baumann, a friend of Kachalov, had been assassinated in a
Moscow street by the fascist Black Hundred organisation and
the first-night audience was distracted by rumours that they
planned to invade the theatre as a patriotic protest against
Gorky's revolutionary activities. When the first sounds of the
rioting workers were heard offstage in Act Four panic broke
out in the auditorium, many fled for the exits, and others
rushed towards the stage to protect the actors. The curtain
was hastily lowered and the audience did not calm down until

Kachalov had demonstrated to them that it was only as Protassov that he had suffered injury.

Once again, the critics saw little in the play but a straightforward lampoon of intellectual attitudes, ignoring Gorky's protestations that what he was calling for was an alliance of the masses and the intelligentsia in order to release the true potential of humanity. In January 1906 *Children of the Sun* was staged by Max Reinhardt at the Kleines Theater in Berlin. After seeing the production a few weeks later Gorky said in a newspaper interview:

> However deep the gulf that separates the intelligentsia from the proletariat and however difficult it might be to bridge that gulf, I remain convinced that we shall succeed in doing so. This is the task that confronts those who have risen from the ranks of the proletariat to achieve the heights of knowledge. Our sick society will not become healthy until the sources of light, beauty and wisdom have become accessible to everyone.[18]

The following year, however, Gorky admitted in a letter to Lunacharsky (December 1907) that he had failed in his play to find the solution to this problem since none of his 'children of the sun' were capable of rising to the challenge. By now Gorky had met Lenin and committed himself to the Bolshevik faction of the Social Democratic Party. The answer, he was convinced, lay with the revolutionary proletariat, a class that he depicted first in his novel *The Mother* and in *Enemies*, both completed in the late summer of 1906.

Barbarians had been published in the March of that year, having been written more or less concurrently with *Children of the Sun*, between February and October 1905. Just as *Summerfolk* had been prompted by Gorky's own encounter with dacha life and *Children of the Sun* harked back to the cholera epidemic of 1892, so 'Verkhoplye', the setting for *Barbarians*, was clearly based on Arzamas, where he had spent several months in exile in 1902. However, the coming of the railway, the confrontation between ancient 'wooden' Russia and the new 'iron' age, recalls the 'dark kingdom' depicted in the plays of Alexander Ostrovsky. In the first draft of the text far more prominence was given to the conflict between the reactionary patriarchal mayor, Redozubov, and the energetic 'new man', Cherkoon. Later, however, Gorky developed the character of the radical student, Stepan Lukin, who threatens to mobilise the workers at the local factory. Correspondingly, the progress represented by Cherkoon and Tsyganov emerges as unprincipled and thoroughly destructive in its effect on the local community. The period may be the nineteenth century, but once again Gorky is pointing a finger at his own contemporaries with their lack of moral purpose, and by the end of the play one is left in little doubt as to the identity of the true barbarians.

Blok was no less dimissive of *Barbarians* than he was of Gorky's other work, describing it as 'a play of types and characters written carelessly and with an incredibly large cast, many of whom are simply repeated from before.' At the same time, he was compelled to acknowledge the hypnotic power of one character, Nadezhda Monakhova. 'Everything about her is strangely and beautifully consistent,' he wrote; 'she has a great strength that is both attractive and repellent. She is powerful with a kind of severe, animal fascination. I sense that the whole play was written for the sake of this one character.'[19] For Lunacharsky too Nadezhda was no less captivating; he found it 'difficult to recall any other dramatic character of recent years to rank alongside her'. Yet, at the same time, he discerned a more lasting significance in *Barbarians*:

> Possibly, in the clamour of the political moment these socio-psychological scenes from provincial life might seem irrelevant to matters of current concern. But the moral struggle being waged throughout Russia between industrial capitalism and the petty bourgeoisie will not be quick to subside. The writer helps us to understand and assess the mighty phenomenon of this war between the two forms of barbarism through the direct experiences of real people, through their ephemeral, empty victories and their wretched, tragic disasters.[20]

For reasons that are not clear neither the Moscow Art Theatre nor Komissarzhevskya pursued plans to stage *Barbarians*; it was first presented in March 1906 in Riga and then in numerous provincial theatres throughout Russia. Gorky seems to have quickly lost faith in the play, describing it to one potential director as 'old-fashioned and ponderous', and advising him to choose *Enemies* instead. There is no record of any major Soviet production until the 1930s, but since then it has entered the repertoire of most major companies.

As early as 1901 Gorky had mentioned to his publisher, Piatnitsky, an idea for a play about the urban proletariat, but dismissed it because he felt it stood no chance with the censor. The project surfaced again shortly after his release from prison in 1905 during that remarkably productive period when he was working on both *Children of the Sun* and *Barbarians*. At that time Gorky did not progress beyond a preliminary list of characters and a synopsis of part of the action. In early January 1906 he was forced to leave Russia following his involvement in the December uprising in Moscow. Between March and September he was in the United States and it was there that he completed both *The Mother* and *Enemies*, which was published in December in Stuttgart and Petersburg.

Through his close personal contact with the Social Democratic Party, Gorky was very familiar with the pattern of revolutionary agitation and disruption in Russian industry. Thus, the action of *Enemies* closely resembled the events of recent months, notably a series of disturbances between February and November 1905 at the vast Morozov textile plant in Orekhovo-Zuyevo which involved some 20,000 workers. Similarly, the 'Bryansk works', where Sintsov alias 'Maxim Markov' was previously active (Act Three), refers to the Bryansk metallurgical works in Yekaterinoslavl, the major centre of revolutionary activity in Southern Russia. Some years earlier the censor had issued a directive categorically forbidding the performance of any play dealing with industrial unrest, so there was no possibility of *Enemies* passing scrutiny. In February 1907 it was rejected with the following comments:

These scenes present a clear picture of the irreconcilable enmity between workers and employers, with the former portrayed as resolute fighters advancing clear-sightedly towards their declared aim of the overthrow of capital, and the latter shown as narrow-minded egotists. Furthermore, in the words of one of the characters, it is immaterial what kind of man the boss is; it is enough that he is 'the boss' for him to be the enemy of the workers. The author . . . predicts victory for the workers. These scenes are an outright provocation against the ruling class and therefore cannot be authorised for performance.[21]

Six months later the published text was suppressed as well, but not before a production in Poltava in the Ukraine and another in Central Asia had somehow escaped the authorities' notice. Soviet sources refer to a production in German of *Enemies* on 16 February 1907 at Max Reinhardt's Kleines Theater in Berlin. Whilst German scholarship on Reinhardt makes no reference to any production by him of the play, the leading contemporay Marxist theoretician, Plekhanov, suggests that it was staged in Berlin that winter. Recalling Reinhardt's earlier success with *The Lower Depths*, he writes:

Whereas a well-portrayed down-and-out (of the Lumpen-proletariat) is likely to intrigue the bourgeois patron of the arts, a well-portrayed class-concious worker is bound to provoke all kinds of unpleasant thoughts. And as regards the Berlin proletariat, they wouldn't have had time for the theatre this winter.[22]

Plekhanov's article offers a detailed analysis of the means by which Gorky gives dramatic shape to the psychology and tactics of the revolutionary proletariat. In particular he admires his success in conveying collective action through the characters of the individual workers, notably the portrayal of Levshin and Ryabtsov. Significantly, the one play he chooses for comparison is Schiller's *Wilhelm Tell*, completed in 1803. With the obvious exception of Hauptmann's *The Weavers* (1893), which the author himself described as 'certainly social but not socialist', *Enemies* was the first play of any consequence to take industrial conflict as its central theme. In more ways than one it marked the end of the cycle that had begun with *Philistines*: consistent with the advance of events in Russia, the workers now were present onstage in greater numbers and with far clearer purpose than their predecessors in the earlier plays. With few exceptions, the critics interpreted this as proof of Gorky's final capitulation to Marxist ideology and his demise as a serious dramatist. Blok spoke for many when he wrote:

> This is simply the labour question treated crassly in dramatic form. There are no longer any of the real contradictions that one associates with art in general and drama in particular. On the one hand, we have angelic workers who strike in the name of justice, never betray their comrades, and take the boss's children for walks; on the other hand, there are the capitalists, intellectually feeble or mindlessly cruel, and the police, portrayed with the same intolerable banality, straight out of a newspaper exposé. Whilst all this is very moving and sentimental, it has nothing to do with art.[23]

With Gorky's departure from Russia in 1906 his name disappeared completely from the repertoire, but throughout his exile on Capri and following his return under a general amnesty in 1913 he continued to write for the theatre. In 1912 *Vassa Zheleznova* was awarded the Griboyedov Prize by the Society of Russian Dramatists but received only one production. Of the five plays he completed during this period all but one went unperformed until after the Revolution.

In the early years of the Soviet period the Moscow Art Theatre was not alone in neglecting all his work but *The Lower Depths*. The opinion that it was outmoded and untheatrical persisted until after his final return to Russia in 1931. Two years earlier the first Five-Year Plan had been announced, and at the same time the Party had adopted measures to ensure far closer control of the arts and to eliminate what were now denounced as the 'leftist' deviations of the permissive N.E.P. period. Theatre censorship was placed in the hands of a new Central Repertoire Committee or

'Glavrepertkom' and each theatre's artistic policy was subject to the control of a Party-dominated 'Artistic Council'. As a result many theatres reluctant to compromise their artistic standards were faced with a repertoire crisis. For example, in two seasons from 1930 to 1932 the Moscow Art Theatre and Tairov's Kamerny Theatre succeeded in putting on only three new productions each. The position became more critical still in 1934 when, at the inaugural congress of the new Writers' Union, Zhdanov formulated the stifling principles of the now mandatory Socialist Realism and laid down the guide lines for the elimination of formalism. Alone amongst leading directors, Meyerhold refused to yield and within four years his theatre was liquidated, having added only one further production to its repertoire.

In these coercive circumstances the Soviet theatre began its reappraisal of Gorky the dramatist, stimulated in 1932 by the appearance of *Yegor Bulychov and Others*, the first of a trilogy of plays set against the background of events from 1917 up to 1930. (The other two were *Somov and Others* and *Dostigayev and Others*.) A complex, often bizarre tragedy, *Yegor Bulychov* deals with a wealthy provincial merchant alienated from his own class and struggling for understanding as he dies of cancer during the last days of the Romanov dynasty.

Encouraged by Boris Zakhava's vivid production at the Moscow Vakhtangov Theatre, directors started to look afresh at Gorky's earlier works. The following year, within a single month there were revivals of *Enemies* at the Pushkin Theatre in Leningrad and at the Maly and the Trade Union Theatre in Moscow. Gorky's position in the Soviet repertoire was confirmed finally in October 1935 with the production of *Enemies* at the Moscow Art Theatre by Nemirovich-Danchenko and Mikhail Kedrov; it was performed 275 times and was taken to the Paris International Exhibition of 1937. For the 1933 production Gorky extensively revised *Enemies*, aiming principally to reduce the audience's sympathy for the Bardins, to raise the political consciousness of Levshin, and to shift emphasis away from Nadya and onto the workers at the play's conclusion.

However, it was the times rather than the text that demanded these 'improvements' since there is little justification in denying Nadya her final insight and Levshin's endorsement of her. It may not have suited the 1930's version of Russian history for a member of the intelligentsia to manifest this degree of revolutionary understanding and commitment, but there can be no doubt that in 1905 a character such as Nadya was by no means the product of Gorky's wishful thinking.

When Chekhov read the first draft of *Philistines* in 1901 he was full of praises for its content but criticised the conservatism of its form. 'You make these new, original people sing their songs to second-hand music', he told Gorky.[24] It is certainly true that compared to Chekhov's own work, or the late Ibsen or Strindberg, there is little in Gorky that stretches the resources of the stage. Yet as an actor's dramatist he is perhaps the equal of any of them, and his representations of class conflict marked an advance that has hardly been surpassed eighty years on.

Edward Braun

Notes

1 Quoted in E. Braun, *The Theatre of Meyerhold* (1979), p.23
2 Ibid.
3 All dates are old style, 13 days behind the modern calendar.
4 Letter to Sumbatov-Yuzhin, 26 February 1903.
5 Complete Works (Moscow, 1970), vol. VII, p.606.
6 Ibid., p.614.
7 Interview in *Peterburgskaya gazeta*, 15 June 1903.
8 Letter to Piatnitsky, 15 July 1902.
9 Letter, 16 February 1903.
10 *Complete Works*, VII, p.630. His words are echoed by Pustobaika in Act Three.
11 Pelican ed., 1973, p.59.
12 *Complete Works*. VII, p.639.
13 Ibid., p.640.
14 *Pravda*, January–April 1905.
15 *Zolotoe runo*, No.7–9, 1907.
16 *Rus*, 13 October 1905.
17 Quoted in Gorky, *Complete Works*, VII, p.647.
18 *Neue Freie Presse*, Vienna, 11 March 1906.
19 Blok, op.cit.
20 *Vestnik zhizni*, 1906, No 2.
21 *Teatralnoe nasledie* – 1, (Leningrad, 1934), p.223.
22 'On the psychology of the Working-Class Movement', *Sovremenny mir*, 1907, No.5.
23 Blok, op.cit.
24 Letter, 22 October 1901.

THE LOWER DEPTHS

This translation of The Lower Depths *was first performed by the Royal Shakespeare Company on 29th June 1972, at the Aldwych Theatre, with the following cast:*

MIKHAIL IVANOV KOSTYLIOV, *aged 54,*
        landlord of a doss-house   Tony Church
VASSILISSA KARPOVNA, *his wife, aged 26*   Heather Canning
NATASHA, *her sister, aged 20*   Lisa Harrow
ABRAM IVANICH MEDVEDIEV, *their uncle,*
        a policeman, aged 50   Richard Mays
VASSILY PEPEL, *aged 28*   Mike Pratt
ANDREY MITRICH KLESHCH, *a locksmith,*
        aged 40   Morgan Shepherd
ANNA, *his wife, aged 24*   Lynn Dearth
NASTYA, *a streetwalker*   Alison Fiske
KVASHNIA, *a dumpling peddler, aged 40*   Lila Kaye
BUBNOV, *a cap-maker, aged 45*   Peter Geddis
BARON, *aged 33*   Richard Pasco
SATIN, *aged close to 40*   Bernard Lloyd
ACTOR, *aged close to 40*   Peter Woodthorpe
LUKA, *aged 60, a palmer*   Gordon Gostelow
ALYOSHKA, *aged 20, a cobbler*   Nicholas Grace
TARTAR   } *'hook-men', or porters*   Robert Ashby
KRIVOY ZOB   David Calder
Various paupers, without names or speech   Ted Valentine
                                       Marion Lines

    Directed by David Jones
    Designed by Timothy O'Brien
    Costumes by Tazeena Firth and Timothy O'Brien

Act One

A cellar, which looks like a cave. The ceiling consists of heavy stone arches, black with smoke and with the plaster falling. The light comes in from the audience, and downwards from a square window on the right. The right-hand corner is taken up by PEPEL's *room, separated from the rest by a thin partition, close to the door of which is* BUB-NOV's *plank bed. In the left-hand corner is a large Russian stove; in the stone wall, left, a door leads to the kitchen in which* KVASHNIA, *the* BARON *and* NASTYA *live. Against the wall, between the stove and the door, stands a wide bed covered with a dirty chintz canopy. Plank beds stand all the way around the walls.*

In the foreground by the left wall stands a block of wood with a vice and a small anvil fixed to it; in front of it is another, slightly smaller, block, on which KLESHCH *is sitting, trying keys in old locks. At his feet lie two large bunches of keys of different sizes, held together by rings made of bent wire; a battered tin samovar; a hammer; files. In the middle of the lodging house stand a large table, two benches, and a stool, all unpainted and dirty. At the table* KVASHNIA *is in charge of the samovar, the* BARON *is chewing black bread, and* NASTYA, *on the stool, is reading a tattered book, her elbows on the table. On the bed covered by the canopy* ANNA *is lying, and can be heard coughing.* BUBNOV *sits on his bed, holding a hat-block between his knees, and trying to work out how best to cut the old, unpicked pair of trousers which he has pulled over the block. Beside him lie a cardboard hat-box – torn to make cap peaks – some pieces of oil-cloth, rags.* SATIN *has just woken up. He lies on his plank bed, growling. On the stove, out of sight the* ACTOR *is tossing and coughing.*

Early Spring. Morning.

BARON. Further – further!
KVASHNIA. Well, so I said, 'Oh no, my dear,' I said, 'you get

away from me with all that kind of talk,' I said, 'I've been through all that once, and I'm not going through it again. You won't catch me taking that bridal veil again, not for a hundred baked crabs I won't!'

BUBNOV (*to* SATIN). What are you snorting about?

SATIN *snorts some more.*

KVASHNIA. 'I'm a free woman,' I said, 'I earn my own living,' I said, 'why should I go and get myself written into another body's passport? Lock myself up in some man's rotten dungeon?' I said. 'Oh, no!' No, I tell you, I wouldn't marry him, not if he was an American prince.

KLESHCH. You're lying.

KVASHNIA. Wha-a-at?

KLESHCH. You're a liar. You'll marry Abramka.

The BARON *grabs* NASTYA's *book and reads the title.*

BARON. 'Fatal Love'.

He roars with laughter. NASTYA *reaches for the book.*

NASTYA. Give it here, give it back! Come on, stop bloody fooling!

The BARON *watches her, waving the book about beyond her reach.*

KVASHNIA (*to* KLESHCH). You red-headed goat, I'll give you 'liar'! You've got a nerve, talking to me like that!

BARON (*bringing the book down on* NASTYA's *head*). You're an idiot, Nastya.

NASTYA. Give it here. (*She grabs the book.*)

KLESHCH. Oo, the grand madam! But you'll marry Abramka. It's all you've been waiting for.

KVASHNIA. Oh yes, of course! Naturally! What else? And there's you, driving your little wife there till she's half dead . . .

KLESHCH. Belt up, you old bitch, that's none of your business.

KVASHNIA. Ha! Can't take a spot of truth, eh!

BARON. There they go. Well, Nastya, where've you got to?

NASTYA (*without looking up*). Eh? . . . Oh, go away!

ANNA *puts her head out from under the canopy.*

ANNA. Oh God, the day's started! For pity's sake don't shout, don't start rowing.

KLESHCH. She's whining again.

ANNA. Every single God's day the same! Can't you even let me die in peace?

BUBNOV. Noise don't get in the way of death.

KVASHNIA *goes over to* ANNA.

KVASHNIA. How did you ever put up with such a useless animal, girl?

ANNA. Leave off. Leave me be.

KVASHNIA. Well, well, there's a patient little martyr, then! How's the chest now, any easier?

BARON. Kvashnia! Time to go to market!

KVASHNIA. Just coming. (*To* ANNA.) Why don't I give you some nice hot dumplings, now?

ANNA. No, don't . . . Thank you. What's the point of me eating?

KVASHNIA. You just eat them, now. Something hot softens your insides. I'll put them in a bowl and leave them here, then if you feel like it you can have them. (*To* BARON.) Come on then, your lordship. (*To* KLESHCH.) You – you're a nasty piece of work, you are. (*She exits to the kitchen.*)

ANNA. (*coughs*). Lord . . .

The BARON *nudges the back of* NASTYA's *neck.*

BARON. Give it up, stupid girl.

NASTYA (*mutters*). Get away . . . I'm not hurting you.

The BARON *follows* KVASHNIA *into the kitchen, whistling.* SATIN *props himself up on his bed.*

SATIN. Who was it beat me up last night?

BUBNOV. Does it make any difference?

SATIN. Maybe not. But why did they do it?

BUBNOV. Did you play cards?

SATIN. I did.

BUBNOV. That's why you got beaten, then.

SATIN. Bastards.

The ACTOR *sticks his head over the top of the stove.*

ACTOR. One of these times they do you in, they'll do you in for good.

SATIN. And you are an imbecile.

ACTOR. Why?

SATIN. Because you can't be done in more than once.

ACTOR (*after a pause*). I don't understand. Why can't you?

KLESHCH. You get yourself down off that stove and clear this place up. What do you think you're doing, fondling yourself up there?

ACTOR. Mind your own business.

KLESHCH. You wait till Vassilissa comes in, she'll soon learn you whose business it is.

ACTOR. Vassilissa can go to hell, it's the Baron's turn to clear up today. (*Shouts.*) Baron!

The BARON *comes out of the kitchen.*

BARON. I've no time for housework. I'm going to the market with Kvashnia.

ACTOR. You can go to Siberia if you like, it's nothing to me, but it's still your turn to sweep the floor. I'm not going to do other people's work for them.

BARON. May you be damned, then. Nastionka'll do the sweeping – Hey, Fatal Love, wake up! (*He snatches* NASTYA's *book away.*)

NASTYA (*getting up*). What d'you want? Give it here, you cheeky lout! Call yourself a gentleman!

BARON (*giving her the book*). Sweep the floor for me, Nastya, there's a good girl!

NASTYA (*going into the kitchen*). Oh, yeah, that's all I need.

KVASHNIA (*from the doorway, to the* BARON). You come along now, they'll get the floor swept without you. (*To* ACTOR.) Why don't you do as you're asked, it won't break your poor little back will it?

ACTOR. It's always me. Why is it always me?

The BARON *comes out of the kitchen carrying a yoke hung with baskets in which there are earthenware pots, each covered with a cloth.*

BARON. Seems heavy today, somehow.

SATIN. Fat lot of good it did you, being born a baron.

KVASHNIA (*to* ACTOR). See you get that floor swept, now.

She exits into the passage, allowing the BARON *to go through the door in front of her. The* ACTOR *climbs down from the stove.*

ACTOR. I oughtn't to breathe dust, it's bad for me. (*With pride.*) My organism is poisoned with alcohol.

SATIN. Organism ... organon ...

ANNA. Andrey Mitrich ...

KLESHCH. What is it now?

ANNA. Kvashnia left some hot dumplings ... You take them, you eat them.

KLESHCH goes over to her.

KLESHCH. Won't you have some?

ANNA. I don't want any. Why should I eat? You're a working man, you must have something to eat.

KLESHCH. You scared? Don't be scared. Maybe you'll still ...

ANNA. Go and eat the dumplings! I feel bad. I don't think it'll be long now.

KLESHCH (*walking away*). Never mind. Maybe you'll get up again. It happens sometimes ...

He goes into the kitchen.

ACTOR (*loudly, as if he is just waking up*). Yesterday at the clinic the doctor said to me, 'Your organism,' he said, 'is completely poisoned with alcohol'.

SATIN (*smiling*). Organan.

ACTOR (*firmly*). Not organon. Organism.

SATIN. Sycamore ... sycambro ...

ACTOR (*waving his hands dismissively*). Oh, nonsense! I'm serious, I tell you. If my organism is poisoned it must be bad for me to sweep the floor ... breathe in all that dust ...

SATIN. Microbiotins ... ha!

ACTOR. What? What are you mumbling about?

SATIN. Words. Words. And then there's ... trans-cend-dental-istic!

BUBNOV. What's that, then.

SATIN. Don't know. Forgotten.

BUBNOV. Why say it, then?

SATIN. Because. I'm sick of all these everyday words. Sick of them. I must have heard every one of them a thousand times.

ACTOR. There's a line in 'Hamlet' – 'Words, words, words'. It's a good piece. I played the gravedigger.

KLESHCH *comes out of the kitchen.*

KLESHCH. When are you going to play with that broom?

ACTOR. Mind your own business. (*He strikes a pose, hand on breast.*) 'Ophelia! Ah ... remember me in thy orisons ...'

Offstage, in the distance, muffled sounds, shouting, a police whistle. KLESHCH *sits down to his work, scraping away with a file.*

SATIN. I like ... rare words, words you can't understand. When I was young I had a job in a telegraph office ... used to read books ... lots of books ...

BUBNOV. So you were a telegraphist too, were you?

SATIN. I was ... (*He gives a short laugh.*) There are some very good books, you know ... and lots of curious words. I was an educated man, d'you know that?

BUBNOV. I've heard it a hundred times. Well, all right, so you were. Very important. And me, I had my own establishment – a master furrier, I was. My forearms were all yellow, from the dye, I used to dye the furs, and my hands and arms were so yellow, you know, right up to the elbow, I used to think I'd never get it washed off. Thought I'd die with yellow hands. And now here they are, look, same hands – just dirty. Yeah.

SATIN. Yes – well?

BUBNOV. Well – er – that's all.

SATIN. What are you trying to say?

BUBNOV. Just . . . thinking it out. It means, however much you paint yourself up on the outside, it all gets rubbed off . . . all gets rubbed off . . . hm.

SATIN. [I'm stiff. My bones ache.]

ACTOR (*sitting with his arms clasped round his knees*). Education . . . is bunk. What matters is talent. I knew an actor, he had to spell out his part syllable by syllable . . . could hardly read. But when he went out there and gave his performance, the whole theatre crackled and shook with excitement.

SATIN. Bubnov – let me have five kopeks.

BUBNOV. I've only got two.

ACTOR. What I say is, *talent* is what you need to be a star. And talent means believing in yourself, in your own strength . . .

SATIN. Give me five kopeks and I'll believe you're a talent, a star, a crocodile, a police inspector . . . Kleshch give us a five!

KLESHCH. Go to hell. There's too many of your sort here . . .

SATIN. No need for the abuse! I know you're cleaned out.

ANNA. Andrey Mitrich, I can't breathe, it hurts to breathe.

KLESHCH. What can I do about it?

BUBNOV. Open the door into the passage.

KLESHCH. Oh, fine. There's you, sitting up on your bed, and I'm down here on the floor. Change places, then you can open the door . . . I'm bloody freezing.

BUBNOV (*calmly*). I don't need to have it open. It's your wife that needs it.

KLESHCH (*gloomily*). Who cares who needs what?

SATIN. My head's splitting . . . Oooh! Why do people have to go about bashing each other on the head?

BUBNOV. They'll bash you on anything they can get hold of if you give them the chance. (*Gets up.*) Well, got to go and buy some thread. [What's happened to those landlords of ours today? Maybe they've up and died, at last.]

> BUBNOV *goes off.* ANNA *coughs;* SATIN *lies motionless, his hands behind his head. The* ACTOR *looks round unhappily, and goes over to* ANNA.

ACTOR. Feeling bad?

ANNA. Can't . . . breathe . . . in here.

ACTOR. Shall I take you out in the passage? Come on – up . . . up!

> *He helps her get up, throws a ragged garment over her shoulders, supports her out to the passage.*

Walk, dammit! I'm ill myself – poisoned with alcohol.

> KOSTYLIOV *appears in the doorway.*

KOSTYLIOV. Off for a walk, eh? Pretty little pair – the ram and his little ewe lamb!

ACTOR. Out of the way – can't you see we're invalids?

KOSTYLIOV. Of course, of course, come along then!

> KOSTYLIOV *sings something liturgical under his breath, looking round suspiciously, inclining his head on one side as if listening for something from Pepel's room.* KLESHCH *rattles his keys furiously and scrapes away with the file, furtively watching the landlord.*

KOSTYLIOV. Scrape-scraping, huh?

KLESHCH. What?

KOSTYLIOV. I said, you're *scraping*!

> *Pause.*

Ah – the – ugh – what was it I was going to ask? (*Fast, in a low voice.*) My wife wasn't here, huh?

KLESHCH. Haven't seen her.

KOSTYLIOV *moves carefully over to the door to Pepel's room.*

KOSTYLIOV. What a lot of space you've got out of me for your two roubles a month! A bed . . . and there you are, sitting about . . . h'm, yes, before God I'd call that five roubles worth of space! We'll have to slip a wee half rouble on you I can see . . .

KLESHCH. Why not slip a noose round my neck and have done with it? You'll be dead soon, and there you're still dreaming about half roubles.

KOSTYLIOV. A noose? What would I do that for? Who'd gain from that? No, no, God's peace on you, man, you live on regardless to your heart's content. But I'll just put that half rouble on you, it'll buy some oil for the sanctuary lamp . . . and my sacrifice will burn before the holy icon, my sacrifice will go up for me, in reparation for my sins, and for yours as well . . . After all, you don't think about your sins for yourself. So there we are. Oh, Andriushka, you're a wicked man! Your wife's dying because of your wicked ways, and nobody loves you, nobody respects you, you just scrape, scrape away, upsetting everybody . . .

KLESHCH (*shouting*). Did you come here just to bait me!

SATIN *growls loudly.*

KOSTYLIOV (*startled*). Oh, dear me, come now . . . !

The ACTOR *comes in from the passage.*

ACTOR. I've settled your woman in the passage, wrapped her up . . .

KOSTYLIOV. There's kindness, brother! That's good, you know, that'll be all on the reckoning for you.

ACTOR. When?

KOSTYLIOV. In the next world, little brother! Everything, all our deeds, all being reckoned up, for reward.

ACTOR. How about you rewarding me here for my 'kindness'?

KOSTYLIOV. How could I do that, now?

ACTOR. Knocking off half my debt.

KOSTYLIOV. He-he! Always joking, dear friend, always play-acting! As if you could compare goodness of heart with money! Goodness – goodness is above all other blessings. And your debt to me – that's still a *debt*! And so you're endebted to repay it. You must show kindness to your elders without looking for rewards.

ACTOR. Elders? You're an old leech!

He goes into the kitchen. KLESHCH *gets up and goes into the passage.*

KOSTYLIOV (*to* SATIN.) Scrape-scrape's taking himself off – he-he! He doesn't like me!

SATIN. Who does? Apart from . . . Satan?

KOSTYLIOV (*with a little laugh*). Oh, you and your abuse! And yet I love you all, I understand you, you're my fallen brothers, lost, good-for-nothing . . . (*Suddenly, quickly.*) Is Vasska in?

SATIN. Look and see.

KOSTYLIOV *goes over to the door and knocks.*

KOSTYLIOV. Vasska!

The ACTOR *appears in the kitchen door. He is chewing.*

PEPEL (*off*). Who's that?

KOSTYLIOV. It's me – me, Vasska.

PEPEL. What d'you want?

KOSTYLIOV (*moving away*). Open the door.

SATIN (*not looking at* KOSTYLIOV). He'll open it, and she'll be in there.

ACTOR *snorts.*

KOSTYLIOV (*anxiously, softly*). Eh? Who's in there? What ... you what? ...

SATIN. What? What – what? ... You talking to me?

KOSTYLIOV. What did you say just then?

SATIN. Just talking to myself.

KOSTYLIOV. You watch it, brother! Watch you don't take your jokes too far. Yes. (*Knocks loudly on the door.*) Vasska!

PEPEL *opens the door of his room.*

PEPEL. Well? What d'you want now?

KOSTYLIOV (*peering into the room*). I – er – you see, I – er –

PEPEL. You brought the money, then?

KOSTYLIOV. There's something I've got to see you about ...

PEPEL. Have you brought the money?

KOSTYLIOV. What money? Now wait a ...

PEPEL. The money, the seven roubles. For the watch. Well?

KOSTYLIOV. What watch, Vasska? Oh, you mean ...

PEPEL. Now you look here! I sold you a watch yesterday, in front of witnesses, for ten roubles, right? I've had three, so you just hand over the other seven! [What are you gawping at? Hanging about here disturbing people, and don't even know your own business!]

KOSTYLIOV. Sh – sh! Don't be angry now, Vasska. That watch is ...

SATIN. Stolen.

KOSTYLIOV (*severely*). I don't accept stolen goods. How can you ...

PEPEL *grabs him by the shoulders.*

PEPEL. Why d'you come down here, badgering me? What d'you want?

KOSTYLIOV. But ... Oh, nothing, I'll go away ... if you're so ...

PEPEL. Bugger off and get the money, go on.

KOSTYLIOV. What coarse people, really! (*He exits, tut-tutting.*)

ACTOR. A comedy!

SATIN. Splendid! I like it!

PEPEL. What's he doing in here? What's he want?

SATIN (*laughing*). Don't you know? Looking for his wife, of course. Why don't you knock him off, Vasska?

PEPEL. Catch me messing my life up over a shit like that.

SATIN. You could do a neat little job . . . then – marry Vassilissa – be our landlord!

PEPEL. Perfect joy, yes. You lot'd piss away all my property in a bar, and me too, like as not, in my loving kindness. (*He sits down on a bed.*) Old bastard . . . woke me up . . . Oh! and I was having this great dream! I was fishing, and I hooked this enormous great carp, you know, the sort of carp you only get in dreams, and there I was, playing him, playing him, and, you know, scared the line would snap, and I had the landing net all ready . . . now, now, I thought, any moment now . . .

SATIN. That wasn't a carp, it was Vassilissa.

ACTOR. He hooked Vassilissa years ago.

PEPEL (*angrily*). Ah, go to hell – and take Vassilissa with you.

KLESHCH *comes in from the hall.*

KLESHCH. Bloody perishing out there.

ACTOR. [Why didn't you bring Anna in? She'll freeze.

KLESHCH. Natasha took her up to the kitchen with her.

ACTOR. The old man'll chuck her out.

KLESHCH *sits down to work.*

KLESHCH. Then Natasha'll bring her down here.]

SATIN. Vasska, give me five kopecks!

ACTOR (*to* SATIN). Five! Really! Vasska, give us twenty.

PEPEL. I'd best let you have it fast or you'll take me for a rouble . . . Here.

SATIN. Giblartarr! Oh, there's no one in the world better than a thief!

KLESHCH (*gloomily*). Money comes easy to them, they don't have to work for it.

SATIN. Money comes easy to lots of folk, but it's not so easy to part them from it. Work? Make it pleasant for me, I might start working. I might, you know! When work's a pleasure, life's worth while, when work's a duty, life's a trial. (*To the* ACTOR.) Hey, Sardanapaulous, come on!

ACTOR. Come on then, Nebuchadnezor! Oh, I'm going to get as drunk as – as forty thousand alcoholics!

SATIN *and the* ACTOR *go out.*

PEPEL. Well – (*yawns.*) How's your wife?

KLESHCH. Can't be long now . . .

Pause.

PEPEL. I watch you – scraping away . . . It's pointless.

KLESHCH. What else should I do?

PEPEL. Nothing.

KLESHCH. How'd I eat, then?

PEPEL. People live.

KLESHCH. This lot? People? What sort of *people* are they? Ragbags, cacklebums, gutterscum . . . People! I'm a working man . . . I feel ashamed just to look at them . . . I been working since I was so high . . . Think I'm not going to get out of here? I'll scramble out, don't you worry, if it tears my skin off of me I'll scramble out . . . You wait . . . the wife'll die . . . six months, I've lived here six months, feels like six years . . .

PEPEL. You're no better than anyone else here. You got no business talking like that.

KLESHCH. No better –! People with no honour, no conscience . . . !

PEPEL (*indifferently*). What do you want with honour and conscience? You can't put them on your feet instead of boots. Honour and conscience! They're for the strong and powerful, not for us.

Enter BUBNOV.

BUBNOV. Oooh. (*Shivers.*) I'm freezing.

PEPEL. Bubnov, you got a conscience?

BUBNOV. Eh? Conscience?

PEPEL. That's it.

BUBNOV. Conscience? Me? What for? I'm not rich.

PEPEL. What I was saying, see? It's the rich who can use honour and conscience, right? Kleshch here's been going on about us how we've none of us got any conscience.

BUBNOV. Why? Does he want to borrow some?

PEPEL. No, he's got plenty of his own, he says.

BUBNOV. So he's selling some? Well, he'll get no buyers in here. A few cardboard cartons, now, I might buy those – on tick, mind you.

PEPEL (*sententiously, to* KLESHCH). [You're a fool, Andriushka. You ought to talk to Satin – or the Baron – if you want to know about conscience.

KLESHCH. I got nothing to say to those two.

PEPEL. They're brainier than you, that's why. Even if they are drunkards.

BUBNOV. A brainy man who's on the booze
           Has a double stake to lose.

PEPEL. Satin says, everybody wants his neighbour to have a conscience, but nobody's got any use for one himself. And that's the truth.]

> NATASHA *comes in, followed by* LUKA *with a stick in his hand, a bundle on his shoulder, a kettle and a tea-pot hung from his belt.*

LUKA. Good health to you, honest people.

PEPEL (*stroking his moustache*). A-ah, Natasha!

BUBNOV. Honest people, huh! – the spring before last, maybe.

NATASHA. Here's a new lodger.

LUKA. It's all one to me, I've as much respect for a scoundrel.

The way I see it, there's no such flea as a bad flea – they're all blackies, and all jumpies. Now, my dear, where do I fit myself in here?

NATASHA *points to the kitchen door.*

NATASHA. In there, grandpa.

LUKA. In she says and in I go. For an old man, wherever it's warm, that's home.

LUKA *goes off into the kitchen.*

PEPEL. That's an amusing little old ferret you've brought us, Natasha.

NATASHA. More amusing than you. Andrey – your wife's up in our kitchen with us, you come and fetch her soon, will you?

KLESHCH. All right, I'll come.

NATASHA. It wouldn't hurt you to show a bit of love, now. It can't be long, you know.

KLESHCH. I know.

NATASHA. You know! It's not enough to know, you must try to understand. It's frightening to die.

PEPEL. I'm not afraid of death.

NATASHA. Oh no, of course not! Ah, such a brave big man!

BUBNOV [(*whistles*). And this thread is rotten . . .

PEPEL. It's true. I'm not afraid. I could take death in my arms right now – this very minute. Take a knife, plunge it into my heart – I'll die without a murmur . . . in fact I'd die with joy if death came from such a pure hand.

NATASHA (*going off*). Ah, go and try it on somebody else!]

BUBNOV (*drawling*). And this old thread is rotten . . .

NATASHA (*at the door to the hall*). Don't forget your wife, Andrey.

KLESHCH. All right.

NATASHA *goes out.*

PEPEL. She's a good little maid.

BUBNOV. The lass is all right.

PEPEL. But why does she have to be like that with me – putting me down all the time? She's a lost cause here anyway.

BUBNOV. And you're the one'll lose it for her.

PEPEL. Why me? No, I'm really sorry for her.

BUBNOV. [Like the wolf's sorry for the lamb.

PEPEL. Don't talk cock! I . . . I feel really sorry for her. It's awful for a girl like that to live in a place like this. I can see that.]

KLESHCH. Wait till Vassilissa catches you talking to her.

BUBNOV. Vassilissa? Mm – yes – that one won't give up what's hers too easy. A fearsome woman.

PEPEL *lies down on a bed.*

PEPEL. Ah, to hell with both of you! Prophetic pricks!

KLESHCH. Just wait and see, that's all.

LUKA *is heard singing in the kitchen.*

LUKA. 'In the dark of the night with the path disappearing . . .'

KLESHCH (*going into the hall*). Hark at him bawling . . .

PEPEL. Oh, it's all so bloody boring! Why do I get so bored? You go on living and living and everything seems fine, then suddenly, pow! like catching a cold – you're bored.

BUBNOV. Bored, huh?

PEPEL. Stiff.

LUKA (*sings*). 'Oh the path disappearing behind and before . . .'

PEPEL. Hey, you! Old man!

LUKA (*looking through doorway*). Would that be me?

PEPEL. You. Don't sing.

LUKA (*coming in*). Don't you like it?

PEPEL. When someone sings well I like it.

LUKA. Do I sing badly?

PEPEL. That must be it.

LUKA. Well fancy that, now! And I really thought I sang well! It's always that way. A man thinks to himself, Aha, I'm really doing well, and then, lo and behold! – nobody else is pleased with him at all!

PEPEL (*laughing*). That's true enough!

BUBNOV. You say you're bored with everything, and there you are, laughing.

PEPEL. What's that to you, brown owl?

LUKA. Who here is bored?

PEPEL. I am.

Enter the BARON.

LUKA. Fancy! And there in the kitchen a young lass sits, reading a book and – weeping! Truly! Real tears flowing . . . I say to her, what is it then, my dear, eh? and she says, Ah, she says, it's sad! What's sad? I say and she says, Here, she says, in the book. And so that's what she finds to busy herself with. That must be out of boredom, too.

BARON. That one's a fool.

PEPEL. Baron, have you had your morning tea?

BARON. I have. Further. Further!

PEPEL. Would you like me to stand you – a little half bottle?

BARON. Naturally. Further!

PEPEL. Get down on all fours and bark like a dog.

BARON. Imbecile! What are you – my employer? Or just a drunk?

PEPEL. Oh, come on! Bark for me! It'll amuse me. You're a nobleman. Time was when you didn't look on people like us as human at all. And all that.

BARON. Yes. And further?

PEPEL. What more? Now I'm going to make you bark like a dog. And you'll do it, won't you? You will.

BARON. All right, I will. Imbecile! What kind of satisfaction can you get from that when I am perfectly aware that by now I have become almost lower than you? You should have made me crawl on all fours when I was still not yet your equal.

BUBNOV. He's right.

LUKA. I'd call that right.

BUBNOV. What's gone is gone. All that's left is candle-droppings. There's no lords-and-ladies here, all's been shucked off, nothing left but the naked man.

LUKA. So all are equal ... And were you really a baron, my dear?

BARON. Whatever's this? Who are you, pigwigeon?

LUKA (*laughing*). I've seen a count, and I've seen a prince, but this is the first time I've set eyes on a baron – and it has to be a mouldy one.

PEPEL (*laughing*). Baron! For a moment there you had me shamed.

BARON. Time you got smarter, Vasska.

LUKA. Dear, dear! (*Shakes his head.*) I look at you, brotherkins, and your life is ... Oh ... (*Shakes his head again.*)

BUBNOV. ... a life where you quake the minute you wake.

BARON. We've all lived better. True. Once upon a time I woke in the morning to hot coffee and cream. Cream – yes.

LUKA. And yet we're all still just – humans. Pretend how you like, wriggle how you like, we die as we're born – just humans. And it seems to me people are getting cleverer all the time, more interesting ... and though they live worse and worse, they all want something better ... A stubborn lot.

BARON. Who are you, old man? Where did you spring from?

LUKA. Me?

BARON. You're a pilgrim – a traveller?

LUKA. We're all travellers on this earth. I've heard tell even our earth is a traveller in the heavens.

BARON (*severely*). That is so. But what about a passport? Do you have one?

LUKA (*after a pause*). And are you a 'detective', then?

PEPEL (*joyfully*). Ah, that's a crafty one! [This time the Baron's walked into it.

BUBNOV. Uhu, it's the nobleman's turn now.]

BARON (*embarrassed*). Oh, come now! I was only joking, old one, I don't have any papers myself ...

BUBNOV. Liar.

BARON. Well, yes, I have *papers* – but they're none of them any good.

LUKA. That's the way it is with papers – none of them are any good.

PEPEL. Hey, Baron! You coming down for that drink?

BARON. I'm with you. Well, goodbye, old one. You're a rascal, you know that?

LUKA. Everything's possible, my dear.

PEPEL (*at the door*). Come on, then.

PEPEL *goes out, followed quickly by the* BARON.

LUKA. Was that one really a baron?

BUBNOV. Who knows? He was a gent, that's for sure. Even now, sometimes, he'll suddenly give you a glimpse of it . . . He's not lost the touch.

LUKA. Maybe being a gentleman is like having the smallpox – a man gets better, but the marks remain.

BUBNOV. He's all right. He just gives a little kick like that sometimes, the way he did about your papers.

ALYOSHKA *comes in, drunk, with his accordion in his hand. He's whistling.*

ALYOSHKA. Hey, you monsters of the deep . . . !

BUBNOV. [What are you yelling for?

ALYOSHKA. Oh! Sorry! Excuse me! As a man of manners . . .]

BUBNOV. Been on the booze again.

ALYOSHKA. Booze? On the house! You know that inspector Medyakin? He just threw me out of the police station. And make sure, he says, there's not even a whiff of you on the streets of this town! Uh-uh! (*Wags a finger reprovingly.*) Not a whiff! Now I – am a man – of character. And that boss of mine . . . *snarls* at me! And what is he, this . . . boss? Aargh! A mis-con-cep-tion! He's a drunkard, this boss! And I – I am the sort of man . . . who doesn't wish for a thing. I don't want *anything* –

full stop! Come on, you can have me for twenty roubles – no.
No. I don't want a thing.

NASTYA *comes in from the kitchen.*

Offer me a million – I *don't want* it! And for me, a man of
character, to be bossed about by a drunk – I don't want that
either. I don't want it.

NASTYA, *standing by the door, shakes her head as she looks
at* ALYOSHKA.

LUKA (*good-naturedly*). You're in a proper muddle, aren't you,
lad?
BUBNOV. All men are fools.

ALYOSHKA *lies down on the floor.*

ALYOSHKA. There you are. Eat me up! I don't want – a single
thing! I tell you, I am a desperate man! Tell me this – who . . .
is better than me? Or – why . . . am I any worse than anyone
else? You see! And that Medyakin says, don't you go out on the
streets or I'll bash you to . . . smithereens! But I'm going! Oh,
yes, I'm going! I'll lie down in the middle of the street . . . run
over me if you like . . . I don't want a thing!
NASTYA. Poor silly kid – look at the state he's in!

ALYOSHKA *sees her, and kneels.*

ALYOSHKA. Miss! Mamzell. Parley francey? Weiner Shnitzel?
Quanta costa? Che bella fräulein! – I've been drinking . . .
NASTYA (*loud whisper*). Vassilissa!

VASSILISSA *opens the door quickly, speaks to* ALYOSHKA.

VASSILISSA. You here again?
ALYOSHKA. Ah – good day to you, madam! Please do come in!
VASSILISSA. I told you not to set foot in here again, you young
puppy, and here you are . . .
ALYOSHKA. Vassilissa Karpovna, wouldn't you like me . . . to
play you a funeral march?

VASSILISSA *gives him a shove on the shoulder.*

VASSILISSA. Get out!

ALYOSHKA *moves towards the door.*

ALYOSHKA. No – wait – don't be like that! The funeral march! I
only just learnt it! A brand new piece! You mustn't be like that!

VASSILISSA. I'll give you *mustn't*! I'll set the whole street on you,
you filthy blabbermouth! You're too young to go round yapping
about me!

ALYOSHKA (*running out*). I'm going, I'm going!

VASSILISSA (*to* BUBNOV). You see he doesn't set foot in here
again, understand?

BUBNOV. I'm not your watchdog.

VASSILISSA. I don't care who you are, you're living here on
charity don't forget! How much do you owe me?

BUBNOV (*calmly*). Haven't counted.

VASSILISSA. You watch it, or I will!

ALYOSHKA *opens the door, shouts.*

ALYOSHKA. Vassilissa Kar-pov-na! I'm not af-RAID of You-ou!
Not af-rai-aid!

He disappears. LUKA *laughs.*

VASSILISSA. And who might you be?

LUKA. A passer-by.

VASSILISSA. Spending the night, or staying?

LUKA. I'll see.

VASSILISSA. Passport.

LUKA. You'll get it.

VASSILISSA. Give it me now.

LUKA. I'll bring it – bring it to your very door.

VASSILISSA. [A passer-by, indeed! Pilferer would be more like it.

LUKA (*sighing*). Ah, you've an unkindly way with you, motherkin.]

VASSILISSA *goes over to the door into Pepel's room.*
ALYOSHKA *looks in through the kitchen door, whispers:*

ALYOSHKA. Psst! Has she gone.

VASSILISSA *rounds on him.*

VASSILISSA. You still here?!

ALYOSHKA *whistles, disappears;* NASTYA *and* LUKA *laugh.*

BUBNOV (*to* VASSILISSA). He's not there.
VASSILISSA. Who isn't?
BUBNOV. Vasska.
VASSILISSA. Who asked you?
BUBNOV. I see you looking round and about.
VASSILISSA. I'm looking to see if everything's in order, all right?
Why hasn't the place been swept yet? How often have I got to
tell you to keep the place clean?
BUBNOV. It's the actor's turn to sweep up.
VASSILISSA. I don't care whose turn it is! If those sanitary
inspectors come round and I'm fined, out you go – the lot of
you!
BUBNOV (*calmly*). Then what'll you live on?
VASSILISSA. It's got to be spotless – spotless! (*She goes into the
kitchen; to* NASTYA.) What are you hanging about here for?
Why are your eyes all swollen like that? Don't stand there like a
tree stump – sweep the floor! Have you seen Natasha? Has she
been in here?
NASTYA. I don't know. I haven't seen her.
VASSILISSA. Bubnov! Was my sister in here?
BUBNOV. Uhu. She brought him in.
VASSILISSA. Was that thing home?
BUBNOV. Vasska? Yes. But she was talking to Kleshch, Natasha
was.
VASSILISSA. Did I ask who she was talking to? Ugh! Filth
everywhere! Filthy! Pack of pigs, you are! See it's cleaned up
you hear?

VASSILISSA *goes out quickly.*

BUBNOV. She's vicious, that one.

LUKA. A severious little ladybug.

NASTYA. Anyone'd get vicious, leading her life. Tie any living thing to a man like hers . . .

BUBNOV. She's not tied that tight.

LUKA. Does she always . . . explode like that?

BUBNOV. Always. She came to see her lover; you see, and he wasn't here . . .

LUKA. And that was an offence. Ah-ha. Dear me, all these different souls on this earth, all trying to order things the way they want, and frightening each other with all sorts of fears . . . and for all that, there's no order in life, nothing's clean-cut and pure.

BUBNOV. Order we want, brew it we can't. However, there's sweeping to be done. Nastya! Why don't you get on with it?

NASTYA. Oh, yes, of course! I'm your chambermaid, aren't I?

Pause

I'm going to get drunk today. Stinking drunk.

BUBNOV. Ah, well, of course, that's a serious business too.

LUKA. Why do you want to get drunk, lass? A while ago there you were, weeping. And now you say you want to get drunk!

NASTYA *(defiantly).* I'll get drunk – and then I'll have a cry again. That's all.

BUBNOV. It's not much.

LUKA. But what's the reason for it, my dear? You don't get blisters without bad boots, do you?

NASTYA *is silent, shaking her head.*

Well, well – *(He tut-tuts.)* – ah, people, people – what's to become of you? As for me, I might as well sweep up the floor for you – where's the broom?

BUBNOV. In the passage, behind the door.

LUKA *goes out into the passage.*

Nastionka!

NASTYA. What?

BUBNOV. Why did Vassilissa lay into Alyoshka like that?

NASTYA. He's been going around saying that Vasska's tired of her
and would like to drop her and take up with Natasha instead.
I'm getting out of here. Find myself another place.

BUBNOV. What? Where?

NASTYA. Anywhere. I'm sick of all this . . . I don't belong here.

BUBNOV (*calmly*). You don't belong anywhere. Nobody on earth
belongs anywhere.

> NASTYA *shakes her head, goes out quietly into the hall. Enter*
> MEDVEDIEV, *followed by* LUKA *with the broom.*

MEDVEDIEV. I don't seem to know you.

LUKA. And the others – you know all of them?

MEDVEDIEV. It's my job to know everyone in my parish. And I
certainly don't know you.

LUKA. That, uncle, is because the whole world hasn't quite been
got into your parish – a mite's been left out in the cold.

> LUKA *goes out into the kitchen.* MEDVEDIEV *goes up to*
> BUBNOV.

MEDVEDIEV. My parish isn't all that big, it's true – but it's far
worse than any of the big ones. A few minutes ago [– just before
I came off duty,] I had to take that cobbler, Alyoshka, into the
station. He was laying down in [the street, you know, laying
there in] the middle of the street, playing that accordion of his
and singing out I DON'T WANT ANYTHING, I
DON'T WANT A SINGLE THING! [And there was
all the traffic going past him, horses trotting along and everything,] he could have got run over or something! [He's wild,
that boy!] Well, so I took him in. He likes to make a disturbance.

BUBNOV. Coming in for a game this evening?

MEDVEDIEV. Might as well – Mm – yes. What's Vasska up to?

BUBNOV. Nothing. Same as usual.

MEDVEDIEV. He's living all right, is he?

BUBNOV. Why not? He's allowed to live.

MEDVEDIEV (*doubtfully*). Don't know about that.

LUKA *passes through to the hall, carrying a bucket.*

Mm – yes . . . There's a lot of talk, you know . . . about Vasska. Have you heard?

BUBNOV. I hear quite a bit of talk.

MEDVEDIEV. About Vassilissa and . . . Haven't you noticed?

BUBNOV. Noticed what?

MEDVEDIEV. Oh . . . just – things . . . in general . . . Perhaps you know it all and you're lying? *Every*body knows! (*Severely.*) You mustn't lie, my friend.

BUBNOV. Why should I lie?

MEDVEDIEV. That's it. Why? Oh, the bastards! [They're all saying Vasska and Vassilissa, they say . . .] what's it got to do with me, I'm her uncle not her father, why laugh at me?

KVASHNIA *enters.*

That's the way people are these days, they'll laugh at anything . . . (*Sees* KVASHNIA.) Aah, there you are!

KVASHNIA. Ha – my precious police force! You know what, Bubnov! He was going on at me again, down at the market, about me marrying him!

BUBNOV. Do it. Why not? He's got a bit of money, and I'm sure he's still got plenty of juice in him.

MEDVEDIEV. Who, me? (*He chortles.*)

KVASHNIA. Listen, you looby, don't you touch me there, I tell you, not on my sore spot now! I been through that one, my pet. Getting married's like jumping through a hole in the ice for us poor women – you do it once and you remember it for the rest of your life.

MEDVEDIEV. Hold on now! Husbands aren't always the same, you know!

KVASHNIA. But I'm always the same. When my dear departed

husband finally went to his grave – may his soul never find rest – I spent the whole day just sitting alone with my job, I tell you I just couldn't believe my luck.

MEDVEDIEV. If your husband used to beat you for no good reason you should have complained to the police.

KVASHNIA. I complained to God for eight years – he didn't help.

MEDVEDIEV. Wife-beating's prohibited now, there's a decent severity and order in everything. Nobody can be beaten for nothing, only for the sake of law and order.

LUKA *comes in, supporting* ANNA.

LUKA. There now, we've crawled our way in somehow . . . Deary me, you shouldn't be out and about in your feebleness! Which is your place?

ANNA *points to her bed.*

ANNA. Thank you, grandpa.

KVASHNIA. There's a married woman for you. Look at her!

LUKA. The little ladybug has an extremely feeble debilitution. She was creeping along the passage, clutching the wall and groaning . . . Why do you let her go out there by herself?

KVASHNIA. Ah, forgive us our wickedness, little father! Madam's personal maid must have gone out for a walk.

LUKA. All right, laugh about it – but how can you abandon a soul like that? Everybody, whatever he is, has his own worth.

MEDVEDIEV. Not enough surveillance! What if she died? There'd be a lot of bother. Got to keep a watch on things.

LUKA. Very true, sergeant.

MEDVEDIEV. H'mm, yes . . . though I'm not – er – quite a sergeant.

LUKA. Truly? Well, well, but your bearing is ever so sergeantic, sir.

Noise and footsteps from the hall, muffled shouts.

MEDVEDIEV. Not another brawl?

BUBNOV. Sounds like it.

KVASHNIA. Best go and see.

MEDVEDIEV. Suppose I must – duty's duty. Why do people have to be separated when they start fighting? [They'd stop of their own accord, sooner or later.] After all, people get tired when they fight, so why not let them bash each other about to their heart's content, till they've had enough? [That way they'd fight less because they wouldn't forget what a real beating feels like . . .]

BUBNOV (*climbing down off the bed*). You go and tell your chief that . . .

> KOSTYLIOV *flings open the door, shouting:*

KOSTYLIOV. Abram! . . . Quick! Vassilissa is . . . she's killing Natasha! Go on, quick!

> KVASHNIA, MEDVEDIEV *and* BUBNOV *rush out.* LUKA *looks after them, shakes his head.*

ANNA. Oh God! Poor little Natasha.

LUKA. Who's fighting up there?

ANNA. Our landladies – sisters.

> LUKA *goes over to* ANNA.

LUKA. What are they dividing up then?

ANNA. Oooh – you know – That's the way it is. They're both well fed, big healthy girls . . .

LUKA. What's your name?

ANNA. Anna. Look at you – you're just like my old father – just as gentle, just as tender . . .

LUKA. I've been well trampled, that's why I'm tender.

> *He gives a cackling laugh.*

CURTAIN

Act Two

The same set as Act One. Evening.

On plank beds round the stove SATIN, BARON, KRIVOY ZOB *and* TARTAR *are playing cards.* KLESHCH *and the* ACTOR *are watching the game.* BUBNOV *is sitting on his plank bed playing draughts with* MEDVEDIEV. LUKA *is sitting on a stool beside* ANNA'*s bed. The dosshouse is lit by two lamps, one hanging on the wall beside the card-players, the other on* BUBNOV'*s bed.*

(KRIVOY ZOB. Bloody hell, they've done us again, Assan!)
TARTAR. [One . . . stay.]
       (One more time, then finish.)
BUBNOV. Flopchin – sing!

    (*He sings.*)

  'Though the bright sun may be shining . . .'*
KRIVOY ZOB (*joining in*). 'My dungeon stays as dark as night.'
TARTAR (*to* SATIN). Shuffle! Shuffle 'em good! We know about you.
BUBNOV   'The prison guard stands by my window
KRIVOY ZOB (*together*).   – oh – oh
                And with his body steals my light.'
ANNA. Beatings. Curses. I've never known anything else. I haven't!
LUKA. Ah, little ladybug, don't be sad!
MEDEDIEV. Where are you going with that? Careful, now!
BUBNOV. Aha! Right, right!

    TARTAR *shakes his fist at* SATIN.

TARTAR. You try to hide card, [huh? I see you! You . . .]

* The full text of the song appears on page 90.

KRIVOY ZOB. Leave him, Assan. They'll outswindle us any case. Hey, Bubnov! [Sound off!]

KRIVOY ZOB *and* BUBNOV *sing*.

ANNA. I don't remember ever having enough to eat. Every bit of bread I've ever eaten I've shook over, been shaking all my life in case I was taking more'n my share . . . Gone about in rags all my life . . . all my rotten life. What did I do?

LUKA. Ah, childerkin! Tired, are you? Never mind.

ACTOR (*to* KRIVOY ZOB). The jack – you've got to play your jack, dammit!

BARON. Although we have a queen.

KLESHCH. They always win.

SATIN. It's become a habit.

MEDVEDIEV. And now – there's a king!

BUBNOV. Two can play at that . . .

ANNA. I'm going. Dying.

(KRIVOY ZOB. Hey, Assan, come on! One more time!)

KLESHCH (*to* TARTAR). Have some sense, Prince, don't go in again! Get out of the game I tell you!

ACTOR. Has he no mind of his own?

BARON. Careful now, Andriushka, or I'll put the evil eye on you!

TARTAR. Deal again! Pitcher keeps going to well and . . . pitcher break himself! Same as me.

KLESHCH, *shaking his head, goes over to* BUBNOV.

ANNA. And I keep thinking, Lord, Lord, surely I'm not going to be punished in the next world as well? Not there too, surely?

LUKA. There won't be anything at all. Lie still now and don't you worry a whit. [Nothing at all. You'll rest there. Bear up a bit longer.] Everybody has to bear his life, each in his own way.

LUKA *gets up and walks out quickly into the kitchen*.

BURNOV (*sings*). 'Guard me, though I need no guarding –'

KRBVOY ZOB (*sings*). 'I can't hope to break this chain . . .'

BUBNOV   'But stand aside from my
KRIVOY ZOB   (*sing together*).   window – oh – oh That I
                                       may see the sun again.'

TARTAR (*shouts*). Hey! You shove card up your sleeve!

BARON (*embarrassed*). Well, where would you like me to shove it – up your arse?

ACTOR (*firmly*). No, Prince, you're mistaken, no one would dream of . . .

TARTAR. I saw! Is cheat! No more play.

SATIN (*collecting the cards*). Oh, come off it, Assan. You know we're villains – so why play with us?

BARON. You lose forty 'pecks and make enough noise for three roubles . . . really, for a Prince . . . !

TARTAR (*angrily*). Must play honest!

SATIN. Whatever for?

TARTAR. How that, whatev' for?

SATIN. What I say – whatever for?

TARTAR. You don' know?

SATIN. I don't. Do you?

    The TARTAR *spits furiously. They all laugh at him.*

KRIVOY ZOB (*amiably*). You are a prick, Assan! Don't you see, if they started to be honest they'd starve to death in three days.

TARTAR. Is nothing to me. I say man must live honest!

KRIVOY ZOB. Doesn't he keep on! Why don't we go and get some tea? Buben –

    Sings.

'Oh you chain, you heavy mooring . . .'

BUBNOV (*sings*). 'Oh you cru-el iron bond . . .'

KRIVOY ZOB. Come on, Assanka!

    He goes out singing.

'I can never shake nor break you-oo-oo.'

BUBNOV   (*together*).   'And roam the sunlit world beyond.'
KRIVOY ZOB

The TARTAR *shakes his fist at the* BARON *and follows his friend out.*

SATIN [(*to the* BARON, *laughing*). Well, your lowness, thou hast once again solemnly plonked thyself in the shit. An educated man, and can't even palm a card!

BARON (*shrugging*). God knows what happened.

ACTOR. No talent – not enough faith in yourself! Without that, nothing. No faith, no success – nothing!

MEDVEDIEV. I've got one king and ... H'm. You've got two.

BUBNOV. Just one can survive, if his brain is alive. Go on. Move!

KLESHCH. You've lost, Abram Ivanich.

MEDVEDIEV. Mind your own business. Understand? And shut up!

SATIN. The winnings – fifty-three kopecks.

ACTOR. The three 'pecks for me ... though come to think of it, what do I want three kopecks for?]

    LUKA *comes out of the kitchen.*

LUKA. Well, did you take the Tartar? You'll be going for a drop of vodka now, then?

BARON. Come along with us.

SATIN. It'd be worth it, to see what you're like when you're drunk.

LUKA. No better than when I'm sober.

ACTOR. Come on, old one. I'll give you a few couplets.

LUKA. What are they?

ACTOR. You know – verses.

LUKA. Ah, *ve-ers*es! But what good are they to me, verses?

ACTOR. They can make you laugh. Or sad, sometimes.

SATIN. Come on, coupleteer. (*To* BARON.) You coming?

    SATIN *exits with the* BARON.

ACTOR. You go on, I'll catch you up. Listen, old one, I'll give you some lines from a poem ... I forget how it begins ... H'm ... forgotten ... (*He rubs his forehead.*)

BUBNOV. That's it! There goes your king. Your move.

MEDVEDIEV. Dammit, he went wrong there somewhere . . .

ACTOR. Before my organism was poisoned with alcohol, old one, I
had an excellent memory. But it's finished now, everything's
finished for me. I used to declaim that poem with enormous
success . . . to tumultuous applause! You wouldn't know what
applause means . . . it's like vodka, brother! I'd make my
entrance, take up my pose . . . (*Poses*.) So! I'd stand there, so,
and . . . (*He is silent*.) Don't remember any of it. Not a word.
Just – don't remember. And it was the poem I loved the best
. . . Is that bad, old one?

LUKA. What could be good about it, if you've forgotten something
you loved? Your whole soul goes into what you love.

ACTOR. I've drunk my soul away, old one. Done myself in. Done
for – and why? Because I had no faith. I'm finished.

LUKA. Why? Cure yourself! They can cure you of drunkenness
now, you know. Cure you free of charge, brotherkin! There's a
sort of clinic been built for drunkards, to cure them, you know,
for free. They've allowed that a drunk is a human soul same as
anyone else, and they're actually pleased if he wants to get
himself cured! Well there you are then! You go!

ACTOR (*thoughtfully*). Go? Where? Where is it?

LUKA. Oh, it's in a town – now, what is it? It's called . . . some-
thing-or-other. Oh, I'll see you get the name all right. Now,
here's what you do. First you prepare yourself. Try and keep
away from it . . . get a grip on yourself, and – bear with it. Then
one day you'll be cured and begin to live all over again . . . it's
good, brotherkin, all-over-again is good! Just make up your
mind . . . two easy steps . . .

ACTOR (*smiling*). All-over-again, eh? Right from the start. That's
good, yes. All over again? (*Laughs*.) Oh . . . yes! I can? I can,
can't I?

LUKA. Why not? A human soul can do anything – if he really
wants to.

ACTOR (*suddenly, as if waking up*). You're a comic aren't you?
Goodbye for now – (*He whistles*.) Goodbye, old one!

ANNA. Grandpa!

LUKA. What is it, little one?

ANNA. Talk to me.

LUKA crosses to her bed.

LUKA. All right, let's talk together, then.

KLESHCH looks round, goes silently over to his wife, looks at her, and makes movements with his hands as if he wants to say something.

What, brother?

KLESHCH (*in a low voice*). Nothing.

He slowly goes over to the door into the hall, stands in front of it for a few moments, then goes out.

LUKA (*looking after* KLESHCH). It's painful for that little husband of yours.

ANNA. I'm past caring about him.

LUKA. Did he beat you?

ANNA. Did he ever! It was him started me on the coughing.

BUBNOV. My wife . . . had a lover. Very handy at draughts, he was, the villain.

MEDVEDIEV. H'mm.

ANNA. Grandpa . . . talk to me, dear. I feel so sick.

LUKA. It's nothing. It's only – death's beginnings, little pigeon. It's nothing, my dear. Just hope. You'll do a little dying that's all and then you'll be wrapped in the long peace . . . [nothing more asked of you, nothing to fear! Silence, peaceness, you just lie.] Death – quietens everything, she strokes us to sleep . . . Blest in their rest are the dead, they say, and that's true, my dear, for where is there here for a soul to rest?

Enter PEPEL. He is slightly drunk, dishevelled, and gloomy. He sits down on the plank bed by the door and remains silent and motionless.

ANNA. But how will it be there? More miseries?

LUKA. Nothing! There'll be nothing! Believe me. Peaceness – and nothing else. You'll be called before the Lord and they'll say, Lord, look here on your servant Anna . .

MEDVEDIEV. How do you know what they're going to say there? You . . .

> PEPEL *looks up at the sound of* MEDVEDIEV'*s voice and starts listening.*

LUKA. It must be – that I know, sergeant.

MEDVEDIEV (*conciliatory*). H'm, yes. Well, that's your line I suppose . . . (*mumbles*) . . . not . . . exactly . . . uh . . . sergeant.

BUBNOV. Double jump!

MEDVEDIEV. Oh, you . . . May you be . . .!

LUKA. And the Lord's eyes will stroke you, and he'll say, I know this Anna! Now, He'll say, you take this soul, Anna, into paradise, let her be soothed . . . I know how hard her life's been, she's tired, let Anna rest . . .

ANNA (*sighing*). Oh grandpa, good grandpa . . . if only it could be like that! if only there'll be peace . . . not to feel anything . . .

LUKA. You won't. There'll be nothing – believe that! Die with joy, without fear . . . for I tell you, death to us is like a mother to her little children.

ANNA. But perhaps . . . perhaps . . . I'll get better?

LUKA (*with a short laugh*). What for? More 'miseries'?

ANNA (*grunts*). Just a . . . a little more . . . if only I could live . . . just a little bit more! If there's not going to be any torment there, I could bear it here for a while . . . I could!

LUKA. There'll be nothing! Just . . .

PEPEL (*loudly*). True! Or perhaps – not true!

ANNA (*fearfully*). Oh God!

LUKA. Hello, handsome.

MEDVEDIEV. Who's shouting?

> PEPEL *goes up to* MEDVEDIEV.

PEPEL. I am. So what?

MEDVEDIEV. You got no business shouting, that's what. A soul should behave peaceably.

PEPEL. Ah, you dumb ox! Fine big uncle you are, aren't you?

LUKA (*quietly, to* PEPEL). Listen, don't shout. The little woman here's dying, her lips are already tasting the loam. Don't disturb her.

PEPEL. Oh, dutiful respects, grandpa. You're a fine old feller too. I can see that. You lie well, that's the thing – tell pleasant little tales. You lie on regardless, then – there's none too much in this world that's pleasant.

BUBNOV. Is she really dying, that one?

LUKA. Doesn't look as if she's joking.

BUBNOV. Then she'll stop coughing. She was always coughing – very unrestful it was. Double jump.

MEDVEDIEV. Oh, you should be shot through the heart!

PEPEL. Abram.

MEDVEDIEV. I'm not Abram to you

PEPEL. Abrashka – is Natasha poorly?

MEDVEDIEV. None of your business.

PEPEL. No, tell me – did Vassilissa knock her about badly?

MEDVEDIEV. That's none of your business either. It's family business. Who do you think you are?

PEPEL. Whoever I think I am, I could make sure none of your lot saw Natasha again if I wanted to.

MEDVEDIEV (*stops playing*). You . . . What did you say? What are you talking about? My youngest niece could . . . you . . . you're just a thief!

PEPEL. A thief, perhaps – but not one you've caught.

MEDVEDIEV. You wait! I'll catch you soon enough!

PEPEL. You'll be sorry if you do, you and your whole tribe. You don't imagine I'd keep my mouth shut in front of the magistrate do you? You can't keep a fox in a box! Who started you thieving, they'll ask, who gave you the tip-offs? Mishka Kostyliov and his wife! And who received the stolen goods? Mishka Kostyliov and his wife!

MEDVEDIEV. Liar. They'd never believe you.

PEPEL. They'd believe me – because it's true. Oh, and I'll drag
you into it too ... Ha! I'll destroy the whole rotten pack of
you, you wait and see!

MEDVEDIEV (*at a loss*). Liar! And – and – liar! And – and – what
harm have I ever done you? You're like a mad dog!

PEPEL. What good have you ever done me?

LUKA. Ah-a.

MEDVEDIEV (*to* LUKA). What are you grunting about, what's it
got to do with you? This is family business.

BUBNOV (*to* LUKA). [Leave it. They're not tying nooses for our
necks.

LUKA (*serenely*). Didn't say a word. All I do say is, if someone has
done nothing good to a person, then they've done bad.

MEDVEDIEV (*not understanding*). That's it, you see, all of us here,
now, we know each other and . . .] Who are you, anyway?

He snorts angrily, goes out quickly.

LUKA. He's lost his temper, that official gentleman. Tsk-
tsk! I can see your affairs are in a muddle, brothers.

PEPEL. He's gone off to snivel to Vassilissa.

BUBNOV. You're acting like a fool, Vasska. You keep your end up
all right – but you watch it. [Boldness is all very well when
you're off to the woods with a girl to gather mushrooms – but
it won't do here, on your own doorstep.] That lot'll rip your
guts out in no time.

PEPEL. We-e-ell – as a matter of fact, no. You can't take a man
from Yaroslavl with your bare hands. When it's war, we fight.

LUKA. But it's true, brotherkin – you should get away from this
place.

PEPEL. Where to? Got anything in mind?

LUKA. Take yourself off to Siberia.

PEPEL. Ha! No, if it's going to be Siberia, I'll wait to be sent at
Government expense.

LUKA. No, listen, you take yourself off there! [You could find a road for yourself there, you're just the kind of man they need there.

PEPEL. My road was laid down for me long ago. My father spent his whole life in jail, and booked the same berth for me. Even when I was a kid I was called thief and son-of-a-thief.]

LUKA. It's a good part of the world, though, Siberia, a golden part. Anyone strong and in his right mind can make himself a nice snug bed there, and grow like a cucumber.

PEPEL. Why do you lie all the time, old one?

LUKA. Eh?

PEPEL. Gone deaf suddenly? Why do you lie, I said?

LUKA. Lie? When've I lied?

PEPEL. All the time. You say it's wonderful here, wonderful there, and you're lying. What for?

LUKA. Just believe me. You trot off and see for yourself. You'll thank me. What are you hanging around here for? And why are you so keen on the truth. Think now – the truth is a blade that can turn.

PEPEL. It's all one to me. If the blade turns, it turns.

LUKA. Ah, you're all dreams! What's the point of letting oneself be killed?

BUBNOV. What are you two drivelling on about? I don't understand. What truth do you want, Vasska, and what for? You know the truth about yourself and so does everyone else.

PEPEL. Wait, stop croaking, Bubnov. Just let him tell me . . . Listen, old one – does God exist?

LUKA *smiles, says nothing.*

BUBNOV. People's lives are just chips on the water – the house gets built, but the chips float away.

PEPEL. Well? Does he? Go on.

LUKA (*in a low voice*). If you believe – he does. If you don't – he doesn't. Whatever you believe in, exists.

PEPEL *gazes intently at* LUKA, *in silence, astonished.*

BUBNOV. I'm going for some tea. Come on – hey!

LUKA (*to* PEPEL). What are you staring at?

PEPEL. So that . . . wait a minute . . . that means . . .

BUBNOV. Ah well, I'll go by myself.

> BUBNOV *goes towards the door, where he is met by* VASSILISSA.

PEPEL. What you mean is . . .

VASSILISSA (*to* BUBNOV). Is Nastya here?

BUBNOV. No.

> BUBNOV *goes out.*

PEPEL. Oh, you're here.

> VASSILISSA *goes over to* ANNA.

VASSILISSA. Still alive?

LUKA. Don't disturb her.

VASSILISSA. What are you hanging about here for?

LUKA. I can go if necessary.

> VASSILISSA *goes over to the door of* PEPEL's *room.*

VASSILISSA. Vasska. There's something I want to talk to you
about.

> LUKA *goes to the hall door, opens it, then shuts it loudly again.*
> *He then stealthily climbs on to a bed and from there on to the*
> *top of the stove.* VASSILISSA *calls from Pepel's room.*

Vasska! Come here.

PEPEL. I won't. Don't want to.

VASSILISSA. Why not? Why are you so cross?

PEPEL. I'm tired of it – sick of all the fuss.

VASSILISSA. And tired of me?

PEPEL. Tired of you, too.

> VASSILISSA *pulls her shawl tightly about her shoulders, pressing*
> *her hands to her chest. She goes over to* ANNA's *bed, looks care-*
> *fully behind the canopy, and goes back to* PEPEL.

Go on, then.

VASSILISSA. What can I say? You can't be forced to love ... and it's not my way to beg for kindness ... Thank you for the truth.

PEPEL. What truth?

VASSILISSA. That you're tired of me ... or perhaps you aren't?

PEPEL *looks at her in silence. She moves up to him.*

Why are you staring? Don't you recognize me?

PEPEL (*sighs*). You're a fine-looking woman, Vassilissa.

She puts her arm around his neck, but he shrugs it off with a movement of his shoulder.

But you never came near my heart. I lived with you and all that ... but I never cared for you.

VASSILISSA (*quietly*). I see. So ...

PEPEL. So we've got nothing to talk about. Nothing. Just leave me alone.

VASSILISSA. Is there someone else?

PEPEL. None of your business. If there was, I wouldn't use you as a go-between.

VASSILISSA (*significantly*). You'd be wrong about that. I might be the very person who could do it.

PEPEL (*suspiciously*). What d'you mean?

VASSILISSA. You know – why pretend? Vasska, I'm a straight-forward person .... (*Quietly*). I won't try to hide it – you've hurt me ... for no reason at all ... as if you'd lashed at me with a whip. Saying you loved me and then suddenly ...

PEPEL. Not suddenly. For a long time I've ... There's no heart in you, woman! A woman must have heart in her! We're wild animals, we need ... we have to be trained, and you – what kind of training did you give me?

VASSILISSA. That's all past and done. I know we're none of us our own masters. You don't love me any more – all right, that's it.

PEPEL. Well, that's the end, then. We're parting peacefully, without a fuss, and that's fine.

VASSILISSA. No, wait, I'm not finished. When – when I was with you – I was always – waiting. Hoping you'd help me to get out of this – cesspit, get away from my husband, my uncle, this whole rotten way of life. [I don't know, but maybe it wasn't really you I loved at all, Vasska, maybe it was just this – this hope, this idea – I was loving and seeing in you.] Do you understand? I was waiting for you to drag me out of here.

PEPEL. I'm not a pair of pincers. No, what I thought was, what with you being so smart . . . because you are smart, Vassilissa, I grant you that, you're clever . . .

VASSILISSA (*leaning close to him*). Vasska! We could – help each other . . . Couldn't we?

PEPEL. How?

VASSILISSA (*quietly, insistently*). My sister – you like her, don't you?

PEPEL. That's why you knock her about so savagely, isn't it? You watch it, Vassilissa! Keep your hands off her!

VASSILISSA. [Wait, please,] don't get angry. It could all be arranged quietly, smoothly. You want to marry Natasha – all right, I'll give you money as well! Silver roubles . . . three hundred of them! And more, when I can save more!

PEPEL (*moving away*). Hey, now, hold on! What d'you mean, what are you getting at?

VASSILISSA. Free me . . . from that man. Take that . . . noose off my neck!

PEPEL (*whistles softly*). So that's it! Oh, yes! That's a smart bit of thinking, all right! Your husband to his grave, your lover to jail, and yourself . . .

VASSILISSA. No, Vasska! No need for jail! You could get friends to do it – and even if it was you, who'd ever find out? Think of Natasha – think! And the money . . . you'll be able to get away somewhere . . . and I'll be free for ever . . . and Natasha would be better off away from me . . . I can't look at her without

burning with hatred, and then I can't stop myself, I torture
the poor girl, because of you, beat her, beat her until I'm
weeping with pity for her ... but I keep on beating her. And
I'll go on beating her.

PEPEL. You're a savage. [It's nothing to boast about.]

VASSILISSA. [Not boasting – speaking the truth.] Think, Vasska!
Twice now you've been to jail because of my husband, because
of his greed! [He fastened on me like a leech – he's been
sucking my blood for four years now. What sort of a husband is
he?] And he bullies Natasha, [ridicules her,] tells her she's a
beggar! He's poison for everyone, he's just poison.

PEPEL. Cunning, the way you twist your snares.

VASSILISSA. I've been straight enough with you – only a fool
could get me wrong.

KOSTYLIOV *comes in carefully and steals forward.*

PEPEL. You'd better go.

VASSILISSA. Think, Vasska! (*She sees her husband.*) What is it?
Come for me, huh?

PEPEL *starts, and looks wildly at* KOSTYLIOV.

KOSTYLIOV. It's me, yes! And here you are, alone together, eh?
Talking together?

He suddenly stamps his foot and squeals loudly.

You slut! You selfish tramp!

*He is alarmed by his own shouting, which the others meet with
silence, remaining motionless.*

God forgive me, Vassilissa, you've led me into sin again! I've
been looking for you everywhere ... (*Shrieking again.*) It's
bedtime! And you've forgotten to put oil in the votive lamps!
Oh, you tramp, you sow!

*He makes a dismissive downward movement of his trembling
hands.* VASSILISSA *walks slowly over to the door, looking back
at* PEPEL.

PEPEL (*to* KOSTYLIOV). Get away from here.

KOSTYLIOV (*shouting*). It's my house! Get away yourself, thief!

PEPEL (*in a stifled voice*). Watch out, Mishka.

KOSTYLIOV. Don't you dare ... I'll ... You'll ...

> PEPEL *grabs him by the scruff of the neck and shakes him. Loud scuffling noises and howling yawns start from on top of the stove.* PEPEL *lets go of* KOSTYLIOV, *who scampers out with a cry.* PEPEL *jumps up on to a bed.*

PEPEL. Who's that? Who's up there?

> LUKA *sticks out his head.*

LUKA. Eh?

PEPEL. You.

LUKA (*calmly*). None other. Oh, Lord Jesus Christ!

> PEPEL *closes the door, looks for a bolt but can't find one.*

PEPEL. Bastards! Come down, old one.

LUKA (*drawling*). I'm coming.

PEPEL (*roughly*). What were you doing up on the stove?

LUKA. Where else should I have gone?

PEPEL. But ... you went outside ... ?

LUKA. Brotherkin, outside's too cold for an old man like me.

PEPEL. You heard?

LUKA. I heard. Couldn't help it. I'm not deaf. [Ah, luck's on your side, young one, luck is really on your side.

PEPEL (*suspiciously*). What d'you mean? What luck?

LUKA. Me, up on the stove.]

PEPEL. Why did you suddenly start making all that noise?

LUKA. Started getting too hot ... [your orphan luck again.] And then, I was figuring, what if the young one made a mistake ...? What if he accidentally strangled that old man?

PEPEL. I could've, too. I hate him.

LUKA. Isn't it natural? Nothing more easy! Mistakes like that happen all the time.

PEPEL (*smiling*). Maybe you made a mistake yourself, once?

LUKA. Young one, you listen to what I got to say: that woman, you keep her away from you. (*He wags his finger.*) Don't you let her come anywhere near you! She'll harry her husband to his grave neater than you can. Don't you listen to the witch. Look – see how bald I am? And why? Because of women of all sorts, I must have known more of these women than maybe there were hairs on my head and I tell you, that Vassilissa, she's worse than a scyllaritdis!

PEPEL. I don't know. Do I say thank you? Or are you another?

LUKA. Don't say anything. You won't say better than me. Just hear me – the one you want here, take her arm, and quick march, away from here! Get away from here, right away!

PEPEL (*gloomily*). How can you tell about people – which are good and which are bad? I don't understand a thing.

LUKA. There's nothing to understand. Men live every which way, according as his heart is set so a man lives, good today, bad tomorrow ... If that lass has got severiously into your heart, get away with her and have done. Otherwise, go alone. You're young, you've time enough to acquire a woman.

PEPEL *takes* LUKA *by the shoulders.*

PEPEL. No, why are you giving me all this ...?

LUKA. Wait – let go. I must have a peek at Anna. She was breathing a bit heavy, somehow ...

He goes over to ANNA's *bed, opens the canopy, looks in, and touches her with his hand.* PEPEL *watches thoughtfully, with a puzzled air.*

All-merciful Jesus Christ, receive with mercy the newly departed soul of thy servant Anna!

PEPEL (*quietly*). Is she dead?

Without going nearer, he stretches up to look over to the bed.

LUKA. She's suffered her way out of it. Where's that old whinger of hers?

PEPEL. Drinking, most likely.

LUKA. Must tell him.

PEPEL (*shuddering*). I don't like dead bodies.

LUKA (*going to door*). Why should you? It's the living you should like, the living!

PEPEL. I'm coming with you.

LUKA. Afraid?

PEPEL. Don't like it.

> *They go out hurriedly. The place is quiet and deserted. Beyond the hall door can be heard muffled sounds – it's not clear what they are. Then the* ACTOR *enters. He stops on the threshold with the door open, hanging on to the door frame. Shouts:*

ACTOR. Old one! Hey! Where are you? I've remembered! Listen!

> *Swaying, he takes two steps forward, strikes a pose, and declaims:*

'If the world, my friends, should fail to find
The road to sacred truth,
All honour to that fool whose mind
With golden dreams wraps round mankind.'

> NATASHA *appears in the doorway behind the* ACTOR.

Old one! Listen!
'If tomorrow, my friends, the sun should seem
Too tired to light the earth,
Some madman's mind would dream a dream
More dazzling than the sun's own beam.'

NATASHA (*laughing*). You scarecrow, you're drunk again!

> *The* ACTOR *turns round to her.*

ACTOR. Aha, you're there, are you? But where's the old one – the nice little old man? Looks as if there's no one here. Well, Natasha – goodbye! Yes – farewell!

NATASHA comes further in.

NATASHA. You haven't said hello yet, and now you're saying goodbye.

The ACTOR bars her way.

ACTOR. I'm leaving – going away! Spring will arrive – and find me gone!

NATASHA. Let me by. Where are you off to?

ACTOR. To look for a town . . . to get myself cured . . . You should go away too – Ophelia! get thee to a nunnery! And somewhere in the world, you see, there's a clinic, a clinic for organisms! For drunken organisms! Oh yes, a fabulous clinic, with . . . marble . . . yes, marble floors! Light, clean and everything – food and everything – free! And . . . and marble floors, yes. And I shall find it, I shall get myself cured, and once again I shall be . . . all-over-again . . . I am on the road to rebirth, as – ah – King – ah – Lear said! On the stage, Natasha, my name was Sverchkov-Zavolzhshky – no one knows that, Natasha, no one! I don't have any name at all here. Can you imagine how that hurts – to lose your name? Even dogs have names.

NATASHA walks carefully round the ACTOR, stops beside ANNA's bed, looks in.

No name – no man.

NATASHA. Look – Oh my dear, she has done it; she has died!

ACTOR (*shaking his head*). No-o-o . . .

NATASHA (*stepping back*). Before God – look!

BUBNOV (*in the doorway*). Look at what?

NATASHA. Anna. She's dead.

BUBNOV. Stopped her coughing, has she?

He goes over to ANNA's bed, looks at her, and then goes to his own place.

Better tell Kleshch. That's his business.

ACTOR. I'll go and ... and tell him that ... that she's lost her name.

The ACTOR *goes out.*

NATASHA (*in the middle of the room*). That's how it'll be with me some day ... end up ... in a basement ... beaten ... smashed ...

BUBNOV [(*spreading rags out on his bed*). What? What are you mumbling about?

NATASHA. Just ... talking to myself.

BUBNOV. Waiting for Vasska, are you? You be careful – he'll be the end of you, that one.

NATASHA. I'd as soon it was him as another.

BUBNOV (*lying down*). Well, it's your own business.

NATASHA. She's better off dead, of course, but it's sad all the same ...] Lord, what was it for – a life like that?

BUBNOV. It's the same for everyone – they're born, they live for a bit, then they die. I shall die. So will you. What's sad about it?

Enter LUKA, *the* TARTAR, KRIVOY ZOB *and* KLESHCH. KLESHCH *comes in behind the others, slowly, his shoulders hunched.*

NATASHA. Ssssh! Anna ...

KRIVOY ZOB. Yeah, we heard. Lord have mercy on her.

TARTAR (*to* KLESHCH). Humped out there must be – pulled out in hall. Here not possible dead person, here live persons sleep.

KLESHCH (*quietly*). We'll take her out.

They all go over to the bed. KLESHCH *looks at his wife over the others' shoulders.*

KRIVOY ZOB (*to the* TARTAR). You afraid she'll smell? She won't, you know. She was all dried up already before she died.

NATASHA. Oh God, if only there was a drop of pity somewhere ... if only one of you had a single kind word! Oh, you ...!

LUKA. Don't take on burdens, little one. It's nothing. How can they – how can any of us pity the dead when we can't even pity ourselves?

BUBNOV (*yawning*). And then again, death don't wince at words. An illness might, but not death.

TARTAR (*stepping back*). Police must . . .

KRIVOY ZOB. Police – right! Kleshch! You told the police?

KLESHCH. No. And there's the burial . . . I've only got forty kopecks.

KRIVOY ZOB. For a thing like this, you got to borrow. [Or p'raps we'll have a whip round – five from one, so much from another . . .] But you got to tell the police, quickly, else they'll start saying you killed her or something . . .

He goes over to the TARTAR's *bed and prepares to lie down beside him.* NATASHA *goes over to* BUBNOV's *bed.*

NATASHA. And now I shall dream about her. I always dream about dead people . . . I'm scared to go back alone – it's dark in the hall.

LUKA (*watching her*). You watch out for the living, that's all I say.

NATASHA. See me back, grandpa.

LUKA. Come on with you, then, I'll see you back.

They go out together. Pause.

KRIVOY ZOB. Oh-oh-ooh! Assan! It'll be spring soon, man! Warm living again! They're already mending their ploughs in the villages, all set for turning the soil again . . . Aah! . . . ye-e-es! And how about us, Assan . . .? Jesus, fucking Mahommed's asleep already.

BUBNOV. Tartars love to sleep.

KLESHCH *stands in the middle of the room, gazing stupidly in front of him.*

KLESHCH. What do I do now?

KRIVOY ZOB. Lie down and sleep. What else?

KLESHCH (*quietly*). But . . . she . . . How can I?

Nobody answers him. Enter SATIN *and the* ACTOR.

ACTOR (*shouts*). Hey, old one! Here, my faithful Kent!

SATIN. Here comes our brave explorer! Ho-ho!

ACTOR. It's all settled and decided, old one! Where's that town of yours? Where are you?

SATIN. Off to Phantasmagoria! Crap! – The old one lied to you, there's nothing! No town, no people, no clinic – nothing!

ACTOR. Liar!

TARTAR (*jumping up*). Where landlord? I go landlord! Not possible sleep, not possible pay rent . . . Dead persons, drunk persons . . .

Muttering, he goes out quickly. SATIN *whistles after him.*

BUBNOV (*sleepily*). Lie down, you lot, don't make such a row . . . night . . . must sleep.

ACTOR. Aha, yes . . . here . . . the dead! 'Let the dead past bury its dead.' A p-poem by . . . Béranger.*

SATIN (*shouts*). The dead can't hear! The dead can't feel! Shout – howl – the dead can't hear!

LUKA *appears in the doorway.*

CURTAIN

---

* The Actor actually quotes a poem of Pushkin's which is very well known in Russia: 'Daddy, daddy, our nets have dragged in a dead man!' But unless the quotation is a familiar one, the misattribution to Béranger is lost. Hence our borrowing from Sir Walter Scott.

Act Three

'The Waste Land' – a patch of yard littered with all kinds of rubbish and overgrown with weeds. At the back is a high brick wall which blocks out the sky. Elder bushes grow beside it. To the right, the dark wooden wall of some outbuilding – a barn or a stable. To the left, the grey wall – with its few remaining patches of stucco – of the building of which KOSTYLIOV's dosshouse is the cellar. It stands at an angle, so that the back corner comes almost into the middle of the patch, forming a narrow passage between this corner and the red brick wall. There are two windows in the grey wall, one level with the ground, the other about five feet higher and nearer the brick wall. Against this wall lie wide, low sledges, their runners uppermost, and some planks, about nine feet in length. To the right by the wall, lies a heap of old boards and joists.

Evening. The sun is setting, casting a reddish glow on the brick wall. It is early spring, and the snow has recently melted. There are no buds yet on the black elder twigs.

On a log NATASHA and NASTYA are seated side by side. LUKA and the BARON are sitting on a sledge, and KLESHCH is lying on the pile of wood to the right. In the ground level window can be seen BUBNOV's face. NASTYA, with her eyes closed, speaks in a sing-song voice, shaking her head in time to her words.

NASTYA. And so, at dead of night, into the garden he came, to the summer-house, as had been arranged between us. I had long been awaiting him there, trembling with fear and grief. He too was trembling all over and as white as a sheet, and there . . . in his hands . . . a revolverer!

> NASTASHA is chewing sunflower seeds, breaking off the husks with her teeth and spitting them out.

NATASHA. It's right, then, what they say, they are a wild lot, those students!

NASTYA. And in a fearful voice he says to me, 'Ah, my precious love, my pearl without price!'

BUBNOV. Ho, ho! Without price!

BARON. One moment! If you don't like the story don't listen, but don't interrupt the recitation. Further!

NASTYA. 'My sweetest love,' he says. 'My parents,' he says, 'will not give their consent to our marriage, and,' he says, 'they say they will curse me for all eternity because of my love for you. On which account,' he says, 'I am obliged to take my life.' And he had this revolverer, an enormous great thing it was and loaded with ten bullets. 'Farewell!' he says, 'gentle friend of my heart! I have taken an irreversal decision, for I cannot possibly live without you.' And I answered him, 'Oh, my never to be forgotten friend, Raoul . . .'

BUBNOV (astonished). What? Growl?

BARON (laughing). But, Nastya, last time it was Gaston!

NASTYA (jumping up). Shut up . . . you . . . you mangy dogs! How could you ever understand love – true love? And that's what mine was – true! (To the BARON.) You – you're nothing! Supposed to be an educated man, supposed to have drunk coffee in bed with cream in it . . .

LUKA. Now now, you two, wait, wai-ai-ait! (Drawling the word out soothingly.) Don't interfere. 'Tisn't the word that matters. But why has the word been spoken, that's what matters. Tell on, then, girl.

BUBNOV. Go on, then. Paint your feathers, draggletail.

BARON. Yes, yes! Further!

NATASHA. [Don't you listen to them, Nastya. They don't mean a thing. They're just jealous, that's all. They've got nothing to tell, themselves.]

NASTYA sits down.

NASTYA. Shan't tell any more. Don't want to. If they're not going to believe me, if they're going to laugh at me . . .

Suddenly breaking off, NASTYA is quiet for a few seconds and then, closing her eyes again, she starts to talk passionately and loudly, her hand beating time to her words, as if she is listening to music in the distance.

And so I answered him, 'Oh light of my life! heart of my heart! No more could I possibly live in this world without you, for I love you quite insanely, and ever will I love you while my heart beats within my breast! But,' says I, 'do not, oh do not take your own young life, for your dear parents so badly need you to live, you who are their only joy! No, no, rather leave me, forget me, rather let me perish with grief over the loss of you who are my whole life . . . I am alone in the world . . . let me be . . . forsaken . . . doesn't matter . . . I'm no good . . . nothing . . . I'm nothing . . . there's nothing here for me . . . nothing . . .'

NASTYA covers her face with her hands and cries silently. NATASHA turns away from NASTYA, says quietly:

NATASHA. Don't cry. Don't!

LUKA, smiling, is stroking NASTYA's hair.

BUBNOV (*laughing loudly*). Oh, isn't she the bloody limit, though?
BARON (*also laughing*). Hey, grandpa, you don't think it's all true, do you? She got it all out of that book – *Fatal Love*! It's a lot of nonsense! Don't waste your time on her!
NATASHA. What's it got to do with you? Shut up, can't you? Just because you're feebleminded yourself you . . .
NASTYA (*furious*). You – you – you're lost – empty – you're . . . what happened to your soul?

LUKA takes NASTYA by the hand.

LUKA. Come away, my dear. Pay no heed. Calm down now. I understand, I believe. It's your truth, not theirs. If you believe you've known true love, then you have, you have! [But don't be angry with him, you live with him, you mustn't quarrel with him. Maybe . . . he was only laughing . . . because he's jealous. Maybe he never had anything real happen to him, nothing at all!] Come away now!

NASTYA (*pressing her hands to her breast*).   Before God, Grandpa, it *did* happen, it all really happened! He was a student, a French student, called Gaston, and he had a little black beard and he – he went about in – in patent-lacquered boots . . . and – may I be struck down if I lie – he *loved* me, he loved me so much!

LUKA. I know. Never mind, I believe you. And patent-lacquered boots, eh? Fancy that! And you loved him too . . . ?

They disappear round the corner.

BARON. Really, how stupid she is, that girl! Kind, perhaps, but unbearably stupid!

BUBNOV. Funny how people can get so fond of lying. She goes on as if she was always up in front of the magistrate. It's a fact!

NATASHA. It's obvious lies are more pleasant than the truth. I too . . .

BARON. Well? You too what? Further!

NATASHA. Well I . . . daydream . . . imagine things and . . . wait.

BARON. For what?

NATASHA (*smiling bashfully*). Just . . . well, I think, tomorrow, perhaps tomorrow someone will come, somebody . . . special will come. Or else, maybe, something will happen, that's never happened before. I wait – I've been waiting a long time, I'm always waiting, and of course, really and truly, what is there to wait for?

Pause.

BARON (*with a mocking smile*). Nothing. There's nothing to wait for. I'm not waiting for anything. Everything's already happened. It's over, finished! All right – further!

NATASHA. Or sometimes I think, tomorrow . . . perhaps tomorrow I'll suddenly die! And that makes me feel . . . all shivery. Summer's a good time for imagining about death, there's thunderstorms in summer, there's always a chance of death, when there's a thunderstorm.

BARON. You don't have much of a life, do you? That sister of yours – my God, she's vicious!

NATASHA. Who does have much of a life? As far as I can see it's bad for everyone.

Up to now KLESHCH *has been motionless and has taken no part in the conversation. Now he starts up.*

KLESHCH. Everyone? That's a lie! It's not bad for everyone! If it was, all right, that'd be the way of things, and it wouldn't all be such a bloody insult!

BUBNOV. Who got his teeth in you then? Yelping like that!

KLESHCH *lies down again, grumbling to himself.*

BARON. Suppose I'd better go and make my peace with Nastionka . . . if one doesn't go and make up one can't even get the price of a drink out of her . . .

BUBNOV. H'm . . . people do love telling lies, though . . . You can understand it with Nastya, she's used to painting her face, and she'd like to paint her soul as well, dab a bit of rouge on her soul. But what about the others – look at Luka, for instance, he's always telling lies and he gets nothing out of it. And he's an old man, that one. What does he do it for?

BARON (*with a smile, going out*). Everyone in the world's got a grey little soul – we'd all like to touch them up a bit.

LUKA *reappears from around the corner.*

LUKA. Why do you nag at the poor girl, sir? You should leave her be, let her weep away and amuse herself, she only does it for her own pleasure. What harm does it do you?

BARON. It's stupid, old one, and it's a bore. Today it's Raoul, tomorrow Gaston, and it's always the same stupid rubbish! Anyhow, I'm going to make it up with her.

The BARON *goes off.*

LUKA. Off you go then, and be gentle with her. It never does any harm to be gentle with a person.

NATASHA. You're kind, grandpa. Why are you so kind?

LUKA. Kind, am I? Well, all right, yes, if you say so.

From over the red wall come soft sounds of an accordion, and someone singing.

Somebody has to be kind after all, my dear. People need pity. Didn't Christ pity us all, and tell us to pity each other? I can tell you, it's good when you take pity on someone in time! For instance – I was once working as caretaker in a villa outside Tomsk. Belonged to an engineer. Right. Now this villa stood all alone in the forest – very lonely spot it was too! Winter in Siberia. And there I was, alone in the villa. All fine and good. But then, one day . . . there's this noise! Someone trying to climb in!

NATASHA. Thieves?

LUKA. Just that. So there they were, climbing in. I picked up a gun, and out I went. Looked round. Two of them there were, trying to open up a window – so busy working away at it they never even saw me. So I shouted. 'Hey! You! Get away from there!' They turned round – and come straight at me with an axe. 'Stop!' I warned them, 'Or I'll shoot!' And I kept moving the gun, now on one, now on the other. And down they went, down on their knees, begging me to let them go. Then I – well, I lost my temper. You know, because of the axe. 'I told you to go,' I said, 'and instead you come at me like limbs of satan. So now,' I said, 'You over there, you break off that branch of twigs!' So he broke off the branch. 'And you,' I said, 'you lie down there, face down. Right. Now you – whip him!' And they did as I told them, and gave each other a whipping. And when the whipping was done they said . . . grandpa, they said, for the love of Christ, they said, give us a crust of bread! We haven't had a bite since we started out . . . There's thieves for you, my dear! (*He laughs.*) There's coming at you with an axe! Yes, good little fellers they were, the pair of them. [You should've asked me for bread straight off, I told them, but they said, Ah, we've had enough of that, asking and asking and nobody giving a crumb, it's insulting to a man . . .] And so they stayed with me the whole winter. [One of them, Stepan, he'd take the gun and go off hunting. The other one, Yakov, he was always sick, coughing all the time. So there we were, the three of us, looking after the villa.] When spring came it was, 'Goodbye, grandpa!' and off they went, making tracks back to Russia.

NATASHA. Were they on the run? Convicts?

LUKA. Just that. They'd run away from a penal colony. [Good little fellers they were.] But if I hadn't taken pity on them, they'd have maybe come back and killed me or something, and then it would have been the courts again, and prison again, and Siberia . . . and what's the sense in it all? Prison doesn't teach a man to be good, no more does Siberia. Only another poor soul can do that. It's true. One soul can teach good to another soul. It's simple.

   Pause.

BUBNOV. H'm. Well, me, I can't tell lies. What's the point, anyway? The way I see it, let's have the whole truth coming out just as it is. Why shy away from it?

   KLESHCH *again suddenly jumps up as if he'd been scalded, shouting.*

KLESHCH. Truth! What truth? Where's the truth! Here . . . (*He pulls at the rags he's wearing.*) There's the truth for you! Got no work . . . no strength left . . . there's the truth. No shelter, no place to go, might as well lie down and die, that's it, that's the truth of it. Shit! – what's the good of it to me, the truth? – it's shit! Let me get my head out and breathe! What have I done wrong, to be given the truth! Ah, Christ, living, living's just bloody impossible. And that's it. That's the truth of it.

BUBNOV. Whew! The devil's really nipped his arse this time!

LUKA. Lord Jesus! Listen, my dear, you . . .

KLESHCH (*trembling with excitement*). You and your *truth*! You just want to make everyone feel good, you old fool! Well, I'll tell you, I hate every last one of you, and as for the truth, may it be damned to hell. Got that? Well, just you get it!

> KLESHCH *runs off round the corner, glancing back as he goes.*

LUKA (*tut-tuts, shaking his head*). Tsk-tsk! Fancy getting so excited! Where's he run off to now?

NATASHA. You'd think he'd gone off his head.

BUBNOV. What a performance! [He could have been on the stage.] It happens like that with him. He's not used to being alive yet.

> PEPEL *comes slowly round the corner.*

PEPEL. Greetings, all. Well, Luka, you old rascal – still telling stories?

LUKA. You should've been here just now. Poor soul was shouting his head off.

PEPEL. Kleshch, you mean? What's up with him now? He was running like a scalded cat.

LUKA. When something gets too close to your heart – you run.

PEPEL. I don't like him. He's too proud, proud and bitter. (*Imitating* KLESHCH.) 'I'm a working man . . .' – as if he was any better than the rest of us. [All right, work, if that's what you like, but it's nothing to be proud about. If you're going to judge by work, horses are better than any man . . . slave all day, and never say a word.] Natasha. Your people at home?

NATASHA. They've gone to the cemetery . . . Then they were going to evening service.

PEPEL. Ah, that's it. I saw you were free for once.

LUKA (*thoughtfully, to* BUBNOV). Look, what you were saying, about the whole truth . . . you know, truth isn't always the right medicine for a man, you can't always cure a sick soul with the truth. For instance, here's a case ... I knew this man who believed in the land of the righteous ...

BUBNOV. The *what*?

LUKA. The virtuous land. There must be a virtuous country somewhere in the world, he said, a place where a special kind of people go to live, good people, who respect each other and help each other, just like that, quite simply ... and all's fine and lovely amongst them. And so this man was all ready to go off and search for the virtuous land. He was a poor man, lived a hard life, but whenever things got so bad for him that he might just as well lie down and die, he'd never lose heart, he'd just smile to himself and he'd say, 'It's nothing, I can bear it, I'll just hang on a bit longer and then I'll be away, away from all this, away to the virtuous land.' It was his one joy, the thought of that land.

PEPEL. Well? Did he go?

BUBNOV. Go where? Ho-ho!

LUKA. And then one day – all this happened in Siberia – this exile arrived. A scientist, he was. And he'd brought with him all his books and his plans, had this scientist, and his maps and all manner of learned things. So this man says to the scientist, 'would you be so good,' he says, 'as to show me where the land of the virtuous lies, and how I can find my way there?' So the scientist straightway opens up his books, and he looks ... but the land of the virtuous was nowhere to be found! All was correct, every country in the world was shown, everything there in its proper place ... but among them, no virtuous land!

PEPEL (*quietly*). What? Nowhere at all?

BUBNOV *laughs loudly*.

NATASHA. No, wait. Go on, grandpa.

LUKA. Well – this man just didn't believe it. 'It must be there,' he says, 'you go on and take a better look, because otherwise,'' he says, 'if they don't show where the virtuous land is, all your books and maps are completely worthless!' The scientist was very offended. 'My maps,' he says, 'are exact and true, and there is no land of the virtuous anywhere there at all!' Well, the man got very angry when he heard this. 'What!' he says, 'here I've lived and suffered and endured all this time, believing that there is, and now your maps make out that there isn't! I've been robbed!' he says to the scientist, 'Oh you swine,' he says, 'you're a crook not a scientist!' And with that he fetched the scientist a clout across the ear, and then another cross the other. (LUKA *is silent for a moment.*) Then he went home and hanged himself.

They are all silent. LUKA, *smiling, looks at* PEPEL *and* NAT-
ASHA.

PEPEL (*quietly*). Mother of God – that's not a very cheerful story.
NATASHA. He couldn't bear being cheated . . .
BUBNOV (*glumly*). It's all just – stories.
PEPEL. We-e-ell – so much for the virtuous land. Turns out there isn't one.
NATASHA. It's sad . . . poor man.
BUBNOV. It's all just make believe. Go on, then – ho-ho! – the virtuous land! That's the place to go! Ho-ho-ho!

BUBNOV *disappears from the window.* LUKA *shakes his head in that direction.*

LUKA. He's laughing – oh well. (*Nods in direction of* BUBNOV's *window.*) Hey-ho! – live richly, my friends! I'll be leaving you soon.
PEPEL. Where are you off to now?
LUKA. To Little Russia. Hear they've discovered a new religion there, must go and have a look. Must go, yes. People are always searching, always asking for . . . something better. God give them patience.
PEPEL. You think they'll find it?
LUKA. They're human – they'll find it. He who seeks, finds. He who wants strongly enough, gets.

NATASHA. If only they would find something – think up something – better.

LUKA. They'll think it up. Only – we have to help, my dear. We have to respect them.

NATASHA. How could I help? I'm helpless myself.

PEPEL (*resolutely*). Natasha – I – I've spoken to you about this before, and I'm going to again – now, in front of him. He knows . . . all about it. Natasha – come away with me.

NATASHA. Where? Round the prison yards?

PEPEL. I told you, I'll give up thieving! I will, before God, I'll give it up! I've said I will, and I will. I can read and write – I'll get work. The old man here told me I should get myself to Siberia of my own free will – let's go there together, eh? You don't think I'm not sick of the kind of life I lead here, do you? Oh, Natasha, I know it all, I'm not blind! [Of course I say to myself, what about all those people who steal lots more than I do, and still have everyone looking up to them . . . but it doesn't help, that isn't the point.] Mind you – I'm not sorry about anything, and I still don't believe in conscience – but I do know this: I've got to live different somehow, got to live better, got to live somehow so I can have a bit of respect for myself.

LUKA. I'd call that right, my dear. [God grant it and Christ aid it! A man's got to respect himself and that's the truth of it.]

PEPEL. I've been a thief since I was that high. Vasska the thief – everyone always called me that – Vasska the thief's son, Vasska the thief. [So all right then, if that's the way it is – I'm a thief! You see –] maybe I'm only a thief because nobody ever thought to call me different – out of spite, sort of. Natasha – you could call me . . . something different. Well?

NATASHA (*sadly*). Somehow I can't believe any . . . words . . . today. I feel uneasy, my heart feels heavy – as if I was expecting something. I wish you hadn't started talking about all that today.

PEPEL. When, then? It's not the first time I've talked about it . . .

NATASHA. Why should I go with you, anyway? I don't love you –

well, not all that much ... occasionally, perhaps, I quite like you, but other times it makes me sick to look at you, so I can't love you, can I? – [because people, when they love, can't see anything bad in the person they love. And I can.]

PEPEL. You'll come to love me, I promise! I'll teach you to! [Oh, Natasha, you only have to agree ...! I've been watching you for over a year now and I know you ...] you're good – very firm with yourself – reliable – and – and ... I've come to love you very much.

VASSILISSA, *in her best clothes, appears at the window, and stands by the amb, listening.*

NATASHA. So – you've come to love me. And what about my sister.

PEPEL (*embarrassed*). Well, what about her? There's plenty of her sort around ...

LUKA. Never you mind old history, my dear. If a man can't get bread he'll eat pigswill ... if there's really no bread at all. Forget all that.

PEPEL (*morosely*). Have a heart, Natasha – my life's been bare enough, God knows. There's not much joy in living like a wolf, with a criminal record and your passport marked ... it's like drowning in a bog, wherever you step you go deeper in, whatever you grab at comes away in your hands, it's all stinking rotten ... Your sister, I thought she was ... turned out she was rotten too. If she hadn't been so bloody greedy ... I'd have done anything for her ... if she could have been mine, just for me, not for ... but, no, she was after more than me, she was after money, and freedom – yeah! freedom to whore about all over town! No, she could never be any help to me ... But you, Natasha, you're like a young fir tree – if a man clings to you, you may prick his hands but you hold up firm.

LUKA. And I tell you too, marry him, girl, get in behind him! He's all right, this lad, he's a good one. Only you got to keep reminding him, often, that he's a good one, so he won't go forgetting it! Just you tell him now and then, 'Vasska, you're a good man, you know – and don't you forget it!' And think, my dear – where else can you ever go? Your sister's a vicious beast, and her husband – [well, there aren't any words I'd want to waste on that one ... And this life here, all this – where could it ever take you? And this lad is strong ...]

NATASHA. No, there's nowhere to go. I know that, I've thought that too. It's just – I don't trust anyone ... But it's true – there's no way I can go ...

PEPEL. There's only one road. But I won't let you take that one. I'd rather kill you.

NATASHA [(smiling). There. I'm not even your wife yet, and you're talking about killing me already.

PEPEL (embracing her). Stop it, Natasha! All the same, I would ...]

NATASHA (pressing close to him). There's ... just one thing ... I must say ... and, Vasska, I say this before God! – the very first time you hit me, or – or – hurt me ... any way at all ... I swear I won't spare my own life, I – I'll either hang myself or – or ...

PEPEL. May my arm wither, if I ever touch you!

LUKA. Don't you worry, my dear – trust him! He needs you more than you need him.

VASSILISSA (from the window). So there they are – the happy couple! For richer, for ... poorer ...

NATASHA. Oh my God, they're back! They saw! Oh, Vasska ...!

PEPEL. What are you scared of? Nobody'll dare touch you now.

VASSILISSA. You needn't worry about him, Natasha, he won't beat you. He can't beat a woman any more than he can love one ... I should know!

LUKA (softly). Poisonous woman. Viper.

VASSILISSA. He's only big with words.

KOSTYLIOV (coming out). Natasha! What do you think you're doing, you idle tramp! Gossip-mongering, eh? Complaining about your family? Yes, and with the samovar not ready and the table not laid, eh?

NATASHA (*going out*). You said you wanted to go to church . . .

KOSTYLIOV. What we do's none of your business, you should be attending to your own business, doing what you were told to do!

PEPEL. Pack that in! She's not your servant any more . . . Natasha, don't go, don't you do anything!

NATASHA. It's too soon for you to start giving me orders.

PEPEL (*to* KOSTYLIOV). That's enough! You've been trampling on her long enough. She's mine now.

KOSTYLIOV. You-ou-ours? (*Drawled mockingly.*) When did you buy her? How much did you pay?

    VASSILISSA *laughs loudly.*

LUKA. Vasska! Get away from here!

PEPEL. You – you watch out! You can laugh now – watch out you don't end weeping!

VASSILISSA. Ooh, how terrifying! Ooh, I am scared!

LUKA. Vasska, get away! Can't you see she's just goading you on, trying to get you mad – don't you understand?

PEPEL. Yes – aha! – yes! But she's got it all wrong! (*To* VASSILISSA.) You and your filth! What you want isn't going to happen, see!

VASSILISSA. What I don't want isn't going to happen either, Vasska!

PEPEL (*shaking his fist at her*). We'll see about that!

    PEPEL *exits.*

VASSILISSA (*disappearing from window*). I'll arrange a nice little wedding for you.

KOSTYLIOV (*going up to* LUKA). Well then, old one?

LUKA. Nothing then, old one.

KOSTYLIOV. So. You're going, I hear?

LUKA. It's time.

KOSTYLIOV. Where to?

LUKA. Where my eyes lead me.

KOSTYLIOV. Tramping, in other words. It doesn't suit you to stay in one place, then?

LUKA. A stone that never moves, they say, kills the grass it lies on.

KOSTYLIOV. That's for stones. But humans should live in one place, it's not right for people to live like cockroaches, crawling off every which way whenever they want. A man must root himself in his place, not go traipsing aimlessly about the face of the earth.

LUKA. What if there's a place for a man wherever he goes?

KOSTYLIOV. Then he's a tramp, a waster, useless! There must be some service come out of everyone, some work . . .

LUKA. So you say.

KOSTYLIOV. Yes, I do! Now, a pilgrim, a palmer – he's different, a strange man, not like other people at all . . . if he's truly seeking for something, knows something, has found out something or other . . . which no one else needs to know . . . well, so maybe he's found out the truth somehow, all right, but not every truth needs to be known, that's certain, so let him keep it to himself, keep quiet about it! If he's a true palmer, I mean, he keeps his silence . . . or . . . or he speaks so nobody can understand him . . . and he's not after anything, he doesn't interfere with anything, doesn't go stirring people up when he's not been asked to! It's not his business how other people live, his business is pursuing the paths of righteousness . . . he should live in forests . . . thickets . . . out of sight! And not disturb anybody, or judge anybody, no, but just pray . . . pray for everyone, for all the sins of all the world, for my sins and your sins, for everybody's sins! Yes! That's why he flees from wordly vanities, yes, in order to pray! And that's it.

Pause.

But you . . . what sort of a palmer are you? You haven't even got any papers. A decent person must have a purseport, all decent people have their purseport papers, oh yes!

LUKA. There are people – and there are human beings.

KOSTYLIOV. Don't start being clever! I don't need riddles from you, I'm just as intelligent as you are! What d'you mean, people and human beings?

LUKA. Where's the riddle? [I only say, some ground's good for sowing – what you sow, sprouts. And some ground's bad. That's all.

KOSTYLIOV. Well? What's the point of that?]

LUKA. Take you, for instance – if the Lord God himself said, 'Mikhail, be human' – well, even that wouldn't do any good – such as you are, so you'd remain.

KOSTYLIOV (*grunts menacingly*). . . . and do you know that my wife's uncle is a police officer, and if I . . .

VASSILISSA (*coming in*). Mikhail Ivanich, the tea is ready.

KOSTYLIOV (*to* LUKA). Now listen, you . . . you get out of here! Clear right out of these lodgings!

VASSILISSA. Yes, just you clear off, old one! Your tongue's a sight too long – and anyway, how do we know you're not on the run from somewhere?

KOSTYLIOV. I want you out of here today, understand? Otherwise I'll . . . well, you watch out!

LUKA. You'll call uncle? Call uncle, then, tell him you've caught a runaway. You never know, uncle might get a reward . . . three kopecks or so.

BUBNOV (*appearing at the window*). Hello, what's being sold out here? Three kopecks for what?

LUKA. They're threatening to sell me.

VASSILISSA (*to* KOSTYLIOV). Come on.

BUBNOV. For three kopecks? You be careful, old one. They'd sell you for one kopeck.

KOSTYLIOV (*to* BUBNOV). You . . . came popping out there like a hoblin out of the hearth!

VASSILISSA (*leaving*). The world seems to be full of stupid people. Every kind of crook you can imagine.

LUKA. Enjoy your tea.

VASSILISSA (*turning*). Hold your tongue, you poisonous toad-stool!

VASSILISSA *and* KOSTYLIOV *go out*.

LUKA. Tonight . . . I shall leave.

BUBNOV. It's the best way. It's always best to leave in time.

LUKA. I'd say that's true.

BUBNOV. I know it. I probably missed a spell in Siberia by leaving in time.

LUKA. Is that so?

BUBNOV. It's the truth. It was like this – my wife had got herself mixed up with my master-furrier – first-class furrier he was, too, you should've seen the way he'd dye a dog-skin to turn it into racoon . . . or . . . or cat-skins into kangaroos, muskrats, whatever you like . . . Oh, he was a real craftsman! Well, so my wife gets herself mixed up with him, and there they were, thick as thieves the pair of them, and it wasn't going to take much for them to decide to poison me, or shuffle me out of the world some way or other. I took to beating my wife. Then the furrier took to beating me – vicious old fighter he was, too, one time he pulled out half my beard and broke one of my ribs. So I turned nasty too. One day I whacked my wife over the head with an iron scraper . . . and altogether there was a fine old war getting going between us. But no good was going to come of it, I could see that – they were getting the best of it. So one day I thought, right, well I'll have to kill the wife. Had a good hard think about that for a while . . . Then I saw sense, and came away.

LUKA. That was the best way. Let them go on turning cats into kangaroos.

BUBNOV. Only thing was, the workshop went to the wife of course, and I was left – as you see. Though, to be honest, I'd only have drunk the business away. I'm a drinker, you see.

LUKA. A drinker? A-ah.

BUBNOV. Terrible drinker. Once I start swilling it, I go on till I'm soaked, nothing left but a skinful of vodka ... I'm lazy, too. Terrible ... the way I hate work.

Enter SATIN *and the* ACTOR, *arguing.*

SATIN. Rubbish! You're not going anywhere, it's just the drink talking! Hey, old one! What's all this hot air you've been pumping into this fag-end?

ACTOR. Liar! I am going! Grandpa, tell him he's lying! I'm going. I worked today – swept the street – didn't touch a drop of vodka! How about that, then? Look at this. (*Jingles coins.*) Thirty pretty 'pecks – and I'm sober!

SATIN. Ridiculous, that's what it is. Give 'em here, I'll drink them for you ... or lay them on a card.

ACTOR Get away! They're towards my journey.

LUKA (*to* SATIN). Why do you keep trying to sap his strength?

SATIN. 'Tell me, Oh, Sorcerer, beloved of the gods, What will befall me on my weary way?' Brother, I have been wiped out, picked clean, every last 'peck. All is not yet lost for the world, grandpa, while there's niftier cardsharpers in it than me.

LUKA. When you're merry, Konstantin, you're good company.

BUBNOV. Actor! Come over here.

The ACTOR *goes over to the window and squats on his haunches in front of* BUBNOV. *They talk in low voices.*

SATIN. When I was young, brother – yes, I was really good company then! It's good to think back on it – Oh, I was a ball of fire! Dance splendidly, acted, loved to make people laugh ... It was good, all that.

LUKA. How did you come to lose your way?

SATIN. Nosey old greybeard, aren't you? There's nothing you wouldn't like to know. What for?

LUKA. I like to understand ... why people do what they do. I look at you and ... don't understand. You're a fine manly fellow, Konstantin ... clever ... no fool, anyway ... and yet ...

SATIN. Prison, grandpa. I spent four years and seven months in prison. After prison – there's no way up.

LUKA. A-ha. What were you in for?

SATIN. For a louse. Killed a louse in a fit of rage. It was in prison I learned to play cards.

LUKA. And you killed him because of some woman.

SATIN. Because of my sister . . . and that's enough, now. I don't like being questioned. And it was all a long time ago . . . nine years . . . my sister died nine years ago . . . she was a wonderful little creature, that sister of mine.

LUKA. You bear up well under life. And there was that locksmith a while back – you should have heard him howling, oh dear, oh dear!

SATIN. Kleshch?

LUKA. That's him. He was yelling, 'there's no work, there's no nothing!'

SATIN. He'll get used to it. What should I do with myself, I wonder?

LUKA (*softly*). Look. He's coming back.

Enter KLESHCH *slowly, his head bowed.*

SATIN. Well, widower, why've you got your snout in the dust? What's on your mind?

KLESHCH. I'm thinking . . . trying to think . . . what to do. My tools are all gone. The funeral ate up everything.

SATIN. I'll give you some good advice: don't do a thing. Just . . . be a burden on the world.

KLESHCH. You can talk like that . . . I've got my pride in front of people.

SATIN. Give it up! Why feel ashamed? – nobody's ashamed that your life's worse than a dog's, nobody gives a damn! Just think – if you stop working, and I stop, and hundreds of thousands of others stop – everyone, understand? – if everyone stops working, no one moves a finger . . . what'll happen then?

KLESHCH. They'll all die of hunger.

LUKA (*to* SATIN). You should join the Runners, the way you talk. (They're a sect that doesn't accept any earthly things. The police find them harmful – so they run.*)

SATIN. I know. They're no fools, grandpa.

From KOSTYLIOV's *window come* NATASHA's *screams.*

NATASHA (*off*). No! What for? What have I done!

LUKA (*anxiously*). Is that Natasha screaming? Oh God . . .

From the KOSTYLIOV *apartment, noise, sounds of struggle, broken crockery, and the high-pitched shouting of* KOSTYLIOV.

KOSTYLIOV. Oh – you – you heathen! you blasphemous whore! – you filthy slut!

VASSILISSA. Stop . . . wait . . . I'll get her . . . there . . . there . . .

NATASHA. Help! They're beating me, they'll kill me!

SATIN (*shouts in at the window*). Hey, you there . . .!

LUKA (*fussing*). Vasska . . . call Vasska . . . Oh God! Brothers . . . friends . . .

ACTOR (*running out*). I'll go . . . I'll get him . . .

BUBNOV. They beat her a lot these days.

SATIN. Come on, grandpa – we can be witnesses . . .

LUKA (*following* SATIN). What good would I be as a witness? No . . . better get Vasska as quick as possible . . . Tsk-tsk!

Exits tut-tutting behind SATIN.

NATASHA. No, Vassilissa! – aah – Vassi-aah . . .

BUBNOV. They've gagged her. I'm going to have a look.

The noise from the KOSTYLIOVS' *room dies down, apparently moving from the room into the hall. A shout from the old man of 'Stop!' A door slams loudly, cutting off the noise as if with an axe. On stage it is quiet. Evening twilight.* KLESHCH,

---

* This explanation of 'The Runners' is taken from Gorky's autobiographical volume *My Apprenticeships.*

taking no part, is sitting on the sledge. He rubs his hands hard, starts muttering, unintelligibly at first, then :

KLESHCH. Well, what then? Got to live somehow. (*Loudly.*) Got to have a place! Eh? – there's no place. Nothing. There's nothing. A man's alone, that's what it comes to. Alone. No help. There's no help.

He goes out slowly, head bowed.
A few seconds of sinister silence, then, somewhere in the passage, vague noises start up, a chaos of sounds. It grows and comes nearer. Individual voices can be heard.

VASSILISSA. I'm her sister! Let go of me!
KOSTYLIOV. What right have you got . . .?
VASSILISSA. Jailbird!
SATIN. Get Vasska – quickly – Zob – sock him!

A Police whistle. The TARTAR *runs out. His right hand is in a sling. He is followed by* KRIVOY ZOB *and* MEDVEDIEV.

TARTAR. What law say okay kill in daytime?
KRIVOY ZOB. Oh, I didn't half thump him!
MEDVEDIEV. You – how dare you – fighting like that!
TARTAR. And you, hey? What about your duty, hey?
MEDVEDIEV (*chasing* KRIVOY ZOB). Hey, stop! Give me back my whistle!

KOSTYLIOV *runs on.*

KOSTYLIOV. Abram! Catch him! Take him! He's a killer . . .

From behind the corner appear KVASHNIA *and* NASTYA, *supporting* NATASHA, *bedraggled.* SATIN *comes on backwards, pushing at* VASSILISSA, *who is waving her arms about, attempting to get past him and hit her sister.* ALYOSHKA *is jumping around her like one possessed, whistling in her ears, shouting, howling. Subsequently a few more men and women in rags crowd in through the corner.*

SATIN (*to* VASSILISSA). Keep back, bloody screech-owl!

VASSILISSA. Get out of my way, jailbird! I'll tear that slut to ribbons if I have to die for it!

KVASHNIA *leads* NATASHA *out of range.*

KVASHNIA. Stop it now, Karpovna, you should be ashamed! Behaving like a wild beast!

MEDVEDIEV *catches hold of* SATIN.

MEDVEDIEV. Aha! Got you!

SATIN. Krivoy Zob – get at them! Vasska! Vasska!

They are all crowded together in swirling confusion in the entrance to the passageway. NATASHA *is led further away and sat down on a pile of wood.* PEPEL *bursts through the crowd, out of the passageway, pushing everyone aside with powerful gestures, saying nothing.*

PEPEL. Where is she? Where's Natasha? You ...

KOSTYLIOV *slips round the corner.*

KOSTYLIOV. Abram! Get Vasska! Help him, lads, help take Vasska, he's a robber, a thief.

PEPEL. Ah you ... old bugger, you!

PEPEL *strikes* KOSTYLIOV *a powerful blow. The old man falls so that only the top half of him is visible round the corner.* PEPEL *rushes to* NATASHA.

VASSILISSA. Get him – get Vasska! Oh, my good friends, hit him, hit the thief!

MEDVEDIEV (*shouting at* SATIN). Keep out of this, this is a family affair, they're relations, what's it got to do with you?

PEPEL. How ... what did she get you with? A knife?

KVASHNIA. [Just look at that,] look what the brutes did! Scalded the girl's legs with boiling water!

NASTYA. Tipped the samovar over her.

TARTAR. May be accident . . . got to know sure . . . not say if not know!

NATASHA (*almost fainting*). Vasska . . . take me away . . . hide me . . . I want to die!

VASSILISSA. Merciful heavens! Look – come and see – he's dead! He's been killed!

All crowd into the passageway around KOSTYLIOV's *body.* BUBNOV *emerges from the crowd and crosses quickly to* PEPEL, *speaks to him in a low voice.*

BUBNOV. Vasska! The old rascal, he's – he's finished.

PEPEL (*staring at* BUBNOV *as if not understanding the words*). Go and call . . . we must get her to hospital. I'll deal with them.

BUBNOV. Listen, I tell you, someone's finished off the old man!

The noise on the stage dies down, like fire doused with water. Murmurs here and there, variously: 'He never is!' 'Oh Jesus' 'Hell!' 'Here, let's get out of here!' 'Bugger this!' 'Better watch out' 'Come on, let's get out before the police come!' The crowd becomes smaller. BUBNOV *and the* TARTAR *go out.* NASTYA *and* KVASHNIA *rush over to* KOSTYLIOV's *body.*

VASSILISSA (*rising from the ground, shouting triumphantly*). They've killed him! They've killed my husband – and there – there's the one that did it! I saw him! Oh, my good friends, I did, I saw! Well, Vasska? It's the police now!

PEPEL *moves away from* NATASHA.

PEPEL. Let go. Get away. (*He looks down at the body; to* VASSILISSA:) Well? Pleased? (*He touches the body with his foot.*) So the old dog dropped dead – it's worked out just the way you wanted. Huh! Why don't I do you in too?

He goes for her, and is grabbed quickly from behind by SATIN *and* KRIVOY ZOB. VASSILISSA *hides in the passageway.*

SATIN. Have some sense, Vasska.

KRIVOY ZOB. Who-ah! Where are you galloping off to!

VASSILISSA (*reappearing*). Well, Vasska, my sweetheart? You won't escape what's coming to you! Police . . .! Abram – blow your whistle!

MEDVEDIEV. They've snatched my whistle, the villains!

ALYOSHKA. Here it is.

> ALYOSHKA *blows the whistle;* MEDVEDIEV *gives chase.* SATIN *leads* PEPEL *back to* NASTASHA.

SATIN. Nothing to be afraid of, Vasska – killing a man in a fight – it's nothing. They don't give you much for that.

VASSILISSA. Hold on to Vasska! He killed him! I saw!

SATIN. I hit the old fraud two or three times myself. He didn't need much to go down. Call me as a witness, Vasska.

PEPEL. I want – I don't want to clear myself – I just want to drag Vassilissa into it, and I will – I'll drag her in all right! This is just what she wanted – she tried to talk me into killing her husband, she'd been working on me to do it . . .

NATASHA (*suddenly, loudly*). Ah – now I understand! So that's it, is it, Vasska? Listen, everyone – they were in it together, these two, my sister – and him! They're together! They arranged the whole thing! Isn't that right, Vasska? All you said to me earlier – it was just so she'd hear and . . . Listen, everyone, she's his mistress, you all know that, and – and – they're in it together! She . . . she talked him into it . . . killing her husband . . . he was in their way . . . and I was in their way too so . . . so they did this to me . . .

PEPEL. Natasha! What are you – what . . .?

SATIN. What the hell . . .!

VASSILISSA. Liar! She's lying . . . I . . . he . . . Vasska killed him!

NATASHA. They're in it together. God damn your souls, both of you!

SATIN. Jesus, what a performance! You watch out, Vasska, they'll drown you between the pair of them.

KRIVOY ZOB. Can't understand a word of it. Crazy business!

PEPEL. Natalia – you can't – mean all that? You can't believe I'm
    in with – her!
SATIN. For God's sake, Natasha – think!
VASSILISSA (*in the passage*). My husband's been killed, sir. It was
    Vasska Pepel, the thief, inspector, he killed him. I saw it,
    everyone saw it . . .
NATASHA (*throwing herself about, almost in a faint*). Listen, every-
    one . . . my sister and Vasska killed him! Listen, you policemen!
    [that one there, my sister, she coached him, she persuaded him
    . . . he's her lover . . . that's him, there, damn him!] They
    killed him . . . take them both . . . try them . . . take me too . . .
    take me to prison . . . Oh, for the love of Christ, take me to
    prison!

CURTAIN

Act Four

The same setting as the first Act, only Pepel's room is no longer there, the partition has been taken down. And in the place where Kleshch sat, the anvil has gone. In the corner where Pepel's room used to be the TARTAR *is lying, restlessly, groaning from time to time.* KLESHCH *is seated at the table, mending an accordion, now and again trying the notes. At the other end of the table,* SATIN, *the* BARON, *and* NASTYA. *In front of them, a bottle of vodka, three bottles of beer, a large hunk of black bread. On the stove the* ACTOR *is tossing restlessly and coughing. Night.*

The stage is lit by a lamp in the middle of the table. Noise of the wind outside.

KLESHCH. Yes ... he took himself off while all that fuss was going on ...

BARON. Melted before the police like ... smoke before the fire.

SATIN. Even as sinners do flee before the face of the righteous.

NASTYA. He was a good old man! And you – you're not men, you're maggots.

BARON. Your health, mademoiselle!

SATIN. He was a funny old bugger all right. Nastionka even managed to fall in love with him.

NASTYA. Yes, I did fall in love with him. I do love him, it's quite true. He saw everything, understood everything ...

SATIN (*laughing*). And altogether – for a lot of people – he was like pap for the toothless.

BARON (*laughing*). Like a poultice for boils!

KLESHCH. He – he had some pity. You lot haven't got an ounce of pity in you.

SATIN. What good will it do you if I pity you?

KLESHCH. At least you know how ... well, I won't say pity, but you should know how not to hurt a person ...

The TARTAR *sits up on his plank bed and rocks his wounded hand like a child.*

TARTAR. Old man was good. He has law in his soul. Who has law in his soul is good. Who loses law – loses his life.

BARON. What law, prince?

TARTAR. That one – different kinds – you know what.

BARON. Further, further!

TARTAR. Not to harm another being. That law.

SATIN. That's known as 'The Code of Criminal and Corrective Penalties.'

BARON. [Or sometimes – 'Statute of Penalties to be imposed by Provincial Magistrates'.]

TARTAR. Is called Koran . . . Your Koran must be law, soul must be Koran. Yes!

KLESHCH (*trying the accordion*). Still hissing, the bitch. But the prince is quite right. Man should live by the law. By the Gospel.

SATIN. Do it.

BARON. Try.

TARTAR. [Mahomet gave Koran and say, 'Here is law, do as written here.' One day time come when Koran not enough . . . that time must give own law, new law . . . Every time give its own law.

SATIN. Ab-so-lute-ly! A time came and gave us the Code of Penalties' – a nice tough law! You won't wear that one out in a hurry.]

NASTYA *suddenly bangs her glass down on the table.*

NASTYA. And why – why – do I go on living here? With you lot? What for? I'll go away . . . go off somewhere . . . to the ends of the earth!

BARON. With no shoes, mademoiselle?

NASTYA. Stark naked! I'll crawl on all fours!

BARON. How picturesque that will be, mademoiselle! On all fours . . .

NASTYA. I shall. I'll crawl. Anything not to have to see your ugly mug again . . . Oh, it all makes me so sick! All this . . . this whole life and . . . and everyone.

SATIN. If you do go, take the Actor along with you. He's thinking of going to the same place. He's heard that only half a mile or so from the ends of the earth there's a clinic for the treatment of organons . . .

The ACTOR *raises his head from the stove.*

ACTOR. Organisms – imbecile!

SATIN. For organons poisoned by alcohol. . . .

ACTOR. Yes! And he'll go there, too – he'll go, you wait and see.

BARON. And who is *he*, monsieur?

ACTOR. Me!

BARON. Grazie, good servant of the goddess – what's her name? The goddess of drama, tragedy? What was she called . . .?

ACTOR. The muse, idiot! Not a goddess – a muse!

SATIN. Lachesa, Here, Aphrodite, Atropos . . . God only knows . . . It's all the old man's doing, you know what I mean, Baron? He screwed the Actor up to this.

BARON. The old man's a fool.

ACTOR. Ignoramuses! Barbarians! Mel-po-me-na! Soulless wretches! He'll go – just you wait and see! 'Devour yourselves, benighted minds!' A poem by . . . Béranger. Yes! He'll find a place for himself where there's no . . . no . . .

BARON. Nothing at all, monsieur?

ACTOR. Yes! Nothing! 'This pit is all the grave I need, Here I die, a broken reed!' Why live at all? What for?

BARON. All right, Edmund Kean, [you dissipated genius –] that's enough of your yelling!

ACTOR. Rubbish! I shall yell!

NASTYA *raises her head from the table and makes a gesture of dismissal with both hands.*

NASTYA. Go on, shout away. You tell 'em.

BARON. Where's the sense of it, mademoiselle?

SATIN. Leave them, Baron. To hell with them! Let 'em shout, let 'em split their heads open, let 'em do it! There *is* sense to it ... don't interfere with a person; as the old man used to say ... It's him, old yeasty-beard, who's started all our lodgers fermenting.

KLESHCH. He set them off somewhere – but he never showed them the road.

BARON. The old man's a fake.

NASTYA. Liar! Fake yourself!

BARON. Down, mademoiselle!

KLESHCH. Didn't care for the truth, that old man ... dead set against the truth! Quite right too. What would we do with it if we had it? Even without it, we can't breathe! Look at the prince there – had his hand crushed at work, it's going to have to be cut right off, understand? Right off! There's the truth for you!

SATIN (*banging the table with his fist*). Shut up! You ... cattle! Sods! Shut up about the old man! (*More calmly.*) You, Baron – you're the worst of the lot. You don't understand anything about anything, you just talk rubbish! The old man is not a fake! [What ... is ... the truth? A human being – that's the truth! He understood that, and you don't. You're thick as bricks, the lot of you! I understand the old man . . .] all right, yes, he lied – but that was out of pity for you, damn you! There are people, lots of people, who lie out of pity for their neighbour. I know about that – I've read books – and their lies are beautiful, inspired, exciting! They have a lie that comforts, that – that reconciles ... But there's another lie. It's – it can justify the load that crushed a workman's hand, and it – it blames the man who's dying of hunger! I know that lie! Whoever's weak in the soul, and lives off the sap of others, he needs that lie! Some are supported by the lie, others hide themselves away underneath it ... but whoever's his own master, independent, not leeching on someone else – what does he need a lie for? Lies – they're the religion of slaves and bosses! The only god for a free man is the truth.

BARON. Bravo! Well said! I agree! Spoken like a gentleman!

SATIN. Why shouldn't a cheat speak like a gentleman when gentlemen speak like cheats? Yes, I've forgotten a lot, but I still know something. The old man? He's a clever one. He scoured my soul the way acid scours a dirty old coin – let's drink to his health! Fill 'em up!

NASTYA pours some beer and gives it to SATIN.

(*Smiling.*) The old man lives from what's in himself – looks at everything with his own eyes. Once I asked him – Grandpa, what do people live for?

He tries to imitate LUKA's voice and mannerisms.

'Ah', he says, 'Ah, now, people live for something better, brotherkin. Now you take some carpenters, let's say, a lot of carpenters and all their rubbishy stuff. And now, from among this lot, there's born a carpenter – ah, such a carpenter as never before was seen on this earth, there's not another carpenter to match him! He makes his mark on the entire carpentry trade – and straightway it moves forward twenty years! Better, every last one of them! It's the same with all the others, locksmiths, if you like, cobblers, bakers, the rest of the workers . . . and all the peasants . . . and even the gentry . . . all living for something better! Each one of them thinks he's living just for himself, and it turns out he's living for something better! Each one of them living on for a hundred years or more – for the sake of a better man!

NASTYA gazes into SATIN's face. KLESHCH stops working on the accordion and also listens. The BARON, head bowed low, drums with his fingers quietly on the table. The ACTOR, emerging from the stove, is about to climb carefully on to the plank bed.

'Everyone, brotherkin, everyone there is, lives towards something better! That's why every soul must be respected, for it's

not for us to know who he is, what he was born for or what he
may do ... maybe he was born for our happiness, to bring
some sort of good to us? Above all, the children must be respected – the little ones! The little ones need *space*! Don't interfere
with them, don't hinder them in their living ... respect the
childerkin!'

SATIN *laughs. A pause.*

BARON (*thoughtfully*). Mm – yes ... for something better, eh?
Reminds me of my own family ... an old name – dates from
the time of Catherine the Great – nobles, warriors ... an old
French line. They served the Czar, rose higher and higher ...
Under Nicholas the first my grandfather, Gustave Debile, held
– uh – a post – most important post ... yes – wealth ... hundreds of serfs ... horses ... chefs ...

NASTYA. Liar! There was not!

BARON (*jumping up*). Wha-a-at! Well ... further!

NASTYA. None of it happened!

BARON (*shouting*). A house in Moscow! A house in Petersburg!
Carriages – carriages with coats of arms!

KLESHCH *picks up the accordion, walks over to one side,
watches the scene from there.*

NASTYA. Never happened.

BARON. Down! I tell you – dozens of lackeys!

NASTYA (*with relish*). Not true.

BARON. I'll kill you!

NASTYA (*making as if to run away*). There weren't any carriages!

SATIN. Stop it, Nastionka! don't tease him.

BARON. Wait – listen – you little bitch! – my grandfather ...

NASTYA. No grandfather – no carriage – no lackeys – nothing!

SATIN *roars with laughter. The* BARON, *tired from his burst of
temper, sits down on a bench.*

BARON. Satin ... tell her ... tell that whore ... Are you laughing
too? Don't you believe me either?

He shouts with despair, banging his fists on the table.

There *was*, damn and blast the lot of you!

NASTYA (*triumphantly*). A-ha, you can howl, too! Now you know what it's like when you're not believed!

KLESHCH (*returning to the table*). I thought there was going to be a fight.

TARTAR. O-oh, stupid people! Very bad!

BARON. I – I cannot permit anyone to mock me! I have . . . proof . . . documents, damn it!

SATIN. Throw them away! And forget about grandpapa's carriages – they won't take you anywhere now.

BARON. But still, how *dare* she . . .

NASTYA. Just listen – how dare I!

SATIN. You see – she dares. Why not? Is she any worse than you? She may not have any carriages or grandfathers – probably not even a father or a mother – but . . .

BARON (*calming down*). Damn you, Satin – you know how to discuss things calmly . . . I don't seem to have any character.

SATIN. Acquire some. It comes in handy.

Pause.

Nastya – are you going to the hospital?

NASTYA. What for?

SATIN. To see Natasha.

NASTYA. Come on! She's been out of there for ages – came out, and just disappeared. Vanished.

SATIN. So she's gone for good.

KLESHCH. Wonder whose axe will go deepest – Vasska's into Vassilissa, or hers into him?

NASTYA. Vassilissa's bound to snake out of it somehow – she's crafty. And Vasska will get sent to forced labour.

SATIN. It's only prison if you kill in the course of a fight.

NASTYA. Pity. Forced labour's what he needs – you all ought to be sent to forced labour . . . sweep you up like a pile of rubbish and into the rubbish pit with you!

SATIN (*surprised*). What's got into you? Gone out of your mind?

BARON. Oh, now I'm going to box her ears for her damned impudence!

NASTYA. You try! Just you touch me!

BARON. I will, I'll . . .

SATIN. Pack it in! Keep your hands off her . . . don't interfere with a person! I just can't get that old man out my head! (*Laughs.*) Don't interfere with a person – and if I've been interfered with once and for all . . . what do I do? Forgive? Never. Nobody. Not for a thing.

BARON (*to* NASTYA). You've got to understand that you're not my equal. You're just . . . dirt.

NASTYA. You poor idiot, aren't you living off of me like a maggot off an apple?

A friendly burst of laughter from the men.

KLESHCH. Oh you fool! Some apple!

BARON. One really can't be angry – she's such an idiot!

NASTYA. Laughing, are you? Liar! – you don't really think it's funny!

ACTOR (*gloomily*). Go on – bowl them down.

NASTYA. If only I could I'd –

She takes a cup from the table and smashes it to the ground.

– that's what I'd do to you!

TARTAR. Why breaks pots? Eh – stupid!

BARON (*getting*). No, now I really must teach her some manners.

NASTYA (*running off*). You go to hell!

SATIN (*calling after her*). Hey, that'll do! Who are you trying to scare? What's all this about?

NASTYA. Dogs! May you all drop dead, dogs!

ACTOR (*gloomily*). Amen!

TARTAR. O-oh, Russian woman – savage woman! Rude . . . free! Tartar woman not – Tartar woman know Tartar law!

KLESHCH. She needs a good hiding.

BARON (*hisses*). S-s-s-slut!

> KLESHCH *tries out the accordion.*

KLESHCH. Finished! No sign of the owner, though. The little fellow's out on the tiles again.

SATIN. Now – have a drink!

KLESHCH. Thanks. Time to turn in, then.

SATIN. Getting used to us?

> KLESHCH *drains his cup, then goes over to his plank bed in the corner.*

KLESHCH. It's all right. There's people all over the place. You don't see it at first, but then ... you take a closer look ... turns out they're all human ... all of them all right, really ...

> *The* TARTAR *spreads something out on his plank bed, kneels down, prays. The* BARON *points to the* TARTAR, *addressing* SATIN.

BARON. Look.

SATIN. Leave him. He's all right, don't interfere with him. (*Laughs.*) I'm in a kind mood today, God knows why!

BARON. You're always kind when you've been drinking. Kind – and clever.

SATIN. When I'm drunk – I like everything! Mmm-ye-e-es. So – he's praying? Fine – a man can believe, or not believe – that's up to him. Man is free. Whatever he does, he has to pay for himself – for believing, for not believing, for loving, for thinking – man pays for it all himself, and that's why he's free. Man! There's the truth for you! What is Man? It isn't me – or you – or them ... no! It's you and me and them and the old man and Mahomet ... all rolled into one! (*He draws the figure of a man in the air.*) You see? It's tremendous! All the beginnings and all the ends are here – everything, in Man – everything, for Man! Only Man exists, everything else is the work of his hand and brain! Hu-man-kind! – it's magnificent! It sounds so proud! Man! Man ... must be respected – not pitied, not humiliated with pity! Respected! Let's drink to Man, Baron! (*He stands up.*) Ah, but it's good – to feel you're a man! I'm an old lag, a murderer, a cardsharper – well, yes, all right. When I walk along the street, people [see me as a crook, and edge away. They] glance back over their shoulders at me . . . and sometimes they shout, 'Layabout! Bum! Get some work!' Work? What for? To stuff my gut full of food? (*He laughs.*) I've always despised people who worry too much about being well-fed – that's not the point, Baron! That's not the point! Man is above that . . . man is above . . . being well-fed!

BARON (*shaking his head*). You can work things out – that's good. It must warm the heart. I don't have that . . . I . . . can't. (*He looks round – in a low, careful voice.*) I feel scared, dear chap . . . sometimes. D'you understand? I'm afraid! Because . . . what . . . further . . . is there?

SATIN (*walking about*). Rubbish! Who is there to be afraid of?

BARON. You know, ever since I can remember . . . there's always been a sort of fog in my head. I've never understood anything. I feel . . . out of place . . . somehow. I seem to have done nothing all my life but change one lot of clothes for another. And what for? – I don't understand it! I went to school, wore the uniform of the Noblemen's Academy . . . but what did I study? Don't remember. Got married – put on a frock coat, then a dressing-gown . . . married some nasty female – what was that about? I don't understand. I went through my fortune, ended up wearing some sort of old grey coat and faded trousers . . . and how did I come to be ruined? Never noticed. I worked in the department of the exchequer, wore a uniform with a cockade on my cap . . . helped myself to a bit of public money . . . then they dressed me in convict's overalls . . . finally put on these things. And it's all passed like a dream . . . Well? Does that seem – ridiculous?

SATIN. Not really. Stupid, more like.

BARON. Yes. I think it's stupid, too. But I must have been born for some reason, mustn't I?

SATIN (*laughing*). Very likely. Man is born – for something better! (*He nods.*) Yes, that's – that's good.

BARON. That Nastya – where did she run off to? I'd better go and see. After all, she . . .

The BARON *exits. Pause.*

ACTOR. Tartar!

Pause.

Prince!

The TARTAR *turns his head.*

Pray for me.

TARTAR. What?

ACTOR (*quietly*). Pray . . . for me.

TARTAR (*after a moment's silence*). Pray for yourself.

The ACTOR *climbs quickly down from the stove, goes over to the table, pours some vodka with a trembling hand, drinks it – and almost runs into the hall.*

ACTOR. Going . . . gone!

SATIN. Hey – you – sycambro! Where?

SATIN whistles. Enter MEDVEDIEV, *in a woman's padded jerkin, and* BUBNOV, *carrying a bundle of pretzel rolls in one hand and some fish in the other; a bottle of vodka is under his arm, another in his jacket pocket.*

MEDVEDIEV. The camel, now – the camel is a sort of donkey. Only without ears.

BUBNOV. Shut up. You're a sort of donkey yourself.

MEDVEDIEV. The camel – has no ears at all. He hears with his nostrils.

BUBNOV (*to* SATIN). My friend! – I've been looking for you under every barrel in town! [Take a bottle, my hands are full.

SATIN. If you put the rolls down on the table you'd have one hand free.

BUBNOV. True.] Hey – you – Sheriff! Look – there he is, our own clever boy!

MEDVEDIEV. Crooks are all clever – don't I know it! [They have to be. A good man's still good even if he's stupid, but a bad one – has simply got to be clever.] But about the camel . . . you're wrong, you know. He's a riding animal. Hasn't got any horns . . . nor any teeth . . .

BUBNOV. Where is everyone? Why's nobody here? Hey, come on out, it's my treat! Who's that in the corner?

SATIN. How soon will you have drunk yourself into the gutter? Scarecrow!

BUBNOV. Soon enough. This time I've amassed a . . . modest little capital. Krivoy Zob! Where's Krivoy Zob?

KLESHCH *comes up the table.*

KLESHCH. Not here.

BUBNOV. Grrr-uff! Grrr-uff! Down, you old watchdog! Don't bark, don't growl – sing, enjoy yourself, keep that old snout out of the dirt! Come on, it's my treat – I like to treat . . . *everyone*! If I was rich I'd . . . keep a free bar! Yes, before God I would! – with music and – and – fine singers! Come on, I'd say, drink up, all of you, eat, [let's have some songs,] let yourselves go! Roll up, you poor devils, roll up to my free bar! [Satin! I'd . . . for you I'd . . . Here, look – take half of my entire capital . . . there . . . just like that!

SATIN. Give me the lot, straight off.

BUBNOV. All my capital? Straight off? All right – here! – one rouble . . . and another . . . twenty kopecks . . . a five . . . a two . . . that's the lot.]

SATIN. [Fine. It'll be safer with me. I'll put it on a card.

MEDVEDIEV. I'm a witness to that. Money's been handed over for safe-keeping, to the tune of . . . how much was it?

BUBNOV. You're a camel, not a witness. We don't need witnesses.]

ALYOSHKA *enters, barefoot.*

ALYOSHKA. Comrades! . . . I've got my feet wet!

BUBNOV. Come on and get your throat wet. That'll fix you.
You're a nice lad – you play and sing, and that's good. But you
drink too much. It's bad for you, brother – drinking's bad for
you!

ALYOSHKA. I can see that from you. You're only human when
you're drunk. Kleshch! Have you mended my squeeze-box?

He sings, dancing a few steps.

> Oh, if this old mug
> Weren't so fine to see
> My sister wouldn't open
> Her legs for me!

I'm frozen, brothers. It's c-c-c-cold!

MEDVEDIEV. H'm. And might I ask – who is your sister?

BUBNOV. Leave him be. You've had your lot, brother, you're not
Sheriff any longer. It's all finished. Not a policeman, and not an
uncle.

ALYOSHKA. But just – auntie's husband!

BUBNOV. One of your nieces is in jail. The other's dying.

MEDVEDIEV (*disdainfully*). Nonsense! She is not dying. She has
. . . disappeared without trace.

SATIN *laughs.*

BUBNOV. It's all the same, brother! No nieces, no uncle!

ALYOSHKA. Your Excellency! Retired drummer-boy to the
regimental goat – sah!

> Oh I'm merry and good
> But I haven't a bean
> My sister's got the lolly
> And she's my queen!

It's cold.

Enter KRIVOY ZOB; *then, and until the end of the Act, a few
more men and women. They take their coats off, lie down on the
plank beds, and grumble.*

KRIVOY ZOB. Bubnov! Why did you run away?

BUBNOV. Come here! Sit down ... let's have a song, brother! Our favourite, all right?

TARTAR. Is night. Must sleep! Sing songs in day.

SATIN. Ah, never mind that, prince! You come over here.

TARTAR. How, never mind? Is noisy. When people sing, is always noisy.

BUBNOV (*going over to him*). How's the hand, prince? Have they cut it off?

TARTAR. What for, cut off? Better wait. Maybe not have to cut off. A hand not iron, to be cut off so easy.

KRIVOY ZOB. You're finished, Assanka. Without a hand you're nothing, useless. Us sort, we're only wanted for our hands and our backs – no hand, no man! Your life's a clinker. Come and have some vodka – there's nothing else.

    KVASHNIA *enters.*

KVASHNIA. Ah, my dear little lodgers! Ooh, but outside there, outside! It's so cold and slushy ... Is my little Sheriff here? Constable!

MEDVEDIEV. Here.

KVASHNIA. You traipsing about in my jacket again? You look as if you're a bit ... Well? What do you think you're up to?

MEDVEDIEV. It's on account of ... it's Bubnov's nameday ... and ... er ... it's cold, sleety ...

KVASHNIA. You watch it now – sleety indeed! None of your tricks, just you get off to bed.

MEDVEDIEV (*going into the kitchen*). Bed – I can do that all right. I want to. It's time.

SATIN. Do you have to be so strict with him?

KVASHNIA. No good being any other way, my friend. A husband like that – he has to be dealt with firmly. I took him on as a partner, thought he'd be useful, him being a policeman, with you rowdy lot to handle, and me only a woman ... And what does he do? Drinks! That's no good to me!

SATIN. You chose yourself a bad partner.

KVASHNIA. There wasn't a better one going ... You wouldn't
want to live with me – indeed you wouldn't! And if you did,
inside a week you'd have lost me at cards – me and all my trash.

SATIN (*laughing*). It's true enough, landlady! I'd lose you ...

KVASHNIA. There you are. Alyoshka!

ALYOSHKA. Here [he is! Me!]

KVASHNIA. What's this you've [been tittle-tattling about me?

ALYOSHKA. Me? Everything! Most conscientiously, everything –
just as I see it! Now there, I say – there's a woman! Wonderful!
Meat, fat and bones, all twenty-five stone of it, and not one
ounce of brain among it!

KVASHNIA. Ah, now, there you're quite wrong! I've got plenty
of brain! Well – and why've you] been saying that I beat my
little policeman?

ALYOSHKA. I thought you were beating him that time you pulled
him down by his hair.

KVASHNIA (*laughing*). Idiot! As if you didn't see! Anyway, why
wash dirty linen in public? It hurts his pride – it's because of
your silly tales he's started drinking.

ALYOSHKA. So it's true what they say – even camels drink!

   SATIN *and* KLESHCH *laugh.*

KVASHNIA. Always poking fun, aren't you? What sort of a man
are you, Alyoshka.

ALYOSHKA. Absolutely top quality type man! Of all trades,
Ma'am. Wherever I look, there I'm took!

BUBNOV (*beside* TARTAR'*s plank bed*). Come on, join us. We're
not going to let anyone sleep, anyway. We're going to sing ...
all night long! Zob!

KRIVOY ZOB. Sing? Ay, it's possible.

ALYOSHKA. And I – will accompany you!

SATIN. And we'll listen!

TARTAR (*smiling*). Well, shaitan Bubna, bring out your vodka!
We drink, we make merry, and if death come – we bury!

BUBNOV. Pour him a drink, Satin! Zob, sit down! Well, brothers – a man doesn't need much, does he? Here I am, I've had a drink – and I'm happy! Zob – begin! Our favourite! When I start singing . . . I shall cry.

KRIVOY ZOB (*sings*). 'Though the bright sun may be shining . . .'

BUBNOV (*joining in*). 'My dungeon stays as dark as night . . .'

The door is suddenly opened. The BARON *stands in the doorway and shouts.*

BARON. Hey . . . you . . . come . . . come here! Out there . . . in the yard . . . the Actor . . . He's hanged himself!

Silence. All look at the BARON. *From behind his back* NASTYA *appears, and, slowly, her eyes wide open, makes her way to the table.*

SATIN (*quietly*). Ooh . . . spoilt our song . . . the *fool*!

CURTAIN

Music and full text of the song sung by BUBNOV and KRIVOY
ZOB in Acts Two and Four.

> Though the bright sun may be shining
> My dungeon stays as dark as night
> The prison guard stands by my window – oh – oh –
> And with his body steals my light.
>
> Guard me, though I need no guarding,
> I can't hope to break this chain,
> But stand aside from my small window – oh – oh –
> That I may see the sun again.
>
> Oh you chain, you heavy mooring,
> Oh you cru-el iron bond,
> I can never shake nor break you – oo – oo –
> And roam the sunlit world beyond.

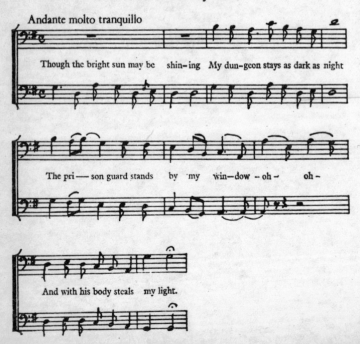

Andante molto tranquillo

Though the bright sun may be   shin-ing My dun-geon stays as dark as night

The pri —— son guard stands   by my   win-dow – oh –   oh –

And with his body steals   my light.

SUMMERFOLK

The British première of Summerfolk *was given by the Royal Shakespeare Company on 27th August 1974 at the Aldwych Theatre, London, with the following cast:*

SERGEI VASSILICH BASSOV, *a lawyer, aged* 40	Norman Rodway
VARVARA MIKHAILOVNA, *his wife, aged* 27	Estelle Kohler
KALERIA, *his sister, aged* 29	Susan Fleetwood
VLASS MIKHAILICH, *Varvara's brother, aged* 25	Mike Gwylim
PYTOR IVANICH SUSLOV, *an engineer, aged* 42	Tony Church
YULIA FILIPOVNA, *his wife, aged* 30	Lynette Davies
KIRILL AKIMOVICH DUDAKOV, *a doctor, aged* 40	Patrick Godfrey
OLGA ALEKSEYEVNA, *his wife, aged* 35	Janet Whiteside
YAKOV PETROVICH SHALIMOV, *a writer, aged* 40	Ian Richardson
PAVEL SERGEYICH RYUMIN, *aged* 32	Robert Ashby
MARIA LVOVNA, *a doctor, aged* 37	Margaret Tyzak
SONYA, *her daughter, aged* 18	Louise Jamieson
SEMYON SEMYONICH DVOETOCHIE, *Suslov's uncle, aged* 55	Sebastian Shaw
NIKOLAI PETROVICH ZAMISLOV, *Bassov's assistant, aged* 28	David Suchet
MAXIM ZIMIN, *a student, aged* 23	Michael Ensign
PUSTOBAIKA, *watchman of the villas, aged* 50	Norman Tyrrell
KROPILKIN, *a watchman*	Gavin Campbell
SASHA, *the Bassov's maid*	Annette Badland
WOMAN WITH BANDAGED CHEEK	Maroussia Frank
SEMYONOV	Albert Welling
LADY IN A YELLOW DRESS	Janet Chappell
YOUNG MAN IN A CHECKED SUIT	Wilfred Grove
YOUNG WOMAN IN BLUE	(not cast)*
YOUNG LADY IN PINK	Deborah Fairfax
CADET	Mark Cooper
GENTLEMAN IN A TOP HAT	Roger Bisley
BEGGARS	Doyne Byrd, John Labanowski

(The section YOUNG MAN IN A CHECKED SUIT through GENTLEMAN IN A TOP HAT is bracketed as *Amateur actors*.)

Directed by David Jones
Designed by Timothy O'Brien *and* Tazeena Firth

(*the YOUNG WOMAN IN BLUE appears in Gorky's cast list but not in the text. She must be one of the TWO GIRLS mentioned in the stage direction on page 143)

Act One

The Bassovs' villa.

A large room in which dining-room and drawing-room are combined. In the rear wall, left, an open door leads into BASSOV's *study; the door on the right leads into his wife* VARVARA's *room. These two rooms are separated by a passage, the entrance to which is covered by a heavy curtain. In the right wall is a window and a wide door leading on to the verandah; in the left wall, two windows. A large dining table stands in the middle of the room. There is a grand piano opposite the study door. The rest of the furniture is made of wicker, summer-house style, except for a wide sofa in front of the passage entrance, which is covered in grey material.*

Evening. BASSOV *is sitting at the desk in his study, a reading lamp with a green shade in front of him. He is writing, sitting sideways to the door. Now and again he hums to himself quietly; and sometimes turns his head to stare into the darkness of the big room.*

VARVARA MIKHAILOVNA *comes noiselessly out of her room, lights a match, holds it in front of her, and looks around. The match goes out. As she makes her way quietly towards the window in the darkness, she stumbles against a chair.*

BASSOV. Who's that?

VARVARA. Me.

BASSOV. Oh . . .

VARVARA. Did you take the candle?

BASSOV. No.

VARVARA. Ring for Sasha.

BASSOV. Has Vlass arrived?

VARVARA (*by the terrace door*). I don't know.

BASSOV. Stupid house . . . electric bells all over the place, but the walls are full of cracks . . . floor creaks . . . (*He hums a cheerful tune*.) Varya – you still there?

VARVARA. I'm here.

BASSOV *collects his papers and puts them away.*

BASSOV. Do the draughts whistle through your room?

VARVARA. They whistle.

BASSOV. There you are.

Enter SASHA.

VARVARA. Bring in a light, Sasha.

BASSOV. Sasha – has Vlass Mikhailich arrived?

SASHA. Not yet.

SASHA *goes out, returns with a lamp which she puts on the table by the armchair. She wipes the ashtray and straightens the table cloth on the dining table.* VARVARA *lets down the blind, takes a book from the shelf and sits down in the armchair.*

BASSOV (*amicably*). He's become rather sloppy lately, Vlass has . . . unpunctual . . . lazy . . . Yes. Indeed, he's been behaving altogether . . . absurdly. It's a fact, you know.

VARVARA. Will you have some tea?

BASSOV. No. I'm going over to the Suslovs.

VARVARA. Sasha, go over to Olga Alekseyevna and ask her if she'll come and have tea with me.

Exit SASHA.

BASSOV *puts his papers into the drawer of his desk.*

BASSOV. Well, that's done.

BASSOV *comes out of his study, straightening his back.*

You might speak to him, Varya. I mean, you know, tactfully.

VARVARA. Speak to him about what?

BASSOV. Oh, you know – about being more . . . conscientious . . . over his work? Mm?

VARVARA. All right. Only I don't think you ought to talk about him like that in front of Sasha.

BASSOV (*looking round the room*). Why not? You can't hide anything from the servants, you know. It's very *bare* in here, isn't it? You ought to hang something on the walls, you know, some sort of frame or . . . a little picture or something . . . It's not very cosy, is it? Well, I'm off . . . give me your little paw then . . . you're very withdrawn, you know – why's that, huh? And you look so bored . . . Why? Tell me!

VARVARA. Are you in much of a hurry to get to Suslov's?

BASSOV. Yes, must get going . . . haven't played chess with him for ages . . . come to that, haven't kissed your little paw for ages . . . why's that, d'you think? Strange.

VARVARA (*hiding a smile*). Then we'd better postpone our little talk about me and my moods until you're not so busy. It's not important, after all.

BASSOV (*reassuringly*). No, no, of course not. Just remarking, that's all, nothing serious. You're a splendid woman . . . clever, sincere . . . and all that. It's a fact. If you'd got anything against me, you'd say, wouldn't you? Yes. Why are your eyes glinting like that? Aren't you well?

VARVARA. I'm perfectly well.

BASSOV. You know, you ought to find something to occupy yourself with, my dear. There you are, always reading, you read much too much. Any excess is harmful, you know. It's a fact.

VARVARA. I hope you'll keep that fact in mind when you're drinking with Suslov.

BASSOV (*laughing*). Ha! – that's a sharp one! But honestly, you know, all these heady books people read these days do far more harm than wine. It's true. There's something . . . narcotic about them. Must be written by a bunch of gloomy neurotics . . . (*yawns*) And soon we're to have what children would call 'a real live writer' descending on us . . . it'll be interesting to see what he's like now. Conceited, I expect. All these celebrities are morbidly obsessed with their reputations. An abnormal lot, altogether. Karelia's not normal, come to that, though she hardly counts as a writer, really . . . She'll be glad to see Shalimov. Now, wouldn't it

be an idea for her to marry him! Too old, I suppose, yes, a
bit too old . . . and always moaning, as if she had chronic
toothache. Not exactly a beauty, either.

VARVARA. What a lot of unnecessary things you say, Sergei.

BASSOV. Oh, come, surely not? Well, anyway, it doesn't
matter, we're alone and . . . yes, it's true, I do love to
chatter.

A dry cough is heard behind the curtain.

Who's that?

SUSLOV (*off*). Me.

BASSOV (*going to meet him*). I was just on my way over to you.

SUSLOV *greets* VARVARA *in silence.*

SUSLOV. Let's go, then. I came over to fetch you. You weren't
in town today, were you?

BASSOV. No. Why?

SUSLOV (*with a crooked smile*). Seems that assistant of yours
won two thousand roubles at the club . . .

BASSOV. Did he, indeed!

SUSLOV. . . . from some extremely drunk merchant.

VARVARA. You always put things . . .

SUSLOV. How?

VARVARA. Like that . . . he won some money . . . and then
you underline that it was from a drunk.

SUSLOV (*grinning*). I don't underline.

BASSOV. What's so special, anyway? Now if he'd said that
Zamislov had made the merchant drunk first and *then*
cleaned him out – well, that of course would have been bad
form, but . . . Come on, Pyotr, let's go. Varya, when Vlass
comes . . . ah, here he is.

VLASS *enters, with an old brief-case in his hands.*

VLASS. Did you miss me, *mon cher patron?* Good – it's nice to
be missed. (To SUSLOV, *clowning, in a mock-threatening
voice.*) You are being sought after by some man, evidently a
new arrival – he's going around all the villas asking
everybody very loudly where you live. (*Goes up to his sister*).
Hello, Varya.

VARVARA. Hello.

SUSLOV. Oh, damn! Probably my uncle.

BASSOV. I'd better not come over, then?

SUSLOV. Why on earth not? – You don't imagine I want to be left alone with an uncle I hardly know? I haven't seen him for ten years.

BASSOV (*to* VLASS). Come into my room, would you.

He takes VLASS *into the study.*

SUSLOV (*lighting a cigarette*). Won't you come over with us, Varvara Mikhailovna?

VARVARA. No, thanks. Is your uncle poor?

SUSLOV. No, he's rich. Very rich. Do you suppose I only dislike relations if they're poor?

VARVARA. I don't know.

SUSLOV (*with a peevish cough*). That Zamislov of yours is going to get Sergei into trouble one of these fine days. You'll see. He's a real villain! Don't you agree?

VARVARA (*calmly*). I'd rather not discuss him with you.

SUSLOV. Very well then. So be it. (*Pause*). You know, you make rather a show of this candour of yours. But you be careful – the role of plain dealer isn't an easy one, to play it even passably needs a lot of personality, courage, intelligence . . . You're not taking offence?

VARVARA. No.

SUSLOV. And you don't want to argue about it? Or maybe in your heart of hearts you agree with me?

VARVARA (*simply*). I don't know how to argue. I don't really know how to talk at all.

SUSLOV (*morosely*). Don't mind me. I just don't like admitting that there might be people with the courage to be themselves.

SASHA *enters.*

SASHA. Olga Alekseyevna says she's just coming. Shall I make tea?

VARVARA. Yes please.

SASHA. And Nikolai Petrovitch is coming over.

SASHA *exits.*
SUSLOV *goes over to the study door.*

SUSLOV. Sergei, you coming? I'm off.
BASSOV. Now, this very minute . . .

Enter ZAMISLOV.

ZAMISLOV. Greeting, milady bountiful! Good evening, Pyotr Ivanich!
SUSTOV (*clearing his throat*). My respects. What a mayfly you are!
ZAMISLOV. Yes, indeed, light as a feather! Light of heart, light of pocket and light of head!
SUSTOV (*rather rudely, sarcastically*). I won't argue about your heart and your head, but as for your pocket – I hear you cleaned someone out at the club last night.
ZAMISLOV (*gently*). When speaking of me, you should say 'won'. 'Cleaned out' is said of card-sharpers.
VARVARA. One's forever hearing sensational stories about you. They say that's true only of people who are out of the ordinary.
ZAMISLOV. I can tell you that when I hear the gossip about myself I become increasingly convinced of my own extraordinariness. Unfortunately I didn't win much – forty-two roubles.

SUSLOV *with a dry cough walks over to the left and looks out of the window.* BASSOV *enters.*

BASSOV. Is that all? And there was I with visions of champagne . . . Well now, is there anything you need to tell me? I'm in a hurry.
ZAMISLOV. Are you off? It can wait then, there's nothing urgent. Varvara Mikhailovna, what a pity you weren't at the play! Yulia Filipovna was quite entrancing! Wonderful.
VARVARA. I always enjoy her acting.
ZAMISLOV (*with enthusiasm*). Oh, she has such talent! Off with my head if I'm not right!
SUSLOV (*laughing*). But what if you're wrong? Very awkward, going around without a head . . . Well, come on, Sergei.

Goodbye, Varvara Mikhailovna. (*He bows to* ZAMISLOV.)
Goodbye.

> BASSOV *looks into the study where* VLASS *is sorting out
> papers*

BASSOV. So I can hope you'll have all that written out by nine
tomorrow morning?

VLASS. Hope, yes. And may you be tortured by insomnia, *cher
patron*.

> *Exit* SUSLOV *and* BASSOV.

ZAMISLOV. I must go, too. Your hand, Varvara
Mikhailovna.

VARVARA. Stay and have tea, won't you?

ZAMISLOV. If I may, I'll come back later. Just now, I must
go.

> *He exits quickly.* VLASS *appears from the study.*

VLASS. Varya! Will there ever be any tea in this house?

VARVARA. Call Sasha. (*She puts her hands on his shoulders.*)
Why are you looking so shattered?

> *He rubs his cheek against her hand.*

VLASS. I'm tired. I was in court from ten until three. From
three to seven I was running about all over town . . . Didn't
even get time for lunch.

VARVARA. A clerk. Really, Vlass, it's beneath you, you know.

VLASS. Oh, I know – one must reach for the heights and all
that. But Varya – you know how I love examples – think of
the chimney sweep, right up on the roof – he's climbed
higher than anyone else, but he can't climb higher than
himself.

VARVARA. Oh do stop fooling! Why don't you look for some
other kind of work – something useful, something meaning-
ful?

VLASS (*in mock indignation*). My dear lady! I make a vital –
albeit oblique – contribution to the defence and protection
of the sacred institution of Property – and you call that

useless? Such depravity!

VARVARA. I wish you'd be serious.

Enter SASHA.

VLASS (*to* SASHA). Honoured madam, we beg your indulgence in the matter of – bring me in some tea, and something to eat!

SASHA. Straight away. Would you like a cutlet, sir?

VLASS. I'd like a cutlet, and everything else cutlet-like. I'm waiting!

Exit SASHA.
VLASS *puts his arm round* VARVARA's *waist and walks around the room with her.*

Well? What's up?

VARVARA. I don't know. I'm very down for some reason, Vlassik. You know, sometimes, when you're not thinking about anything in particular, you suddenly feel with your whole being that you're in a prison . . . everything seems alien, hostile and . . . meaningless. Unwanted. And somehow no one seems to be living seriously . . . You're always joking, acting the buffoon.

VLASS (*striking a comic pose*). Do not rebuke me, friend.
              For so much jesting.
              Behind my wall of mirth
              Sorrow lies resting.

A poem of my own manufacture – and a great deal better than Kaleria's poems. But I shan't recite the rest of it – it must be five yards long. Darling sister! – you want me to be serious, do you? The way a person with one eye, I suppose, wants everyone else to be one-eyed.

Enter SASHA *with the tea things, which she disposes neatly on the table. The watchman's rattle can be heard.*

VARVARA. Stop it, Vlass! Stop . . . *prattling!*

VLASS. Very well, he said, and sadly fell silent. But you know, little sister, you're not being very kind. All day long I'm quiet, copying out people's slanders and libels . . . it's only natural that in the evening I should want to talk.

VARVARA. You know, I'd like to go away. Go somewhere where simple, healthy people live . . . where they talk differently, a different language . . . and they're all working at some great, serious project which everybody needs . . . Do you understand?

VLASS (*thoughtfully*). Yes, I understand all right. But you know – you won't go anywhere, Varya.

VARVARA. I might. I just might.

Pause. SASHA *brings in the samovar.*

Shalimov is probably arriving tomorrow.

VLASS. I don't like his recent stuff. Empty. Boring. Limp.

VARVARA. I saw him once, giving a lecture. I was a schoolgirl. I remember him striding out on to the platform, so strong and resolute . . . with thick, unruly hair . . . and a bold, open face, the face of a man who knows what he loves and what he hates . . . who knows his own strength. I looked up at him . . . and trembled with joy to think that such people could exist. It was . . . thrilling. Yes. I remember how he threw back his head, to toss back a lock of dark hair that was falling across his forehead . . . and his inspired eyes . . . That was six or seven years ago. No. Eight years.

VLASS. You're romancing about him like a schoolgirl in love with a new teacher. You be careful. I've heard that writers are experts at seducing women.

VARVARA. That's a horrid thing to say, Vlass. It's cheap.

VLASS (*simply, frankly*). Don't be angry, Varya.

VARVARA. Try to understand. I'm waiting for him as . . . as one waits for the spring. My life is so futile.

VLASS. I do understand, you know. My life's futile too . . . I feel ashamed and . . . awkward, somehow. Where on earth is it all going?

VARVARA. Oh yes, Vlass, yes! But then why do you . . .?

VLASS. Play the clown? I don't want other people to realise I feel futile.

Enter KALERIA.

KALERIA. It's such a heavenly evening! And here you are, sitting indoors, breathing smokey air. . .

VLASS (*rousing himself*). Ah, good evening, Abstractia Vassilevna!

KALERIA. The woods are so quiet and pensive. Spellbound! And the gentle moon throwing shadows like velvet. Day could never be more beautiful than night.

VLASS (*imitating her tone*). Indeed, no, as young girls can never be gayer than old women, nor swallows swifter than crabs . . .

KALERIA sits down at the table.

KALERIA. You don't understand a single thing. Varya, give me some tea. I suppose no one's been here?

VLASS (*with mock tendentiousness*). No one could ever be here, for no one is nowhere.

KALERIA. Do leave me in peace.

VLASS bows and goes silently into the study, where he starts sorting out the papers on the desk. Through the window can be heard the distant rattle of the nightwatchman, and a soft whistle.

VARVARA. Yulia Fillipovna was here, looking for you.

KALERIA. For me? Oh, of course – about the play.

VARVARA. You were in the woods, I suppose?

KALERIA. Yes. I met Ryumin. He talked about you quite a lot.

VARVARA. What did he say?

KALERIA. You know what he said.

Pause. VLASS sings something in a soft, nasal voice.

VARVARA. It's very sad.

KALERIA. For him?

VARVARA. He once said that to love a woman was a man's tragic duty.

KALERIA. Your attitude to him used to be quite different.

VARVARA. Do you blame me for that? Do you?

KALERIA. Oh no, Varya, no!

VARVARA. I tried to cure him of his melancholy, at first. I did pay him a lot of attention, it's quite true. But then I began to realise where it was all leading, and . . . he went away.

KALERIA. Was anything said?

VARVARA. Not a word. Neither from him nor from me.

Pause.

KALERIA. His love must be weak and lukewarm – all fine words, and no joy. For a woman, love without joy is offensive. Hasn't it struck you he's a hunchback?

VARVARA (*surprised*). I hadn't noticed . . . no, surely not! You must be mistaken.

KALERIA. There's something misshapen in him – in his soul. Whenever I see that in a person I start believing he must be physically deformed as well.

VLASS *comes out of the study waving a bunch of papers.*

VLASS. In consideration of the abundance of the attached libels and slanders and as a consequence of said abundance I have the honour to inform you, madam, that despite my having every wish to do so I shall be unable to execute the unpleasant task allotted to me within the time limits specified by *mon patron.* Yours faithfully.

VARVARA. I'll help you, later on. Have some tea.

VLASS. Ah, good sister, you are a true sister! Abstractia Vassilevna, learn the lineaments of true love while my sister and I are still alive to teach you.

KALERIA. You really are a hunchback.

VLASS. From which point of view?

KALERIA. You have a hump on your soul.

VLASS. I trust it doesn't spoil my figure?

KALERIA. Rudeness is as much a deformity as a hump. Stupid people are like the lame . . .

VLASS (*imitating*). And the lame are like your aphorisms.

KALERIA. People who are cheap always strike me as pock-marked. And they're nearly always blond.

VLASS. Brunettes, on the other hand, always marry young, and metaphysicians are always blind and deaf. Such a pity they were given tongues.

KALERIA. That's not a bit witty. And I'm quite certain you don't know anything about metaphysics.

VLASS. Ah, but I do. Tobacco and metaphysics both give pleasure to those addicted to them. I don't smoke, so I know nothing about the ill-effects of tobacco, but I have tried metaphysics. It produces nausea and giddiness.

KALERIA. People with weak heads can get giddy from the scent of flowers.

VARVARA. You two'll end up quarrelling.

VLASS. I'm going to eat. Much more useful.

KALERIA. I'm going to play the piano. Much more entertaining. How stuffy it is in here, Varya!

VARVARA. I'll open the door onto the verandah. Olga's just arriving.

> *Pause.* VLASS *has his tea.* KALERIA *sits down at the piano. Through the window, softly, comes the whistle of a watchman, answered by another in the distance, even softer.* KALERIA *gently fingers the middle keys. Enter* OLGA ALEKSEYEVNA, *quickly pushing the portière, like a large, frightened bird flying in. She throws a grey shawl from her head.*

OLGA. Here I am! Oh, I thought I'd never get away! (*kisses* VARVARA) Good evening, Karelia Vassilevna . . . Oh, go on playing, do, we don't have to shake hands, do we? Hello, Vlass.

VLASS. Evening, materfamilias.

VARVARA. Sit down, won't you? Will you have some tea? What kept you?

OLGA (*agitated*). Wait, wait! Oh dear! out there . . . outdoors . . . it's so scarey . . . as if there's something bad hiding in the woods . . . and the watchmen keep hooting at their whistles, they sound sad and . . . mocking. Why do they do it?

VLASS. Very suspicious, yes! Perhaps they're hooting at us?

OLGA. I wanted to come over straight away, but then Nadya started playing up, she must be sickening for something too . . . Did I tell you Volka's not well? Yes, he's got quite a

temperature . . . And then I had to give Sonya her bath . . .
Misha disappeared into the woods straight after lunch and
only got back a little while ago, all tattered and dirty – and
hungry again, of course . . . Then my husband got back
from town, and he's in a bad mood about something, all
silent and scowling. Oh, it's been such a mad whirl! And
that new maid, she's an absolute torture! She washed the
feeding bottles in boiling water . . . they all broke, of
course.

VARVARA (*smiling*). Oh my dear, you poor thing, you must be
exhausted!

VLASS. Oh Martha, Martha, thou art cumbered about with
much cooking – and that's why everything you do is either
overdone or underdone. Wise words!

KALERIA. Ugly words. 'Cumbered with cooking' – ugh!

VLASS. My apologies. I didn't do the new translation.

OLGA (*rather hurt*). Oh of course I suppose it all just sounds
funny to you, all that, and boring, I understand that. But
there you are – 'Talk spurts from where it hurts' as they say.
Children! – the mere thought of them sets off an alarm bell
inside me – chil-dren, chil-dren! Oh, if you only knew,
Varya, what a trial they are when they're young . . . !

VARVARA. Forgive me, but it always seems to me you
exaggerate about them.

OLGA (*excited*). No, don't say that, don't! You don't know,
you can't judge! You've no idea what a heavy, oppressive
feeling it is . . . to know that you and only you are
responsible for your children . . . One day, you realise,
they're going to come and ask, 'How should we live?' And
what am I going to tell them?

VLASS. Why worry about it before you have to? Perhaps they
won't ask. Perhaps they'll have ideas of their own.

OLGA. Oh, you don't know! They do ask things, they're
asking already . . . terrifying questions which there *aren't*
any answers to . . . I don't know the answers, you don't,
nobody does! . . . Oh, it's such a torment, to be a woman!

VLASS (*quietly, lightly*). One should simply try to be a human
being.

VARVARA. Stop it, Vlass.

>VLASS *goes into the study, sits down at the desk, starts*
>*writing.* VARVARA *gets up, walks slowly over to the verandah*
>*door.*

KALERIA (*dreamily*). But dawn with her smile comes to put
out all the stars.

>KALERIA *leaves the piano and goes to stand beside* VAR-
>VARA *in the doorway.*

OLGA. I seem to have made everybody depressed. Just like an
owl calling in the night. Oh dear. well, don't worry, I shan't
go on about it any more. Varya, why've you gone over
there? Come back to me, dear, or I shall think you can't
stand being near me.

>VARVARA *comes over to her quickly.*

VARVARA. Oh Olga, don't talk such nonsense! It's just . . . I
start feeling this unbearable pity and . . .

OLGA. Don't. You mustn't. You know, sometimes even I see
myself as repulsive and pitiful. My soul seems all wrinkled,
like the muzzle of a little old dog – you know, one of those
vicious little pug-dogs that hate everybody and are always
looking for the chance of a sly nip at your ankles.

KALERIA. The sun rises and the sun sets, but in our souls it is
always twilight.

OLGA. What do you mean?

KALERIA. Me? Oh, I was just talking about myself.

VLASS (*sings to the tune of a funeral dirge*). Family happiness,
family happiness . . .

VARVARA. Vlass, do please be quiet.

VLASS. I'm quiet.

OLGA. It's my fault, I made him like that.

KALERIA. There are some people coming out of the woods.
Look, what a beautiful scene they make! And how
comically Pavel Sergeyich waves his arms about!

VARVARA. Who else is there?

KALERIA. Maria Lvovna, Yulia Filipovna, Sonya, Zimin
and Zamislov.

OLGA (*wrapping herself in her shawl*). And I'm such an old draggletail! That Suslov woman's always so dolled up, she's bound to make me feel a fool. Oh, I do dislike her!

VARVARA. Vlass, go and call Sasha.

VLASS. Please note, *madame*, that you are tearing me away from my specified duties.

He goes to ring for SASHA.

OLGA. That stuck-up woman never does a thing for her children . . . the odd thing is, hers never seem to be ill.

MARIA LVOVNA *enters by the terrace door.*

MARIA. Your husband said you weren't feeling well. Is that true? What's the trouble?

VARVARA. I'm glad you've come, but I'm quite fit, thank you.

Noise and laughter on the terrace.

MARIA. You do look a little strained. (*To* OLGA.) Ah, you're here, too. I haven't seen you for such a long time.

OLGA. Who'd want to see a sour face like mine?

MARIA. Perhaps I like sour things. How are your little ones?

YULIA FILIPOVNA *comes in from the terrace.*

YULIA. Just look how many guests I've brought you! But don't worry, we'll all go away again soon. Hello, Olga Alekseyevna. Oh, why aren't the men coming in? Pavel Sergeyich and Zamislov are out there, Varvara Mikhailovna – may I tell them to come in?

VARVARA. Of course.

YULIA. Come on, Kaleria Vassilevna!

MARIA (*to* VLASS). You've got thinner. Why? ⎫

VLASS. No idea. ⎪ *all*

SASHA (*entering*). Shall I heat the samovar again? ⎬ *together*

VARVARA. Please, as quickly as possible. ⎪

MARIA (*to* VLASS). And why are you pulling faces? ⎭

OLGA. He always does.

VLASS. It's a speciality of mine.

MARIA. Still trying to be witty, are you? And still failing. (*To*

VARVARA): My dear, that Pavel Sergeyich of yours has finally talked himself into the ground.

VARVARA. Why do you say, of mine?

Enter RYUMIN, *then* YULIA *and* KALERIA. VLASS, *frowning, goes into the study and shuts the door behind him.* OLGA *takes* MARIA *to the left and explains something to her inaudibly, pointing to her chest.*

RYUMIN. You must forgive us for invading you at such a late hour . . .

VARVARA. I'm always delighted to have visitors.

YULIA. That's what's so nice about life in these summer villas – it's so informal. Oh, but you should have heard these two arguing – him and Maria Lvovna!

RYUMIN. I can't talk calmly about something when it's really vital to have it out completely.

SASHA *brings in the samovar.* VARVARA, *by the table, quietly gives her orders about the tea things.* RYUMIN, *standing by the piano, gazes at her thoughtfully and intently.*

YULIA. When you get so agitated, you cease to be convincing. (*To* VARVARA.) Your husband is sitting there with my own instrument of torture, knocking back the brandy. I suspect they're going to get themselves thoroughly drunk. My husband's uncle has arrived out of the blue, he's in meat or butter or something, owns a factory anyway, curly grey hair, very noisy, roars with laughter all the time . . . he's quite funny, really. But where's Nikolay Petrovich, my cautious knight?

ZAMISLOV (*from the terrace*). I am here, beneath thy window, fair and fabled princess.

YULIA. Come in here. What have you been talking about out there?

ZAMISLOV (*entering*). I was corrupting the young. Sonia and Zimin were trying to persuade me that the purpose of life is daily exercise in solving problems in the fields of social and personal morality. I was proving to them that life is art. Life, I was telling them, is the art of looking at everything

through your own eyes, of hearing everything with your own
ears.

YULIA. Rubbish!

ZAMISLOV. I've only just thought of it, but I believe that from
now on it's going to be my firm conviction. Life is the art of
finding beauty and joy in everything, in eating, in drinking
. . . Good heavens, they're quarrelling like savages out
there!

YULIA. Kaleria Vassilievna, do make them stop.

ZAMISLOV. Kaleria Vassilievna, I know that you love
everything that is true and beautiful – why don't you love
me? It's a frightful anomaly.

KALERIA. You're so noisy and . . . colourful.

ZAMISLOV. Hmm . . . Still, for the moment that's not the
point, the point is that we – that is, this beautiful princess
and I . . .

YULIA. Oh, do stop it! We've come . . .

ZAMISLOV (*bowing*). To you . . .

YULIA. to ask . . .

ZAMISLOV (*bowing lower*). you . . .

YULIA. Oh really, I can't . . . look, let's go into that lovely
clean room of yours, I love it in there . . .

ZAMISLOV. And out here, the whole world intrudes. Let's go,
then.

KALERIA (*laughing*). Come on then.

They go to the passage doorway.

YULIA. Oh, do listen, that sausage manufacturer or whatever
he is, my husband's uncle, comes from some desert beyond
the Urals. He never stops talking about his money and
wears the most extraordinary hats . . .

ZAMISLOV. Nothing wrong with Siberian money. You can
keep the hats.

Laughing, they disappear behind the portière.

OLGA. She's always so cheerful, and yet, as we all know, life
isn't all that rosy for her. She and her husband . . .

VARVARA (*coldly*). I don't think it's anything to do with us,
Olga.

OLGA. I wasn't saying anything bad, was I?

RYUMIN. Family dramas have become almost a daily occurrence with us.

SONYA *looks in at the door.*

SONYA. Mamaskha! I'm going for a walk.

MARIA. Another walk?

SONYA. Yes, another. This place is full of women, and they're always so boring.

MARIA (*joking*). You be careful what you say. Your mother's a woman too, you know.

SONYA *runs in.*

MARIA. Oh no, Mama? Really? Since when?

OLGA. What nonsense she talks.

VARVARA. And she might say hello.

MARIA. Sonya, you're a monster!

SONYA (*to* VARVARA). But we've said hello once today, haven't we? But I don't mind, I'll give you another kiss with pleasure, I'm always kind and generous when it gives me pleasure – as long as it doesn't cost me anything . . .

MARIA. Sonya, stop talking nonsense and remove yourself.

SONYA. But how about my mamashka, then! Suddenly she's calling herself a woman! I've known her for eighteen years and it's the first time I've heard it! Very significant, that!

ZIMIN *puts his head through the portière.*

ZIMIN. Well, are you coming or aren't you?

SONYA. May I introduce my slave?

VARVARA. Aren't you going to come in? Do, please.

SONYA. He's not fit to be seen in decent society.

ZIMIN. She's torn the sleeve off my jacket, that's all.

SONYA. That's all, indeed! He hasn't had enough, it seems he wants some more. Ah well, I suppose I'd better go and listen to him telling me all about eternal love.

ZIMIN. You'll have a long wait if that's what you're expecting.

SONYA. We'll see about that, youngster. Goodbye. Is there

still a moon?

ZIMIN I'm no youngster. In Sparta I'd . . . hey, you can't go pushing a man who . . .

SONYA. . . . . isn't a man yet. Forward, Sparta!

> SONYA *exits with* ZIMIN; *their voices and laughter can be heard from the house for some time.*

RYUMIN. You have a lovely daughter, Maria Lvovna.

OLGA. I used to be like that.

VARVARA. You have such a nice relationship – I like to watch you. Come on, sit down and have some tea, everyone.

MARIA. Yes, we're friends.

OLGA. Friends . . . How does one achieve that?

MARIA. What?

OLGA. Friendship with one's children.

MARIA. It's very simple: be frank with them, never try to hide the truth from them, never deceive them.

RYUMIN (*with a laugh*). But you know, that's very risky! The truth is crude and cold, and hidden within it there's always the subtle poison of scepticism. You can poison a child at a stroke by revealing to him the terrifying face of truth.

MARIA. You prefer to poison him by degrees? . . . so that you never actually have to see the harm you're doing him?

RYUMIN (*hotly, nervously*). Now wait a minute, that's not what I said! It's just that I'm against all this laying bare of the truth, all these silly, unnecessary attempts to strip life of its poetry, of the beautiful clothes that cover its crude and often unattractive body . . . Life needs to be adorned, not stripped, and we must have new and lovelier garments ready for it before the old ones are thrown away . . .

MARIA. What on earth are you talking about? I don't understand a word.

RYUMIN. I'm talking about a person's right to look for a little deception! You're always talking about 'Life'. Well, what is it, this 'Life'? When you talk about it, I always see it as a huge, shapeless monster, eternally demanding human sacrifice, day after day devouring the brains and muscles of human beings, forever drinking our blood . . .

VARVARA *listens intently to* RYUMIN, *with a steadily growing expression of perplexity; she makes a gesture, as if she wants to stop him.*

And what's it all for? I see no sense in it. I only know that the longer a man lives the more he sees himself surrounded by filth, bourgeois mediocrity, crudity, nastiness . . . and the more he longs for all that is beautiful and bright and pure! He can't get away from life's contradictions, and he hasn't the strength to purge it of all its evil and filth – so don't rob him of his right not to see all the things that poison the soul! Allow him his right to turn aside from what offends him! He wants to rest, he wants to forget . . . Yes, to rest in peace is what man wants!

He meets VARVARA's *gaze, shudders, and stops.*

MARIA (*calmly*). Is he spiritually bankrupt, then, your 'man'? What a shame! That sems to be the only explanation of his right to 'rest in peace'. Not very flattering.

RYUMIN (*to* VARVARA). I – I'm sorry I raised my voice like that . . . I can see you're upset . . .

VARVARA. But not because you got so agitated . . .

RYUMIN. Why, then? Why?

VARVARA (*slowly, very calmly*). I remember your saying something quite different two years ago – and just as sincerely, just as vehemently.

RYUMIN (*excited*). But a man changes, develops, and his ideas advance too.

MARIA. They rush about like frightened bats, those dark little ideas!

RYUMIN (*as excited as ever*). They advance in a spiral, it's true – but rising higher and higher all the time. Maria Lvovna, you doubt my sincerity, is that it?

MARIA. Me? Certainly not! I can see that you . . . shout . . . sincerely enough, and although for me hysteria is not an argument, I think I understand . . . something has given you a very severe fright, and now you'd like to hide from life . . . and of course you're not alone in that. There are plenty of frightened people.

RYUMIN. Indeed there are – because people are becoming more and more keenly sensitive to the horrors of life! Everything in life is strictly pre-determined – the only thing that's accidental, meaningless and aimless is human existence itself!

MARIA (*calmly*). If you would try to elevate the accidental fact of your existence to the level of society's needs, your life might take on some meaning.

OLGA. Oh dear! Whenever I hear anything severe or accusing said I always cringe, as if it was me that was being condemned! There's so little gentleness in life . . . Well, it's time I went home. It's always so good in your house, Varya . . . one always hears something that touches the best part of one's soul for a moment. But it's late enough already, I must go.

VARVARA. You stay where you are, my dear! Why go dashing off, suddenly? If they need you they'll send over for you.

OLGA. Yes, they'll send over . . . Oh, all right then, I'll stay a bit longer.

OLGA *goes over and sits on the sofa with her legs curled up under her.* RYUMIN *drums his fingers nervously on the window pane, standing by the terrace door.*

VARVARA (*pensive*). Strange, the way we live . . . We go on talking and talking and . . . that's all. It's just talk. We amass any number of opinions and keep on changing them – it's very bad, the way we pick things up and drop them so quickly . . . But as for any real desires, any clear, strong desires – not a single one!

RYUMIN. You're talking about me, I suppose?

VARVARA. I'm talking about everyone. We lead such boring lives, without sincerity, without beauty.

YULIA *comes in quickly.*

YULIA. Help me, everybody!

KALERIA *follows her in.*

KALERIA. No, really, this is silly . . .

YULIA. She's written a new poem, and she's promised to read it at our evening in aid of the Children's Home, but I want her to read it to us now, here! Do make her!

RYUMIN. Yes, do read it. I love your gentle poems.

MARIA. I'd like to hear it, too. Arguments leave one feeling coarse. Read it, my dear.

VARVARA. Something new, Kaleria.

KALERIA. Yes. Prose. Very dull.

YULIA. Go on, dear – read it! It won't cost you anything . . . let's go and get the others.

YULIA goes out, taking KALERIA *with her.*

MARIA. Where's Vlass Mikhailich?

VARVARA. In the study. He has a lot of work to do.

MARIA. I was a bit abrupt with him . . . It's irritating one's only allowed to see him as a clown.

VARVARA. Yes, it's a pity. You know, if you could just be a little gentler with him . . . He's sweet, really. Plenty of people preach at him, but no one ever shows him any affection.

MARIA (*smiling*). Of course. It happens to all of us. That's why we're all so sharp and unfeeling . . .

VARVARA. He lived with father, who was always drunk and always beating him . . .

MARIA. I'll go and see him.

She goes to the study door, knocks, and goes in.

RYUMIN (*to* VARVARA). You and Maria Lvovna are getting closer all the time, aren't you.

VARVARA. I like her . . .

OLGA (*softly*). She talks so severely about everything . . . always severely.

RYUMIN. Maria Lvovna has the cold cruelty of your true believer – cold, blind and ruthless. How can you do that?

DUDAKOV appears from the passage.

DUDAKOV. Oh, um – excuse me – um, good evening . . . Ah, Olga, here you are! Coming home soon?

OLGA. Straightaway, if you like. Have you been for a walk?

VARVARA. A glass of tea, Kiril Akimovich?

DUDAKOV. Tea? Er – no, I don't drink tea in the evening . . .
Pavel Sergeyich, I need to talk to you. Can I come over
tomorrow?

RYUMIN. Certainly.

DUDAKOV. It's about the home for juvenile delinquents. More
trouble, damn them. Seems they've been beating the kids,
and you and I were getting the blame for it in yesterday's
paper.

RYUMIN. In point of fact, I haven't been near the place lately.
Never seem to have the time . . .

DUDAKOV. Ye-es, well . . . none of us has any time, really.
Everybody's bustling about, but nothing ever seems to get
done. Why's that, d'you think? And I get so tired . . . Just
now I've been loafing about in the woods – that calms one
down . . . a bit, anyway . . . My nerves are in shreds.

VARVARA. You do look a bit drawn.

DUDAKOV. I'm not surprised. There was another bit of – um
– nastiness today, too. That fool of a mayor accusing us of
being uneconomical at the hospital. Seems the patients eat
too much, and we use too much quinine. Imbecile! For one
thing, it's none of his business, and for another, if he'd
drain the lower part of the town properly I wouldn't need to
touch his blasted quinine. What does he think, that I drink
it all myself? I loathe quinine . . . and insolence.

OLGA. Why do you let yourself be upset by such little trifles,
Kyril? You ought to be used to them by now.

DUDAKOV. And what if the whole of life is made up of such
little trifles? Eh? What do you mean, 'used to them'? Used
to what? To the fact that any idiot who wants to can shove
his nose into your work, interfere with your life? Well, look
at me – I'm getting used to that all right! So the mayor says
we've got to economise – all right, I'll economise! It may be
bad for my work, for my patients, but I'll do it. I've got no
private practice so I can't give up this stupid job . . .

OLGA (reproachfully). . . . because of your large family, is that
what you mean, Kyril? Oh, I know, I've heard it all before,

you needn't have started going on about it here . . . you're
so coarse and tactless!

Throwing a shawl over her head she walks quickly over to
VARVARA's *room.*

VARVARA. Olga! What are you saying?
OLGA (*almost sobbing*). Oh, leave me . . . let me go . . . I know
what he . . . I've heard . . .

They disappear into VARVARA's *room.*

DUDAKOV (*dismayed*). Would you believe it? And I didn't
mean anything of the sort . . . Oh! Pavel Sergeyich, I do
apologise, I really couldn't have known she . . . I'm . . . it's
all so confusing . . .

He goes out quickly, colliding with KALERIA *and* YULIA *in
the doorway.*

YULIA. What on earth's the matter with the doctor? He nearly
knocked us over.
RYUMIN. Nerves.

Enter VARVARA.

RYUMIN. Has Olga Alekseyevna gone?
VARVARA. She's gone, yes.
YULIA. I don't trust that doctor, he's unhealthy. Stuttering
away . . . And he's so absent-minded – puts his teaspoon in
his spectacle case and stirs his tea with that little hammer of
his – he could just as easily muddle a prescription and give
one something poisonous.
RYUMIN. I believe he'll end up putting a bullet through his
head.
VARVARA. You say that so calmly.
RYUMIN. Suicide is common among doctors.
VARVARA. Words move us more than people, isn't that the
trouble?
RYUMIN (*shudders*). Oh, Varvara Mikhailovna!

KALERIA *sits down at the piano, with* ZAMISLOV *standing
beside her.*

ZAMISLOV. Comfortable?

KALERIA. Thank you.

ZAMISLOV. Ladies and gentlemen – your attention, please!

Enter MARIA *and* VLASS, *very animated.*

VLASS. Aha! So we're to have a poetry reading, are we?

KALERIA (*annoyed*). If you want to listen you'll have to stay quiet.

VLASS. Spirits of liveliness – perish!

MARIA. We'll be quiet, we'll be quiet.

KALERIA. Good. This – is a poem in prose. It will eventually be set to music.

YULIA. A recitation to music! – how lovely! I simply adore anything really original, I'm just like a child, anything can delight me, even things like picture postcards, motor cars . . .

VLASS (*imitating her*). . . . earthquakes, gramophones, influenza . . .

KALERIA (*loudly and coldly*). May I begin?

They all sit down quickly. KALERIA *runs her fingers over the keys.*

It's called Edelweiss.

Eternally mantled are the peaks of the Alps in their pure shroud of snow, and over them all reigns coldness, reigns silence: the wise silence of proud heights.

Limitless is the wilderness of the heavens above the mountaintops, limitless the sad eyes of the stars gazing down upon the snowy peaks.

At the foot of the mountains, there where the crowded plains of the earth begin, Life stirs and grows, trembling with fear, and Man, the weary Lord of the Plain, suffers and endures.

From the dark pits of the earth come groans, comes laughter, come cries of anger, murmurs of love – the grim many-tongued music of earthly life! But the mountain peaks are mute, the stars remain aloof, untouched by the heavy moaning of man.

Eternally mantled are the peaks of the Alps in their pure
shroud of snow, and over them all reigns coldness, reigns
silence: the wise silence of proud heights.

But as if to bear witness to the miseries of earth, to the
torments of life, to the weariness of man, there at the edge of
the ice-cap, in the eternal kingdom of wise silence, there
grows, a solitary mute sentinel, the sad-eyed mountain-
flower – the Edelweiss.

And high above it, in the limitless wilderness of the heavens,
proudly and silently floats the sun, sadly and dumbly drifts
the moon, mute and a-tremble burn the stars. And all this
cold tumult of silence descends from the heavens to embrace
the day, to embrace the night, to embrace the lonely little
flower – the Edelweiss.

*Pause. All sit deep in thought. In the distance the sound of the
watchman's rattle, and a faint whistle.* KALERIA, *her eyes
wide open, gazes straight ahead of her.*

YULIA (*softly*). How wonderful! So sad and pure . . .

ZAMISLOV. Listen! You ought to recite that in a costume . . .
white . . . very wide . . . diaphonous . . . like the Edelweiss!
Can't you see it? That would be fantastically beautiful,
magnificent!

VLASS goes over to the piano.

VLASS. I liked it, too. I did, honestly. (*He laughs self-
consciously.*) It really gave me pleasure . . . a treat . . . like a
glass of cranberry water on a hot day!

KALERIA. Go away!

VLASS. But I mean it! Don't be angry.

SASHA (*entering*). Mr. Shalimov has arrived.

General stir. VARVARA *goes towards the door but stops at the
sight of* SHALIMOV *as he enters. He is bald.*

SHALIMOV. Do I have the honour of . . .?

VARVARA (*softly, after a moment's hesitation*). Please . . . do
come in Sergei will be here in a little while . . .

CURTAIN

Act Two

The meadow in front of the verandah of BASSOV's *villa.*

It is surrounded by a dense ring of pines, firs and birches. Downstage left are two pines, below them a round table with three chairs. Behind them is a low terrace, covered with an awning. Opposite the terrace is a group of trees, among these a wide bench with a back. Behind these trees is the road into the woods. Further back, right, is a small open-air stage shaped like a shell, from which – from right to left – runs a road to the SUSLOV *house. At the front of the stage a few benches.*

Evening. The sun is setting. In the BASSOVS' *house* KALERIA *is playing the piano.* PUSTOBAIKA *is moving slowly and ponderously about the meadow, arranging the benches.* KROPILKIN *is standing by the two pines, a gun slung across his back.*

KROPILKIN. And what about that villa over there – who's taken it this year?

PUSTOBAIKA (*in a thick, gloomy voice*). An engineer. Suslov.

KROPILKIN. New people again?

PUSTOBAIKA. What?

KROPILKIN. New people, I said. Not the same as last year.

PUSTOBAIKA (*taking out his pipe*). They're always the same. Even when they're different, they're the same.

KROPILKIN (*sighing*). At's it, at's all your . . . town money, in'it?

PUSTOBAIKA. Ah. Summer folk. Villa people. All the same. Past five years I seen more of 'em 'n you could count up of stars. Like bubbles on a puddle in wet weather they are. Up she pops. Burst. Up she pops. Burst. At's it.

Round the corner of BASSOV's *villa, laughing noisily, comes a group of young people carrying mandolins, balalaikas, guitars. They pass along the road and into the woods.*

KROPILKIN. Look at 'em. (*Music, off.*) Off to their play-acting, are they?

PUSTOBAIKA. Ah, they'll do that. Why not? Well-fed people, they are.

KROPILKIN. At's a thing I never seen, now. Summer folk at their play-acting. At's funny, I doubt? You seen at?

PUSTOBAIKA. I seen. I seen it all, lad.

From the right comes a booming laugh from DVOETOCHIE.

KROPILKIN. Ah? Well? What they do then?

PUSTOBAIKA. Not much. Dress 'emselves up in all different kinds of clothes. Say all different sorts of words, whatever each one likes to say, at's what he say. Shout, fuss about, as if they was up to something, angry or something. And then they play-act at each other. One play-acts 'Me, I'm honest,' and another, 'Me, I'm clever,' or again, 'Me, now, I'm unhappy' . . . just whatever one of 'em feels is right, that's what he play-acts.

Off left, someone whistles for his dog and shouts: 'Bayan! Bayan! Here, boy!' PUSTOBAIKA *hammers at a bench with the back of his axe.*

KROPILKIN. Why, is that . . .? Well! They sing songs too, then?

PUSTOBAIKA. Songs they don't sing that much. The engineer's wife, that one warbles a bit . . . ah, but at's a watery little voice she got.

KROPILKIN. They're coming.

PUSTOBAIKA. Ah, let 'em come.

Enter DVOETOCHIE *from the right, near the little stage, followed by* SUSLOV.

DVOETOCHIE (*amiably*). You've got no call to go laughing at me. There's you, only just past forty, and bald as an egg, while I'm pushing sixty and still got a headful of curls on me – they may be grey, but better than none at all. (*He laughs.*)

PUSTOBAIKA *goes on lazily and clumsily arranging the*

benches by the stage. KROPILKIN *slips off carefully behind the stage.*

SUSLOV. Just your good luck . . . But go on, I'm listening.

DVOETOCHIE. Let's sit down. Well, so these Germans come along . . . My little old factory was way out of date, the machinery was a load of rubbish, while theirs was all the very latest thing, and . . . well, I couldn't compete, their stuff was better than mine, and cheaper, I could see myself going right up the spout . . . So I thought, right, can't beat those Germans, I'd do better to sell 'em the whole caboodle.

SUSLOV. Did you sell the lot, then?

DVOETOCHIE. The lot. Kept the house in town, though. Big old place. So now I've got nothing to do but sit and count my money. (*He laughs.*) Truth is, I'm an old fool – soon as I'd sold up I felt like an orphan. I'm bored stiff, don't know where to put myself – know what I mean? Look at these hands of mine – before, I never used to notice them, now I keep seeing them as a couple of useless objects just cluttering the place up . . .

He laughs again. Pause. VARVARA *comes out on the terrace and walks slowly and thoughtfully about with her hands behind her back.*

There's Bassov's wife. What a woman, eh? A magnet! If only I was ten years younger . . .

SUSLOV. But you're already married, surely?

DVOETOCHIE. Was. Several times, in fact. But some of my wives popped off, some of them upped and left me. There were children, too . . . couple of little girls – they both died . . . and a young shaver of a boy . . . he was drowned, you know. But as regards women, I've been very lucky. Always picked them up here, in Russia . . . it's too easy, getting your wives off you Russians. You make rotten husbands. I used to come in from Siberia, you know, have a bit of a look round, and I'd think, right, now *there's* a woman worthy of a bit of attention . . . She'd have a husband, some nobody in a silly hat, but I'd straighten that out pretty smartly . . . (*He laughs.*)

VLASS *comes out on to the terrace from indoors and stands looking at his sister.*

Yes, there was all that . . . and now, nothing . . . there it is . . . nothing and nobody.

SUSLOV. So what are you thinking of doing?

DVOETOCHIE. Don't know. Advice, please! But you know, that fish soup of yours is no good, it's rubbish, and fancy serving pork cutlets! Eating pork in the summer – that's what's called an anachronism . . .

VLASS. How's it going, Varya?

VARVARA. Oh . . . all right, really. (*Pause.*) So . . . I'm a pathetic picture, am. I?

VLASS *puts his arm round her waist.*

VLASS. If I could, I'd say something comforting . . . Don't know how, though . . .

VARVARA. Leave me alone, darling.

DVOETOCHIE. That young Chornov's coming over.

SUSLOV. Oh, that clown . . .

DVOETOCHIE. Lively little lad, but not much of a do-er it seems.

VLASS (*approaching*). Who isn't?

DVOETOCHIE. My nephew here! (*Laughs.*) But you're not doing all that much yourself by the look of it, eh?

VLASS. From what little I've learned of you so far, sir, by the word 'doing' I understnad you to mean, squeezing the juice out of your neighbour. In that sense, alas! It is true: I do nothing.

DVOETOCHIE. Ha! Don't let it get you down, my boy! It's all a bit difficult when you're young, you know, the conscience hasn't hardened and there's pink blancmange where your brains should be. But once you grow up you'll find yourself straddling someone's neck with the greatest of ease. (*Laughs.*) Yes, on your neighbour's neck, that's the way to travel in comfort!

VLASS. I believe you, sir. You are obviously a very experienced rider.

VLASS *bows and walks away.*

DVOETOCHIE (*laughing*). Gives me a rap over the knuckles, and off he goes, pleased as punch. Ah, bless 'is heart, thinks 'e's a real little hero now, I don't doubt. Well, let 'im then, let the young cub have 'is bit of fun . . .

Head bowed, he sits in silence. KALERIA *comes out on to the verandah.*

KALERIA. And you still can't accept how much he's changed?
VARVARA (*softly*). No. No, I can't.
KALERIA. Who will you wait for now?
VARVARA. I don't know . . . I don't know.

KALERIA *shrugs, goes down the terrace steps to the left, and disappears round the corner of the house.*

DVOETOCHIE. H'm, yes. Well, now, Pyotr . . . how am I going to live, then, eh?
SUSLOV. That won't settle itself . . . you'll have to think it over.
DVOETOCHIE. Won't settle itself, eh? Ho-ho! Oh, you're a . . . What? What?
SUSLOV. Nothing. I wasn't saying anything.
DVOETOCHIE. Ha. And you'll go on not saying anything too. That's obvious.

BASSOV *and* SHALIMOV *come out of the woods, right, bow to the others, and go and sit down at the table under the pine trees.* BASSOV *has a towel round his neck.*

Here comes the writer, and the lawyer . . . Been out for a walk, then?
BASSOV. We had a swim.
DVOETOCHIE. Water cold?
BASSOV. Not too bad.
DVOETOCHIE. I could do with a swim myself. Come on, Pyotr. Maybe I'll drown, and you'll lay hands on my money all the sooner, eh?
SUSLOV. I can't just yet. I must have a talk with these two.

DVOETOCHIE. Well, I'm off anyway.

He gets up and goes off into the woods, right. SUSLOV *stares
after him, then with a short laugh goes over to* BASSOV.

BASSOV (*to* VARVARA). Varya, ask Sasha to bring us a bottle
of beer – no, better, three bottles . . . Well, how is it with
your uncle?

VARVARA *goes indoors.*

SUSLOV. He's beginning to get on my nerves a bit.
BASSOV. Yes. Old people aren't much fun.
SUSLOV. I think he wants to live with us.
BASSOV. He does? H'm. Well, how do you feel about it?
SUSLOV. Oh . . . God knows. I expect it'll go the way he
wants.

SASHA *brings in the beer.*

BASSOV. Yakov . . . you're very silent?
SHALIMOV. Feeling a bit battered. What was the name of
that belligerent lady . . .?
BASSOV. Maria Lvovna. My God, Pyotr, you should have
heard the battle we had at lunch today!
SUSLOV. Oh well – Maria Lvovna!
SHALIMOV. She's a ferocious woman, believe me.

VARVARA *comes slowly out on to the terrace again.*

SUSLOV. I can't stand her.
SHALIMOV. I'm a mild sort of man, but I can tell you I only
just managed not to be rude to her.
BASSOV (*laughing*). Which is more than she did with you!
SHALIMOV (*to* SUSLOV). Put yourself in my place: here's a
man writing something, getting all worked up by it, and
when he finishes, frankly, he's exhausted. So he comes to
his friend's house to have a bit of a rest, let his hair down,
collect his thoughts . . . and suddenly he's pounced on by
some female who proceeds to cross-examine him: what do
you believe in, what do you aspire to, why do you write
about this, why don't you write about that? Then she goes

on to say you weren't clear about this, you didn't tell the truth about that, and you didn't find any beauty in the other. Oh God! – go on, madam, go on and write yourself, and make everything clear and true and beautiful, write like a genius if you can, but just leave me to rest in peace!

BASSOV. That's your bed and you have to lie on it. When people travel down to Volga, everybody absolutely has to eat sturgeon; if they meet a writer, everybody absolutely has to show off their intellect. You'll just have to put up with it.

SHALIMOV. It's so bad-mannered and stupid. Do you often have her in your house?

BASSOV. No . . . that is . . . well, I suppose, quite often. But I don't care for her myself . . . she's as stiff as a poker. It's my wife who's friendly with her – and I don't like it, she's a bad influence. (*He looks round and sees* VARVARA.) Oh – Varya – you're here, are you?

VARVARA. As you see.

> ZAMISLOV *and* YULIA *come quickly down the road from* SUSLOV'*s house. They are laughing.* SHALIMOV *grins at* BASSOV'*s embarrassment.*

ZAMISLOV. Varvara Mikhailovna! We're arranging a picnic – a boating picnic!

YULIA. My dear, hello.

VARVARA. Let's go inside.

> *They go in.* SUSLOV *gets up and follows them slowly.*

ZAMISLOV (*going in*). Is Kaleria Vassilevna at home?

SHALIMOV (*laughing*). Sergei, you seem to me to be a bit afraid of your wife?

BASSOV (*sighing*). Ah, it's nothing, really. She's a good wife to me.

SHALIMOV (*grinning*). Why do you say that so sadly?

> BASSOV *gestures towards the disappearing* SUSLOV.

BASSOV. He's jealous. Jealous of my assistant. Understand? That wife of his – well, you want to keep an eye open for her. Fascinating woman!

At the end of the meadow, SONYA *and* ZIMIN *walk past.*

SHALIMOV. Indeed? I shall make a note. Although that Maria Lvovna is a powerful deterrent against getting involved with the local women, I can tell you.

BASSOV. Ah, but this one's something altogether different! This one's . . . whew! Well, you'll see. (*Pause.*) Yakov, you haven't published anything for a long time. You writing a major work?

SHALIMOV (*irritably*). Frankly, I'm not writing anything at all. No. What the hell can you write when it's impossible to understand anything? Somehow everyone seems to be in a tangle with themselves, they're slippery, impossible to grasp . . .

BASSOV. Write that, then. Write: "I don't understand a single thing." After all, the main thing for a writer ought to be *sincerity*.

SHALIMOV. Thanks for the advice. But no, sincerity – that's not the point. Perhaps the one sincere thing I could do would be to give up writing entirely and plant cabbages, like Diocletian.

Behind the house some beggars are chanting softly.

BEGGARS. Good people, kind people, a little crust for Christ's own sake, alms for the love of Christ, a crust for the feast of Corpus Christi, bountiful ladies, benefactors, protectors, a little crust on the feast of remembrance, for the love of God, for the love of Christ and Christ's holy body, alms for the feast of Corpus Christi . . .

PUSTOBAIKA *appears from behind the stage and goes to chase the beggars away.*

SHALIMOV. But one has to eat, so one has to write. But for whom? I no longer know. One must have a clear image of one's reader – what is he? Who is he? Five years ago I was quite certain I knew my reader, knew exactly what he wanted from me. And then, suddenly, I lost him. Yes. Lost him. That's the calamity, you see. Now they're saying there's a new type of reader around . . . but who is he?

BASSOV. I don't follow you. What do you mean, you've lost your reader? What about me? And all the rest of us, all the educated people in the country . . . aren't we readers? It doesn't make sense. How can you lose us?

SHALIMOV (*pensively*). Oh of course . . . educated people, intellectuals, I'm not talking about them. No, it's these others, this . . . new reader.

BASSOV (*shaking his head*). Really? I don't understand.

SHALIMOV. I don't, either. But I feel it. I walk down the street and I see people . . . certain people . . . and their faces have something quite special – different – in them . . . And their eyes . . . I look at their eyes and I think, they're not going to read me, I'm not what they want at all. Last winter I was giving a reading, and there were all these eyes, looking up at me, attentive, curious . . . and they were alien to me, all those faces. They don't like me, these new people, I'm as unnecessary to them as . . . Latin. In their eyes, I'm old . . . all my ideas are old. I don't understand who they are. What *do* they like? What is it they want?

BASSOV. H'm. Yes. Very curious. But you know, I think it's just your nerves. It's a fact – just nerves. Look, you stay on here for a bit, have a rest, calm down – you'll find your reader again. The main thing in life is to maintain a calm attitude to everything . . . That's what I believe, anyway. Come on, let's go inside . . . Oh, and Yashka, could I just ask you to – you know – be a bit of a peacock . . . ?

SHALIMOV (*amazed*). Be a . . . ? What do you mean, be a peacock? What on earth for?

BASSOV. Oh, you know, spread your tail a bit, show off your feathers . . . in front of my wife. Just for Varya's sake. Distract her, make her take an interest in something. I would appreciate it . . .

SHALIMOV (*after a pause*). In other words, you want me to act as a lightning conductor, is that it? (*Laughing.*) You old lunatic! Oh, all right, then, I'll try.

BASSOV. Oh, but you mustn't start thinking . . . I mean, she's a good wife, you know, but it's just that she seems to find something lacking all the time . . . Everyone seems to find

something missing these days . . . all these moods . . .
strange conversations . . . very peculiar goings on altogether. By the way, are you married? I mean, I had heard
that you and your wife were divorced . . .

SHALIMOV. Yes. And I married again, and got divorced
again. It's very difficult, let me tell you, to find a true friend
in a woman.

BASSOV. That's true, yes. That's very true.

They go indoors. LADY IN YELLOW DRESS *and* YOUNG
MAN IN CHECKED SUIT *come out of the woods.*

LADY. There you are – nobody here yet! And it was supposed
to be at six o'clock! How do you like that!

YOUNG MAN. The fact is, I'm basically a romantic actor . . .

LADY. Are you? That's just what I'd have guessed!

YOUNG MAN. Yes, a romantic actor . . . and she goes and
gives me these little comic parts! Really! It's too absurd,
isn't it?

LADY. Of course, they always keep the juicy parts for
themselves . . .

They go off into the woods, right. SONYA *and* ZIMIN *appear
from the other side. At the back of the stage* SUSLOV *walks
slowly in the direction of his own villa.*

ZIMIN (*in a hushed voice*). Wait, Sonya, I'm not coming in . . .
So, there we are: tomorrow I'll be gone.

SONYA (*same tone*). That's right, yes – you go. But do please
be careful, Max!

ZIMIN (*taking her hand*). You too – please.

SONYA. Goodbye, then. We'll see each other in about three
weeks . . . no sooner, I suppose?

ZIMIN. No, no sooner. Goodbye, darling Sonya. While I'm
gone you won't . . .

He breaks off, self-conscious.

SONYA. What?

ZIMIN. Nothing . . . something silly. Goodbye, Sonya.

SONYA *holds him back by his arm.*

SONYA. No, say it . . . While you're gone I won't – what?

ZIMIN (*quietly, head bowed*). . . . won't get married.

SONYA. Don't you dare talk like that, Maxim! – or even think such a thing! You hear? It's silly and . . . well, even nasty. Do you understand?

ZIMIN. No need to get cross. I'm sorry, but all sorts of wild ideas drop into one's head without being invited . . . They do say a person isn't complete master of his own feelings.

SONYA (*heatedly*). That's not true! That's a lie, Maxim, you must know it's a lie! It's just an excuse someone thought up to justify their own weakness – I don't believe it, Maxim! Remember that! Go on, now.

ZIMIN (*squeezing her hand*). All right. And I will remember, Sonya, I promise! Goodbye, my wonderful one!

> ZIMIN *walks quickly away around the corner of the villa.* SONYA *gazes after him, then walks slowly on to the terrace, and then indoors.* DUDAKOV, VLASS *and* MARIA LVOVNA *come out of the woods, right, followed by* DVOETOCHIE. MARIA *sits down on the bench,* DVOETOCHIE *sits beside her. He yawns.*

DUDAKOV. How is it that people can be so frivolous, when life's so difficult?

VLASS. That's something I couldn't tell you, doctor. Anyway, I shall continue. So, you see, my father was a chef, a man with an imagination. He loved me cruelly, and dragged me about everywhere with him – like his pipe. Several times I ran away from him, ran back to my mother, but he'd turn up there at her laundry, beat up anyone he could lay hands on, and take me back into captivity. The fatal notion that he ought to do something about my education came to him while he was cooking for a bishop, so of course I soon found myself in a theological school, but a few months later he left the bishop and went to work for an engineer, so there I was at a technical school . . . Before the year was up I was at agricultural school, because my father had got a position with the chairman of the local Land Board. An art school and a commercial college also had the privilege of seeing me pass briefly beneath their roofs . . . In short, by the time I was seventeen I'd developed such an aversion to knowledge of all kinds that I was quite incapable of learning anything at all – even how to play cards or smoke a pipe. Why are you looking at me like that, Maria Lvovna?

MARIA (*thoughtfully*). It's all very sad . . .

VLASS. Sad? Oh, but it's all in the past.

WOMAN WITH BANDAGED CHEEK (*runs on puffing and panting*). Oh, madam, and master, sir, would you have seen our little Zhenichka, at's a little boy he is, and 'is fair hair, in 'is little straw hat, did 'e ever come running this way then?

MARIA. We haven't seen him.

WOMAN. Oh mercy, at's a sin! Belong to the master and madam Rozov 'e do, at's such a lively little lad with 'is . . . Eh?

VLASS. We haven't seen him, granny.

Muttering, the woman runs off into the woods.

DVOETOCHIE. You know what, Mr. Chornov, you, er . . . you know . . .

VLASS. What? I don't know, you know.

DVOETOCHIE. I like you.

VLASS. Go on.

DVOETOCHIE. It's true.

VLASS. I'm very happy for you.

DVOETOCHIE *laughs loudly.*

DUDAKOV. You're going to have a hard time of it, Vlass.

VLASS. When?

DUDAKOV. Always, with everything.

DVOETOCHIE. Of course he'll have a hard time. You get a straight man, there's fun for everybody – come on, folks, let's see if he'll bend!

VLASS. That remains to be seen. Why don't we go and have some tea, it must be ready by now.

DUDAKOV. Good plan.

DVOETOCHIE. I wouldn't mind either, but . . . d'you think a

stranger'd be welcome?

VLASS. Very welcome, grandpa, I promise. I'll run on ahead.

He runs towards the villa, the others follow more slowly.

DVOETOCHIE. Nice youngster.

MARIA. Yes, he is nice. It's a pity he's so affected.

DVOETOCHIE. Doesn't matter. That'll pass. Main thing is, he's honest, deep down inside. Usually people have their honesty tacked on to the outside, like a necktie or something, and go about shouting 'I'm honest, honestly, I'm ever so honest!' But you know it's like when a girl keeps on saying, 'I am but a young girl, I am but a young girl' – you can be sure she's already moved on to join the ladies. (*Roars with laughter.*) Begging your pardon, Maria Lvovna.

MARIA (*smiling*). It's just what I'd expect from you.

They go up on to the terrace and are just going indoors when SUSLOV *meets them on the way out.*

DVOETOCHIE. Where are you off to, Pyotr?

SUSLOV (*shrugs*). Oh . . . just coming out for a smoke.

They go inside. SUSLOV *walks slowly towards his villa. The* WOMAN WITH A BANDAGED CHEEK *comes running up to meet him. The* MAN IN THE TOP HAT *comes out of the woods, stops, and shrugs his shoulders.*

WOMAN. Oh, good master, sir, would you ever've seen our little boy, Zenichka 'at is . . . in his little jacket and . . .

SUSLOV (*in a low voice*). No. Go away!

She runs off. The MAN IN THE TOP HAT *gives* SUSLOV *an elegant bow.*

MAN. Excuse me, sir. Am I, perhaps, the person for whom you are looking?

SUSLOV (*bewildered*). I'm not looking for anybody. The old woman there is.

MAN. I was invited, don't you see, to play the lead in the . . .

SUSLOV (*walking away*). That's no concern of mine.

MAN (*offended*). No, wait . . .! Whose concern is it, then?

Where is the producer, for heaven's sake? I've been wandering about looking for him for the past two hours and . . . Walked off, the lout!

He goes towards the stage and disappears behind it. OLGA *comes along the road from* VARVARA's *house.*

OLGA. Hello, Pyotr Ivanich.

SUSLOV. Oh – good evening. Muggy, isn't it?

OLGA. Muggy? I hadn't thought so . . .

SUSLOV (*lighting a cigarette*). Suffocating . . . There's a horde of lunatics tearing about the place looking for play producers and little boys in jackets . . .

OLGA. Yes, yes, of course . . . Are you feeling tired? Your hands are shaking.

OLGA *accompanies* SUSLOV *back towards* BASSOV's *villa.*

SUSLOV. I drank too much last night . . . and slept too little.

OLGA. Why do you drink?

SUSLOV. Have to get some joy out of life.

OLGA. Have you seen my husband?

SUSLOV. He's having tea with the Bassovs.

VARVARA *appears on the terrace.*

VARVARA. Are you coming in to see me, Olya?

OLGA. I was just out for a walk.

VARVARA. What took you away from us, Pyotr Ivanich?

SUSLOV (*little laugh*). My own two feet on the solid earth, as always. I'd had enough of listening to speeches from the man of letters and the esteemed Maria Lvovna.

VARVARA. Really? Didn't it interest you at all? I'd still like to go on listening.

SUSLOV (*shrugging*). You're welcome to it. As for me, I'm off. Goodbye.

He goes off towards his villa.

OLGA (*softly*). Why is he like that, do you think?

VARVARA. I don't know, and frankly, I don't care. Shall we go in?

OLGA. Sit with me out here for a while. They'll manage without you.

VARVARA. I'm sure they will. Are you upset again?

OLGA. How can I help it, Varya? He got back from town, popped into the house for one minute, and then disappeared. That's hardly likely to make me happy, is it?

VARVARA. He's been with us.

They walk slowly over to the group of firs.

OLGA (*irritably*). He's running away from me and the children . . . Oh, I know, he's been out earning our living and deserves a rest, but then I'm tired too . . . Oh, if you knew how tired I am! I can't do anything, nothing seems to go right, and it makes me so furious! He can't seem to realise that I sacrificed the whole of my youth and strength for his sake.

VARVARA (*gently*). Darling Olya, you do love complaining, don't you?

From indoors comes the muffled sounds of voices raised in argument; it gets louder and louder.

OLGA. I don't know . . . maybe. But I've got to tell him . . . it would be better if I went away. With the children, of course.

VARVARA. Yes, that's what you should do. Have a rest from one another. Yes, you go. I'll find the money for you.

OLGA. Oh, but I owe you so much already!

VARVARA. It's nothing, don't fret about it. Let's sit down – and calm down.

OLGA. I hate myself for not being able to manage without your help. Hate myself! Do you think it's easy for me, to accept money from you – your husband's money? If you can't manage your own life, if you've always got to have someone helping you, supporting you, you can't respect yourself. Do you understand? Sometimes I even hate *you* too – for being so calm and rational about everything, and never really living, never *feeling* anything!

VARVARA. But, darling, I only manage by being quiet and not allowing myself to complain. That's my way, that's all.

OLGA. In their heart of hearts, people who help must despise those who are helped. I want to be the one who does the helping.

RYUMIN *walks quickly up to the* BASSOVS' *villa.*

VARVARA. So that you can despise people?

OLGA. Yes! Yes! I don't like people! I don't like Maria Lvovna – why does she have to judge everyone so severely? I don't like that Ryumin – he never stops philosophising but hasn't the guts to *do* anything – can't do anything. And I don't like your husband either, he's soft as dough and he's afraid of you – that's not very admirable, is it? And your brother. He's in love with that vicious loud-mouthed shrew Maria Lvovna . . .

VARVARA (*surprised and reproachful*). Olga! What's got into you? That's very wrong of you, you know . . .

OLGA. All right, so it's wrong of me. I don't care. And that stuck-up Karelia – talks about 'beauty' all the time – all she wants is to find herself a husband!

VARVARA (*severely and coldly*). You mustn't let yourself give way to these feelings, Olga. They'll lead you into dark places . . .

OLGA (*softly, but with force and venom*). I don't care! I don't care where they lead me so long as it's away from this intolerable boredom! I want to live! I've got as much right as anyone else has! I'm not stupid, I can see what's going on . . . yes, even you – Oh I know, you lead a good life, well, of course, you've got a rich husband, haven't you? – yes, and not all that scrupulous in his affairs either . . . everyone says that about him, you must know that! And you, yes – you arranged things somehow so that you couldn't have children . . .

VARVARA *gets up slowly and gazes at* OLGA, *her eyes wide with amazement.*

VARVARA. Arranged things? You . . . what do you mean?

OLGA (*embarrassed*). I don't mean anything in particular . . . I only meant . . . well, my husband says there's lots of women who don't want to have children . . .

VARVARA. I don't understand you, but you seem to suspect me of something disgusting . . . I don't want to know exactly what, but . . .

OLGA. Varya, don't speak in that tone . . . don't look at me like that . . . After all, it's true, they do say awful things about your husband . . .

VARVARA (*with a shudder, thoughtfully*). You and I, Olga – we were like sisters, once. So close . . . If I didn't know how hard your life is . . . didn't understand how you once dreamed – we dreamed together – of a quite different kind of life . . .

OLGA (*sincerely*). Oh, forgive me, Varya, please forgive me. I'm a monster.

VARVARA. We dreamed together of a good life, a radiant life . . . and wept together when the dreams decayed . . . I'm hurt now, Olga. Is that what you wanted? I'm hurt.

OLGA. No, don't say . . . don't say that, Varya!

VARVARA. I must go.

OLGA *gets up.*

No, don't follow me. I don't want you.

OLGA. You mean . . . Never, Varya? Never again?

VARVARA. Don't ask me that . . . I can't understand why you had to say such things.

DVOETOCHIE *comes quickly down the steps from the terrace, roaring with laughter, comes up to* VARVARA, *takes her by the hand.*

DVOETOCHIE. I've run away, Ma'am! That philosophising little beauty, Mr. Ryumin, drove me into a corner, got me all confused. I don't have the head for these oracles, couldn't stand up to the fellow, just got stuck in his speeches like a cockroach in treacle . . . So, to hell with him, I've run away! Do a sight better chatting with you . . . old fossil I may be, but I really like you, you know. Ah, but why's the little face gone all droopy now?

Catches sight of OLGA, *clears his throat in embarrassment.*

OLGA (*meekly*). Am I to go, Varya?

VARVARA (*firmly*). Yes.

> OLGA *goes off quickly.* VARVARA *looks after her, then turns to* DVOETOCHIE.

I'm sorry . . . You were saying . . .?

DVOETOCHIE (*with friendly simplicity*). Oh dear, Ma'am, I look at you . . . It's bad for you here, you know. Bad, isn't it, eh? (*He roars with laughter.*)

VARVARA (*looking him up and down; calmly, evenly*). Would you explain, Semyon Semyonich, what gives you the right to take that strange tone with me?

DVOETOCHIE (*laughing*). Oh, give over, ma'am! I'm given the right by my advanced years and my extensive experience!

VARVARA. I'm sorry, but I don't think that's sufficient excuse for such an intrusion.

DVOETOCHIE (*good-naturedly*). I'm not intruding into anything. But I can see you don't really belong here . . . and no more do I . . . so, well, there it is, I felt like saying something but obviously I didn't know how to put it right, and if that's it, well then I'm sorry.

VARVARA (*with a short laugh*). I'm sorry too. I'm afraid I spoke rudely, but it did seem rather odd . . . I'm not used to being talked to like that.

DVOETOCHIE. No, of course not, I can see you're not used to it – how could you be, in this place? Come on, let's have a walk. Make an old man happy, eh?

> SEMYONOV *comes flying in on his bicycle and rides straight over to stop at* DVOETOCHIE's *feet.*

DVOETOCHIE (*in alarm*). Where do you think you're off to, young man? What's all this?

SEMYONOV (*panting*). I beg your pardon . . . Is it all over?

DVOETOCHIE. Is what all over? Get along with you.

SEMYONOV. Such rotten luck – I had a puncture! I'm Semyonov. I was supposed to be at two rehearsals today, you see, and . . .

DVOETOCHIE. What's it go to do with me?

SEMYONOV. Oh, but aren't you in it? I'm sorry, I thought you
were in make-up . . .

DVOETOCHIE (*to* VARVARA). What on earth's he talking
about?

VARVARA (*to* SEMYONOV). Are you here for the rehearsal?

SEMYONOV. Yes, and on the way you see . . .

VARVARA. They haven't started yet.

SEMYONOV (*joyfully*). Oh, marvellous, thank you! What a
nuisance, really – I'm always so punctual!

DVOETOCHIE. What is the nuisance now?

SEMYONOV (*amiably*). I mean, it would have been a nuisance
if I had been late. (*Bows.*) My apologies, excuse me.

He walks away, bowing, towards the stage.

DVOETOCHIE. What a monstrous little insect. Comes
crashing down on us, and we're supposed to be fascinated.
Let's get away from here, Varvara Mikhailovna, before
some other prancing earwig drops on us.

VARVARA (*absently*). Come on, then . . . I'll just get a shawl.
Wait a moment.

She goes into the villa. SEMYONOV *comes up to*
DVOETOCHIE.

SEMYONOV. There's some others riding over . . . two girls,
and a cadet.

DVOETOCHIE. Aha! Riding over, are they? That will be nice
for us!

SEMYONOV. They should be here any minute now . . . The
cadet, you know, is the one whose sister shot herself.

DVOETOCHIE. That one, eh? Think of that!

SEMYONOV. Yes, quite a sensation, wasn't it? Just a girl, and
all of a sudden, there she is shooting herself!

DVOETOCHIE. H'm, yes. That would be a – sensation.

SEMYONOV. Fancy me thinking you were wearing make-up!
But honestly, your hair and your skin are just like make-up!

DVOETOCHIE. I thank you most humbly.

SEMYONOV. Truly, I'm not flattering you, I did think . . .

DVOETOCHIE. Oh, I believe you. I just don't understand how

it could be flattering.

SEMYONOV. Oh, but of course it is! A person's always better-looking when they've got make-up on! Tell me, you don't just happen to be the scene painter, do you?

> SUSLOV *comes out of the woods; at the back of the stage appear the* LADY IN YELLOW *and the* YOUNG MAN IN THE CHECK SUIT.

DVOETOCHIE. No. I just happen to be that gentleman's uncle.

LADY. Mr. Sazanov!

SEMYONOV. They're calling me, I must go. It's strange, you know – I have such a simple name, but nobody ever seems to get it right. Goodbye.

> *He goes off to where he's being called, bowing to the* LADY *with animation.* SUSLOV *comes up to* DVOETOCHIE.

SUSLOV. Have you seen my wife?

> DVOETOCHIE *shakes his head and gives a sigh of relief.*

SUSLOV. The place is swarming with actors.

DVOETOCHIE. That little burr stuck to me like a birch leaf to a bare bum in a bath-house. Called me a scene painter. Spindle-shanked sissy, taking up room on the earth! – And that lot are at their arguing again. I don't know!

> *From the villa emerge* KALERIA, SHALIMOV, RYUMIN, VARVARA. DVOETOCHIE *goes towards them, listening attentively to their argument.* SUSLOV *sits down on a bench, gazing morosely at the others.*

SHALIMOV (*wearily*). No, frankly I'd rather run to the North Pole to get away from her – she's too hot for me.

RYUMIN. What makes me so furious is that she's so didactic. Intolerance of that degree is positively criminal. Why do people like that assume that everyone else must accept their beliefs?

VARVARA (*looking at them all intently*). You must show them something greater and more beautiful than what they believe in.

KALERIA. Cold dreams about full stomachs for all – dreams
without the smallest touch of poetry – is that what you call
'great and beautiful'?

VARVARA (*excited*). I don't know, but I don't see anyone
offering anything more exciting. I don't know how to
express myself properly . . . but I feel with all my heart how
essential it is to awaken in people – in everybody – a sense of
their own value and dignity . . .

SHALIMOV *is listening to her with close attention.*

We none of us know how to respect each other . . . and
that's so painful, so . . . insulting.

KALERIA. But good God, it's not Maria Lvovna who'll teach
us to do that!

VARVARA. You're all so hostile towards her. Why?

RYUMIN. She's the one who's hostile! She's maddening.
Whenever I hear someone trying to explain the meaning of
life I feel as if I'm being crushed in a steely embrace by
someone who wants to squeeze me into a different shape.

KALERIA. It's so confining, having to live among such people.

VARVARA. And having to live among people who are always
complaining – is that freedom, Kaleria? Be fair – surely it
isn't good to be surrounded by people who are forever
moaning and whining about themselves and their troubles,
making life a dustbin for their complaints and contributing
nothing, but nothing else to it at all? What do any of us here
contribute to life, you or I or anyone?

RYUMIN. And what does Maria Lvovna contribute? Hostility.

KALERIA. And a few old clichés that were best forgotten. The
living can't be guided by the maxims of the dead.

The amateur actors start gathering around the stage. PUSTO-
BAIKA *arranges chairs on the stage.*

DVOETOCHIE. Ah, now, Varvara Mikhailovna, why upset
your good-self, eh? Why not drop the whole foolish thing
and come for a walk, eh? You did promise!

VARVARA. Yes. Yes – I'll come. I don't know how to say what
I feel, what I want, anyway . . . I just can't do it. It's
terrible, being such an intellectual mute.

SHALIMOV. I testify, Varvara Mikhailovna, that you are not. May I join you on your walk?

VARVARA. Of course.

DVOETOCHIE. Let's go down to the summerhouse by the stream . . . Why do you let yourself get so worked up, my dear?

VARVARA. Oh . . . I feel . . . I don't know . . . there's some sort of tragic misunderstanding . . .

They walk off along the road into the woods. SUSLOV *gazes after them and grins.*

RYUMIN (*also looking after them*). The arrival of that man Shamilov has certainly put some life into her! Talking nineteen to the dozen . . . and after all, what is he? – a burnt-out writer who can't feel the ground beneath his feet any more – surely she can see that? The more conviction he speaks with the more he's lying to himself and deceiving others.

KALERIA. She knows that. I saw her just after her conversation with him last night. She was weeping like a little child. Yes . . . Of course, he looked so strong and fearless from a distance, she thought he was bound to bring a new dimension to her barren life.

Round the corner of BASSOV's *villa came* ZAMISLOV *and* YULIA. *He whispers something to her and she laughs.* SUSLOV *sees them.*

RYUMIN. Let's go inside. I feel like some music – will you play something?

KALERIA. All right, let's go in. Yes, it's sad when everything around you is so . . .

YULIA. Oh, look, our actors have arrived! The rehearsal was called for six, and now it's . . .

ZAMISLOV. Half-past seven. It used to be only you who was late, now they all are. That's your influence.

YULIA. Is that an impertinence?

ZAMISLOV. A compliment. I'll just slip in and see my master for a moment, if you'll allow me?

YULIA. Quick as you can, then.

> ZAMISLOV *goes into the villa;* YULIA, *humming, crosses to the group of trees. She sees her husband.*

SUSLOV. M'm – and where have you been?

YULIA. Round and about.

> *The* LADY IN YELLOW, *the* YOUNG MAN, SEMYONOV, *the* CADET *and* TWO GIRLS *are standing beside the stage. On the stage* PUSTOBAIKA *is noisily dragging a table into position. Laughter, and odd scraps of conversation.*

'Listen, everyone!' 'Where's the producer?' 'Mr. Stepanov!' 'He's here, I saw him'. 'We're late!' 'We'll never get back to town.' 'Can't we get started?' 'Excuse me, my name's Semyonov, not Stepanov!'

SUSLOV. And with him all the time, I suppose? With that . . . that . . . and so openly . . . What do you think you're doing, Yulia? Don't you understand that people are already laughing at me?

YULIA. Already laughing? H'm, that's bad.

SUSLOV. We must have this out with each other. I simply can't allow you to be . . .

YULIA. – the wife of a man people laugh at? No, the role doesn't suit me, either.

SUSLOV. Be careful, Yulia! I'm quite capable of . . .

YULIA. . . . behaving like a drunken peasant. Yes, I know.

SUSLOV. How dare you speak to me like that, you – you strumpet!

YULIA (*softly, calmly*). We'll finish this scene at home. There's some people coming, you'd better go. Your face is . . .

> *She shudders, fastidiously.* SUSLOV *takes a step towards her, but retreats again quickly, disappearing into the woods, muttering.*

SUSLOV. One day . . . one day – I shall shoot you.

YULIA (*calling after him*). Not today, then? No? (*She sings softly*). 'Now the weary sun is sinking . . .' (*Her voice trembles.*) 'Soon to drown in blood-red sea.'

She stares ahead, eyes wide open, and then slowly lowers her head. From BASSOV's *villa appears* MARIA LVOVNA, *very agitated, followed by* DUDAKOV *and* BASSOV, *carrying fishing rods.* BASSOV *is struggling to untangle his line.*

BASSOV. But, my dear good lady, you ought to be more gentle – kinder to people. We're all only human, you know . . . Damn and blast whoever got my line all tangled up!

MARIA. Now wait a moment . . .

DUDAKOV. You see, people get tired . . .

BASSOV. No, you simply can't go on the way you do! According to you, if someone's a writer he absolutely has to be some sort of, I don't know, hero or something, a god. But you know, not every writer wants to be like that.

MARIA. We must go on demanding more of life, and more of people.

BASSOV. Of course. Demand more – yes, but within the limits of the possible. Everything must be accomplished, gradually – evolution, not revolution! That's what we must never forget.

MARIA. I am not demanding the impossible. But we live in a country where the only person who can be a herald of truth, a dispassionate judge of his people's vices, and a fighter for their true interests . . . is the writer. Only he can be that, and that's what the Russian writer must be.

BASSOV. Well, yes, of course . . . All the same . . .

MARIA (*coming down from the verandah*). And I don't see any of that in your friend. No, none of it. What does he want? What are his ideals? What does he hate? Or love? Where is his truth? Is he my enemy, or my friend? I don't understand who he is.

She goes quickly round the corner of the villa.

BASSOV (*untangling his line*). Maria Lvovna, of course I have to admire you for your . . . er . . . enthusiasm, but . . . er . . . Oh. Gone, has she? Well, really! Why do you suppose she has to get so worked up? Dammit, every schoolboy knows that a writer's supposed to tell the truth and . . . well . . . be interested in good causes and all that . . . just as a soldier's supposed to be brave, and a lawyer clever . . . but this damned spitfire has to keep on bludgeoning us over the head with it . . . Come on, doctor, let's go and catch some perch . . . Wish I knew who got this line in such a tangle, dammit!

DUDAKOV. Ye-es . . . um . . . she talks a lot of brainy stuff, though . . . of course, things are easy for her, she's got a private practice, no real demands on her time . . .

BASSOV. But that Yakov, now – he really is a slippery customer, you know. Did you see how neatly he wriggled out of it when she'd got him cornered. (*He laughs.*) Oh yes, he's a lovely talker once he gets into his stride. However, lovely talker or not, after the death of his first wife – and he only lived with her for six months before he chucked her out . . .

DUDAKOV. Divorced. Before they got divorced, you should say.

BASSOV. All right, divorced . . . anyway, now she's dead he's trying to get his hands on her nice little estate. Pretty smart, eh?

DUDAKOV. B-but . . . no, not smart, really – going a bit far, isn't it?

BASSOV. Well, there it is – he doesn't think it's going too far at all . . . Well, come on, let's get down to the river . . .

DUDAKOV. But you know, actually . . .

BASSOV. What, actually?

DUDAKOV (*slowly, thoughtfully*). Don't you think it's strange . . .or, rather, doesn't it surprise you, that we haven't all grown to hate one another?

BASSOV (*stopping*). Wha-at? You're not serious, are you?

DUDAKOV. Perfectly serious. We're a pretty empty lot, aren't we? – doesn't it strike you?

BASSOV (*walking on*). No it does not strike me. I am a perfectly normal healthy man – with your permission.

DUDAKOV. No, look, don't joke about it . . .

BASSOV. Joke? Look here, doctor, you – er – well, you need – well, in a word, physician, heal thyself! Eh? Could I just ask, by the way – you won't push me into the river, will you?

DUDAKOV (*seriously, shrugging his shoulders*). Why should I?

BASSOV (*walking on*). Just that you seem to be in a very odd mood altogether.

DUDAKOV (*morosely*). It's difficult to have a serious conversation with you.

BASSOV. Don't try. Absolutely not. You have such very original ideas about serious conversation, so – let's not talk seriously.

> *Exit* BASSOV *and* DUDAKOV. *From the right* SONYA *and* VLASS *enter.* ZAMISLOV *comes out of* BASSOV's *villa and runs hurriedly to the stage, where he is greeted noisily. The actors crowd round him closely while he explains something.*

SONYA. I don't believe you're really a poet, Vlass.

VLASS. Aha, but you're quite wrong. Some of my pieces display enormous talent. For instance:

> The pineapple and the peach, alas!
> Are not for peasants of my class.
> Others may guzzle, but for Vlass
> The peach and pineapple must pass.

SONYA (*laughing*). Why do you waste your time on such nonsense? Why won't you take yourself seriously?

VLASS (*quietly, mysteriously*). Ah, Sonya, all-seeing Sonya, even that I have attempted – and indeed have written a song about the attempt:
(*He sings in a low nasal voice.*)
I'm much too big for hole-and-corner solutions
But much too small to help with revolutions . . .

SONYA (*seriously*). Stop it, Vlass! You don't really want to fool about all the time, I'm sure. What *do* you want, though, I wonder?

VLASS (*fervently*). To live well – I want to live *well*!

SONYA. And what are you doing about it?

VLASS (*sadly*). Nothing. Not one single thing.

MARIA (*calling from the woods*). Sonya!

SONYA. Hello! I'm here. What is it?

MARIA. There's some people come to see you – friends of yours – they're up at the villa.

SONYA. All right, I'll go . . .

Enter MARIA.

I'll turn this performer over to you. He's been talking utter nonsense, he's just asking for a good beating . . .

She runs off.

VLASS (*meekly*). Well, go ahead. (*Imitates country accent.*) At ole fledging o yourn, at's been a-chewing' on me all down at long rud from station, but I be a-breathin' yet.

MARIA (*gently*). Vlass, dear, why make yourself into a clown? Why degrade yourself? Who needs it?

VLASS (*not looking at her*). Who needs it? I don't know . . . But nobody ever laughs. I want people to laugh! (*Suddenly he becomes fervent, simple, sincere.*) I'm sick of it, Maria Lvovna, it all seems utterly absurd to me . . . All these people, I don't love them, don't respect them, they're pathetic, insignificant, like a cloud of mosquitoes . . . how can I talk seriously to them? They're all so affected that I get this nasty urge to be even more obviously affected than they are . . . My head's cluttered up with all their junk, I feel like groaning, cursing, complaining or . . . I don't know . . . damn it, maybe I'll just take to drink. I can't . . . don't know how to . . . live differently from them, so I'm becoming a monster . . . poisoned by their vulgarity. Oh God, listen, there they are, they're coming . . . Sometimes I look at them with such sick horror that . . . Quick, let's go, I've really *got* to go on talking to you!

MARIA (*taking his arm*). If you only knew how happy I am to see you like this.

VLASS. Sometimes . . . I look at them . . . and I just want to shout at them – something vicious, insulting . . .

They go off into the woods. SHALIMOV, YULIA *and* VARVARA *appear on the right.*

SHALIMOV. No, no! No more serious talk, please. I've had all the philosophy I can take. Let me just vegetate, and give my poor nerves a rest . . . I want to do nothing more taxing than drift about flirting with the ladies . . .

YULIA. And flirting with ladies doesn't tax your nerves? You must be very unusual. Tell me, why have you not flirted with me?

SHALIMOV. I shall not fail to take advantage of your kind permission.

YULIA. I wasn't giving my permission, only asking . . .

SHALIMOV. Nevertheless, I insist on regarding it as your kind permission.

VARVARA. Oh very well, we'll leave that one . . . But answer my first question – truthfully, now.

SHALIMOV. Certainly. I admit the possibility of friendship with a woman, but not as something that can endure. Nature will not be denied.

YULIA. In other words, you only see friendship as a prelude to love?

SHALIMOV. Ah, now, love – that's a serious matter. When I love a woman I want to raise her high above the earth and deck her with the finest flowers of my thoughts and feelings . . .

ZAMISLOV (*calling*). Yulia Filipovna! Could you come up here, please?

YULIA. Coming! Goodbye for the moment, Mister Floricultu-ralist! You go and tidy up your conservatory.

She goes up on to the stage.

SHALIMOV. Oh, but at once, immediately! . . . What a vivacious little thing! Why the strange look, Varvara Mikhailovna?

VARVARA. Your moustache suits you perfectly.

SHALIMOV. Really? My humble thanks. But my tone doesn't suit you at all, does it? You're very severe. But honestly, somehow it's impossible to talk to her in any other tone.

VARVARA. I seem to be losing my capacity for surprise.

SHALIMOV. Ah, I see – you think it's odd that I should be the way I am? But everyone can't be quite as vociferously candid as that hysterical Mr. Ryumin, can they? Oh, I do beg your pardon! – I believe he's your . . . friend?

VARVARA (*shakes her head*). I have no friends.

SHALIMOV. I value the inner world of my soul too much to put it on show to the first caller. The followers of Pythagorus only revealed their secrets to the chosen few.

VARVARA. Now your moustache is beginning to seem superfluous.

SHALIMOV. Oh, damn my moustache, leave it in peace! You know the saying: live with the wolves, howl like a wolf; or, when in Rome . . . good advice, both of them, especially for someone who's drunk the cup of loneliness to the bitter dregs. You obviously haven't had your fill of it yet, so it's difficult for you to understand a man who . . . However, I mustn't detain you . . .

He bows, and crosses to the stage where the audience is gathering, watching in silence as ZAMISLOV, *a book in his hand, creeps across the stage, demonstrating to* SEMYONOV *how a scene is to be acted.* BASSOV *comes hurrying towards the villa with his fishing rod.*

BASSOV. Varya! The fishing! Amazing! Even the doctor, for all his bungling, hooked one straight off – whoops! And how about that, there's a perch for you. And Pyotr's uncle got three . . . (*He glances round.*) Listen, as I was on my way back here just now, coming past the summerhouse near that dead pine, suddenly, can you imagine, there was Vlass down on his knees in front of Maria Lvovna, kissing her hands! How about that, eh? Darling, you'll have to speak to him – the boy's only a baby, isn't he? She's old enough to be his mother, isn't she?

VARVARA (*softly*). Sergei, listen to me – please say nothing about this – not a word – to anybody. You don't understand, you've got it all wrong. I'm afraid you'll go and tell everybody, and that would be quite dreadful, you must understand that.

BASSOV. What are you getting so worked up about? All right, then, if I mustn't, I won't. But isn't it ridiculous, eh? And Maria Lvovna . . .

VARVARA. Sergei, you must promise that you'll forget all

about it. Give me your word of honour. Please!

BASSOV. Word of honour? Oh, all right, to hell with them! But just explain to me . . .

VARVARA. I can't explain. But I just know that it's not what you're thinking. It's not an affair.

BASSOV. Aha. Well. Not an affair, eh? H'm. Then what is it, Varya, eh? Oh, all right, all right, I'll keep quiet, no need to get excited! I went off to catch perch and . . . didn't see a thing. Oh, but wait a minute, listen – that Yakov! What a swine, eh?

VARVARA (*alarmed*). What is it, Sergei? What's happened?

BASSOV. What are you so jumpy about? This is something quite different . . .

VARVARA. Please, I don't want to hear it, Sergei . . . Can't you understand? I don't want to!

BASSOV (*surprised, hurriedly*). But it's nothing very special! You're so peculiar – what's the matter with you? It's just that Yakov's trying to swindle his first wife's sister out of the bits of land she inherited – and he was only . . .

VARVARA (*fastidiously, with pain*). Please! Will you please be quiet! Please! Can't you understand, I don't want to hear any more, Sergei?

BASSOV (*offended*). You ought to do something about your nerves, Varya! I'm sorry, but you're behaving very strangely . . . in fact, almost offensively. Did you know that?

He goes out quickly. VARVARA *goes quietly towards the verandah. Around the stage there is noise and laughter.*

ZAMISLOV. Where's the lantern? Bring the lantern!

YULIA. Mr. Somov, where's my part?

SEMYONOV. Semyonov, if you don't mind?

YULIA. Not a bit.

ZAMISLOV. Quiet, everybody, quiet, please! We're about to begin!

CURTAIN

Act Three

A glade in the woods.

At the back, under the trees, around a carpet spread with hors d'oeuvres and bottles, are gathered, BASSOV, DVOETOCHIE, SHALIMOV, SUSLOV *and* ZAMISLOV. *To their right on one side is a large samovar; close to it* SASHA *is washing dishes.* PUSTOBAIKA *is lying smoking a pipe; beside him are oars, baskets, an iron bucket. Towards the front, left, is a broken hay-rick, and a large tree stump with its root pulled out of the earth. On the hay are sitting* KALERIA, VARVARA *and* YULIA. BASSOV *is telling a story in a low voice, the other men listening attentively. From the right* SONYA'S *voice can be heard now and then, and the strumming of a balalaika and a guitar. It is early evening.*

YULIA. This picnic . . . is boring.

KALERIA. Like our lives.

VARVARA. It's fun for the men.

YULIA. They've all had lots to drink – now I expect they're telling each other dirty stories.

Pause.

SONYA (*off*). No, not like that – slower.

The guitar strums. DVOETOCHIE *roars with laughter.*

YULIA. I've been drinking too, but it hasn't made me cheerful. On the contrary, when I've had a strong drink I always feel more moody . . . living seems a more difficult business . . . and I feel like doing something mad and wild.

KALERIA (*thoughtfully*). Everything's so muddled . . . and blurred . . . It frightens me.

VARVARA. What frightens you?

KALERIA. People. They're all unreliable, there isn't anyone you can really trust.

VARVARA. Yes, that's it – unreliable. I understand you.

BASSOV (*in a thick accent*). But vy, my liddle pettikins? I yam evrzo perveckly commvable like zis!

All the men laugh.

KALERIA. No you don't, you don't understand me, and I don't understand you, and nobody understands anybody else, and don't even want to try . . . People are just drifting about like ice-floes in the Arctic, bumping into one another . . .

 DVOETOCHIE *gets up and walks off to the right.* YULIA *sings softly.*

YULIA. Now the weary sun is sinking
  Soon to drown in blood-red sea . . .

When VARVARA *starts talking* YULIA *stops singing and stares intently into her face.*

VARVARA. Life's just like a street market – everybody wants to cheat everyone else, get as much as possible, give as little as possible.

YULIA (*sings*). Purple shadows lengthen, darken,
   Soon to wrap their shrouds round me . . .

KALERIA. What would people have to be like, I wonder, for it to be less . . . boring . . . just to look at them.

VARVARA. More honest. More couragous.

KALERIA. No – more definite, Varya. In everything they do or say, people should define themselves.

YULIA. Oh, do stop philosophising, it's not a bit amusing! Let's sing.

VARVARA. That duet you sang the other day was lovely, Yulia Filipovna.

YULIA. Yes, it's beautiful, isn't it? So pure! I love everything that's pure – don't you believe me? But I do, I love pure sights, pure sounds . . .

 She laughs.

KALERIA. There's a sort of grey anger growing inside me, Varya – grey, like rainclouds in autumn . . . heavy clouds

of anger weighing down on me . . . I don't love anybody,
and I don't want to love anybody! I shall die a ridiculous old
maid.

VARVARA. Oh do stop, my dear! It's so depressing.

YULIA. Anyway it's a doubtful pleasure, being married . . . If
I were you I'd marry Ryumin. He's a bit dour but . . .

SONYA (off). No, wait. All right – begin . . . No, mandolin
first . . .

Mandolin and guitar play a duet.

KALERIA. He's made of rubber.

VARVARA. There's a sad little song that keeps coming back to
me for some reason. The washerwomen in the laundry
where my mother worked used to sing it. I was just a girl
then, studying at the gymnasium. I remember how I used to
arrive home and the laundry would be full of grey,
suffocating steam with these half-naked women weaving
dimly about in it and singing in their soft, tired voices;

Oh pity me, mother,
Your lonely young daughter
A slave among strangers,
My tears have run dry

I'd cry whenever I heard that song.

BASSOV. Sasha! Bring us some beer – and some port.

VARVARA. It was good, the way I lived then. Those women
loved me – in the evenings, when they'd finished work, they
used to sit down to drink tea round a huge well-scrubbed
table, and they'd sit me down beside them, like an
equal . . .

KALERIA. Varya, you're being a bore – as bad as Maria
Lvovna.

YULIA. My dears, it's bad, the way we women live now.

VARVARA (thoughtfully). Yes, it is. Terrible. And we've none
of us any idea how to live better. My mother worked hard
all her life, but she was always cheerful and kind,
everybody loved her. She made sure I got an education – she
was so thrilled and proud when I qualified from the

gymnasium! She could hardly walk by that time, she was crippled with rheumatism . . . She died calmly, and she said: 'Don't cry, Varya, it's nothing. For me, it's time. A bit of life, a bit of work, and that's it.' Her life had more meaning than mine. I live so – clumsily. I feel as if I'd stumbled into a strange country, full of strange people, and I don't understand the way they live . . . I don't understand this sort of life, the way of educated people, it seems to me precarious, unstable, not meant to last – thrown together hurriedly like booths at a fair . . . no, it's like ice on the surface of a strongly flowing river – it looks all shiny and firm, but underneath it's full of dirt, full of shameful ugly things . . . And when I read a book that's really honest and courageous, I feel that the hot sun of truth is rising and will melt the ice and release all that filth, and soon the waters of the river will break it up, shatter it, wash it all away . . .

KALERIA (*with distaste, impatient*). Why don't you leave that husband of yours? Vulgar thing – he's irrelevant to you.

VARVARA *gazes at* KALERIA *in perplexity.*

(*insistently*). Leave him, go away somewhere, go off and study, fall in love . . . anything, just go.

VARVARA *stands up, annoyed.*

VARVARA. You're very crude.

KALERIA. You could do it. You don't mind a bit of dirt, you get on with washerwomen – you could live anywhere . . .

YULIA. What a nice way to talk about your brother.

KALERIA (*calmly*). I'll talk about your husband in just the same way if you like.

YULIA (*laughing*). Oh, carry on, I don't imagine you'd offend me. I often tell him things about himself which drive him mad – and then he tries to pay me in the same coin. The other day he told me I was a strumpet . . .

VARVARA. You . . . what did you say?

YULIA. Nothing. I didn't argue. I'm not sure what a strumpet is, but I do know I'm very curious – I have a sort of nasty keen curiosity about men.

VARVARA *gets up and walks two or three steps to one side.*

I'm beautiful, that's my trouble. I was still only in the third
form when the masters started to look at me in a way that
made me feel ashamed – I'd blush, and that delighted them
– they'd grin with relish, like gluttons outside a delicatessen.

KALERIA (*shudders*). Ugh, how revolting!

YULIA. Yes. And then my married friends enlightened
me . . . But I'm indebted to my husband most of all, he
really fouled up my imagination, he's the one who made me
so curious about men.

She laughs. SHALIMOV *moves away from the group of men
and comes slowly over towards the women.*

So in return I foul up his life. There's a saying: if you've
caught a caning, give back a belting.

SHALIMOV (*arriving*). A splendid saying too! No doubt
invented by a very kind a generous man. Varavara
Mikhailovna – would you care to stroll down to the river?

VARVARA. Perhaps . . . yes, all right.

SHALIMOV. May I offer you my arm?

VARVARA. No thank you – I don't like to.

SHALIMOV. What a mournful face! – you're not a bit like
your brother, he's a jolly youngster, very amusing . . .

They go off to the right.

KALERIA. There's not one of us here who's contented with
their life. Look at you, always so cheerful, but at the same
time . . .

YULIA. Do you like that man? I feel there's something false
about him. Something cold, like a frog . . . Let's go down to
the river too.

KALERIA (*getting up*). All right. It's all the same to me.

YULIA. He seems to be rather attracted by her. But really,
how remote she is with everyone! She has such a strange,
inquisitive way of looking at one – what is it she's looking
for? I like her, but . . . I'm afraid of her, too. She's so strict
and pure . . .

They go out. From the right come loud shouts and laughter.

VOICES. Quick, the boat! Where's the oars? Bring the oars!

> PUSTOBAIKA *slowly gets up, puts the oars on to his shoulder, and is about to start off.* SUSLOV *and* BASSOV *run in the direction of the shouts.* ZAMISLOV *rushes up to* PUSTO-BAIKA *and snatches the oars away from him.*

ZAMISLOV. Move, dammit! Can't you hear, there's going to be an accident and you just stand there like a dummy!

> *He runs off.* PUSTOBAIKA *follows him, grumbling.*

PUSTOBAIKA. At's no accident, at'd never be shouting like that for an accident, don't you worry yoursen . . . Little hero, leapin' about . . .

> *The stage is empty for a few moments. Shouts can be heard:*

VOICES. No, don't throw stones at it! Catch it! Use the oars!

> *Laughter. From the left appear* MARIA LVOVNA *and* VLASS, *both agitated.*

MARIA (*excited, but in a low voice*). No, you mustn't, I won't listen to such things! Don't you dare to talk to me like that again! Have I ever given you the slightest reason to . . .?
VLASS. I will say it! I will!

> MARIA *thrusts her hands forward as if wanting to push* VLASS *away.*

MARIA. I demand that you treat me with respect!
VLASS. I love you! Yes, love you! Insanely, with all my heart and soul, I love the way you think, love the way you feel . . . and love that stern lock of grey hair, and your eyes, and your voice . . .
MARIA. No, no, be quiet, how can you!
VLASS. I can't live . . . I need you as I need . . . air!
MARIA. Oh my God! Isn't it possible without all this . . .?
VLASS (*clutching his head*). You've given me back my self-respect . . . I was in darkness, wandering in darkness, aimlessly . . . but now you've taught me to believe in my own strength . . .

MARIA. Go away! Don't torture me – you mustn't torture me, my dear!

VLASS (*on his knees*). You've given me so much already, but even that's not enough. Please, be generous, give me more! I've got to believe . . . I've got to know that I'm worthy, not just of your attention, but of your love! Please, I implore you – don't reject me!

MARIA. No, it's me that's imploring you – go away, go away! Later . . . I'll answer you later . . . not now. And stand up! Please, please stand up!

VLASS (*stands*). But you must believe me – your love is absolutely vital to me . . . My heart is so soiled from living among all these pathetic people . . . I need your fire to cauterise it of all its dirt and rust.

MARIA. Please, you must have a little respect for me! After all, I'm an old woman, surely you can see that? And I insist that you go away, now, this instant. Go on, go!

VLASS. Very well, I'll go. But later . . . you will tell me, later . . .

MARIA. Yes, yes, later! But now, go!

VLASS *goes quickly into the woods on the right, colliding with* VARVARA *as he goes*.

VARVARA. Careful! What's the matter with you?

VLASS. Oh, it's you. Sorry.

MARIA *stretches her hands towards* VARVARA.

MARIA. Varya – come here.

VARVARA. What's happened? Has he offended you?

MARIA. No . . . that is, yes . . . I don't know. Did he offend me? I don't understand anything at all.

VARVARA. Sit down. Now – tell me what happened.

MARIA. He told me – (*She laughs, looking at* VARVARA, *bewildered*.) He told me that he – loves me! Me, with my grey hair and my false teeth – my three false teeth! My dear, I'm an old woman, surely he can see that. I've got a daughter of eighteen! Oh, it's impossible, it's absurd!

VARVARA (*agitated*). Oh my dear, my darling, you needn't be upset, you can tell me, you're such a . . .

MARIA. Such a nothing. Like all the rest of us, just an
unhappy female! Help me, Varya. He must be rebuffed,
but I can't do it . . . I shall have to go away.

VARVARA. I see. You feel sorry for him, but you don't like him
. . . Poor Vlass!

MARIA. Oh, I keep misleading you! It's not him I feel sorry for
– it's myself!

VARVARA (quickly). No! Why?

> SONYA comes out of the woods and stands for a few moments
> behind the hay-rick. She has flowers in her hands, which she is
> on the point of scattering over her mother and VARVARA. She
> hears her mother's words, makes a movement towards her, and
> then turns round and goes silently away.

MARIA. I love him. Does that seem ridiculous to you? Well, all
right, but . . . I do love him. Grey hairs, yes . . . but I want
to live, still, I'm still hungry for life, that's the trouble. I've
never really lived. My marriage was three years of torture.
I've never loved, never been loved. And now, I'm ashamed
to admit it, but . . . I long so much for some tenderness,
some strong and loving tenderness! Oh, I know, it's too late,
it's too late! Darling Varya, please help me! Persuade him
that he's made a mistake, that what he feels isn't really love
. . . I've been unhappy once, I suffered a lot . . . I don't
want any more.

VARVARA. But, darling, I don't understand what you're
afraid of! If you love him, and he loves you . . . well, why
not? You're afraid of suffering in the future, but after all,
that could be a long long way ahead!

MARIA. You really think it's possible? What about my
daughter, my Sonya? And my age, my wretched age? These
grey hairs . . .? He's so terribly young! A year, perhaps –
and then he'd leave me. No. No, I don't want that
humiliation.

VARVARA. Why weigh things up, why calculate everything?
We're so afraid just to live. It's ridiculous, the way we all
pity ourselves! Oh, I don't know what I'm saying, perhaps

it's wrong of me, perhaps I shouldn't be talking like this, but I . . . Oh, I don't understand, I feel like a stupid great bluebottle beating and beating against a window pane, longing to get out, to be free . . . I can feel your pain, and I would so like you to have even just a little happiness . . . And I'm sorry for my poor brother! You could do him so much good . . . he never had a mother, and he's suffered so much misery and humiliation . . .

MARIA (*bowing her head*). A mother . . . yes. Only a mother. I understand. Thank you.

VARVARA (*hurriedly*). No, no, you're misunderstanding me, I wasn't saying . . .

RYUMIN *comes out of the woods from the right, sees the women, stops, and coughs. They don't hear him. He comes closer.*

MARIA. You didn't mean to, no, but in fact without meaning to you spoke the simple, sober truth . . . I must be a mother to him. Yes. A mother and a friend. Darling Varya, I want to cry, I'll go . . . somewhere else . . . Oh, look, there's Ryumin over there . . . My face must be a sight . . . the old woman's gone off her rocker . . .

Quietly, wearily, she goes off into the woods.

VARVARA. Wait, I'll come with you.

RYUMIN (*quickly*). Varvara Mikhailovna, please, stay for a moment, I won't keep you long!

VARVARA. I'll catch you up, Maria Lvovna. Go to the lodge. Well, Pavel Sergeyich, what did you want to say?

RYUMIN (*glancing round*). I'll tell you . . . in just a minute.

He bows his head and is silent.

VARVARA. Why did you look round so mysteriously? What is it?

At the back of the stage SUSLOV *walks past from right to left, humming.* BASSOV *can be heard shouting.*

BASSOV (*off*). Hey, Vlass, where do you think you're off to?

You were going to recite some verses for us!

RYUMIN. Now . . . Now I can . . . I can begin. You've known me a long time, Varvara Mikhailovna . . .

VARVARA. Four years. But what on earth's the matter with you?

RYUMIN. I'm sorry, I'm . . . I'm not quite myself, I'm afraid. I can't seem to . . . bring it out . . . I want . . . I want you to . . .

VARVARA. I don't understand. What have I got to do?

RYUMIN. Guess . . . try to guess.

VARVARA. Guess what? Can't you talk more directly?

RYUMIN. About what I've been wanting to tell you for – Oh, such a long time! Now . . . surely you've understood now?

Pause. Frowning, VARVARA *looks severely at* RYUMIN *and moves slowly off to one side.*

VARVARA (*involuntarily*). What a strange day!

RYUMIN (*in a low voice*). I feel that I've loved you all my life. Before I met you, before I even saw you – I loved you! You were the woman I used to dream of . . . that wonderful image one creates in youth . . . and searches for, sometimes for a lifetime, sometimes in vain . . . But my search wasn't in vain. I met my dream . . .

VARVARA (*calmly*). This is not something that can be talked about, Pavel Sergeyich. I do not love you. No.

RYUMIN. But . . . perhaps . . . allow me to say . . .

VARVARA. What? And why?

RYUMIN. Well . . . but what am I to do? (*He laughs quietly.*) So it's over. Done. And all so simple! I've been steeling myself to tell you this for so long. I looked forward to the moment when I would tell you that I love you with both joy and terror . . . And now . . . I've said it.

VARVARA. But, Pavel Sergeyich . . . what can I do?'

RYUMIN. Oh, I understand, of course, yes . . . yes . . . But you must see that I'd placed all my hopes on you – on your response – and now those hopes are dead – my life is dead too.

VARVARA. You must stop talking of this . . . It's very painful for me. Surely none of it is my fault?

RYUMIN. It's much more painful for me! I'm crushed by the burden of unfulfilled promise . . . When I was young I made solemn vows to myself and to others, I vowed that I'd dedicate my whole life to fighting for everything that seemed to me then to be honest and right. And here I am now with my best years already behind me – and I've done nothing, nothing at all! At first I was always just gathering myself, waiting for the right moment, measuring up to things . . . But without quite noticing it . . . You see how sincere I'm being? Please don't take that away from me – the joy of being sincere! I'm ashamed of what I'm saying, but along with the shame there's the sharp sweetness of confession.

VARVARA. But . . . what can I do for you?

RYUMIN. It's not your love I'm asking for – it's your pity. Life, with all its insistent demands, frightens me . . . I try to skirt round them, and hide myself behind a screen of abstract theories – you understand that, I know you do. When I met you, this beautiful vivid hope flowered in my heart . . . that you'd help me to fulfil my vow, you'd give me the strength and the desire to work for a better life!

VARVARA (*emphatically, with sadness and annoyance*). But I can't – you must understand that! I can't! I'm a pauper myself, I'm as bewildered by life as you are! I keep on looking for some sort of meaning in it all, but I can't find any. It's not really life at all, is it, the way we live? Surely we can't go on living like this? Oh, it's revolting, sickening, shameful! Everyone's afraid of something, people clutch at each other, groaning and shouting, crying for help . . .

RYUMIN. Yes. I am, too. At the moment I'm weak and irresolute, but if you wanted . . .

VARVARA (*forcefully*). No, that's not true. I don't believe that! that! That's just another way of complaining! Supposing I am a strong person – I can't transfer my heart into your chest, can I? I don't believe that any outside power can regenerate a person – either it's in him or it's not! But I'm not going to talk any more, I can feel myself growing hostile . . .

RYUMIN. Towards me? Why?

VARVARA. Oh, no . . . not specially towards you . . . towards everyone! We live like aliens on the earth, strangers . . . We don't know how to make ourselves necessary, useful . . . and it seems to me that soon, perhaps even tomorrow, some quite different kind of people, strong, bold people, will come and sweep us off the earth like so much litter. Yes, I'm growing hostile to all our lies and deceptions . . .

RYUMIN. But I want to be deceived, I want my illusions! Now that you've shown me the truth . . . I've nothing more to live for!

VARVARA (*almost with revulsion*). Don't bare your soul in front of me. I feel sorry for a pauper if he's been robbed of his money – but if he's run through it himself, or if he was born a pauper, I can't feel sorry for him.

RYUMIN (*insulted*). That's cruel. After all you're sick yourself, you're wounded . . .

VARVARA (*strongly, almost proudly*). A wounded person is not sick – it's just that his body is torn. Those who are poisoned are sick.

RYUMIN. Show a little mercy, can't you? I am human, you know.

VARVARA. And I? Surely I'm human too? Or am I just some object you need to make your life easier? Is that it? And isn't that cruel? Oh yes, I understand you! But you aren't the only one who made solemn vows and promises in their youth – there must be thousands of you, who've betrayed your vows.

RYUMIN (*beside himself*). Goodbye . . . I understand, now, yes, I came to you too late, yes, of course . . . but you know, that Shalimov, too . . . yes, you look at him, take a good look . . . hasn't he . . .

VARVARA (*coldly*). Shalimov? You've no right to –

RYUMIN. Goodbye! I can't – no . . . goodbye.

> RYUMIN *walks off quickly into the woods, left.* VARVARA *makes a movement as if to follow him, but immediately shakes her head and sits down on a tree stump. At the back of the stage, near the carpet with the food on it,* SUSLOV *appears,*

and helps himself to some wine. VARVARA *stands up and walks off into the woods to the left.* RYUMIN *walks in quickly from the right, looks round with a gesture of annoyance, and sits down on the hay.* SUSLOV, *slightly drunk, goes up to* RYUMIN, *whistling.*

SUSLOV (*thickly*). You hear it?

RYUMIN. What?

SUSLOV (*sitting down*). The argument.

RYUMIN. No. What about?

SUSLOV (*lighting a cigarette*). Vlass, with that writer, and Zamislov.

RYUMIN. No.

SUSLOV. Pity.

RYUMIN. Don't set the hay alight!

SUSLOV. Ah, to hell with the hay. Yes, quite an argument they had. But it's all humbug, the lot of it. I know. I did my bit of philosophising myself, once. I've used all the fashionable words in my time – conversation, intelligentsia, democracy and all the rest – I know just what they're worth. Dead ideas. Lies, every one of 'em. Man is first and foremost a zoological species – that's the truth and you know it. However much humbug you talk you can't escape the fact that what you basically want is to eat, drink . . . and have a woman. That's your dialectical truth for you. Ye-es . . . I can understand Shalimov wanting to arguefy, he's a literary man, playing with words in his trade . . . And it's all right for Vlass, he's young and stupid . . . But when Zamıslov starts spouting – that swindler, that bloodsucker – I want to ram my fist down his throat! Have you heard? He's got Bassov mixed up in some dirty business – they stand to pocket a sweet fifty thousand on it, Bassov and that dirty swindler, but their names will never be clean again after this! And that proud Varvara, who can't make up her mind who to choose as a lover . . .

RYUMIN. You're talking filth.

RYUMIN *walks quickly away.*

SUSLOV. Spineless jellyfish!

PUSTOBAIKA *appears from the right, takes his pipe from his mouth and stares at* SUSLOV.

SUSLOV. What are you gaping at? Never seen a human being before? Bugger off!

PUSTOBAIKA. At's what I'll do.

He goes off slowly. SUSLOV *lounges back on the hay, sleepy.*

SUSLOV. 'God hath made Man upright . . .' (*He coughs.*) All scoundrels under the skin. 'The love of money is the root of all evil . . .' Rubbish. Money's nothing . . . When it's there . . . (*He dozes.*) Being afraid of what people think of you, though . . . that's something . . . if you're sober . . . but you're all . . . I tell you . . . you're all scoundrels under the skin . . .

SUSLOV *falls asleep.* DUDAKOV *and* OLGA *come in quietly, walking arm in arm. She is pressed against his shoulder, gazing into his face.*

DUDAKOV. And . . . of course . . . both of us were in the wrong, really . . . fussing and floundering about . . . somehow we lost our respect for each other . . . Don't know why you should respect me anyway. After all, what am I?

OLGA. My darling Kirill, you're the father of my children . . . And I do respect you. I love you.

DUDAKOV. I get tired and just let go . . . can't control myself . . . And you take everything so much to heart . . . and so we create hell for ourselves . . .

OLGA. You're all I have in the whole world – you and the children. I've nothing else at all . . .

DUDAKOV. Do you remember, Olga, how we once . . . well, we certainly didn't dream of a life like this, did we?

YULIA *and* ZAMISLOV *appear from behind the trees, left.*

No, not like this.

OLGA. But there's nothing we can do, is there? What could we do? There's the children – we have to think of them.

DUDAKOV. Yes, the children. I know. But sometimes I can't help thinking . . .

OLGA. My poor darling . . . whatever are we to do?

They go off into the woods. YULIA *is laughing as she comes forward.*

YULIA. What a solemn and touching little scene! And a lesson for me!

ZAMISLOV. That's the overture to the fifth little Dudakov – or is it six already? Well, Yulia darling . . . so I can expect you?

YULIA (*teasing*). I'm not so sure about that now . . . They were so sweet! Perhaps I should return to the path of virtue too. Do you think I should, stupid?

ZAMISLOV. Afterwards, Yulia.

YULIA. Yes, afterwards. I resolve to stay on the path of vice and let my summer-house affair live out its natural life. What were you shouting about with Vlass and that writer?

ZAMISLOV. That Vlass – he's like some sort of lunatic today. The conversation turned to matters of faith . . .

YULIA. Oh yes – and what do you believe in?

ZAMISLOV. Me? Only in myself, Yulia – only in my right to live as I please!

YULIA. And I, as you know, don't believe in anything.

ZAMISLOV. I have a hungry childhood behind me, Yulia . . . a hungry youth too, full of humiliations. Yes, hard times to look back on, my dear, I've seen too much hardship and dirt. I've been through a lot . . . But now I'm the judge, I run my own life now. That's all. Well, I'm away – goodbye, my precious! We ought to be a little more careful, you know – not be seen together quite so much . . .

YULIA (*melodramatically*). Together, apart – what boots it, fair knight? Fearless we are, who love so insanely!

ZAMISLOV. My treasure, I vanish, your bidding is law!

ZAMISLOV *goes off into the woods.* YULIA *gazes after him, glances round the glade, sighs deeply and freely. She goes over to the hay-rick, singing softly.*

As a mother soothes her baby,
Soothe my pining anguished soul . . .

She sees her husband; stops, shudders and stands motionless for a few moments looking at him; is about to walk away but then turns and sits down with a smile beside him; tickles his face with a stalk of grass. He moans.

YULIA. Very musical.

SUSLOV. Wha – ? What the hell? Oh, it's you.

YULIA. You stink of wine. A whole haystack can't drown it. You're going to ruin yourself with all this expensive wine, my friend.

SUSLOV (*stretching his arms towards her*). You . . . so close! I've forgotten, Yulia . . . I can't remember when we last . . .

YULIA. And there's no point in trying to, my friend. Listen – do you want to give me pleasure?

SUSLOV. How? Tell me! I'm ready, Yulia, I promise you, I'm ready to do anything for you . . .

YULIA. Just as a loving husband should be.

SUSLOV (*kissing her hands*). Tell me, then – tell me what you want?

YULIA *takes a small revolver out of her pocket.*

YULIA. Let's shoot ourselves. First you, then me.

SUSLOV. Yulia! That's a foul joke! Throw that beastly thing away! Go on, please – throw it away.

YULIA. No, wait – take your hand off! You don't like my little proposition, then? But after all, you said you were going to shoot me, didn't you? I'd shoot myself first, only I'm afraid you might cheat and stay alive. I don't want to be cheated again, and I don't want to be separated from you . . . we're going to be together for a very, very long time. Does that please you?

SUSLOV (*crushed*). Listen, Yulia, you can't do that . . . it's forbidden!

YULIA. Oh, but I can! You'll see that I can! Well – do you want me to shoot you myself?

SUSLOV *shields himself from her with his hand.*

SUSLOV. Don't look at me like that! God knows what all this is about . . . I'll . . . I'll go away, I can't . . .

YULIA (*cheerfully*). Go on, then. I'll shoot you in the back. Oh dear, I can't just now – Maria Lvovna's pacing about over there . . . Now, there's a nice woman, why don't you fall in love with her, Pyotr? She's got beautiful hair!

SUSLOV (*softly*). You're driving me out of my mind! Why? Why do you hate me?

YULIA (*carelessly*). I don't. You're not worth hating.

SUSLOV (*in a low voice, breathing heavily*). Why do you torture me? Why? Tell me?

> MARIA LVOVNA *enters thoughtfully, head bowed low.* SUSLOV *stands opposite his wife, staring at the revolver in her hand.*

YULIA. Maria Lvovna! Come over here! (*To* SUSLOV.) You've turned me into a vile woman, Pyotr. Now get away from me, go on, go! (*To* MARIA.) Are we going home soon?

MARIA. I don't honestly know. Everyone's scattered all over the place . . . Have you seen Varvara Mikhailovna?

YULIA. She's probably with that writer. (*To* SUSLOV.) You wanted to go to the river, didn't you? Well, go then. We can manage quite well without you.

> SUSLOV *goes off silently.*

MARIA (*absently*). You're very hard on him.

YULIA. It's good for him. I'm told some philosopher's advice to men was: when you go near a woman, take your whip with you . . .

MARIA. That was Nietzche.

YULIA. Really? He was insane, wasn't he? Well, I don't know any philosophers, sane or insane, but if I were one myself, my advice to women would be: if you go near a man, take a good heavy club with you.

> *From the left, at the edge of the glade, appear* OLGA *and* KALERIA. *They sit down by the carpet.*

I've also heard about a tribe of savages who have a really splendid custom. Before plucking the flowers of pleasure, the man beats the woman over the head with a club. In our

more civilised society, we don't get beaten until after the
wedding night. Were you beaten over the head with a club?

MARIA. Certainly.

YULIA (*smiling*). The savages are more honest, aren't they?
Why are you looking so gloomy.

MARIA. Don't ask. Is your life very unhappy?

Enter DVOETOCHIE *from the right, hatless, with a fishing
rod in his hand.*

YULIA (*laughing*). Has anyone ever heard me complain? I'm
always cheerful, aren't I? Ah, here comes uncle – do you
like him? I do, very much.

MARIA. Yes, he's very pleasant.

DVOETOCHIE (*coming up*). Lost me hat . . . floated off down
the river, it did. Some youngsters went off after it but only
succeeded in sinking it! Has anyone got a scarf I could tie
over my head? – keep the mosquitos out of my hair.

YULIA (*standing*). Wait . . . I'll fetch something.

DVOETOCHIE. Young Vlass was making us all laugh just
now. Nice little fellow he is.

MARIA. Is he . . . cheerful?

DVOETOCHIE. Wonderfully cheerful! Sparkling with fun!
Kept on reciting his verses . . . some young lady asked him
to write in her album, so he spoke as he wrote: 'Your gaze
was aimed at my eyes,' he says, 'But struck to my heart's
core,' he says, 'Now the weeks waft by on my sighs,' he
says, 'And, madam, I sleep no more.' Well, you know . . .
Oh, and then . . .

MARIA (*hurriedly*). Don't go on, Semyon Semyonich. I know
that poem . . . Tell me, will you be staying here for long?

DVOETOCHIE. Well now, I'd thought about settling down
with my nephew for the rest of my days . . . but he doesn't
seem too anxious to encourage the idea. I've got nowhere
else to park myself, though . . . no family, apart from him.
Got lots of money, but nothing else!

MARIA (*absently, not looking at him*). Are you really rich, then?

DVOETOCHIE. Got about a million, if you must know. (*He
chortles.*) Yes, about a million. When I die it'll go to Pyotr –

but that doesn't seem to interest him – in fact he's not a bit
loving with me, you know, not a bit. All in all he's a bit of a
nothing, there's nothing he wants, nothing he needs . . . I
don't understand him. Suppose he knows he'll get the
money anyway, so why should he bother. (*He chortles
again.*)

MARIA (*with great interest*). Oh, you poor thing! Why don't you
use your money for some sort of social work? Wouldn't there
be more point in that?

DVOETOCHIE. H'm, yes. Maybe. There was a certain
monsewer who advised the same thing. But I don't like him.
Makes himself out a liberal, you know, but I can see he's
just another red-headed swindler. No, but speaking quite
frankly, I'm not entirely happy about leaving it all to Pyotr.
What does he need it for, after all? He's far too full of
himself already.

MARIA *laughs.* DVOETOCHIE *looks at her attentively.*

What are you laughing at? Think I'm stupid, do you? Well,
I'm not. It's just – well, I'm not used to living alone. Ah, me!
(*He sighs stagily.*) You whine and you sigh and you pine till
you die . . . You start thinking too much, you end up being
sorry for everybody. But, you know . . . you're all right, you
are! (*He laughs.*)

MARIA. Thank you!

DVOETOCHIE. Not at all. In fact, thank *you*! You just called
me 'poor' (*Chortles.*) – never heard that one before! They all
say I'm rich (*Chortles.*) . . . thought I was rich myself! Turns
out (*Chortles.*) . . . I'm poor!

YULIA *comes up with a scarf in her hands.*

YULIA. Are you declaring your love, Uncle?

DVOETOCHIE. Ah, devil take it! I'm not in the running, am I?
All I can ask for these days is a bit of respect. Now then, tie
it nice and prettily . . . thank you. Think I'll go and have a
bite for the road.

YULIA. There! It suits you very nicely.

DVOETOCHIE. Don't tease. My face is a masculine face.

Come and have a snack with me . . . Listen, I've been
wanting to ask you ever since I arrived – you don't love your
husband, do you?

YULIA. Do you think it would be possible to love him?

DVOETOCHIE. What did you go and marry him for, then?

YULIA. He made himself out to be interesting.

DVOETOCHIE (*laughing loudly*). Oh, bless your silly little
heart!

> *The three of them go to the back of the stage, and their quiet
> talk and laughter continues. From the left appear* BASSOV,
> *drunk,* SHALIMOV, DUDAKOV *and* VLASS. VLASS *goes to
> the back of the stage while the other three go over to the hay-
> rick.* ZAMISLOV *shouts from the woods:*

ZAMISLOV (*off*). Hey, everybody! Time to go home!

BASSOV. Lovely spot, this, isn't it, Yakov? Yes. Splendid little
excursion, eh?

SHALIMOV. All you've done is brood over a bottle all day –
just sitting and drinking and getting sodden.

> SONYA, *now at the carpet, is re-tying the scarf round*
> DVOETOCHIE's *head. Laughter.* ZAMISLOV *comes out of
> the woods near the carpet, picks up a bottle of wine and some
> glasses, and goes over to* BASSOV, *followed by*
> DVOETOCHIE, *who is waving his arms about, trying to
> escape from* SONYA. BASSOV *sits down on the hay-rick.*

BASSOV. Yes, and I'm going to do some more of the same.
One can only admire nature . . . from a sitting position.
Yes. Nature . . . forests, trees . . . hay . . . I love nature!
(*In a sad voice.*) And I love people! I love my poor, vast,
ridiculous country . . . my Russia! I love everybody and
every thing! My soul . . . my soul is as tender as a peach!
Yakov, that's good, you can use that, it's a good simile: a
soul as tender as a peach.

SHALIMOV. Very well, thank you. I shall use it.

SONYA. Semyon Semyonich, please . . .

DVOETOCHIE. No, that's enough, you've teased the old man
quite enough! I shall take offence! (*He chortles.*)

BASSOV. Ah, wine! Lovely! Here, give me some. Isn't this fun, my friends! Ah, what a splendid thing life is . . . for anyone who's prepared to look at it in a simple, trusting way, that is. Yes. One's attitude to life must be simple and trusting, my friends! Look it in the face with trusting, childlike eyes . . . and everything will be absolutely splendid!

DVOETOCHIE *stands by the tree trunk, roaring with laughter at* BASSOV's *drunken chatter.*

Friends! Let us look with . . . with our clear, childlike eyes, deep into each others' hearts! That's all we have to do! Nothing more! And there's uncle, laughing. Uncle caught a merry young perch . . . and I took his merry young perch and gave it back its freedom, released it into its . . . native element. Yes. Because I am a pantheist. It's a fact. Pantheist. And I love perches. And uncle's hat got drowned. So there.

SHALIMOV. Sergei, you're just chattering.

BASSOV. Judge not, that ye be not judged. And I don't chatter any worse than you. You are a man of many fine words, and I am a man of many fine words . . . There, I can hear Maria Lvovna talking . . . Excellent woman. Yes. Worthy of the deepest respect.

SHALIMOV. I don't like that machine-gun. Generally speaking I'm no admirer of women worthy of respect.

BASSOV (*joyfully*). Absolutely right! Women unworthy of respect are much better than worthy ones! Much better! It's a fact!

DVOETOCHIE. How can you say that when you're married to . . . well, to a queen . . .

BASSOV. My wife? Varya? Ah – now there's a purist! A puritan! Yes, she's an amazing woman, a saint. But living with her is a dull business. She's always reading, or quoting from the epistle of some apostle. Let's drink to her health.

SHALIMOV. An unexpected conclusion. But that Maria Lvovna, now . . .

BASSOV (*interrupting*). You know what? She's having an affair with my clerk. It's a fact. I saw him declaring his love to her!

DVOETOCHIE. H'm . . . Best not to talk about that, I'd have thought.

He walks away.

BASSOV. Oh yes, of course. It's a secret!

KALERIA (*coming up*). Sergei, have you seen Varya?

BASSOV. Aha, my sister, my nice little poetess! Yakov, has she recited any of her poems to you? Oh, you should hear them! Very nice, they are, all very lofty . . . clouds . . . mountains . . . stars . . .

KALERIA. You've been drinking, haven't you?

BASSOV. Only one glass.

ZAMISLOV. From *this* bottle.

SHALIMOV. I'd be very interested to see your poetic experiments, Kaleria Vassilevna.

KALERIA. Be careful. I might take you at your word and bring you four very fat notebooks!

SHALIMOV. I'm not frightened that easily.

KALERIA. Well, we shall see.

YULIA (*in the woods, singing*). Time to go home, time to go home . . .

KALERIA. Are we going home now?

SONYA. Yes. Everyone's tired.

> KALERIA *crosses to the right to join* SONYA. ZAMISLOV *goes in the direction of* YULIA's *voice.* BASSOV *winks at his back, and, bending towards* SHALIMOV, *whispers something to him.* SHALIMOV *listens and laughs.*

KALERIA. Whenever I leave the house on some excursion I always take with me a sort of vague hope . . . and always come back without it. I suppose that doesn't happen to you?

SONYA. No, it doesn't.

KALERIA. It will.

SONYA (*laughing*). For some reason you seem to get pleasure out of saying sad things.

KALERIA. You think so? No. But I'd like to bring a pensive shadow in your clear eyes . . . I often see you in company with coarse, dirty people, and I'm amazed that you're not afraid. Don't you find them repulsive?

SONYA. It's only surface dirt – it comes off with soap.

They go to the back of the stage and their conversation becomes inaudible.

SHALIMOV. You've got a foul tongue, Sergei. You watch out – you're a husband yourself . . .

BASSOV. Me?

SHALIMOV. Nature's beautiful, but what's the point of mosquitoes? I dropped my rug here somewhere . . .

He goes off to the right. BASSOV *stretches, and hums a song. At the back of the stage* SASHA, SONYA *and* PUSTOBAIKA *are collecting the picnic things. Left, beside the hay-rick,* VARVARA *appears, carrying flowers.*

VLASS (*in the woods*). Who's going in the boat?

BASSOV. Varya! Been for a walk? I'm all alone here . . . everyone's gone off somewhere . . .

VARVARA. You've had a lot to drink again, Sergei.

BASSOV. Not a lot, really.

VARVARA. You shouldn't drink brandy, you'll start complaining about your heart.

BASSOV. I was drinking port, mainly . . . Varya, you mustn't judge me! You're always so strict and severe with me, and I . . . I'm really such a gentle person . . . I love everything, my love's as tender as a child's . . . Sit down with me, my dear, and let's have a heart-to-heart talk at last . . . We really must have a talk . . .

VARVARA. Oh, do stop, Sergei! Everyone's going to go home now. Stand up, come on. And go on down to the boat. Go on, Sergei – go!

BASSOV. Oh, all right . . . I'm going! Where do I go? Over there? Right, I'm going . . .

He walks off, plonking his feet down too heavily. VARVARA *gazes after him, her face severe. Glancing to the right she sees* SHALIMOV *coming towards her. He is smiling affectionately.*

SHALIMOV. What a long, sad face! Are you tired?

VARVARA. A little.

SHALIMOV. So am I. Very. Tired of looking at these people. And I don't like seeing you among them . . . I beg your pardon.

VARVARA. Whatever for?

SHALIMOV. You might have disliked what I was saying.

VARVARA. I'd have told you if I did.

SHALIMOV. I watch you . . . walking silently through that noisy crowd . . . your eyes mutely asking some enormous question . . . For me, your silence is more eloquent than words. I too have felt the heavy chill of loneliness . . .

SONYA (*off, shouting*). Mama! Are you going in the boat?

MARIA (*in the woods*). No, I'll walk back.

VARVARA *holds out a flower to* SHALIMOV.

VARVARA. Would you like it?

SHALIMOV (*bowing, with a smile*). Thank you. I keep a jealous guard over flowers given to me with such simple friendliness.

VLASS (*in the woods, right*). Hey, where's the second pair of oars?

SHALIMOV. It will lie safe in the pages of some book, your little flower. One day I'll pick up the book, see the flower – and think of you. Is that silly? Sentimental?

VARVARA (*softly, dropping her head*). Go on.

SHALIMOV (*looking into her face with curiosity*). It must be miserable for you, being among people who are so tragically incapable of living properly . . .

VARVARA. Teach them how to live better!

SHALIMOV. I don't have the self-confidence of a teacher. I am a stranger on the earth, a solitary observer of human life. I don't know how to make loud speeches; anyway nothing I could say would waken any courage in these people . . . What are you thinking?

VARVARA. Me? There are some thoughts which . . . make people seem repulsive. They have to be killed in embryo.

SHALIMOV. Your mind will become a graveyard if you do that. No, you mustn't be afraid of standing off from people.

Believe me, the air is so much purer and clearer, everything is purer and more definite, when one stands aside from them.

VARVARA. I understand what you mean . . . and I feel as sad as if someone very dear to me had fallen incurably ill . . .

To the right, noisy sounds of departure.

SHALIMOV (*not listening to* VARVARA's *words*). If you only knew how sincerely I mean that . . . You may not believe this, but I'll tell you anyway – being with you makes me want to be sincere, to be wiser and better . . .

VARVARA. Thank you.

SHALIMOV (*kissing her hand, excited*). I feel when I'm with you that I'm standing on the threshold of some unknown happiness, a happiness as deep as the ocean . . . that you possess a magic power which could saturate one to the core . . . as a magnet's power invades a piece of iron . . . And a mad, rash idea has got hold of me . . . I feel that if you were to . . .

He breaks off, glances round. VARVARA *watches him closely.*

VARVARA. If I were to . . . what?

SHALIMOV. Varvara Mikhailovna . . . you . . . you won't laugh at me? Do you want me to say it?

VARVARA. No. I've understood. You're not a very subtle seducer.

SHALIMOV (*disconcerted*). No! You haven't understood! You . . .

VARVARA (*simply, sadly, quietly*). If you only knew how I loved you when I read your books! How I looked forward to your coming! You seemed to me so full of light and understanding . . . I saw you like that too once when you gave a reading at my school. I was seventeen. And ever since then – until we met – you've shone in my memory like a star, as brilliant as a star.

SHALIMOV (*thickly, bowing his head*). Please. You mustn't. I apologise.

VARVARA. Whenever I was suffocated by . . . smallness . . .

I'd think of you, and feel easier. There was at least a certain
hope . . .

SHALIMOV. Please! Try to understand . . .

VARVARA. And then you appeared . . . and you were just like
everyone else! Just the same! It was so painful . . . What
happened to you? Is it really impossible to retain one's inner
strength?

SHALIMOV (*agitated*). Now wait a minute! Why do you apply
different standards to me? Why use a different yardstick to
those you use for other people? All of you here, you live just
as you please, but because I happen to be a writer I'm
supposed to live the way you want me to!

VARVARA. You mustn't talk like that, you mustn't! Throw
away my flower – I gave it to the former you, the one I had
thought was better than the rest of us. Throw it away.

She goes out quickly.

SHALIMOV (*watching her*). To hell with it! (*He crushes the
flower.*). Poisonous!

SHALIMOV, *wiping his face with his handkerchief, goes off in
the same direction as* VARVARA. DUDAKOV *and* OLGA
walk in quickly from the woods on the left.

ZAMISLOV (*singing in the woods*). 'Oh night, come fast, and
draw'

YULIA (*singing in duet*). 'Thy soft diaphanous veil . . .'

VLASS (*in the woods*). Sit down, for heaven's sake!

DUDAKOV. Here we are. We nearly got left behind.

OLGA. Oh, I'm exhausted! Kirill, my darling – you must never
forget today!

DUDAKOV. Nor you . . . and your promises about being more
restrained . . .

OLGA. My dear, I'm so happy! Life's going to be so much
easier for us now.

They go on past and into the woods. PUSTOBAIKA *appears
from the right, carrying a basket. He is looking for something
on the ground.*

PUSTOBAIKA. Look at it! Muck everywhere. At's all you ever leave, in'it, muck 'n' dross. Makin' a midden of the earth . . .

He goes off, left.

YULIA (*in the woods*). Who's not here yet?
SONYA (*off, calling*). Mama! Yoo-hoo!
BASSOV (*off, mimicking*). Yoo-hoo! Mama!

MARIA *enters from the left; she looks tired and bewildered.*

MARIA. I'm here, Sonya!
SONYA (*running in*). Come on, Mama, we're leaving . . . What's the matter?
MARIA. Nothing. I'm going to walk back. Go and tell them not to wait for me. Go on.

SONYA *runs to the side and shouts, her hands cupped round her mouth.*

SONYA. You can go! Don't wait for us, we're walking back . . . What? Goodbye!
DVOETOCHIE (*off*). You'll be whacked!
SONYA. Goodbye!
MARIA. Why didn't you go with them?
SONYA. Because I stayed with you.
MARIA. Well, come along then.
SONYA. No. Let's sit here for a bit . . . Are you down in the dumps, Mama? Sit down . . . there . . . my darling little Mama! Let me give you a hug . . . there! Well, now – tell me what's wrong?

From the woods come noise and laughter; some shouts can be distinguished.

YULIA (*off*). Don't rock the boat!
ZAMISLOV (*off*). No, don't sing – let them play.
BASSOV (*off*). Music, please!

Guitar and mandolin start tuning up.

VLASS (*off*). Cast off!

MARIA. Sonya, darling, if you knew . . .

SONYA (*simply*). I do know.

MARIA. You don't know anything about it.

SONYA. Darling . . . do you remember, when I was little, how
I used to howl my head off because I couldn't do my sums
. . . and you'd come and cradle my head on your breast,
like this, and rock me, and sing a lullaby . . . (*Sings.*)
Lulla-lulla bye-bye
Lulla-bye my baby . . .
It's you who can't do your sums this time, mama.
If you really love him . . .

DVOETOCHIE, *off, laughs.*

MARIA. Sonya! Hush! How do you know?

Guitar and mandolin music, off.

SONYA. Sh-sh! Lie still now.
(*Sings.*)

Lulla-lulla bye-bye
Lulla-bye my mummy . . .
My clever mummy taught me to think simply and clearly.
He's nice, mama. Don't turn him away. In your hands,
he'd get even nicer. You've already produced one good
human specimen – I'm really not a bad little specimen, am
I, Mama? – and now – why not produce another?

MARIA. My own dear love, that's not possible!

SONYA. Sh-sh! He'll be a brother to me. He's got a lot of
rough edges, you'll smooth him down . . . there's so much
tenderness in you. You'll teach him how to work lovingly, as
you do – as you taught me to do . . . He'll be a good
companion for me, we'll make ourselves a beautiful life,
first just the three of us, and then four . . . because, darling
Mama, I intend to marry my funny old Maxim. I love him,
Mama. He's nice too.

MARIA. Ah, Sonya, my baby, you'll be happy, I know you
will!

SONYA. Be still, and listen! He and I will finish our studies,
and then we'll all live happily together, live brilliantly,

properly! There'll be four of us, Mama, four strong, honest people!

MARIA. My darling, my love, there will be three of us: you, your husband, and me. And he . . . if he wants to be with us . . . only as your brother . . . as my son.

SONYA. And we'll live our lives through decently, we'll do something good with them. Yes, we will! But rest now, Mama. There, don't cry.

(*Sings.*)

Lulla lulla bye-bye.

Lulla-bye, my mummy.

SONYA's *voice trembles with tears. In the distance can be heard the guitar and the mandolin.*

CURTAIN

Act Four

The same setting as the second Act. Evening, the sun is going down.
BASSOV *and* SUSLOV *are playing chess under the pine trees.*
SASHA *is setting the table for supper on the verandah. From the
right come husky sounds from a gramophone; indoors* KALERIA *is
playing some sad piece on the piano.*

BASSOV. What our country needs most is . . . benevolent
people. Your benevolent man is an evolutionist – he isn't in
any hurry . . .

SUSLOV. Allow me . . . to take your bishop.

BASSOV. Oh, take him, by all means . . . No, your benevolent man changes the form of life imperceptibly – by stealth
. . . but his is the only sort of change that endures.

DUDAKOV *comes hurriedly round the corner of the villa.*

DUDAKOV. Er . . . Wife's not with you, is she?

BASSOV. Yours? No. Sit down for a moment, doctor.

DUDAKOV. Can't. In a hurry. Got to get the hospital teaching
report ready for the printers.

BASSOV. You had to do that last year too, didn't you?

DUDAKOV (*going*). Since I'm the only one who gets any work
done . . . Plenty of people, not a worker among them –
why's that, eh?

BASSOV. Cuts a ridiculous figure, that doctor.

SUSLOV. Your move.

BASSOV. H'm, yes indeed. So – I move. As I was saying – one
must try to be benevolent. Misanthropy is a luxury, an
excess. Eleven years ago I first appeared in these parts . . .
and my entire possessions consisted of a briefcase and a
carpet. The briefcase was empty and the carpet was
threadbare. I was pretty threadbare myself . . .

SUSLOV. Bang goes your queen.

BASSOV. Eh? Oh, hell! How did your knight get there without me noticing?

SUSLOV. The man who philosophises, loses.

BASSOV. Fact, fact. Fact – fact . . . as the ducks say.

> *They become engrossed in the game. From the right* VLASS *and* MARIA *come out of the woods; the two men are hidden from them.*

MARIA (*in a low voice*). Believe me, my dear – it will soon pass. It will pass. And then . . . in your secret heart . . . you'll thank me.

VLASS (*loudly*). It's hard for me! It's so painful!

> BASSOV *listens, making signs to* SUSLOV *to be silent.*

MARIA. Go away – go away as soon as you can, my dear! I promise to write to you. Work – carve out a place for yourself in the world . . . Be bold. Never give in to the forces of triviality. You're a fine young man and . . . I love you. Yes. Yes, I love you.

> BASSOV's *eyes widen in amazement.* SUSLOV *looks at him with a smile.*

But that's not what you need – and it's frightening for me . . . I'm not ashamed to admit it, it's frightening! You'll soon get over your infatuation, while I – I'd only love you more deeply the longer it went on. And the end could only be ridiculous, even vulgar – in any case, very sad for me.

VLASS. No. I swear to you . . .

MARIA. Don't. There's no need to swear . . .

VLASS. Even if I did stop loving you . . . I'd always respect you.

MARIA. That's not enough for a woman who still loves . . . Anyway, my dear, there's another side to all this – I'd feel ashamed to abandon myself to my personal life . . . maybe that seems funny to you, unnatural even, but in these times it's somehow shameful just to live for one's personal happiness. Go away, my dear. Go. And remember – if you're ever in any difficulty, if you need a friend – come to me, and I'll welcome you as a son – a dearly loved – son. Goodbye!

VLASS. Give me your hand. I want to fall on my knees to you . . . How I love you! I want to cry, too. Goodbye.

MARIA. Goodbye my dear friend. And remember what I said – fear nothing, give in to nothing, never at all – never!

VLASS. I'm going, my love – my first love – my purest love . . . Thank you.

> MARIA *goes quickly into the woods, right.* VLASS *goes towards the villa, sees* BASSOV *and* SUSLOV, *realises they have overheard, and stops.* BASSOV *stands up and bows, is about to say something.* VLASS *goes over to him.*

Quiet. Not a word. Don't you *dare* . . . not a single word!

> VLASS *goes into the house.*

BASSOV (*embarrassed*). F-ferocious!

SUSLOV (*laughing*). Scared you, did he?

BASSOV. No, but how about that, then? I knew it was going on, but that . . . all that nobility! Oh, what comedians, eh?

> BASSOV *laughs loudly.* YULIA *and* ZAMISLOV *appear on the road from* SUSLOV'S *villa.* YULIA *goes over to her husband,* ZAMISLOV *into the villa.*

SUSLOV. And of course it was all quite deliberate – just so she could get a firmer grip on the boy . . .

BASSOV. For God's sake, that's really priceless!

SUSLOV (*gloomily*). She's a sly one, that . . . laid a really filthy trick on me. Persuaded my uncle, you know, to give all his money away . . .

YULIA. Pyotr, there's a man come to see you . . .

BASSOV (*interrupting*). No, wait, you must ask what just happened . . .

SUSLOV. Who's come?

YULIA (*to* BASSOV). What do you mean? (*To* SUSLOV.) Some sort of contractor. He says it's urgent – something's gone wrong somewhere . . .

SUSLOV (*going out quickly*). Lot of nonsense, probably . . .

BASSOV. Imagine, my dear – here we are, sitting around, me and your husband, and suddenly there's Maria Lvovna . . . (*He roars with laughter*). . . . and it turns out they're having an affair!

YULIA. Who are? My husband and Maria Lvovna? (*Laughs.*)

BASSOV. No, no – *Vlass!* That little clown and that . . .

YULIA. Oh, is that all? Thanks to you, everyone's known about that for ages.

BASSOV. Yes, of course, but you see, now all the gory details . . .

> *Round the corner of the house come* DVOETOCHIE, *with parcels in his hands, and* RYUMIN.

DVOETOCHIE. Peace to all here! Is Varvara Mikhailovna at home? Look who I've brought with me!

BASSOV. Hello! The voyager returned, eh? How are you, then? Handsomer, sun-tanned, a bit thinner . . . yes. Where've you come from?

RYUMIN. The south. I saw the sea for the first time . . . Good evening, Yulia Filipovna.

YULIA. Yes, you really are more handsome, Pavel Sergeyich. Perhaps I should go to the sea, too.

DVOETOCHIE. Well, I'm going indoors. (*To* YULIA *as he goes.*) I've brought you some chocolates as a farewell gift, my dear.

BASSOV (*quoting*). 'I saw the sea
With greedy eyes
And took its measure
Testing my spirit's strength
Against its strength . . .'

Isn't that it? Go on, my wife will be delighted.

RYUMIN. It's so good there! Only music, I imagine, could begin to express the beauty and the grandeur of the sea. Like the idea of eternity, it makes man small, an insignificant speck of dust.

> RYUMIN *and* YULIA *go indoors.* VARVARA *comes round the corner of the house.*

BASSOV. Might as well pack up the chess. Varya, did you know Pavel Sergeyich has arrived?

VARVARA. Is he in the house?

BASSOV (*going over to her*). Yes – and he seems to have a whole new supply of fine phrases . . . Oh, but Varya, if you only knew . . . listen! Here we were, Suslov and me, playing chess, when suddenly there's Vlass and Maria Lvovna – ha! And you know, they *are* having an affair! (*Laughs.*) You said it wasn't that, didn't you? But it is, that's just what it is! It's a fact!

VARVARA. Stop it, Sergei! I don't want to hear any more of your vulgarities . . .

BASSOV. But, Varya, I haven't even told you yet what . . .

VARVARA. I asked you to leave the relationship between Maria Lvovna and my brother alone, and you've gone and gossiped to everyone . . . can't you understand how rotten that is?

BASSOV. Oh, God, she's off again! Honestly, it's better not to try to talk to you at all!

VARVARA. You'd do better to talk less altogether, and just for once think about what you're doing, Sergei, and take note of what people are saying about you.

BASSOV. About me? Let them say what they like – I'm above listening to gossip. And I'm surprised that you, Varya, as my wife . . .

VARVARA. The honour of being your wife . . . is not as great as you imagine. A very heavy honour, in fact . . .

BASSOV (*indignant*). Varvara! What are you saying? That's no way to talk . . .

DVOETOCHIE *and* VLASS *come out on to the verandah.*

VARVARA. I'm saying what I think . . . and what I feel.

BASSOV. I think I'm entitled to an explanation.

VARVARA. Very well. I'll explain later.

BASSOV, *snorting, goes into the villa.* VLASS *gives him a hostile look and sits down on the lowest of the terrace steps.*

DVOETOCHIE. Varvara Mikhailovna – I've brought you some chocolates.

VARVARA. Oh – thank you!

DVOETOCHIE *also sits on the terrace steps.*

DVOETOCHIE. I've brought chocolates for all the ladies – so that I'll be kindly remembered – I want to bribe them into liking me, you know. Won't you let me have that little picture of you?

VARVARA. Oh, yes – I'll go and get it now.

VARVARA *goes indoors.*

DVOETOCHIE. Well then, Uncle Vlass, we're off, are we?

VLASS. The sooner the better.

DVOETOCHIE. Less than twenty-four hours to go. H'm, yes. Wish we could lure that sister of yours away, too. There's nothing for her here.

VLASS (*grimly*). There's nothing for any of them here.

DVOETOCHIE. Still, I'm delighted you're coming with me. We've got a pretty little town – woods all around it, and a river . . . My house is enormous – ten rooms. Give a cough in one of them and it rumbles round the whole lot. In winter, when the blizzard's howling, you get a very rumbly lot of rooms altogether. H'm, yes.

SONYA *comes in quickly from the right.*

You know – loneliness is good for a man when he's young, but coming up to old age it's better if there's two of you, i'n'it? (*He chortles.*) Aha, there's my little villain! Goodbye, child! I'll be away tomorrow, and the day after tomorrow you'll have forgotten the old fool as if he'd never poked a finger out into the world.

SONYA. I shan't forget you. You've got such a funny name.

DVOETOCHIE. Ah, and that's all, is it? Well, thanks for that, anyway.

SONYA. No, uncle darling, I really shan't forget you – really I won't. You're simple and good, and I like simple people.

KALERIA *comes out on to the verandah.*

But . . . you haven't seen my mama anywhere, have you?

DVOETOCHIE. I haven't had that pleasure.

VLASS. She's not inside. Come on, let's go and look for her, maybe she's in the summer-house, down by the river.

KALERIA. Do you mind if I come too?

SONYA. No, of course, come on!

The three of them go onto the woods. DVOETOCHIE *gazes after them, sighs, hums a song.* VARVARA *comes out with a photograph in her hand, followed by* RYUMIN.

VARVARA. Here you are, here's the photograph. When are you leaving?

DVOETOCHIE. Tomorrow. I like the inscription – thank you. Oh dear, oh dear, I've got into the way of loving you, little lady!

VARVARA. What would anyone want to love me for?

DVOETOCHIE. People don't love *for* something, surely? They just love, that's all. Real love – why, it's like the sun hanging in the sky, no one knows what keeps it up there.

VARVARA. I don't know about that.

DVOETOCHIE. I can see you don't. You should come away with me – your young brother's coming. You'd find something to do . . .

VARVARA. What could I do? There's nothing I know how to do.

DVOETOCHIE. You've never learnt, that's why you don't know. But you could learn – you could! Vlass and I, you know, we're going to build schools – a boys' school, and a girls' school.

RYUMIN (*absently*). If life's to have any meaning at all one must build something – undertake some enormous task that will leave its trace on the centuries . . . One must construct temples . . .

DVOETOCHIE. Well, that's a slice of divine light that's a bit above me. I didn't even think of the schools for myself, a kindly person had to drop the notion into my ear.

RYUMIN. Even the universities offer us nothing but a string of contradictory theories, nothing but abstract theories about the mystery of life . . .

VARVARA (*irritably*). Oh God, how dreary all that sounds! So shop-soiled and tired . . .

RYUMIN *looks at them all and then gives a strange, soft laugh.*

RYUMIN. Yes, I know. They're all dead words – dead as autumn leaves . . . I just go on saying them from habit I suppose. Don't know why, really. Maybe autumn has set in for me . . . Ever since I saw the sea I've been hearing the pensive sound of those green waves incessantly . . . Every word man has ever said drowns in that music as surely as drops of rain in the ocean . . .

VARVARA. You do seem strange – What's the matter with you?

KALERIA *and* VLASS *appear from the woods, right.*

RYUMIN (*laughing*). Nothing – I promise you, nothing.

KALERIA. Standing firmly on your feet means standing knee-deep in dirt.

VLASS. Would you rather hang in mid-air so's to keep your hem and your soul nice and clean? Who or what needs you so clean and so cold?

KALERIA. I need myself.

VLASS. It's all a delusion! Not even you need yourself . . .

KALERIA (*interrupting*). I don't want to talk to you. You're rude.

She goes quickly into the villa.

DVOETOCHIE. Well, Uncle Vlass? You've told the young lady off and now you're content, eh?

VLASS *sits down on the lowest step at his sister's feet.*

VLASS. I'm fed up with her. (*Imitating* KALERIA.) 'Ah, I am dying of weariness . . .' I told her she must live among people, but die by herself.

RYUMIN (*quickly*). That's true! It's cruel, but you're right – yes, that's it!

BASSOV *and* YULIA *come out on to the verandah.*

VARVARA (*as if to herself*). Life is going on somewhere else –
somewhere outside us – it doesn't touch our hearts. We just
think about it.

BASSOV. Varya, I've arranged for Sasha to lay supper out
here.

SUSLOV *comes in quickly from the direction of his villa.*

Semyon Semyonich, we'll have a little farewell party for
you. I've laid on some champagne – it's a splendid excuse.

DVOETOCHIE. Very touched, I'm sure.

SUSLOV. Yulia, come here a moment . . .

YULIA. What is it?

SUSLOV *leads his wife a little way down the track and
whispers something to her. She starts away from him and stops
walking. He takes her by the arm and leads her to the right,
where they talk for a few minutes in low voices, only returning
to the verandah after* BASSOV *has gone off.*

BASSOV. I shall offer you some sausage, my friends – and
what a sausage! A client of mine in the Ukraine sent it to
me, you know, and . . . Where's that assistant of mine,
though? (*In a low voice.*) Assistant husband to Yulia's
husband, too, as it happens . . .

VARVARA (*indignant, softly*). Sergei! That's beastly!

BASSOV (*provocatively*). But everyone knows that, Varya!
Anyway, why be so spikey? (*Calls.*) Sasha!

BASSOV *goes off into the villa.*

YULIA (*delighted*). Uncle, you know what? A wall in the prison
Pyotr built has fallen down – two of the workers were
crushed.

SUSLOV (*with a short laugh*). And she's delighted!

VARVARA (*alarmed*). Oh no! Where?

SUSLOV. Not here. A little market town.

DVOETOCHIE. Congratulations. Oh, you – you baby! Did
you ever even go near the site?

SUSLOV. Of course. It's the contractor – it's that scoundrel's fault!

YULIA. He's lying. He never went there, not once. Never had time.

DVOETOCHIE. Your sort need a good flogging – what kind of men are you? – living without moving a finger . . .

SUSLOV (*with a laugh*). Maybe I should shoot myself? – that'd be moving a finger.

RYUMIN (*shaking his head*). You won't shoot yourself.

SUSLOV. But if I did . . .?

VARVARA. But Pyotr Ivanich . . . what about the men who were crushed? Are they dead?

SUSLOV (*gloomily*). Don't know. I'll go over tomorrow . . .

> *Enter* OLGA.

VLASS (*loudly*). What a stinking business!

SUSLOV (*baring his teeth*). You keep quiet, young man!

OLGA (*coming up*). Good evening . . . You're all sitting about like . . . birds in autumn. I've seen everyone today. Oh, Pavel Sergeyich! When did you get back?

> SUSLOV *again takes his wife aside and says something to her. His face is angry.* YULIA *bows to him, mocking, and goes back on to the verandah.* SUSLOV, *whistling loudly, goes towards his villa.* DVOETOCHIE *looks at* YULIA, *and then follows* SUSLOV.

RYUMIN. Just today.

OLGA. And here you are already? – Well, you are a devoted friend! Oh, it's so close today! It'll be autumn soon, and then we'll all move back into town and there, behind our stone walls, we'll be further away from each other and more like strangers than ever.

VLASS (*grumbling*). Moaning again . . .

> BASSOV *calls from the terrace door.*

BASSOV. Pavel Sergeyich, could you come here a moment?

OLGA (*to* VLASS). But isn't it true?

> RYUMIN *goes up towards* BASSOV, *passing* KALERIA *and*

SHALIMOV *on the way.* VLASS, *without answering* OLGA, *gets up from the step and goes over to the pine trees.*

SHALIMOV (*in bored, lazy tones*). People expect life to be transformed by democracy, but I ask you, what sort of an animal is he himself, this democrat of yours?

KALERIA (*excited*). Oh yes, yes, a thousand times, you're absolutely right, he's just a barbarian, an animal, whose only conscious aspiration is to be well-fed.

SHALIMOV. And to wear squeaky boots.

KALERIA. What does he believe in? What is his credo?

VLASS (*irritated*). And you? What do you believe in? What's *your* credo?

KALERIA (*not answering* VLASS). People who believe in something bring a new inspiration to life – they are the aristocracy of the spirit . . .

VLASS. Who are these aristocrats? Where do you find them?

KALERIA. I don't want to talk to you, Vlass! Let's go over there, Yakov Petrovich . . .

They come down from the verandah, go over to the fir trees and sit down, talking in low voices. KALERIA *is agitated,* SHALIMOV *calm, his movements languid as if he is very tired.*

VARVARA (*going up to* VLASS). You're terribly irritable today, Vlass.

VLASS (*indistinctly*). I'm miserable, Varya.

YULIA. Vlass Mikhailich – come to the river with me.

VLASS. No . . . I'm sorry, but I don't feel like it.

YULIA. Oh, please! There's something I must tell you . . .

VLASS (*reluctantly*). Very well, then, come on. What is it?

As they go towards the back of the stage YULIA *takes his arm and whispers to him.* VARVARA *goes on to the verandah.* OLGA *catches at her arm.*

OLGA. Varya! Are you still angry with me?

VARVARA (*thoughtfully*). Angry? No.

VLASS *exclaims loudly at the back.*

VLASS. Good God – the dirty rat! If he weren't married to my sister, I'd . . .

YULIA. Shsh!

YULIA *draws him off into the woods.*

VARVARA (*alarmed*). Oh heavens, what's happened now?

OLGA. Just Yulia gossiping again, I expect . . . Varya, I can see you are still angry. But you know, a few words thrown off in a moment of irritation . . .

VARVARA. Please don't go on! I don't like things that are patched up – including patched up friendships . . .

OLGA (*standing*). You're full of rancour, aren't you? Can't you forget . . . perhaps, even, forgive?

VARVARA (*coldly, firmly*). We forgive too much, too easily – it's a weakness, it kills our respect for one another . . . I've forgiven a great deal to one person, and now I'm completely meaningless to him . . .

OLGA (*after a pause*). You mean – Sergei Vassilich?

VARVARA *doesn't reply, but stares into space, slowly shaking her head.*

How quickly people change! I remember him as a student – how fine he was then! – poor, but merry and carefree, all his friends thought he was a ball of fire . . . But you've hardly changed at all, you're just as serious and severe as ever . . . When we heard you were going to marry him I remember Kirill saying, Bassov will be all right with a wife like that, he's frivolous and a bit vulgar – but she . . .

VARVARA (*simply*). Why are you saying all this, Olga? To prove that I too am just a nonentity.

OLGA. Oh, Varya, how can you think such a thing? I was just . . . well, just remembering . . .

VARVARA (*in a low voice, very clearly, as if pronouncing sentence on herself*). It's true. I'm a weak, pathetic person – isn't that what you meant? But I know it, Olga, I've known it for a long time.

SASHA (*on the verandah*). Varvara Mikhailovna, I been sent to call you in.

VARVARA *goes indoors in silence.*

OLGA (*following*). Oh, Varya, listen, you've misunderstood again . . .

KALERIA (*in a low voice*). For me, anyone who thinks the truth has been revealed to them is as good as dead.

Pause. SHALIMOV *smokes.*

Tell me – is yours a sad life?

SHALIMOV. At times, yes, very sad.

KALERIA. Often?

SHALIMOV. Life's never exactly a joy. I've seen too much already to be particularly cheerful – and anyway, frankly, these are not very cheerful times.

KALERIA (*softly*). The life of any thinking person is a . . . tragedy.

SHALIMOV. Yes . . . Tell me . . .

KALERIA. What?

SHALIMOV (*standing*). Tell me frankly – do you like my stories?

KALERIA (*animated*). Oh, tremendously. Particularly the recent ones – they're not so realistic, there's less of the coarse flesh in them. They're so full of gentleness, and a warm melancholy which enfolds the soul as the sun is enfolded by soft clouds at the hour of sunset . . . Not many people are capable of appreciating them, but the few who are do admire you passionately.

SHALIMOV (*smiling*). Thank you. You mentioned some recent poems of your own – won't you read them to me?

KALERIA. Very well. But later.

SHALIMOV *nods in silent agreement. Pause.* VLASS *and* YULIA *come out of the woods, right, and walk thoughtfully over to the pine trees.* VLASS *sits down, puts his elbows on the table, and whistles softly.* YULIA *goes indoors.*

Now, if you like.

SHALIMOV. What? Now . . . what?

KALERIA (*smiling sadly*). Have you forgotten already? How soon!

SHALIMOV (*frowning*). Wait, let me see, it's . . .

KALERIA (*standing*). You asked me to read you my poems. Would you like me to read them now?

SHALIMOV (*quickly*). Oh yes, yes – please! It's such a wonderful evening that . . . yes, that would be lovely. But you're wrong, you know – I hadn't forgotten . . . I was just deep in thought, that's all, and didn't quite catch the question.

KALERIA (*going indoors*). Very well – I'll go and get them. Though I'm sure they're not of the slightest interest to you.

SHALIMOV (*watching her*). Believe me, you're quite wrong.

> KALERIA *runs quickly up on to the verandah.* SHALIMOV *shrugs and pulls a face. Glancing round he sees* VLASS, SUSLOV *and* DVOETOCHIE *appear on the track from* SUSLOV's *villa. They are both angry and silent.*

SHALIMOV (*to* VLASS). Day-dreaming?

VLASS (*not rudely*). Whistling.

> Out on to the verandah come: OLGA, *who sits down in a whicker chair beside the balustrade;* RYUMIN, *who stands to one side of her – she says something to him in a low voice;* BASSOV, *who stops by the table – laid for supper – and examines the hors d'oeuvres.* VARVARA *stands leaning against a pillar of the verandah.* ZAMISLOV *is in front of her.*

BASSOV. Are we all here? What about Vlass? And Maria Lvovna?

VLASS. I'm here.

> YULIA *comes out of the villa, humming softly, and sits down on the steps of the verandah.* DVOETOCHIE *stands listening to* ZAMISLOV. SUSLOV *glances at the speaker, then walks over to where* VLASS *and* SHALIMOV *are sitting in silence under the pines.*

ZAMISLOV. Varvara Mikhailovna, all of us are very complicated people.

BASSOV (*leaning over the balustrade*). Aha, you're here, are you, Yakov? Splendid!

ZAMISLOV. It's precisely that psychic complexity of ours that
makes us this country's elite – the intelligentsia – and
you . . .

From the back of the stage, right, come MARIA LVOVNA *and*
SONYA.

VARVARA (*with irritation*). The intelligentsia! – we're not the
intelligentsia, we're something quite different. We're just
the summer folk of this country – people who've just
dropped by from somewhere else. We bustle about looking
for comfortable little nests for ourselves . . . and do nothing
else but talk a ridiculous amount.

BASSOV (*mocking*). You are yourself brilliant proof of that
statement.

KALERIA *comes out with an exercise book in her hand, stops
by the table and listens.*

VARVARA (*with greater irritation*). And our conversations are
full of lies. We hide our spiritual bankruptcy from each
other by dressing ourselves up in fine phrases and the
tattered remnants of secondhand wisdom, we go on about
how tragic life is without ever having experienced it . . . we
just love whining and groaning and complaining . . .

DUDAKOV *comes out on the verandah, and stands so that his
wife cannot see him.*

RYUMIN (*irritably*). Oh, be fair, now! There can be a lot of
beauty in complaint. It's cruel to doubt the sincerity of a
man's grief.

VARVARA. No, let's have an end to complaining, let's have
the courage to keep silent! We keep silent easily enough
when life seems satisfying, don't we? We all gobble up our
little bits of happiness alone and in secret, but as soon as
there's the tiniest little scratch on our hearts, we rush out
into the streets with it and show it to everybody and weep
and groan about our pain to anyone who'll listen! Just as we
poison the air of our towns with the garbage we throw out of

our houses, so we poison other people's lives with the trash
and nastiness that pours out of our souls. I'm sure that
hundreds and thousands of perfectly healthy people must
perish through being bludgeoned and deafened by our
poisonous complainings . . . Who gave us the right to
poison other people with a display of our own personal sores
and ulcers?

Pause.

VLASS (*quietly*). Bravo, Varya!
DVOETOCHIE. Good girl. True enough.

MARIA *strokes* VARVARA's *hand in silence.* VLASS *and*
SONYA *are also beside her.* RYUMIN *shakes his head angrily.*

RYUMIN. Please, may I speak? Just a word – my last word.
KALERIA. You're supposed to have the courage to keep
silent . . .
OLGA (*to* BASSOV). She has suddenly started talking so boldly
and firmly . . .
BASSOV. Yes. Thus spake Balaam's . . .

BASSOV *breaks off, and covers his mouth with his hand,
fearfully.* VARVARA *is too excited to notice what her husband
has said, but most of the others heard and knew what he
meant ('Numbers 22/28-9').* ZAMISLOV *goes quickly down
the terrace steps and over to the pines, where he laughs loudly.*
SHALIMOV *smiles and shakes his head reproachfully.* VLASS
and SONYA *look at* BASSOV *with contempt; the others
pretend to have noticed nothing. After the brief remarks
provoked by* VARVARA's *speech, an awkward silence reigns.*
SUSLOV *coughs, smiling.* VARVARA, *realising something is
amiss, looks around, bewildered.*

VARVARA. I seem to have said something . . . something
wrong? Was I rude? Why is everyone so strange?
VLASS (*loudly*). It wasn't you who was rude.
OLGA (*with an innocent air*). Why, what's the matter?
MARIA (*fast, quiet*). Please, Vlass – don't!

> MARIA *starts to talk in order to cover up* BASSOV'S
> *exhibition. Then she gets carried away, and speaks with
> conviction and enthusiasm.* SHALIMOV, SUSLOV *and*
> ZAMISLOV *ostentatiously do not listen to her.* DUDAKOV
> *nods affirmatively.* BASSOV *looks at her with gratitude, and
> makes signs to the others to listen.*

We really ought to be different, you know – all of us! We're the children of cooks and washerwomen and decent working people – we *should* be different! This country's never before had an educated class with direct blood ties to the people – surely this blood relationship ought to have nourished in us a burning desire to bring some light and meaning into the lives of our own people, who've known nothing but hard work, in dirt and darkness, all their born days? Not out of pity or charity – it's for our own sakes that we ought to be working for a richer life for them – so's to escape from this damnable isolation of ours, and not to have to see all the time that awful abyss between us, up here on the heights, and our own kith and kin down there in the depths, gazing back up at us with hatred because we live on their labours! They sent us on ahead to seek out a road that would lead them to a better life, and we left them behind, went on and lost our way, and created a lonely wilderness for ourselves, and filled it with hustle and bustle and bitter divisiveness . . . And that's our tragedy. But we made it ourselves – we fully deserve every one of our little torments! I agree with you, Varya – we just do not have the right to deafen everyone with our lamentations.

> MARIA *is tired out by her own excitement, and sits down
> beside* VARVARA. *Silence.* DUDAKOV *gazes slowly round at
> everybody.*

DUDAKOV. There you are. That's it. It's all true.

OLGA (*quickly*). Oh, there you are! Come over here . . .

SHALIMOV (*raising his hat*). Have you finished, Maria Lvovna?

MARIA. Yes.

OLGA *leads her husband to the corner of the verandah.*

OLGA. Did you hear? Did you take it in? What a fool Bassov is.

DUDAKOV (*softly*). What's Bassov got to do with it?

General movement on the verandah. VARVARA *looks at everyone. It is still not clear whether* BASSOV's *remark has been smoothed over and forgotten.*

OLGA. Shush! Varvara was saying lots of wicked things, and he called her Balaam's ass.

DUDAKOV. Oh well, he's an ass himself. You know, Olga, when I left home there was . . .

OLGA. Wait! Kaleria's going to recite some of her poetry . . . No, but it's good, what happened, it's a good thing! Varvara's become such an arrogant creature lately.

RYUMIN, *looking crushed, comes down from the verandah and paces up and down.*

SHALIMOV. Listen everyone – Kaleria Vassilevna has kindly agreed to read us her poems . . .

BASSOV. Yes, you read them, my dear, go ahead.

KALERIA (*bashfully*). Well – well, all right, I'll read them if . . . Very well.

SHALIMOV. Here's a chair for you.

KALERIA. I don't need one. Varya, how do you explain this? This sudden interest in my poetry is rather alarming.

VARVARA. I don't know. I imagine someone said something tactless and everyone's busy trying to cover it up.

KALERIA. Well, I shall read anyway. My verses will meet the same fate as your words, Varya – all swallowed by the endless quicksands of our lives . . .

She reads.

From the cold high branches
The autumn wind shakes
Petals of dead flowers
And a fall of snowflakes.

Below, the soiled earth
Toils, wearies and frets.
Above, the snow swirls, and settles
Like clean, soft coverlets.

Black, the pensive birds,
Black, the stark dead trees.
White, the mute snowflakes
On the cold, healing breeze.

Pause. They all look at KALERIA, *as if expecting some more.*

SHALIMOV. Charming!

RYUMIN (*thoughtfully*). 'On the cold, healing breeze.'

VLASS (*animated*). I write poetry, too. I want to recite some
verses as well!

DVOETOCHIE (*laughing*). Hey, how about that!

SHALIMOV. Splendid – a competition!

VARVARA. Vlass – do we really need this?

ZAMISLOV. If it's amusing, of course we need it!

MARIA. My dear, remember what I said – be yourself.

They all look at VLASS, *who is very excited. Everyone
becomes very quiet.*

VLASS. I want to show you all how easy it is to clutter up
people's heads with verses . . . Your attention, please . . .

He recites, clearly, powerfully, challengingly.

The little boremongers are rife!
With mournful gait they prowl our land,
Each seeking not to understand,
But to retreat from human life.

Cheap happiness is what they're after:
Peace, plenty, and a place to hide.
From suffering they draw aside,
Afraid of pain as much as laughter.

The little boremongers delight
In every moan and groan in fashion.

For safety's sake they shrink from passion
And crawl towards perpetual night.

> *When he has finished he stands motionless and looks in turn at*
> SHALIMOV, RYUMIN, SUSLOV. *Pause. Everyone is*
> *embarrassed.* KALERIA *shrugs her shoulders.* SHALIMOV
> *slowly lights a cigarette.* SUSLOV *is agitated.* MARIA *and*
> VARVARA *go over to* VLASS, *evidently afraid of something.*

DUDAKOV (*softly but audibly*). That's very apt. Yes – yes, it's
horribly true.

YULIA. Bravo! I liked that!

DVOETOCHIE. Well, well – letting fly in all directions! Proper
little beauty, you are!

KALERIA. Vicious and coarse! What for?

ZAMISLOV. Not at all amusing. No.

SHALIMOV. Did you like it, Sergei?

BASSOV. Who? Me? Well, of course, the rhyme-scheme, you
know, well, that was a bit weak, but . . . well, as a bit of
comic verse . . .

ZAMISLOV. As comic verse, not at all amusing.

YULIA (*to* SHALIMOV). Oh, you're so good at pretending!

SUSLOV (*testily*). Allow me, as a little boremonger – whatever
that may mean – to answer that . . . that . . . I'm sorry, I
really don't know what category of verse you'd call it. But
it's not you, Vlass Mikhailich, no, I'm not going to answer
you. I might as well address myself straight to the source of
your inspiration. To you, Maria Lvovna.

VLASS. What's that? You watch what you're saying!

MARIA (*proudly*). To me? How odd. But do go on.

SUSLOV. It's not odd at all. I'm quite aware that you are this
poet's muse.

VLASS. Don't be cheap.

YULIA. He can't help it.

SUSLOV. Stop interrupting. I'll answer for everything I'm
going to say, any way you want. Now, Maria Lvovna,
you're what's known as an idealist. It seems you're involved
in some mysterious work somewhere. For all I know it may
be great and historic, that doesn't concern me. And you

seem to think these activities of yours give you the right to look down on other people.

MARIA (*calmly*). That's not true.

SUSLOV. You try to influence everybody, you want to be everybody's teacher. You've turned this boy here into a self-appointed judge . . .

VLASS. What on earth are you drivelling about?

SUSLOV (*viciously*). Wait your turn, young man! I've put up with your insolence long enough. (*To* MARIA.) What I want to tell you, Maria Lvovna, is that if we don't all live exactly as you'd like us to, we've got our reasons for it. All of us here had quite enough suffering and hunger in our youth. It's only natural that now, in our maturity, we should want to eat and drink and enjoy a bit of leisure – if only to compensate for what we had to put up with when we were young . . .

SHALIMOV (*coldly*). May one ask who, precisely, are 'we'?

SUSLOV (*still more heatedly*). We? Why – you and me, of course, and him and him and her – all of us! Yes, all of us here, we're all children of poor people. We all know what it's like to be hungry, to be insecure. We've earned the right to eat well and take things easy. That's the root of our psychology. You may not like it, Maria Lvovna, but it's perfectly natural, you know, and there's nothing you can do to change it. First and foremost comes basic human nature, and all the other nonsense comes a long way behind. So you just leave us in peace! However much you abuse us, or incite other people to abuse us, however often you call us cowards and idlers, not one of us here is going to go dashing off to do Good Works. No – not one!

DUDAKOV. God, how cynical! Hadn't you better stop!

SUSLOV (*angrier than ever*). And as for myself, let me tell you that I'm no longer a child, Maria Lvovna, and I don't need you to teach me anything. I'm a grown man, an ordinary run-of-the-mill Russian man, a straightforward Russian provincial! Yes, an ordinary Russian provincial, madam, and nothing more! That's what I am, it's what I like being, and what I intend to remain. I shall live exactly as I want to

live, and let me tell you that as far as all your ideas and
slogans and sermons and all the other claptrap is concerned
– I spit on the lot of it!

> SUSLOV *thrusts his hat on his head and makes off towards his
> villa. General consternation.* ZAMISLOV, BASSOV *and*
> SHALIMOV *go to one side, talking animatedly in low voices.*
> VARVARA *and* MARIA *form a separate group;* YULIA,
> DVOETOCHIE *and the* DUDAKOVS *another. Everyone is
> upset.* KALERIA, *crushed, stands alone under the pine.*
> RYUMIN *walks quickly up and down.* VLASS *moves away,
> clutching his head.*

VLASS. I'll be damned! What've I done now?

> SONYA *follows him and says something to him.*

MARIA. That was pure hysteria! Only someone who's men-
tally sick can expose himself like that!

RYUMIN (*to* MARIA). You see . . . do you see now how
dangerous the truth can be?

VARVARA. Oh, this is all so painful!

DVOETOCHIE (*to* YULIA). I don't understand any of it – not a
bit of it.

YULIA (*to* MARIA). My dear, tell me – did he hurt you?

MARIA. Hurt me? No. He hurt himself.

DVOETOCHIE. Wonderful to behold, the way you folk carry
on!

DUDAKOV (*to his wife*). Wait . . . (*To* DVOETOCHIE.)
Something cracked! You know – all these things festering in
his heart, and suddenly – crack! It could happen to any of
us . . . that . . . that . . . that . . .

> *Excited he waves his hands about, and stutters too much to be
> able to continue.*

YULIA. Nikolai Petrovich . . .

> ZAMISLOV *goes over to her.*

ZAMISLOV. Did that upset you?

YULIA. Not in the least. But it's awkward for me to stay here.

See me home, will you?

ZAMISLOV. Stupid business. Pity, too. Bassov had prepared a
delicious surprise for supper.

YULIA. We've had enough surprises, thank you.

   They go off.

SHALIMOV (*going up to* KALERIA). Well then, how did you
like that?

KALERIA. Oh, it's so frightful! It's as if all the mire from the
bottom of a bog had risen up and was choking me . . .
choking me!

   BASSOV *goes up to* VLASS *and takes him by the sleeve, in
   silence.*

VLASS. What do you want?

BASSOV (*taking him aside*). Just a word . . .

RYUMIN (*going up to* VARVARA, *beside himself*). Varvara
Mikhailovna, that torrent of bilious middle-class vulgarity
has – has – overwhelmed me . . . knocked me right off my
feet . . . I – I'm leaving . . . Goodbye! I came over to make
my farewells . . . hoped to spend a quiet evening here – my
last evening with you . . . I'm going away – for good!
Goodbye!

VARVARA (*not listening to him*). You know what I think? I
believe that Suslov's more sincere than any of you. Yes –
yes, truly – more sincere! He spoke very coarsely I know,
but he spoke the bitter truth which no one else would dare to
utter!

RYUMIN (*stepping back*). Is that all? Is that your farewell? My
God!

   He goes off into the woods.

BASSOV (*to* VLASS). Well, my boy, you excelled yourself,
didn't you? Now what? You offended my sister, and Yakov,
who . . . he's a writer, respected writer! And of course,
Suslov, yes, and Ryumin, and . . . well, everybody, in fact!
You'll have to apologise.

VLASS. What!? Me apologise – to them?

BASSOV. Oh, come on, it's not so difficult! All you've got to say is, you know, you just wanted to have a bit of fun, jolly things up a bit, and you're afraid you laid it on rather too strong . . . They'll forgive you, they're all used to your silly pranks – after all, everyone knows you're just a clown, really . . .

VLASS (*shouting*). Go to hell! You're the one who's a clown – you're a buffoon!

SONYA. Heavens above, do be quiet!

VARVARA. Vlass, what's wrong now?

MARIA. This madness appears to be epidemic.

DVOETOCHIE. Vlass . . . Look, boy – go away!

BASSOV. No, hold on! I'm the one who's been insulted this time . . .

VARVARA. Sergei, please! Vlass!

BASSOV. No, young man, I am not a buffoon! I . . .

VARVARA. Vlass, you're not to . . .

VLASS. It's only out of respect for my sister that I don't tell you . . .

KALERIA *comes up to them.*

SASHA (*to* VARVARA). Shall I serve supper?

VARVARA. Go away!

SASHA (*to* DVOETOCHIE). It'd be better to serve it, really – if the master saw the food on the table he'd stop being angry.

DVOETOCHIE. Get away, girl. Go on – shoo!

BASSOV. Look here, you . . . (*Suddenly yells at* VLASS *in fury.*) You're just a young puppy!

KALERIA. Sergei, no, you're going too far!

BASSOV. He's a puppy, that's what he is, a puppy! It's a fact!

SHALIMOV (*taking* BASSOV's *arm and leading him towards the villa*). Stop it, now, that's enough . . .

SASHA *follows them in.*

MARIA. Vlass Mikhailich! How could you!

VLASS. Good God, it wasn't my fault, was it?

SASHA (*to* BASSOV's *back*). Sir! Shall I serve supper now?

BASSOV. Oh, go away! I'm nothing and nobody here, in my

own house I'm . . .

He goes indoors.

MARIA (*to* SONYA). Take him up to our house. (*to* VLASS.) Go on, my dear.

VLASS. I'm sorry – will you forgive me? It was my fault, I know it was – Oh, Varya, you too – please forgive me! You poor thing – you must go, get away from this place!

VARVARA (*quietly*). Where? Where should I go to?

DVOETOCHIE. Why not come with me? Now, really, there's a fine idea!

Nobody hears him. Sighing heavily he goes off quietly towards SUSLOV's *villa.*

MARIA. Varya, you must come over to us, too.

VARVARA. I will. Vlass . . . later on . . . I'll join you.

VARVARA goes into the villa. MARIA follows her. VLASS and SONYA go off into the woods. KALERIA, shattered, staggers towards the villa.

OLGA. What a disgraceful scene! And all of a sudden like that . . . Kirill, did you understand any of it?

DUDAKOV. Me? Understand? Yes, of course I understood. It was only a matter of time before we all became repulsive to one another – and now the time's come. Vlass hit the nail squarely on the head, Olga – right on the head! But you must go home, you know . . .

OLGA. I will soon . . . but it's all so exciting! And something else might happen any moment . . .

DUDAKOV. That's not a good attitude, Olga! Anyway, you must go home, the children are all shouting and crying, and Volka's been rude to Nanny so she's angry, and he's accusing her of pulling him by the ear . . . total chaos, in fact. I've been telling you for ages you ought to go home.

OLGA. That's not true! You didn't tell me!

DUDAKOV. I most certainly did! We were standing over there, and you were going on about Bassov and I told you.

OLGA. Kirill, you never said a single word!

DUDAKOV. I don't know why you're arguing. I distinctly remember – 'Go home' I said.

OLGA. You couldn't have said that. Only children and servants are told to go home.

DUDAKOV. Oh Olga, what a quarrelsome cow you are!

OLGA. Kirill! Really! Aren't you ashamed of yourself? You promised you'd be more restrained and . . .

DUDAKOV (*moving away from her*). Oh do stop, for God's sake. It's all so . . . so stupid! Arguing like a fishwife . . .

OLGA (*following him*). Oh, I'm stupid, am I? And a fishwife? (*With tears.*) Well, thank you very much, I'm sure!

They disappear into the woods. The stage is empty for a few moments. It grows dark. From the house, BASSOV and SHALIMOV come out on to the verandah.

SHALIMOV. You really must try to be more of a philosopher, you know – it's ridiculous to get so worked up over nothing . . .

BASSOV. But it's so infuriating – coming from that milk-sucking little puppy! But I hope you're not angry yourself?

SHALIMOV. Oh, I assure you one can encounter exhibitions like that one by that – that aspiring poet – every single day in the pages of the gutter press. But really, who cares?

They come down from the verandah and stand beside the pines. SUSLOV comes quickly up to them.

SUSLOV. Sergei Vassilich – I've come back to – well, I realise that I owe you an apology. (*To* SHALIMOV.) And you, of course. I rather let go, I'm afraid. But that woman's been getting on my nerves for a long time, there's something . . . organically repellent to me about her and all her kind. I can't stand the way she looks, the way she talks . . .

BASSOV. Quite understand, old boy – understand completely. One wants a woman to be gentle and tactful . . .

SHALIMOV (*coldly*). But you did rather go over the line, you know.

BASSOV (*hurriedly*). Oh, come on – I'd put my name to anything he said, God knows! And as for that woman, honestly . . . Well, really!

SUSLOV. All women are actresses, that's the fact of the matter, and Russian women all see themselves as the heroine . . .

BASSOV. H'm, women, yes. It really is difficult to get along with them.

VARVARA *and* MARIA *appear on the verandah.*

SHALIMOV. It's us that make it difficult. We should remind ourselves more often that women are still an inferior species.

BASSOV. Yes, of course, yes, you're right. (*As if using someone else's words.*) Women are still closer to the beasts than we are. In order to bend a woman to one's will, it's necessary to exercise a strong but gentle despotism over her – a strong but, in that very strength, essentially beautiful despotism.

A shot rings out in the woods. Nobody takes any notice.

SUSLOV. All that's needed is to keep her pregnant as much of the time as possible – then she's entirely in your hands.

VARVARA (*softly, emphatically*). How revolting!

MARIA. My God, it's like seeing something fall apart and rot . . . corpses putrefying under your eyes . . . Varya, you must get away from here!

SUSLOV *walks quietly away, coughing drily.* BASSOV *rushes up to his wife hurriedly.*

BASSOV. Now really, Pyotr, you know, that . . . that's really a bit much, you really have gone a bit too far!

VARVARA (*to* SHALIMOV). You. You!

SHALIMOV (*removing his hat, shrugging his shoulders*). Me . . . What?

MARIA. Come on, Varya, Quickly, now. Come away.

She pulls VARVARA *after her.* BASSOV *looks at them in consternation.*

BASSOV. Hell and damnation! They must have overheard . . . Oh God!

SHALIMOV (*grinning*). Well, a fine friend you turned out to be!

BASSOV (*upset and worried*). What on earth made him go and do that, the stupid oaf! What a poisonous monster he is – you really can't go around saying things like that for anyone to hear! Ugh!

SHALIMOV (*coldly*). I shall leave tomorrow. I'm going in – it's getting damp and chilly out here.

BASSOV (*dismally*). And in there my sister'll be howling her head off. You'll see.

> *They exit. Silence.* PUSTOBAIKA *and* KROPILKIN *appear from behind* BASSOV's *villa, both warmly dressed, carrying rattles and whistles. From* SUSLOV's *villa come sounds of chords played on a piano. Then* YULIA *and* ZAMISLOV *can be heard singing* 'Now the Weary Sun is Sinking' *as a duet.*

PUSTOBAIKA. Right, you take the path down that side. I'll go round by 'ere, we'll just show ourselves, i'n'it, an' be off to the kitchen for a cup of tea with Stephanida.

KROPILKIN. I'm goin'. (*Sighs.*) Ah, dear oh Lord . . .

PUSTOBAIKA. Ah, more of their litter, the pigs. Like corner boys they are, these summer folk. Come along, litter the place up, and they're away. At's all they leave you, the pickin' up an' the sweepin' up . . .

> *He sounds his rattle loudly and vindictively, and whistles.* KROPILKIN *gives an answering whistle.* PUSTOBAIKA *goes off.* KALERIA *appears, and sits under the pines, melancholy, thoughtful. She listens to the singing, softly hums the same song. From the right comes* PUSTOBAIKA's *voice.*

PUSTOBAIKA (*loudly, alarmed, off*). Who's that? What? Oh, God-a-mercy!

> KALERIA *listens apprehensively.* PUSTOBAIKA *comes in, supporting* RYUMIN *under the arms.*

To the Bassovs', is it?

KALERIA (*calls*). Sergei! Sergei!

RYUMIN. A doctor, please! Call a doctor!

KALERIA. Pavel Sergeyich, it's you! What's the matter? Oh, what on earth is the matter with him?

PUSTOBAIKA. I was walkin' my round . . . he come crawling
toward me along the ground . . . says he's wounded . . .

KALERIA. Wounded? (BASSOV *runs on*.) Oh, Sergei, fetch
Maria Lvovna, quickly. We must have a doctor . . .

BASSOV. What's that? What's happened?

RYUMIN. Forgive me.

KALERIA. Who wounded you?

PUSTOBAIKA (*crossly*). Who'd wound a man in these parts?
Who but himself? Here's his pistol.

> *He takes a revolver from inside his coat and calmly and
> intently examines it.*

BASSOV. Oh, it's you! I thought it was Zamislov, I thought
Pyotr must have . . . (*Runs off, shouting*). Maria Lvovna!

> SHALIMOV *appears, wrapped in a rug.*

SHALIMOV. What? Who is it? What's happened?

KALERIA. Is it very painful?

RYUMIN. Shameful . . . it's shameful.

SHALIMOV. It may not be serious.

RYUMIN. Take me away from here. I don't want her to see me
. . . please, take me away!

KALERIA (*to* SHALIMOV). Go on, can't you, go and call . . .

> SHALIMOV *goes into the villa; there's the sound of people
> running, exclamations can be heard. Enter* MARIA, SONYA,
> VLASS *and* VARVARA.

MARIA. You? Oh dear! Sonya, help me – get his jacket off . . .
gently, now, don't worry . . .

VARVARA. Pavel Sergeyich . . .

RYUMIN. Forgive me! I meant to do it first try, but when a
person's heart is small, and is beating very hard, it's
difficult to hit.

VARVARA. Why, though? Why?

KALERIA (*shouting hysterically at* RYUMIN). But it's so cruel!
(*She stops herself.*) What am I saying? I'm sorry.

VLASS (*to* KALERIA). Go away. This isn't for you. Go, please.

> VLASS *goes over to the pines.* SUSLOV *and* DVOETOCHIE

come running up, the latter dressed in his waistcoat with an overcoat thrown on top, and no hat; then ZAMISLOV *and* YULIA, DUDAKOV – *dishevelled and irritated* – *and* OLGA, *timid and lost.*

MARIA. Ah, here it is! Well, that doesn't look too serious.

RYUMIN. There's people coming. Varvara Mikhailovna – give me your hand.

VARVARA. What's all this about?

RYUMIN. I love you! I can't live without you.

VLASS (*through his teeth*). Oh to hell with you and your love!

KALERIA (*in a loud whisper*). Oh you mustn't! You can't attack a dying man!

MARIA (*to* VARVARA). Go away, please. (*To* RYUMIN.) You've nothing to be afraid of, the wound's nothing . . . And here's another doctor.

DUDAKOV. Well, what is it? A bullet wound? In the shoulder, eh? Now who on earth would want to shoot himself in the shoulder? You've got to do it through the heart or the head if you're really serious about it.

MARIA. Kirill Akimich! What do you think you're saying?

DUDAKOV. Oh . . . Yes, yes, I'm sorry. Well . . . er . . . is he bandaged? Well . . . er . . . pick him up then . . .

BASSOV. Take him to our place . . . Our place, Varya?

RYUMIN. Don't hold me . . . I can walk.

DUDAKOV. You can? Splendid.

RYUMIN *staggers;* BASSOV *and* SUSLOV *support him.*

RYUMIN. Yes, well, there you have it – I've been a failure at living, and now I've made a failure of dying – what a pathetic creature!

They take RYUMIN *indoors.*

YULIA. He's right.

ZAMISLOV (*drearily*). What a pitiful farce!

PUSTOBAKIA (*to* DVOETOCHIE). At was me as brought in the gentleman.

DVOETOCHIE. Ah . . . Good, good.

PUSTOBAIKA. By rights a man'd get something for's trouble.

DVOETOCHIE (*reproachfully*). You're a callous character, my friend.

Gives him some money.

PUSTOBAIKA. Thank you, sir.

KALERIA (*to* VARVARA). Is he dying? It should have been me, shouldn't it, Varya?

VARVARA. Oh, be quiet! You mustn't . . . (*Hysterically.*) Oh, how repulsive we all are! Oh why, why?

SHALIMOV (*to* MARIA). Is it a dangerous wound?

MARIA. No.

SHALIMOV. H'm. Unpleasant business . . . Varvara Mikhailovna, may I . . .?

VARVARA (*shuddering*). What? What is it?

SHALIMOV. A short while ago you heard me say something . . .

Enter BASSOV, SUSLOV, DUDAKOV.

BASSOV. Well, we've got him to lie down . . .

VARVARA. No. Stop. I shan't believe anything you . . . I don't want to hear your explanations! I hate you all, from the very bottom of my heart, you miserable, pitiful monsters!

VLASS. Hold on. Let me tell them. I know you now: you're all in fancy dress. And I swear that as long as I live I shall tear off the rags you use to cover up your lies and your vulgarity, your lack of feeling and your twisted, depraved thoughts!

SHALIMOV *shrugs and walks away.*

MARIA. Don't go on. It's useless.

VARVARA. No. Let them hear about themselves. I've paid dearly for the right to tell them what I think of them – they've warped my soul and poisoned my entire life for me! I used not to be like this, surely? I don't believe in . . . there's nothing I believe in any more! I've no strength left, nothing to face life with . . . I didn't begin my life like this, did I?

YULIA (*passionately*). I can say that. I can say that, too.

OLGA (*to* DUDAKOV). Look at Varvara, look at her face! It's quite vicious!

DUDAKOV *pushes his wife aside with his hand.*

BASSOV. Varya, that'll do. Surely, we don't need all this? After all, what's it all about, really? Well, Ryumin's been stupid, but just because of him it surely isn't worth . . .

VARVARA. Go away, Sergei.

BASSOV. My friend . . .

VARVARA. I'm not your friend and never have been, nor you mine. Never! We were just husband and wife, that's all. And now we're strangers. And I'm going away.

BASSOV. Where to? Oh, Varya, you should be ashamed of yourself . . . here, outside, in front of people!

VARVARA. There are no people here.

MARIA. Come on, Varya, let's go.

YULIA. Don't stop her. Let her have her say.

DVOETOCHIE (*sadly*). Oh dear, oh deary me, friends, truly you've hurt my soul!

KALERIA (*to* MARIA). What is it, though? What's it all about?

MARIA. Just keep calm and help me get her away.

VARVARA. Yes! Yes! I'm going away! Far, far away, away from this place, where everything's rotting and putrefying, far away from these idle parasites! I want to live, and I shall live . . . I shall find something .... something to do . . . against you! Yes – against you!

Looks at them all and shouts in despair:

Curse every one of you!

VLASS. Come along, my dear. No more. You've said enough.

He takes her arm and starts to lead her away.

BASSOV (*to* SHALIMOV). Can't you help me stop this?

SHALIMOV (*calmly smiling*). Give her a glass of cold water – what else can you do?

YULIA (*going up to* VARVARA). Oh, if only I could go away too!

BASSOV. Varya! Now then, where are you going! Maria Lvovna, this is very wrong of you, you're a doctor – you ought to be calming her.

MARIA. Get away from me.

DVOETOCHIE (*to* BASSOV). Poor innocent little villain!

He follows VLASS *and* VARVARA *into the woods, right.*

KALERIA (*sobbing*). What about me? Where am I to go?
SONYA (*goes up to her*). Come to us. Come on.

She takes KALERIA *off.*

YULIA (*calmly and somehow ominously*). Well, Pyotr Ivanich –
let's go and get on with our lives . . .

SUSLOV *grinds his teeth silently and follows her off.*

BASSOV. What the devil's going on? Has everyone gone out of
their minds, or what? That stupid Ryumin . . . just because
his nerves suddenly go to pieces . . . Yakov; why don't you
say something? What are you laughing about, eh? Do you
think it's not really serious, is that it? But it was all so
sudden – bang – and all at once everything's blown apart!
What on earth do we do now?
SHALIMOV. Calm down, old chap – just calm down. The
rhetorics of hysteria, that's all that was.

He takes BASSOV *by the arm and leads him towards the
villa.* DUDAKOV, *his hands behind his back, comes out and
walks slowly to the right, to where his wife, standing silently
under the trees, is waiting for him..*

BASSOV. Hell and damnation!
SHALIMOV (*grinning*). Take it easy, now! Look – the Suslovs
have gone off to continue their lives . . . let's go off calmly
and continue ours.
OLGA. Kirill . . . Is he going to die?
DUDAKOV (*gloomily*). No. Come on. No one's going to die.

They exit into the woods.

SHALIMOV. None of it's of any significance, old chap –
neither the people nor the events. Pour me a drop of wine,
will you? Yes, it's all quite unimportant, you know.

*He drinks. In the forest the watchman gives a soft, long-
drawn out whistle.*

CURTAIN

CHILDREN OF THE SUN

The British première of Children of the Sun *was given by the Royal Shakespeare Company on 3rd October 1979 at the Aldwych Theatre, London with the following cast:*

ROMAN, *the yardman*	John Burgess
PAVEL FYODORICH PROTASSOV *a student of Natural Science*	Norman Rodway
ELIZAVETA FYODOROVNA (LISA) *Pavel's sister*	Sinead Cusak
ANTONOVNA, *the Protassovs' Nanny now their housekeeper*	Valerie Lush
YEGOR, *a blacksmith*	Malcolm Storry
BORIS BORISOVICH CHEPURNOY *a Ukrainian veterinary surgeon*	Alan Howard
MELANYA BORISOVNA KIRPICHEVA *Boris's sister, a rich widow*	Natasha Parry
EFIMIA IVANOVNA (FIMA) *the housemaid*	Susan Dury
NAZAR AVDEYICH VIGRUSOV *pawnbroker and owner of Pavel's house*	Arthur White
MIKHAIL NAZAROV VIGRUSOV (MISHA), *Nazar's son, a future man of substance*	Brian Abbott
ELYENA NIKOLAEVNA PROTASSOV *Pavel's wife*	Carmen du Sautoy
DMITRI SERGEYICH VAGUIN *an artist*	John Shrapnel
YAKOV TROSHIN, *Civil Officer 7th Class former Deputy Station Master of Log*	Paul Webster
AVDOTIA, *Yegor's wife*	Jenny Lipman
LUKERIA (LUSHA) *the new housemaid*	Kate Fitzgerald
A DOCTOR	Dennis Edwards
TOWNSPEOPLE AND PEASANTS	Eileen Carrdus
	Philip Foz
	Jimmy Gardner
	Joseph Greig
	Peter Holmes
	Arthur Kohn
	Valerie Testa
	Stuart Organ
	Diana Van Fossen

Directed by Terry Hands
Designed by Chris Dyer

Act One

An old country house. A large, dim room. In the wall, left, a window and a door leading on to the terrace. In one corner, the staircase leading upstairs to LISA's rooms. At the back of the room is an arch, beyond which is the dining-room. In the corner to the right, doors to ELYENA's rooms.

Bookshelves, heavy, old-fashioned furniture; fine books lie on the tables; on the walls, portraits of scientists; on the cupboard stands a white bust. By the window, is a large round table at which PROTASSOV is sitting, leafing through a pamphlet and observing a flask of liquid which is heating over a spirit stove.

On the terrace below the window PROTASSOV. He calls through the window.

PROTASSOV. Hey, you – er – whatsyername . . .

    ROMAN *puts his head through the window.*

ROMAN. What's that?

PROTASSOV. Can't you, you know . . . go somewhere?

ROMAN. Go where?

PROTASSOV. Anywhere. You're distracting me, you know.

ROMAN. Ah no, sir. Orders, sir. Landlord says, get that mended he says.

    ANTONOVNA *comes in from the dining room.*

ANTONOVNA. Oh you mucky thing, you. Moving in here now with your . . .

PROTASSOV. Shut up, Nanny.

ANTONOVNA. As if you didn't have space to spare in your own rooms . . .

PROTASSOV. No, please, don't go in there, I'm making – um – smoke in there.

ANTONOVNA. Yes, and now you're going to bring your stinky things in here, aren't you! At least let me open the yard door . . .

PROTASSOV. No, no, please, don't! Oh really, Nanny! I didn't ask you in here, did I? Why don't you tell that – whatsisname, the yardman – tell him to go away. He moos like a cow all the time.

ANTONOVNA *calls through the window.*

Here, you, Roman, what are you messing at? Go on away with you!

ROMAN. Can't. Landlord says . . .

ANTONOVNA. Never mind what he say. Off you go. Finish 'at later.

ROMAN. Well, I dunno . . . all right then.

ROMAN *goes away with a clatter.*

ANTONOVNA (*grumpily*). One of these days you'll end up choking yourself . . . The cholera's a-coming, they do say . . . Fancy you, a general's son, playing away there at heaven knows what; and all that comes out of that is nasty smells . . .

PROTASSOV. You wait, Nanny, I'll be just as grand as a general one day . . .

ANTONOVNA. You'll be a beggar one day, that's what. You've already frittered the house away with all your chemistry and physistry.

PROTASSOV. Physics, Nanny, not physistry . . . And now, please, leave me in peace.

ANTONOVNA. That rascal's come – Egorka.

PROTASSOV. Ah, good – tell him to come in here.

ANTONOVNA. Pashenka, you got to tell that one off! You give the brute a good talking to, ask him what he thinks he's up to. Beating his poor wife again yesterday he was, he'll finish her off one day.

PROTASSOV. All right, I'll speak to him . . .

LISA *comes silently downstairs, stops in front of the bookcase, quietly opens it.*

ANTONOVNA. But you must really frighten him! I won't half give it you, you tell him . . .

PROTASSOV. Don't worry, Nanny, I'll scare him all right. Now, off you go . . .

ANTONOVNA. You be strict with him now! You always go on with everyone like you was talking to the gentry!

PROTASSOV. Oh, that's enough, Nanny! Is Elyena home?

ANTONOVNA. She is not. She went off to that Vaguin after breakfast and she's not been back since. You want to watch it, Pashenka, you'll fritter that wife of yours away too.

PROTASSOV. Oh, do stop your stupid chatter – you're making me cross!

LISA. Nanny! You're disturbing Pavel, let him get on with his work.

PROTASSOV. Aha, you're here, are you. Are you well?

LISA. All right . . .

PROTASSOV. Good!

ANTONOVNA. Lisa, it's time for your milk.

LISA. I know.

ANTONOVNA. But I'm going to have my say first about Elyena Nikolaevna – if I was in her place I'd go looking for another, at's what I'd do! Poor thing's given no attention at all! You eats up your oats and away the bowl floats – at's about it, eh? And no babbies neither! – where's the joy in that for a woman?

PROTASSOV. Nanny, I warn you, I'm getting very, very cross! Go away, woman! Shoo! Oh God, you're like a great leech . . .

ANTONOVNA. All right, all right! My, you're fierce! You be fierce with Yegorka too, remember. (*Going out.*) Your milk's in the dining room, Lisa . . . did you take your drops?

LISA. Yes, yes.

ANTONOVNA. At's it then.

> ANTONOVNA *exits into the dining room.* PROTASSOV *glances behind him to make sure she's gone.*

PROTASSOV. Extraordinary old bird! As deathless as stupidity

– and just as importunate. How are you feeling, Lisa?

LISA. Well.

PROTASSOV. That's wonderful. (*Singing, in country accent.*) At's wunderful, wunderful, at's wunderful . . .

LISA. But Nanny's right, you know.

PROTASSOV. I doubt it. The old are seldom right. The sovereignty of truth lies with the newly born. Lisa, just look at what this yeast of mine is doing . . .

LISA. Nanny's right when she says you don't pay enough attention to Elyena.

PROTASSOV (*pained, but gently*). How you two do nag me, you and Nanny! Lena's not dumb, is she? Surely she could tell me herself if there was something I . . . if somehow, something wasn't . . . as it should be . . . or whatever. But she hasn't. So . . . what's the problem?

Enter YEGOR *from the dining room, slightly drunk.*

Ah, here's Yegor. Hullo, Yegor!

YEGOR. Good health, squire.

PROTASSOV. Listen, Yegor, what I want is this. I want you to make me a small burner, with a lid, a sort of conical lid, you see, with a hole at the top so that it makes a chimney . . . do you see?

YEGOR. I see. At's all right.

PROTASSOV. I've made a drawing . . . where is it? Come through here . . .

PROTASSOV *takes* YEGOR *into the dining room.* CHEPUR-NOY *knocks on the door from the terrace.* LISA *opens it.*

CHEPURNOY. Ah, you're at home. A very good day to you!

LISA. Good morning.

CHEPURNOY (*sniffing*). To judge by the smell, my learned friend is also at home.

LISA. Where have you been?

CHEPURNOY. On a professional visit, of course. The tail of the dog of the wife of the administrator of the exchequer of the province had been squashed in a door by a maid. So I treated that unhappily flattened extremity. Got three

roubles for it. Here they are. I thought of buying you some
chocolates, but then it occurred to me that it might not be
correct to treat a young lady on dog-money. So I didn't.

LISA. And a good thing too. Won't you sit down?

CHEPURNOY. I must say, to sit anywhere in the vicinity of
that concoction makes accepting your invitation a doubtful
pleasure. (*Calling towards the dining room.*) Hey, professor,
it's boiling!

PROTASSOV *comes running in.*

PROTASSOV. Oh no, it mustn't boil! Oh, look at that! Why
didn't you tell me, the pair of you?

CHEPURNOY. I did. It's boiling, I cried.

PROTASSOV. Yes, yes, but can't you see, I didn't *want* it to
boil!

YEGOR *comes through from the dining room.*

LISA. Who could have known that, Pavel?

PROTASSOV (*grumbling*). Oh, damn it . . . now I'll have to
start all over again.

YEGOR. Pavel Fedor'ich, give me a rouble.

PROTASSOV. A rouble? Ah . . . of course . . . hold on . . .
(*Searches his pockets.*) Lisa, you haven't got a rouble, have
you?

LISA. No. Nanny has.

CHEPURNOY. So have I. I've got three. Here.

PROTASSOV. Three? Let me have them, will you? Here,
Yegor – three roubles. Is that all right?

YEGOR. That'll do fine. We can settle up later. Thank you.
Goodbye.

LISA. Pavel . . . Nanny asked you to talk to him. Remember?

PROTASSOV. Talk to him? Oh! Oh, ah, yes. H'm . . . yes . . .
er . . . Yes! Yegor, sit down for a minute, will you? Please?
Now – er – Lisa, maybe you'd like to tell him?

LISA *shakes her head.*

Ah. Well. Well, you see, Yegor, I've got to tell you . . . That
is, I mean, Nanny asked me . . . well, the thing is, it seems

you beat your wife? I'm sorry, Yegor . . .

YEGOR *gets up from his chair.*

YEGOR. I do.

PROTASSOV. You do? But that's – um – that's very bad, you know! You must understand that!

YEGOR (*sullenly*). Who said it was good?

PROTASSOV. Ah, so you do understand? Why do it then? Why bully her? It's brutal, Yegor . . . Yegor, you must stop doing it . . . You're a *man*, a rational being, Yegor, the most radiant and beautiful phenomenon on earth . . .

YEGOR (*with a laugh*). What – me?

PROTASSOV. Yes, you!

YEGOR. Squire, you might have started by asking – what for do I beat her?

PROTASSOV. No, you must understand, there can be no beating, of anybody, by anybody. A person cannot – must not – beat a person. It's so obvious, Yegor!

YEGOR (*grinning*). They beat me all right. Persons beat me plenty, at that. As to the wife, well, maybe she's not a person at all, maybe she's a devil . . .

PROTASSOV. A devil? – Oh, rubbish!

YEGOR (*decisively*). Goodbye, squire. And I'll keep right on beating that one, I'll beat her until she lays down before me like grass before the wind. (*Exits.*)

PROTASSOV. But, Yegor, listen, you said yourself . . . He's gone. And I think he's offended. Dammit, what a stupid scene. Nanny always manages to drag me into some ridiculous mess . . . Meanwhile, God knows what's happening to my experiment . . .

PROTASSOV *goes crossly behind the portière.*

CHEPURNOY. My learned friend spoke most convincingly.

LISA. Dear Pavel. He's always so funny.

CHEPURNOY. But as for this Yegor, you know. I'd simply give him a damn good thrashing.

LISA. Boris Boris'ich!

CHEPURNOY. What? Oh – Oh, I'm sorry if I spoke coarsely.

But his reasoning is quite correct, you know – He was beaten, therefore he can beat. To take it a step further – he should be beaten more.

LISA. Please! Why do you talk like that?

CHEPURNOY. But why not? Isn't every law-abiding society based on such logic?

LISA. You know very well how much I hate anything crude and nasty . . . and you always seem to tease me deliberately. No, wait . . . That blacksmith, Yegor – he makes me feel afraid. There's so much darkness in him . . . and those huge, insulted eyes . . . I'm sure I saw them . . . once . . . there . . . in that awful crowd.

CHEPURNOY. Oh, don't keep reminding yourself. Forget about it.

LISA. But how can I – how can I forget such a thing?

CHEPURNOY. What's the point of remembering?

LISA. 'From the ground where blood's been shed
      No flower will ever lift its head.'

CHEPURNOY. But they do, you know, they lift their lovely heads like anything!

LISA *gets up and walks about.*

LISA. No. Only hatred grows there. Whenever I hear anything crude or brutal, and whenever I see anything red, I get this terrible feeling of sickness and horror in my heart . . . and at once I see that black, bestial crowd, with blood running down their faces . . . pools of red blood sinking into the sand . . . .

CHEPURNOY. Steady, lass.

LISA. And there at my feet . . . there's a young man with his head smashed in . . . crawling along the ground . . . blood streaming down his cheek, down his neck . . . teeth red with blood . . . and his head falls down . . . face first, face first! . . . down into the sand!

CHEPURNOY *goes up to her.*

CHEPURNOY. Oh dear me, whatever am I to do with you?

LISA. Doesn't it horrify you too?

CHEPURNOY. Er . . . will you not come out into the garden
with me?

LISA. No . . . tell me, you must tell me . . . do you understand
the horror I feel?

CHEPURNOY. I do indeed. I understand it. And I feel it.

LISA. No. No, that's not true. If only you did understand it
would be easier for me to bear. I want to shift some of the
burden from my soul but . . . but there isn't another soul
that would take it on . . . not one!

CHEPURNOY. Ah, come on, little one, stop it, let's go out into
the garden. There's such a stench in here – as if my learned
friend had been frying rubber galoshes in olive oil.

LISA. Yes . . . my head's spinning . . .

ANTONOVNA (*from the dining room*). Lisanka! It's time you
had your drops . . . And you still haven't drunk your milk!

LISA *goes towards dining room.*

LISA. I'm coming.

CHEPURNOY. And how is life with Antonovna?

ANTONOVNA *is clearing the dining table.*

ANTONOVNA. All right. Mustn't grumble.

CHEPURNOY. Grand! Fit as a flea, are we?

ANTONOVNA. Thanks be to God.

CHEPURNOY. What a shame. If you'd been ill, I could have
cured you.

ANTONOVNA. You'd best stay with your puppies. I'm not a
little dog.

LISA *enters.*

CHEPURNOY. But I'd like to cure a nice human being for a
change.

LISA. Are you coming?

LISA *and* CHEPURNOY *go through the door on to the terrace.*
PROTASSOV *appears with a glass vessel in his hands.*

PROTASSOV. Nanny, can I have some boiled water?

ANTONOVNA. There isn't any.

PROTASSOV. Nanny – please!

ANTONOVNA. You'll have to wait for the samovar. Did you speak to that blacksmith?

PROTASSOV. Yes, yes, I spoke to him.

ANTONOVNA. Did you give him a good ticking off?

PROTASSOV. I certainly did! I had him shaking like a leaf! Now look here my friend, I said, you'll find yourself going up before the . . . the whatsit . . . the . . .

ANTONOVNA. The chief of police?

PROTASSOV. No . . . Oh, it doesn't matter . . . I mean the . . . the . . . magistrate.

ANTONOVNA. Better to threaten him with the chief of police . . . Well, what did he say?

PROTASSOV. He said . . . er . . . yes, you know what he said to me, he said, 'Squire, you're a fool!'

ANTONOVNA (indignant). He never!

PROTASSOV. He did. Just like that. You're a fool, he said, going round sticking your nose into other people's business.

ANTONOVNA. Did he say that then? He surely never did, Pashenka!

PROTASSOV (laughing). Of course he didn't, Nanny! I said it to myself. He thought it, and I said it.

ANTONOVNA. Oh, you . . . !

ANTONOVNA is about to go out, indignant.

PROTASSOV. Oh, and Nanny, when the water's ready, will you bring it in yourself? That girl of ours, with all her frills and furbelows, swans about the place like a ship in a storm, she's bound to knock something flying one day. Why we have to have a maid who gets herself up like a fashion plate I really don't know.

ANTONOVNA. Seems that fashion plate of yours is carrying on with the landlord's son – what d'you think about that?

PROTASSOV. Are you jealous, Nanny?

ANTONOVNA. Tfoo! (a contemptuous spitting sound.) But you're her master, aren't you? You should tell that one a decent girl didn't ought to behave like that.

PROTASSOV. Can't you see it's not my business?

ANTONOVNA. What was all that college learning for then? You tell me that!

MELANYA *appears in the terrace doorway.*

PROTASSOV. Go along with you now – here's Melanya Borisovna. Good morning!

MELANYA. Good morning, Pavel Fyodorich.

ANTONOVNA. Who left that door open? (*She closes it.*)

MELANYA. You look very cheerful.

PROTASSOV. Well, I'm glad to see you – Nanny was just giving me a terrible ticking off – and also, I – um – I'm on the point of completing a highly complex and intellectually demanding experiment.

MELANYA. Are you really? Oh, I am glad! I do so want you to be famous!

ANTONOVNA (*grumbling*). He's famous enough already. You should hear what they say about him in town . . .

ANTONOVNA *exits.*

MELANYA. I'm quite convinced you're going to be another Pastiuer.

PROTASSOV. H'm. Not important of course, but, er – Pasteur, it's pronounced Pasteur . . . Is that my book you've got there? Have you read it? Fascinating . . . Hydatopriomorphism – better than a novel, eh?

MELANYA. Oh, yes, yes! Only, you know, all these funny letters . . .

PROTASSOV. The formulae?

MELANYA. Yes. I don't understand those.

PROTASSOV. They just have to be memorised, that's all. Now I'll let you have something on the physiology of plants. But what you must study most attentively of all is chemistry – chemistry! It's an amazing science, you know! Compared with the others it's been very little developed but already it seems to me like the eye of God. It stares boldly and keenly into the fiery mass of the sun and into the darkness of the earth's crust, even into the invisible particles of your heart . . .

MELANYA *sighs*.

it stares into the mysterious structure of a stone, and into the teeming silent life of a tree . . . It looks into everything, and everywhere, everywhere, it discovers harmony . . . as it goes on obstinately searching and searching for the true source of life. And it will find it, believe me, it will find it! Once it has learned the secrets of the structure of matter, chemistry will create, in a glass test tube, a living organism!

MELANYA (*ecstatically*). Dear God above, how absolutely wonderful! But, Pavel Fyodorich – you must give lectures!

PROTASSOV (*embarrassed*). No – er – Oh no! Why?

MELANYA. But you absolutely must start giving lectures! You speak so – so bewitchingly! When I listen to you . . . I want to kiss your hand.

PROTASSOV (*looking at his hands*). I wouldn't advise it. My hands are seldom clean . . . I'm always messing around with all kinds of stuff, you know . . .

MELANYA (*with sincerity*). If only you knew how much I want to be able to do something for you! I'm quite lost in admiration for you, you're so unworldly, so – so godlike! Tell me . . . what do you want? Demand anything of me, *anything*, anything at all!

PROTASSOV. Ah . . . Well now, you could . . . you might . . .

MELANYA. What? What could I do for you?

PROTASSOV. Do you keep hens?

MELANYA. Hens? What sort of hens?

PROTASSOV. You know – domestic birds. Poultry. Cocks and hens, that sort of thing.

MELANYA. Oh, I see. Well, yes, I do. Why? What do you want hens for?

PROTASSOV. My dear, if you could possibly give me some fresh eggs every day – really fresh eggs, new-laid eggs, still warm from the bird! You see, I need an awful lot of egg white, and Nanny's so mean and anyway she doesn't understand about albumen, she gives me eggs that aren't really fresh, and even to get those I have to go on at her for ages . . . and that sour face of hers . . .

MELANYA. Pavel Fyodorich . . . you are cruel.

PROTASSOV. Cruel? Me? Why?

MELANYA. Oh, all right. I'll send you a dozen fresh eggs every morning.

PROTASSOV. That's wonderful. Marvellous! That's just what I need. And I'm very, very grateful! You're a dear, kind person – really!

MELANYA. And you're a child . . . a cruel child. You don't understand anything, do you?

PROTASSOV (*surprised*). I certainly don't understand why I'm cruel.

MELANYA. You will . . . one day . . . Is Elyena Nikolaevna at home?

PROTASSOV. She's sitting for Vaguin.

MELANYA. Do you like him?

PROTASSOV. Vaguin? Yes, of course. We're old friends, you know. We were at school together, then at university. (*He looks at his watch.*) He was a natural scientist too, you know, but he left it for the Academy of Art during our second year.

MELANYA. Elyena Nikolaevna seems to like him very much too.

PROTASSOV. Yes, she does, very much. He's a fine fellow . . . a bit limited, perhaps . . .

MELANYA. And you're not afraid . . .

> CHEPURNOY *knocks on the outer door.*
> PROTASSOV *opens it.*

PROTASSOV. Afraid of what? (*To* CHEPURNOY.) Sorry. Nanny shut it.

MELANYA. Oh, you're here, are you?

CHEPURNOY. And you too. Where can I find some water? Elizaveta wants some water.

PROTASSOV Isn't she well?

CHEPURNOY. She's all right. It's only to take her drops with . . .

> CHEPURNOY *goes into the dining room.*

PROTASSOV. Melanya Borisovna, I'll leave you just for a

moment . . . I must go and see . . .

MELANYA. Of course, go on, go on! And come back as soon as possible.

PROTASSOV. I will, yes. Why don't you go into the garden?

MELANYA. All right.

PROTASSOV. Lisa's there. (*Calling.*) Nanny! Where's my boiled water?

He exits. CHEPURNOY *re-enters.*

CHEPURNOY. Well, Melanya. How are things with you?

MELANYA (*fast, in a low voice*). Do you know what hydatopiromorphism is?

CHEPURNOY. What?

MELANYA. Hydato . . . piro . . . morphism.

CHEPURNOY. God alone knows. It sounds like an aquatic firework.

MELANYA. Are you serious?

CHEPURNOY. Well, you know – hydra is water . . . piro – pyrotechnics . . . and metamorphism is some kind of trick. Why? Is he making you pass an examination?

MELANYA. Never you mind. Off you go now.

CHEPURNOY. When you finally tease him away from his wife, you should set up a soap factory. The chemist won't need a salary.

CHEPURNOY *goes off towards the garden.*

MELANYA. Boris, you are crude!

MELANYA *gets up and looks around.* FIMA *enters.*

FIMA. Elizaveta Fyodorovna was asking if you'd like to join her in the garden . . .

MELANYA. Yes, of course.

ANTONOVNA *appears, carrying a saucepan of hot water.* FIMA *is clattering dishes in the dining room.*

What's that you're carrying, Nanny?

ANTONOVNA. Boiled water for Pashenka.

MELANYA. Ah. That'll be for one of his experiments.

ANTONOVNA. At always is.

ANTONOVNA *puts the saucepan down and exits.* MELANYA
looks into the dining room.

MELANYA. Fima!

FIMA *comes to the doorway.*

FIMA. Yes, Ma'am?

MELANYA. Does your lady visit the artist every day?

FIMA. When it's raining, Ma'am, or looks like rain, she
doesn't go. But then Mr. Vaguin comes here.

MELANYA. Fima . . . You're a smart girl, aren't you?

FIMA. Not stupid, Ma'am.

MELANYA. Well . . . if you happen to notice anything . . .
well, anything at all, really . . . tell me, will you? Do you
understand?

FIMA. Yes, M'm.

MELANYA. And keep quiet about it. Here. (*She hands over
money.*) There's more where that came from.

FIMA. Thank you . . . thank you kindly, Ma'am. He kisses
her hands, Ma'am.

MELANYA. Well, that's not much. A start. Just you keep
watching.

FIMA. Yes, M'm. I understand.

MELANYA. I'm going into the garden. If Pavel Fyodorich
comes out, call me.

FIMA. I will.

MELANYA *exits.* ANTONOVNA *comes in.*

ANTONOVNA. You was banging them dishes about again.
You'll end up smashing them. That's not made of iron.

FIMA. Think I don't know how to handle dishes?

ANTONOVNA. Now then, don't be cheeky What was that
butcher's widow asking you?

FIMA (*going into the dining room*). About Lizaveta Fyodorovna.
Wanted to know how she was.

ANTONOVNA (*following her*). Why didn't that go and see for
'atself then, not go talking to servants.

FIMA. She did go. An a servant's a person like anyone else. You're a servant yourself at that.

ANTONOVNA. I know who I am. But gentry don't chatter with servants, not born gentry don't. They give orders, and that's that. Oh yes. Everybody's looking to be gentry now, but you can't put that where that isn't. (*Calling.*) Who's that?

ANTONOVNA comes out of the dining room. NAZAR enters.

NAZAR. Me it is. Best of the day to you Nyanushka.

ANTONOVNA. What do you want?

NAZAR. Pavel Fyodorich. Got to talk something over with that one.

ANTONOVNA. Oh. I'll go an tell 'm.

ANTONOVNA exits. FIMA looks through the dining room door.

NAZAR. Humble respects to you too, Efimia Ivanovna. Oh you . . . you ripe little schemer, you, you charming little cheat!

FIMA. Now then! You keep your hands to yourself.

NAZAR. Haven't got time for a nice respectable widower, that it? Not even join him for a spot of tea of an evening . . .

FIMA. Sssh!

Enter PROTASSOV, followed by ANTONOVNA

PROTASSOV. Is it me you want?

NAZAR. Just so, sir.

PROTASSOV. What is it?

NAZAR. Just a little word about the rent, sir . . .

PROTASSOV (*slightly irritated*). Look, when I sold you this house I had to wait two full years before I got paid, and now you . . . When's it due?

NAZAR. Yesterday, sir.

PROTASSOV. Oh, really! This is ridiculous . . . Here I am, totally immersed in my work, and you come interrupting me just for that . . . I mean, damn it . . .

NAZAR. Oh, but I didn't just come for that, no, I only just

happened to mention the money in passing, like to remind myself . . .

PROTASSOV. Well, you remind Nanny, or my wife . . . there's some money around here somewhere, goodness knows where exactly . . . in some box or something . . . My wife will send it over . . . Or Nanny here might bring it . . . Goodbye.

ANTONOVNA *goes into the dining room.*

NAZAR. One moment, sir – can I keep you a moment?

PROTASSOV. What is it? Why?

NAZAR. About your little bit of land there, with that old lodge on it . . .

PROTASSOV. Well?

NAZAR. You should sell it.

PROTASSOV. Who'd be idiot enough to buy it? It's no good for anything . . . sand, a few pine trees . . .

NAZAR (*delighted*). Ah, you're right there! At's no good for nothing, that land!

PROTASSOV. There you are then.

NAZAR. There's no one'd buy it, 'part from me.

PROTASSOV. You? What do you want it for?

NAZAR. This and that. I've already bought some land from your neighbour. I want to buy your little bit too.

PROTASSOV. Splendid. You buy it then. Still getting richer, are you?

NAZAR. Well, I'd put it this way. I'm spreading.

PROTASSOV. You're a funny fellow. What do you want with a patch of sand?

NAZAR. Ah well, you see, sir . . . my son studied at the commercial institute, turns out now he's a learned man. Very shrewd, you know, about industry and that. And I've picked up this desire, sir, to help expansify the national economical productivity . . . to the which end, sir, I intend to set up a little factory. Blowing beer bottles, sir.

FIMA *stands listening in the doorway.*

PROTASSOV (*laughing*). You really are an original, aren't you!

Will you be closing down your pawnshop?

NAZAR. Why should I do that? The pawnshop, now – 'at's something for the soul, a charitable institution, 'at is. To do with helping thy neighbour.

PROTASSOV (*laughing*). Is it really? All right then – you buy my land. Goodbye.

PROTASSOV *exits, laughing.*

NAZAR. Ah, but, sir, excuse me, sir . . . Ha – gone! Why's he go like that? To make a purchase, and make a sale, that takes two – and he's gone.

FIMA (*shrugging*). Daft. It's well known.

NAZAR. H'm . . . At's no way to do things. Well, if that's the way it is, I'm off . . . goodbye.

NAZAR *exits.* ROMAN *appears behind* FIMA.

ROMAN. Where's this smoking stove then?

FIMA. Oh! You . . . Whyn't you drop dead! What you want?

ROMAN. What you fussing about? A stove, you hear? Smoking. Where?

MISHA *runs in from the dining room.*

MISHA. Not here, you dumb ox! In the kitchen!

ROMAN. Oh. Thought it was in here. (*Exits.*)

MISHA (*fast*). Well, Fimka, what about it then? A nice room, and fifteen roubles a month. All right?

FIMA. Get off! What you think – you're buying a horse?

MISHA. No need to talk like that. I'm a businessman. Just you think what your prospects are – who you could marry. Some stupid peasant who'd beat you same as the blacksmith beats his wife . . . But I could set you up, in a modest way, somewhere nice and clean, with enough to eat and everything . . . And get busy on your education.

FIMA. At'll do from you! I'm an honest girl, I am. Anyway, that butcher, Khrapov, he offered me a hundred a month, so there!

MISHA. But he's an old man, you fool! Imagine it!

FIMA. I didn't go along with him neither.

MISHA. Well, there you are, you silly thing. I'd let you . . .

FIMA. Give me seventy-five.

MISHA. What-a-at? Seventy-five?

FIMA. And an IOU for all the money I'm due for a year.

MISHA (*astonished*). You mean . . .?

FIMA. Yes, I do.

> *They stare at each other.* YEGOR *enters from the terrace, very drunk.*

FIMA. Shush now. Your da's gone already.

MISHA. Has he? Oh dear – excuse me. (*Exits.*)

FIMA. What you think you're doing? Why can't you come through the kitchen? The master comes in through the kitchen, and there's you . . .

YEGOR. Quiet, girl. Call the master.

FIMA. You're drunk, too! How can the master talk to you when you're drunk?

YEGOR. Never mind. I'll do the talking. Fetch him. Go on.

> FIMA *runs into the dining room, calling.*

FIMA. Nanny! Nyanka!

> PROTASSOV *appears from behind the portière*

PROTASSOV. What's all the shouting about, Fima? Oh, it's you, Yegor. What do you want? I'm busy. Be quick about it.

YEGOR. Wait. I've been drinking . . . a bit. Can't talk without drink . . .

PROTASSOV. All right. What is it then?

> *Enter* ANTONOVNA *from the dining room, followed by* FIMA.

YEGOR. Back there a bit you insulted me in front of people. Talking about my wife, you were. What sort of man are you, insulting me like that?

PROTASSOV. You see, Nanny? Ah, Yegor, I didn't mean to – er – to insult you . . .

YEGOR. No, wait, listen . . . I been living with insults since I was a kid . . .

PROTASSOV. Yes, of course, Yegor, I understand . . .

YEGOR. Shut up. You don't. No one understands me. And no
one loves me. Nor my wife don't neither. No one gives me no
respect, no love!

PROTASSOV. No need to shout.

ANTONOVNA. Lawk, you drunken pig!

YEGOR. Am I a man or am I not? Am I a 'uman person? Why
does everyone insult me? Eh?

ANTONOVNA. Oh Lawks, what's all this?

> ANTONOVNA *runs into the dining room. Her voice can be
> heard calling outside.*

PROTASSOV. Now do calm down, Yegor. You see, Nanny
told me . . .

YEGOR. Nanny . . . must be put aside. At's a full-grown
beard you've got on you . . . a bearded man don't have to
do what his Nanny tells 'm. Listen here – I respect you, sir.
I can see you're a special kind of man, can't I? I can see
that. So it's worse, isn't it, getting insulted by you, 'fore
other people? Ah, you . . .! I could kneel down 'front of you,
I could, just the two of us here, that'd be no offence, but not
'front of that cattle doctor, to go and . . . And the wife now
. . . I'll thrash her, oh yes, I'll mark her I will! I love her, so
she must love me.

> *Enter, running,* CHEPURNOY, FIMA, LISA, ANTON-
> OVNA, FIMA.

LISA. What is it? What's happening?

> CHEPURNOY *restrains her.*

CHEPURNOY. What's the matter? What's going on here?

PROTASSOV. Please, please . . .

MELANYA. Nanny, send for the yardman . . .

> ANTONOVNA *exits. Outside she can be heard shouting.*

ANTONOVNA (*off*). Roman!

YEGOR. The crows come flying, look. You want to shoo that

lot off, Pavel Fyodorich. Shoo 'em off good an proper.

CHEPURNOY. Why don't you take yourself home my good man?

YEGOR. I'm not your good man.

CHEPURNOY (*frowning*). Even so, you should still get yourself home.

MELANYA. It's the police we need.

PROTASSOV. Oh, please, there's no need for anything like that. Yegor, you go on home . . . I'll come over and see you later.

ANTONOVNA *and* ROMAN *appear in the dining room door.*

YEGOR. Ah? You'll come? Truly?

PROTASSOV. Truly.

YEGOR. All right . . . make sure you do. You mean it?

PROTASSOV. I give you my word.

YEGOR. At's it then. Well – goodbye. All these people . . . next to you, they're dust.

YEGOR *exits.*

ROMAN. I'm not needed then?

PROTASSOV. No, you're not. Off you go. Oooh!

PROTASSOV *gives a sigh of exhaustion.* ROMAN *exits.*

You see, Nanny? (ANTONOVNA *sighs.*) That's your handy-work.

LISA. I'm afraid of that man. Afraid of him.

MELANYA. You were so good with him, Pavel Fyodorich.

PROTASSOV. No, I feel rather guilty about him.

LISA. You must get a different blacksmith, Pavel.

CHEPURNOY. They're all drunkards.

PROTASSOV. It gets on my nerves, this sort of thing. It's so tiring. I'm completely out of luck today, it's been one stupid little thing after another. I'm utterly absorbed in an extremely involved, you could almost say critical and even dangerous experiment with acid of cyanogen, a liquid so volatile that . . . Lisa, get me some tea, will you?

LISA. Yes, I'll have it brought in here, I know you don't like the dining room.

PROTASSOV. Yes, good. I don't like dark rooms . . . not that there are any light ones in this house.

MELANYA. Oh I do understand you so well, Pavel Fyodorich!

CHEPURNOY. Melanya, what was that word?

MELANYA. What word?

CHEPURNOY. The one you asked me.

MELANYA. I didn't ask you anything.

CHEPURNOY. You've forgotten? Well, well. You know, professor, whenever she hears an abstruse word from you she comes and asks me what it means.

MELANYA (*offended*). You are a horrible man, Boris. I've got no memory for foreign words – I don't see what's so funny about that.

FIMA *enters, neatly spreads a cloth on the table by the window, and proceeds to bring in the tea things bit by bit.*

PROTASSOV. What was it you asked him?

MELANYA (*shamefacedly*). I'd forgotten what hydatopiro-morphism means.

CHEPURNOY. I told her it was an aquatic firework.

PROTASSOV (*laughing loudly*). A *what*?

LISA *enters, and busies herself about the table.*

MELANYA. You should be ashamed of yourself, Boris.

PROTASSOV. For brother and sister you two have a very odd relationship. Almost as if you didn't like each other. Sorry if I'm being tactless.

MELANYA. It's all right. Boris doesn't care for me, no. We're like strangers together, complete strangers. He was brought up in Poltava, with an aunt. I was with an uncle in Yaroslavl. We're orphans, you know.

CHEPURNOY (*sings*). Leetle child, leetle orphan. Nowhere to lay your leetle head . . .

MELANYA. We didn't meet until we were grown up . . . and then we didn't much like the look of each other. Boris of course doesn't care for anyone. His own life hasn't worked out, so he takes it out on everyone else. He doesn't even come to visit me.

CHEPURNOY. You know, professor, when that poor old rich husband of hers was still alive I'd go over to see her, and he'd ask me to doctor him . . .

MELANYA. Don't talk nonsense . . .

CHEPURNOY. And I'd say to him, there are some dogs I do not treat.

LISA. Boris Boris'ich!

PROTASSOV *gives an embarrassed laugh.*

CHEPURNOY. Have I gone too far again?

LISA. Drink your tea.

CHEPURNOY. And go home? I understand.

MELANYA. Pavel Fyodorich, do you remember, you were going to show me some seaweed under a microscope?

PROTASSOV. Some seaweed cells, it was . . . Er, yes, of course, um, we can do that . . . Now, if you like?

MELANYA. Oh, yes, let's! I'd be so grateful!

PROTASSOV. Come on then . . . Only I warn you, there's a terrible smell in there . . .

PROTASSOV *exits,* MELANYA *following.*

MELANYA. That doesn't matter a bit . . .

CHEPURNOY. What a farce! What does the cow want with seaweed!

LISA (*distressed*). Boris Boris'ich . . . You're truthful, and straight and strong . . . but . . .

CHEPURNOY (*bowing his head*). But . . .

LISA. Why are you always so harsh with everyone?

CHEPURNOY *shrugs.*

So many things in life are hard and cruel . . . so many horrible things . . . We ought to be softer, kinder with each other.

CHEPURNOY. But why tell lies? People are hard and cruel. That's their nature.

LISA. No! That's not true.

CHEPURNOY. In what way is it not true? Isn't it what you

believe yourself? Isn't it how you feel? Aren't you always saying . . . people are beasts, they're coarse and dirty, you're afraid of them? I know it myself. I believe you. But when you say . . . one must *love* people . . . well, then I don't believe you. You're speaking out of fear then.

LISA. You don't understand me.

CHEPURNOY. Perhaps. What I do understand is that one can only really love something that's useful or pleasant – a pig, perhaps, because it provides soft leather and tasty bacon . . . music . . . crayfish . . . a painting. But as for man – he's not useful, and he's not pleasant.

LISA. My God! How can you talk like that?

CHEPURNOY. One must speak as one feels. I have tried kindness. I once took in a boy off the streets. I'll educate him, I thought. He ran off with my watch. Then I took in a girl, also off the streets . . . still quite young. We'll wait a while, I thought, then I'll marry her. One day she drank herself stupid and went for my face with her nails . . .

LISA. Stop, stop! You must not talk about such things – can't you understand?

CHEPURNOY. Why not? That's just what I ought to do one day – tell the whole story of my life. It might cleanse my soul.

LISA. You should get married.

CHEPURNOY. I agree.

LISA. Find a young girl . . .

CHEPURNOY (*calmly*). You know very well, don't you, that I have found a young girl. I've been walking around her for over a year now like a bear round a nest of honey . . .

LISA. Oh dear, there you go again! Dear Boris Boris'ich, please don't! I've said my last word on that subject, and it won't change, ever, not a single syllable of it.

CHEPURNOY. And yet perhaps – who knows? I'm a Ukrainian, and we are a stubborn lot. Perhaps . . .?

LISA. No!

CHEPURNOY. Ah well. All right, let's change the subject.

LISA. You and your stubbornness frighten me.

CHEPURNOY. You shouldn't be frightened . . . you shouldn't

be frightened of anything.

Pause. ROMAN *can be heard grumbling on the terrace.* LISA *shudders and looks out of the window.*

LISA. Why do you treat your sister so badly?

CHEPURNOY. Because she's a fool. A brazen, scheming, pretentious little fool.

LISA. Oh God, no!

CHEPURNOY. All right, all right, I won't. But what about my sister, now, since you're asking? When she was twenty she married a rich old man. Why would a girl do that, d'you imagine? Then she was so miserable – so revolted by the old man's ways – she tried to kill herself. First she had to be cut down from the flue, then she tried drinking ammonia. And now, do you see, the old man's gone, but she's still tortured by demons.

LISA. Perhaps you're to blame? Why didn't you give her some support?

CHEPURNOY. Perhaps I am. Or again, perhaps I did.

LISA. But to be so hard on her just because of that . . .

CHEPURNOY. Not just because of that. You see, you don't know why she comes here so often. But I do.

LISA. Please don't elaborate. You'd do better to ask yourself who gave you the right to judge her.

CHEPURNOY. And who gave you the right to judge mankind? This is a right which everyone always uses without asking anyone's permission. Man can no more live without judging than he can live without breathing.

MELANYA *enters, excited, followed by* PROTASSOV.

MELANYA. Pavel Fyodorich . . . I do understand, I do, but . . . is it really true?

PROTASSOV. Of course it is. Everything lives. Everywhere – there is life. And secrets. Everywhere. To roam about in this world of the wonderful buried mysteries of existence, to spend all one's mental energies uncovering them – there is a life for a man, a really human life! There you can find an inexhaustible source of happiness, of life-giving joy! Man is

truly free only in his capacity to reason – only when he is
thinking rationally is he fully human – and if a man is
rational, then he will be honest and good. Goodness is the
fruit of reason. Without awareness it can never be achieved.

PROTASSOV *takes out his watch and consults it quickly.*

Oh dear, do excuse me, I must go . . . please . . . Oh,
heavens, yes . . .

PROTASSOV *exits hurriedly.*

MELANYA. If only you'd heard what he was saying in there
. . . the way he spoke . . . and just to me, to me alone . . .
to Melanya Kirpicheva. It was the first time in my life that
anyone ever talked to me like that . . . about wonderful
things like that . . . and just to me! Boris is laughing. Well,
Boris – so what? (*With tears in her voice.*) I'm not saying I
understand his ideas, am I? I didn't say that, did I? Oh I'm
a fool, I know – Lisaveta Fyodorovna, am I completely
ridiculous? My darling, just think about it . . . you live and
live and go on living, just like that, as if you were asleep,
and suddenly . . . something happens . . . you open your
eyes . . . it's morning, sunshine! At first you can see
nothing, only light . . . and your whole soul gives a huge
sigh of pure joy . . . just like at the Easter morning
service . . .

CHEPURNOY. What on earth are you talking about?

LISA. Have some tea . . . And sit down. You're all
excited . . .

MELANYA. You wouldn't understand, Boris! No, thank you, I
won't have any tea . . . I'm sorry, Lisaveta Fyodorovna,
I've disturbed you . . . I'll go . . . goodbye. Tell him, will
you, that I've gone . . .? And thank him for me . . . for
giving me such joy . . . he is such a radiant, wonderful
person!

MELANYA *exits on to the terrace.*

CHEPURNOY. What's the matter with her? I don't understand.

LISA. I do. There was a time when Pavel had the same effect on me. He'd talk, and it was as if the scales fell from my eyes . . . everything suddenly became so clear, so harmonious . . . both mysterious and simple, insignificant and enormous! But then I came to know something about real life, full of dirt and brutality and meaningless cruelty . . . and my soul was torn with fear and uncertainty . . . That was when I had to go to hospital.

CHEPURNOY. That's all over.

LISA. For the moment.

ELYENA *and* VAGUIN *appear on the terrace.*

CHEPURNOY. Someone else is coming. Oh, it's Elyena Nikolaevna . . . and the artist . . . time I was going.

ELYENA. Ah, Boris Boris'ich! – is Pavel in his room, Lisa? Give me some tea, will you?

ELYENA *goes in to her husband.*

CHEPURNOY. Why are you looking so ratty, Dmitri Sergeyich?

VAGUIN. Am I? How's your painting coming along, Lisa?

LISA. I haven't done any today.

VAGUIN. You should. The colours are so soothing.

CHEPURNOY. To look at you, one would hardly think so.

VAGUIN. Not all of them, perhaps.

LISA. And not red!

CHEPURNOY. Farewell, my friends. I'm away off to the river. I shall catch some crayfish, and boil them, and eat them, and drink some beer, and have a smoke . . . Oh, please don't see me out . . . I'll be back tomorrow.

Enter ELYENA.

Goodbye, Elyena Nikolaevna!

ELYENA. You're going? Goodbye.

CHEPURNOY *and* LISA *exit.*

VAGUIN. Is Pavel busy?

ELYENA. Yes. But he's just coming.

VAGUIN. He never stops fussing over this ridiculous idea of creating a human being in a test tube.

ELYENA. What a nasty tone – you should be ashamed of yourself.

VAGUIN. Well, it's a nasty, petty little notion. It irritates me. And I can't forgive him for the way he treats you, it's really monstrous.

ELYENA. If you go on like that I shall regret that I allowed myself to be candid with you.

VAGUIN. You have the right to be free. You ought not to have pity on someone who doesn't appreciate you at all.

ELYENA. I shall free myself. You'll see.

VAGUIN. When? What are you waiting for?

ELYENA. I need to know what place I occupy in his heart.

VAGUIN. None!

ELYENA. If that's so, well and good. Everything is simple – he doesn't need me, I go away. But if not? If his love is simply dormant – pushed down into the depths of his heart by the power of the idea that's possessed him . . .? What if I left him, and his love suddenly flared up again?

VAGUIN. You'd like that, wouldn't you?

ELYENA. I hate dramas.

VAGUIN. So it's for him that you're afraid

ELYENA. I certainly don't want to complicate his life.

VAGUIN. You are deliberating. That means you do not want your freedom. Those who truly desire do not deliberate.

ELYENA. That is for beasts. Animals do not deliberate, that is true. But man must act in such a way as to make for less suffering on this earth.

VAGUIN. And sacrifice oneself in the interests of duty, of course. Lisa's sour philosophy has had a bad influence on you.

ELYENA. Suffering is loathsome. In myself, I find it degrading. To give cause for it in others is dishonourable and vile.

VAGUIN. How rational! All the same, it's the soul of a slave that speaks in your voice. You're sacrificing yourself – and for what? For a man who breaks life down into its minutest fragments in the crass hope of finding its origins . . . it's

absurd! He works not for freedom, not for beauty and joy,
but for anti-life. And he has no need of your sacrifice.

ELYENA. Calm down, my dear! I said nothing about a
sacrifice . . . Anyway I've no real reason to be sure of the
strength of your feelings . . .

VAGUIN. You are not sure of my love?

ELYENA. Let's just say, I'm not sure of . . . myself.

Enter LISA.

VAGUIN. You're being very cold.

ELYENA. I'm being candid.

LISA. Pavel's been disturbed all day long today.

ELYENA. By whom?

LISA. Everybody. Nanny, the blacksmith, the landlord . . .
everybody.

ELYENA. Did it upset him?

LISA. I think it did.

ELYENA. How tiresome.

VAGUIN *goes out on the terrace.*

LISA. Forgive me, Elyena, but you pay terribly little attention
to him.

ELYENA. He's never complained to me.

LISA (*getting up*). Perhaps because it's no good complaining to
you?

LISA *exits to her room upstairs.*

ELYENA (*gently*). Lisa! Again you're . . . Lisa, listen to me,
you're wrong . . .

LISA *doesn't answer.* ELYENA *looks after her, shrugs, and
walks, frowning, to the terrace door.* FIMA *comes out of the
dining room.*

FIMA. Madam!

ELYENA. M'm? What do you want?

FIMA. When you was outside Melanya Bovisovna come in and
she say . . .

Pause. ELYENA *looks at her thoughtfully.*

ELYENA. Well? What did she say?

FIMA. At warn't a proper thing to say.

ELYENA. If it was improper, don't say it.

FIMA. *Watch your lady*, she say. Meaning you, Ma'am.

ELYENA. What's that? Oh, you're always inventing all kinds of nonsense, Fima . . . Out you go, please.

FIMA. At's not nonsense, Ma'am, honest! Watch her, she say, and that Mister Vaguin . . .

ELYENA (*quietly*). Get out!

FIMA. At's not my fault! Look you here, she gave me a rouble!

ELYENA. Out!

> FIMA *goes out quickly.* PROTASSOV *hurries out from behind the portière.*

PROTASSOV. What are you shouting about, Lena? Eh? Oh, it's your war with Fima, is it? She really is an extraordinary girl, you know. There's something peculiar about her skirts – catch on everything, knock things over, break things . . . I shall spend exactly . . . ten minutes with you! Give me some tea, will you? How about Dmitri, didn't he come?

ELYENA. He's on the terrace.

PROTASSOV. Is Lisa there too?

ELYENA. She's in her room.

PROTASSOV. You seem to be in a bad mood. M'm?

ELYENA. A bit tired.

PROTASSOV. How's the portrait coming on?

ELYENA. You ask me that every day.

PROTASSOV. Do I really? Ah, here's Dmitri – looking cross, too. Why?

VAGUIN. Oh, . . . you know . . . One day I shall do a painting of your garden . . . at this time of day, look . . . in this evening light.

PROTASSOV. And this is making you cross in advance?

VAGUIN. Is that a joke?

ELYENA. Tea?

PROTASSOV (*gets up*). You're both in a bad mood . . . I'm going into the kitchen, I want to look at my . . . pour me some more tea, Elyena, will you?

PROTASSOV *exits.*

VAGUIN. One day he's going to put you into a test tube, pour some acid over you, and observe your reactions.

ELYENA. Don't be facetious . . .

VAGUIN (*simply, sincerely*). I have never in my whole life experienced so powerful an emotion as my feeling for you. It both torments me and exalts me.

ELYENA. Really?

VAGUIN. When I'm in your presence I want to be better, more brilliant, more inspired than anyone else.

ELYENA. That's good. I'm very glad for you.

VAGUIN. Elyena Nikolaevna, you must believe me . . .

PROTASSOV *speaks from the dining room, then enters, carrying a metal vessel.*

PROTASSOV. Will you stop nagging, woman! And anyway, why a husband as well as a cook? Just take on a cook, as such . . . and leave me alone!

ANTONOVNA *follows him in.*

ELYENA. Nanny, I did ask you . . .

PROTASSOV. There you are, you old limpet!

PROTASSOV *exits.*

ELYENA. I asked you not to bother Pavel.

ANTONOVNA. And I ask you, young madam, – who is in charge in this house? Pashenka's busy, Lisa's an invalid, and you're out of the house for days at a time . . .

ELYENA. But Pavel is not to be pestered.

ANTONOVNA. Well, at's for you to do something about.

ELYENA. That's all I need, to have you start teaching me . . .

ANTONOVNA. What do I do, then, when I see the house going to wrack and ruin and Pashenka not getting no attention . . .

ELYENA (*gently*). Nanny, please will you go?

ANTONOVNA. Very well, Ma'am. But even the General's lady never sent me out of the room.

ANTONOVNA *exits, insulted.* ELYENA *gets up and walks about the room in agitation.* VAGUIN *watches her with a slightly mocking smile.*

ELYENA. Do you find that amusing?

VAGUIN. A little brush with stupidity is always amusing . . . (*Heatedly.*) You must leave this house! You were made for a beautiful free life . . .

ELYENA (*thoughtfully*). Is such a life possible at all . . . when we're surrounded on all sides by barbarians? It's strange – the bigger the man, the more pettiness there is around him . . . just as the wind sweeps all sorts of trash up against the wall of a high building . . .

PROTASSOV *comes in, pale and distressed. There is something childish and helpless about him. Disarmingly candid, he talks in a low voice, as if guilty.*

ELYENA. What is it, Pavel? What's the matter?

PROTASSOV. It's deoxidised. Reduced. Do you understand? You know – gone sour. And yet . . . the experiment was scrupulously prepared . . . I took everything into account . . .

PROTASSOV *looks at his wife, appearing not to see her. He goes over to the table, sits down, drums his fingers nervously. Takes a notebook from his pocket, draws something quickly with a pencil. He is completely absorbed in this activity.* VAGUIN *silently presses* ELYENA's *hand, and goes out.*

ELYENA (*in a low voice*). Pavel . . . (*Louder.*) Dear Pavel are you very upset?

PROTASSOV (*through his teeth*). Wait . . . Where did it go wrong?

CURTAIN

Act Two

To the right, the wall of the house and a wide terrace with a balustrade. Some of the posts of the balustrade have fallen out. On the terrace are two tables, one a large dining table, the other, in the corner, a small one on which are scattered dice and lotto. The far side of the terrace is covered with an awning. An old green trellis – behind which is the garden – runs the whole length of the yard down to the fence at the end. Evening. Round the corner of the terrace come CHEPURNOY *and* NAZAR.

NAZAR. So it's nothing to worry about? It'll pass?

CHEPURNOY. That's right.

NAZAR. At's good. Even though she's only a stupid old horse, she cost money . . . Paid six hundred roubles for her seven years ago, and there's all the hay she's eaten since . . . But if she's not going to get better, you tell me, and I'll sell her.

CHEPURNOY. Why? You think a change of owners will improve her health?

NAZAR. Ah, that won't be my affair then, will it? Er – Doctor?

CHEPURNOY. What?

NAZAR. I got a ticklish little favour to ask you, only I don't quite know how to put it.

CHEPURNOY (*lighting a cigarette*). Put it briefly.

NAZAR. Always highly advisable, yes. This small kindness, if you would have the magnanity to follow me . . .

CHEPURNOY. More briefly.

NAZAR. . . . touches upon Mr. Protassov . . .

CHEPURNOY. H'm. Well?

NAZAR. My son, do you see, has been studying industry at the commercial institute, and he says as how chemistry, somehow, is making great strides these days, at the forefoot of progress that is, and I can see for myself, can't I, how soaps an parfumes an toiletries of ivry kind are moving fast, showing good profits . . .

CHEPURNOY. Come on. More briefly yet.

MISHA *looks round the corner.*

NAZAR. That I can't, not no how. The enterprise is highly elaborated, sir. Take vinegar, for example. Essences of all sorts, multitudinous things . . . An I look at Mr. Protassov here, at uses up materials and time to no profit, the which result is, a man is bound to think, at'll be all used up an spent out soon. And so – you have a talk with him, sir.

CHEPURNOY. A talk about vinegar?

NAZAR. A general talk. You pile it on about how he's soon going to find himself without means . . . and now here's me, wanting to propose a little deal with him. I'll set him up with a factory, and he can do his work making some useful commodity. If he's got no money to put into the partnership, at's all right. I'll take his promise for it at a fair rate.

CHEPURNOY (*smiling*). How kind.

NAZAR. At's a very soft heart I have! Here you are – I see a man stirring an stirring to no profit, straight way I want to set him up in business! And then again, he's a gentleman, a man of note! Oh yes. For the birthday of his lady wife, sir, he made a firework – my Lord! – a work of high art, at was! So you will have a talk with him? Eh?

FIMA *appears on the terrace, preparing the tea.*

CHEPURNOY. I will.

NAZAR. As I see it, sir, you'll be doing him a great lucrament. Humble respects, Doctor, your honour.

CHEPURNOY. Goodbye. (*To* FIMA.) Where are the ladies and gentlemen?

FIMA. The master's in his room, sir. The mistress is in the garden . . . with Mr. Vaguin. Elizaveta Fyodorovna's there too.

CHEPURNOY. I'll go into the garden then.

MISHA *comes quickly round the corner.*

MISHA. Excuse me . . . I don't have the pleasure of knowing your name . . .

CHEPURNOY. Does it matter? I don't know yours either.

MISHA. Mikhail Nazarov Vygrusov – at your service.

CHEPURNOY. Why?

MISHA (*patronisingly*). That's just something we say out of politeness. I was an accidental witness to your conversation with my father.

CHEPURNOY. I observed the accident. Tell me – why are your legs twitching like that?

MISHA. From impatience. I'm a man in a hurry . . .

CHEPURNOY. Oh? Where are you hurrying off to?

MISHA. Eh? What? No, I mean, in general, I'm a lively character altogether.

CHEPURNOY. Ah, I see. Well, goodbye.

MISHA. No, please, I wanted to tell you . . .

CHEPURNOY. Tell me what?

MISHA. About the Guv'nor's proposal. It was my idea, you see, only he didn't explain it to you very well . . .

CHEPURNOY. Oh, I don't know. Seemed clear enough to me.

MISHA. Perhaps you'd do me the honour of being my guest this evening at nine o'clock at the Paris restaurant on the corner of Trinity . . .?

CHEPURNOY. No, do you know, I shan't do even you that honour.

MISHA. That's very sad.

CHEPURNOY (*with a sigh of relief*). For me too . . .

> CHEPURNOY *exits to the garden.* MISHA *looks after him contemptuously.*

MISHA. Ignorant quack!

FIMA. Ah, there there! Won't they even talk to you then?

MISHA. You know what I could do with you, Fima?

FIMA. Nothing, at's whàt.

MISHA. How 'bout if I go and announce you really stole that ring I gave you? That policeman's a friend of mine, the sergeant.

FIMA. At don't scare me. He's courting me, the sergeant.

MISHA. All the worse for you then . . . No, Fima, come on, let's talk serious. Twenty five a month and an apartment –

how about that?

FIMA. Get away! I'm an honest girl.

MISHA. You're a fool, at's what you are. No, listen – I got a friend, Zotikov, handsome and rich he is – you want me to introduce you?

FIMA. You're too late! I already got two letters from him! How about that!

MISHA. You never! I don't . . . why, the dirty pig! Honestly, the way some people . . . What a rotten cheat! An him swearing he never . . . Well! (*Spits.*) Ah, but now you, Fima, you're a lovely girl and I swear I'd marry you tomorrow if only I didn't have to marry money.

FIMA (*softly*). Here they come now . . .

LISA *and* CHEPURNOY *appear from the garden.*

LISA (*to* MISHA). What do you want?

MISHA. I was just impressing upon your maid here how important it is not to empty chemicals out of the window into the garden . . . the vegetation suffers, you know, and moreover these are dangerous days already, with the cholera spreading, as perhaps you've heard . . .

CHEPURNOY. Farewell, young man.

MISHA. Always at your service, sir . . .

MISHA *exits quickly.*

LISA. What a wonderfully brash young man!

FIMA *goes into the house.*

CHEPURNOY. And there's my learned friend, trying to create a living organism in a test tube, and what is the point of that when all about him is the appalling evidence of what an organism can develop into. If it comes to that, look at me, another fully developed organism – and what's the point of me?

LISA. You're in a difficult mood today. Let's finish our game . . . sit down. I'll go on where we left off . . . Six. Twenty-three.

CHEPURNOY. I have a ten . . . twenty-nine.

LISA. You know, I don't understand you . . . eight, thirty-one . . . you're so healthy and strong . . .

CHEPURNOY. Seven, thirty-six . . .

LISA. And yet you're not interested in anything, you don't do anything . . . five, thirty-six . . . Every day life seems to become more difficult . . .

CHEPURNOY. Thirty-six?

LISA. . . . hatred everywhere, and so little love . . .

CHEPURNOY. Ten, forty-one . . .

LISA. And yet there's so much you could contribute, with your work . . . your useful, difficult work . . . eight, I've got, makes forty-four . . .

CHEPURNOY. I'm already forty, you know . . . And seven, forty-eight . . .

LISA. Forty? That's nothing! Ten, fifty-four . . .

CHEPURNOY. And you've spoilt me dreadfully . . . three, fifty-one . . .

LISA. Spoilt you? I have?

CHEPURNOY. All of you, yes. Your brother, Elyena Nikolaevna, you . . .

LISA. Eight . . . I'm out. Let's start again, only don't let's count aloud this time, it gets in the way of the conversation . . . Tell me how we've spoilt you.

CHEPURNOY. Well, you know, before I came here, I approached everything with great curiosity . . .

LISA. With interest?

CHEPURNOY. Ay, if you like, with interest. I was curious to know everything, about everything . . . If I saw a new book, I'd read it, I'd want to know what was new about it, apart from the cover . . . If I saw a man being beaten in the street, I'd stop . . . to see whether he was being beaten hard or not . . . and even sometimes might ask why he was being beaten. And, you know, I studied veterinary surgery with enormous interest.

ANTONOVNA *appears in the doorway.*

ANTONOVNA. Lisanka, have you taken your drops?

LISA. Yes, yes.

ANTONOVNA. Samovar's on the boil, but there's no one at table . . . I don't know . . .

ANTONOVNA *exits to the garden.*

CHEPURNOY. In fact, I looked at everything with great curiosity, and saw that life was very messily arranged . . . People are stupid, you know, and greedy, and I saw that I was cleverer and better than most of them . . . I enjoyed discovering that, and my soul was at peace, even though I could see quite clearly that a man's life was often worse than a dog's life, certainly worse than a horse's. But I explained that by the obvious fact that a man is generally stupider than a dog or a horse.

LISA. Why do you talk like that? You don't believe it, do you?

CHEPURNOY. That was how I lived and thought, and things weren't too bad for me. Then I came across you . . . all of you. I saw one person with his head buried in his science, another raving about vermilion and ochre, and a third pretending that she's a happy, rational being . . . and saw that all of you had once taken a quick, deep look at the world outside and in your hearts were carrying . . . the germ of tragedy.

LISA. But how did we spoil you? Game.

CHEPURNOY. It's difficult to say. At first I enjoyed being with you all so much that I even stopped drinking. I was drunk enough on your conversation. And then, somehow . . . I lost my curiosity, I became restless and fretful. I have lost my peace of mind.

ANTONOVNA *comes in from the garden.*

ANTONOVNA. You should be having your tea.

PROTASSOV *calls from indoors.*

PROTASSOV. Is the tea ready? Oh, good.

He comes out.

Aha! A fellow scientist!

CHEPURNOY. Hello, professor.

PROTASSOV. Is Lyena in the garden?

LISA. Yes.

PROTASSOV. I'll go and call her . . . You're going to lose.

CHEPURNOY. I already have.

PROTASSOV. You're a splendid colour today, Lisa. And your
eyes are nice and clear. That's good.

> PROTASSOV *exits into the garden.*

LISA (*with displeasure*). Why does he always talk to me as if I
were a sick child?

CHEPURNOY. He talks to everyone like that if they're not
interested in protoplasms.

LISA. But they all talk to me like that . . . everyone tries to
remind me that I'm ill.

CHEPURNOY. If you could forget it, so would they.

LISA. Go on with what you were saying . . . about becoming
fretful . . . Why?

CHEPURNOY. Yes . . . and somehow . . . awkward . . . as if
the mechanism of my soul had somehow become rusty.
Elizaveta Fyodorovna, it all seems so absurd to me, and if
you don't help me . . .

LISA. Dear Boris Boris'ich, please stop! I need help myself.
I'm a cripple, a monster . . .

CHEPURNOY (*calmly*). I shall simply die like a fly on a
dunghill.

LISA (*jumping up*). Stop it, you must stop it, you're tormenting
me, can't you see that?

CHEPURNOY (*alarmed*). No, please, forgive me, I won't go on!
I'll be quiet . . . do calm down, please!

LISA. Oh God, I feel so painfully sorry for everyone . . .
helpless and lonely!

> *Pause.*

CHEPURNOY. Once upon a time . . . I used to sleep very well.
But these days, you know, I lie there at night with my eyes
wide open and staring, and fantasise like a love-sick student
– a first year student at that. I want to do something – well,
you know, something heroic, something ennobling and

grand! But I can't think what. All that comes to me is this
image of a huge angry river, with ice floes floating down it,
and on one of the floes . . . there's a piglet! A small, light
red pigling, sitting on the ice and squealing and squealing!
So of course I launch myself into the cataract! Down and
down I go, in the ice-cold water, fighting for breath,
struggling to the surface, thrashing my way, battered by
ice, to the floe where the pigling sits . . . and I rescue that
piglet! Bring it safely to shore! And, do you know – nobody
wants it! Nobody wants to know about it! It's such a shame!
I have to eat that rescued piglet all by myself. With apple
sauce, of course.

LISA (*laughing*). That's funny.

CHEPURNOY. Enough to make you cry . . .

> ELYENA, PROTASSOV *and* VAGUIN *are approaching from
> the garden.*

LISA. Shall I pour out the tea?

CHEPURNOY. Why not? What else is there to do? All the
same, you should marry me, you know, Elizaveta Fyodorovna. Shouldn't we sit out our time on earth together,
matching groan for groan?

LISA. The way you joke . . . it's so harsh and strange.

CHEPURNOY (*calmly*). Still it's worth thinking about . . .
what else is there to do . . . for you and me?

LISA (*fearfully*). Sh'sh, be quiet!

ELYENA. Well, yes, it is beautiful, I agree, but it has no
depth, no real meaning . . . and the subject matter is
accessible to so few . . .

VAGUIN. Art has always belonged only to the few. That's its
pride.

ELYENA. That's its tragedy.

VAGUIN. Popular opinion has it that way, yes – which alone
would be enough to make me oppose it.

ELYENA. Do stop posing! The purpose of art is to enno-
ble . . .

VAGUIN. Art has no purpose.

PROTASSOV. Dmitri, nothing in this world is without purpose.

CHEPURNOY. As long as you don't include the world itself . . .

ELYENA. Dmitri Sergeyich, we all know life is difficult. We get tired of living sometimes, when everything seems so ugly and brutal and there's nowhere to go to rest one's soul. Of course I know beauty is rare, but if you can find it, true beauty lights up the soul like the sun suddenly bursting through the clouds on a dark, grey day . . . If only everybody could learn to understand and love beauty they'd build a whole ethic around it . . . they'd judge their actions purely in terms of beauty and ugliness . . . and then life itself would become beautiful!

PROTASSOV. That's wonderful, Lyena!

VAGUIN. Everybody! What on earth have I got to do with 'everybody.' No, I'll sing my song for my song's own sake, loudly, alone, and for no one but me!

ELYENA. That's enough of that! What do you think words are for? No, what art must reflect is man's eternal striving towards the distance, towards the heights . . . when I can sense the presence of this striving in an artist, when I feel he believes in the sunlike power of beauty, then his picture, his book, his sonata will have real meaning for me, will become dear to me . . . he'll have sounded a harmonious chord in my soul, and if I'm tired I shall feel rested and ready again for life and work and happiness!

PROTASSOV. Splendid, Lyena!

ELYENA. You know, sometimes I imagine a painting like this. A ship comes sailing across a boundless sea. Green, angry, foaming waves suck greedily at the hull. And there, up on the prow, I see a group of figures – strong, powerful men . . . There they stand, with smiles on their bold, open faces, gazing ahead . . . far ahead into the distance, towards their goal – and ready to perish calmly, if need be, in the attempt to get there . . . That's all there is in the picture!

VAGUIN. You've got something there, you know . . .

PROTASSOV. Listen . . .

ELYENA. People like these would walk under a scorching sun

across the desert's yellow sands . . .

LISA (*quietly, involuntarily*). It's red, the sand . . .

ELYENA. It doesn't matter. These would have to be really outstanding men, courageous and proud, unshakeable in their determination . . . and simple, of course, as everything great is simple . . . A picture like that could make me feel proud of mankind, proud of the artist who created it . . . it would remind me of all the great men who have helped us to move on, so far from the animals, and who are still leading us forward towards . . . full humanity.

VAGUIN. Yes, I see, you have got something . . . beautiful!

> YAKOV TROSHIN *appears on the terrace and, unnoticed, stands there open-mouthed.*

Damned if I won't try that!

PROTASSOV. Yes, Dmitri, of course – paint it! Lyena, you're a clever girl, you know! All this is something new in you, isn't it?

ELYENA. How would you know whether it's new or old?

TROSHIN. L-ladies and gentlemen!

> *They all turn to look at him.*

I waited a long time for you to finish your interesting conversation, but – er – quite simply – I'm obliged to interrupt you!

CHEPURNOY. What is it? Are you looking for somebody?

TROSHIN. Ah! I recognise a Ukrainian because – er – quite simply – I was in the Ukraine myself. And I play the flute.

CHEPURNOY. What d'you want?

TROSHIN. Allow me, please! All in order. Let me introduce myself! Civil Officer Seventh Class Yakov Troshin, former deputy station master of Log . . . that same Yakov Troshin, indeed, whose wife and child were run over by a train. Some childerkin remain to me, but – er – quite simply – no wife. And so, and so . . . with whom have I the honour?

PROTASSOV. Wonderful the way drunks talk.

LISA (*reproachfully*). Pavel! Really!

ELYENA. What can we do for you?

TROSHIN (*bowing*). Madam – excuse me! (*He holds out his foot, which is wearing a slipper.*) Sans shoeses – fortune being adverse – Madam! Tell me this – where does Yegor the blacksmith reside? Yegor, yes – I forget his surname. perhaps he has no surname. And perhaps, even, that was a vision I had last night?

ELYENA. Round the corner . . . in the servants' wing, in the basement.

TROSHIN. R-r-r-remerci, madam! I've been looking for him all day. Can hardly stand on my . . . feet? yes, feet. Round the corner, eh? bon voyage! It was only yesterday I had the good fortune to make my acquaintance . . . er – he had the? Yes. And now here I am going to visit him! Round the corner? And, er – quite simply – until our next enjoyable meeting!

PROTASSOV. What a comedian! Sans-shoeses, eh?

LISA. Sh-sh, Pavel!

TROSHIN *walks along, swaying and muttering to himself.*

TROSHIN. Aha? Thought he was a nobody, did you? Ah, no, it's Yakov Troshin, that's who, that knows the proprieties, ah, quite simply – Yakov Troshin!

TROSHIN *disappears.*

PROTASSOV. Wasn't he funny, don't you think, Lyena?

LISA. Where do people like that appear in your painting, Lyena?

ELYENA. They will not be there.

PROTASSOV. They'll stick themselves on to the bottom of the ship like seaweed and barnacles . . .

VAGUIN. And slow it down . . .

LISA. Are they condemned to death, Elyena? Alone and helpless . . . are these people bound to die?

ELYENA. They're dead already, Lisa.

VAGUIN. And we're alone too, just as much as them, alone in the dark chaos of life . . .

PROTASSOV. Those people are just dead cells in a living organism . . .

LISA. Oh, you're all so cruel, I can't listen to you! You're all cruel and blind . . .

> LISA *goes into the garden.* CHEPURNOY *gets up slowly and follows her.*

PROTASSOV (*in a low voice*). You know, Lyena, one really can't talk about anything when she's around. Whatever it is she'll always bring it back to her own sick, dark corner . . .

ELYENA. Yes, it makes things difficult . . . She seems to live in fear of being alive . . .

VAGUIN. Elyena Nikolaevna! There's one man standing all by himself in the prow of your ship . . . He has the expression of someone who has buried all his past hopes on the shore he has left behind him . . . but his eyes are on fire with a great resolution . . . He is sailing on towards the creation of new hopes . . . alone among the lonely . . .

PROTASSOV. And let there be no storm – or, no! No, let's have a storm, but over there, where the ship's heading, the sun is breaking through, laying a bright path across the water! Call your picture, 'To the Sun' – to the source of all life!

VAGUIN. Yes, to the source of life . . . and there in the distance, among the clouds, radiant as the sun, the face of a woman . . .

PROTASSOV. What do you want a woman there for? But among those passengers of yours you could have Pasteur, Lavoisier, Darwin . . . anyway, I'm talking too much, I must go.

> PROTASSOV *exits quickly into the house.*

VAGUIN (*with sincereity*). My dear, I'm bound to you more powerfully with every day that passes . . . I'm ready to pray to you . . .

PROTASSOV (*calling, off*). Dmitri – just a moment!

ELYENA. Thou shalt not bow down thyself to them, or serve them.

VAGUIN. I shall paint that picture for you, you'll see! And its colours will sing a majestic hymn to freedom and beauty . . .

PROTASSOV. Dmitri!

ELYENA. Go on, my dear.

> VAGUIN *exits.* ELYENA *walks thoughtfully up and down the* terrace. CHEPURNOY's *voice comes from the garden.*

CHEPURNOY (*calmly*). But it can't be any other way . . . When he speaks, he's a man, but when he acts, he's an animal.

LISA (*unhappily*). Oh, but when . . . when . . .

> *Their voices fade.* MELANYA *enters, walking across the yard.*

MELANYA. Ah, Elyena Nikolaevna, you're at home!

ELYENA (*coldly*). Does that surprise you?

MELANYA. No – why should it? Good evening.

ELYENA. I'm sorry, but before I shake hands with you . . .

MELANYA. Wha-a-at . . .?

ELYENA. I have to ask you – let's be completely open with each other – you made a proposal to the maid . . .

MELANYA (*quickly*). Oh, the little Judas!

ELYENA (*after a pause*). It's true, then? Melanya Borisovna, do you understand what . . . what your action has to be called?

MELANYA (*sincerely, passionately*). Yes . . . yes, I understand. That doesn't matter. Do let's be completely open . . . Listen. You're a woman, you . . . love, perhaps you'll understand me . . .

ELYENA. Quietly. Your brother's in the garden.

MELANYA. I don't care. Now, listen – I love Pavel Fyodorich . . . There. I love him so much, I'd be happy to be his cook, his servant . . . And you love too – Oh yes, I can see – you love that artist . . . You don't need Pavel Fyodorich. Give him to me! Shall I go down on my knees? I'll kiss your feet . . .

ELYENA (*amazed*). What – what are you saying?

MELANYA. Doesn't matter! I've got lots of money – I'll have a laboratory built for him, I'll build him a tower! I'll serve him, I won't let even the wind touch him, I'll guard his door day and night! You see? What is he to you? But I love him as if . . . as if . . . he was God's best angel!

ELYENA. Do calm down! No, wait, I can't have understood you correctly . . .

MELANYA. Och, my dear good lady! You're clever, you're noble and pure, but me . . . My life has been squalid and hard . . . I've only mixed with . . . low people . . . and there's Pavel . . . Pavel . . . like an innocent babe . . . sublime! At his side I'd be a queen – a slave to him, but a queen to everyone else! And my soul . . . my soul at last . . . could breathe! I want . . . an *innocent* man, a pure man – do you understand me? There.

ELYENA (*moved*). It's . . . difficult for me . . . to understand. We must talk a lot more. My God . . . how unhappy you must be!

MELANYA. Oh yes, yes, you can understand, you must! That's why I'm telling you everything like this, all at once . . . I know you'll understand . . . And don't make a fool of me – perhaps I could become a whole person too, if you don't make a fool of me.

ELYENA. I've no reason to make a fool of you. I can feel the pain in your heart. Come to my room with me. Come along.

MELANYA. What . . .? What are you saying? Is it possible that you . . . that you're really good . . . as well?

ELYENA *takes* MELANYA *by the hand.*

ELYENA. Believe me . . . believe me, if people are sincere with each other – they'll understand each other!

MELANYA (*following her*). Do I believe you or don't I? I don't know. Your words are clear enough, but I don't think I understand your feelings . . . Are you good? Or not? There you are – I'm afraid to believe in goodness – I haven't seen any of it – and me, myself – I'm a dark person, a bad person . . . My soul's been washed in a sea of tears, but I'm still dark . . .

They exit. ROMAN *looks round the corner, with an axe in his hand.* LISA *and* CHEPURNOY *come in from the garden.* ANTONOVNA *appears from the house.*

ANTONOVNA. Just look at that . . . at's all run off now . . . running about like a lot of lunatics . . . Lisanka, why are you always wandering about?

LISA. Nanny, do stop . . .

ANTONOVNA. No call to be cross . . . you've not got the strength for it . . .

She exits, grumbling, into the house.

CHEPURNOY. Bustling old busybody . . . she must be very fond of you.

LISA. No. It's just habit. She's been looking after us for more than thirty years . . . she's obstinate, and dreadfully stupid . . . It's funny, you know . . . Ever since I can remember there's been good music played in this house, and good talk . . . the best thoughts in the world blazing out like beacons . . . and yet Nanny's never got a scrap kinder or cleverer as a result . . .

PROTASSOV *and* VAGUIN *come out of the house.*

PROTASSOV (*to* VAGUIN). You see, when it becomes possible to spin these fibres – the chemically processed wood fibres – you and I will find ourselves wearing waistcoats made of oak, topcoats made of birch . . .

VAGUIN. You and your wooden fantasies . . .! Stop it, it's a bore!

PROTASSOV. Oh you – you're a bore yourself!

CHEPURNOY. Ah, there's my sister's umbrella . . . Professor! Yesterday Melanya asked me what was the relationship between a hypothesis and a molecule. I told her that a molecule is the granddaughter of a hypothesis.

PROTASSOV (*laughing*). Why did you tell her that? She takes such a naive and lively interest in it all . . .

CHEPURNOY. Naive? H'm. But monads and molecules, surely, are the foundlings of science? Aren't they? Ah well, perhaps I muddled the genealogy.

LISA. There you are – whenever you talk about your sister there's contempt and malice . . .

CHEPURNOY. Oh, really, not malice, surely?

LISA (*agitated*). I tell you, there's more and more hatred gathering in the world, more and more cruelty . . .

PROTASSOV. Lisa! Are you spreading your black wings again?

LISA. You be quiet, Pavel. You can't see anything – you look at everything through a microscope . . .

CHEPURNOY. And you . . . through a telescope. You shouldn't, you know. The naked eye is much better.

LISA (*disturbed, neurotic*). You're all blind! Open your eyes! Everything you live by, your thoughts, your feelings – they're like little flowers in a forest of darkness and putrefaction . . . There's so few of you, you're not even noticeable . . .

VAGUIN (*coldly*). What do you notice, then?

LISA. It's the millions on the earth that are noticeable, not the hundreds! And among the millions, hatred is growing. You're so drunk with fine words and fine ideas, you don't see this. But I see it – I've seen hatred bursting out in the streets, people wild, enraged, taking pleasure in destroying each other . . . and one day . . . one day . . . all that malice will sweep down over you . . .

PROTASSOV. It all seems frightening now, Lisa, because, look, there's a storm gathering, it's a muggy day, and it's affecting your nerves.

LISA (*imploring*). Don't talk to me about my illness!

PROTASSOV. But just think, Lisa – why should anyone hate me . . . or him . . . Who? And what for?

LISA. Who? All the people you've moved so far away from . . .

VAGUIN (*with irritation*). What, are we supposed to – to move *back* – for their sake?

LISA. And what for? For your alienation from them, for your not caring about their hard, inhuman lives, for the fact that you're well-fed and well-dressed . . . Hatred is blind, but you shine even in the dark . . . it will see you.

VAGUIN. The role of Cassandra suits you.

PROTASSOV (*excited*). Hold on, Dmitri! (*To* LISA.) You're wrong, you know! We're doing something great, something

important! He's enriching life by creating beauty, and I'm
analysing creation itself . . . and one day the people you're
talking about will understand and appreciate our work . . .

VAGUIN. It's all the same to me whether they appreciate it or
not.

PROTASSOV. You mustn't take such a gloomy view of them
They're better than you think, more reasonable . . .

LISA. You don't know anything, Pavel, not a thing . . .

PROTASSOV. Yes I do, I do know, I can see!

ELYENA *and* MELANYA *appear on the terrace as he starts
talking. Both are excited.*

I see how life grows and develops, how it yields up its
mysterious, wonderful secrets to the stubborn probing of
thought. I see myself already as master of so much – and I
know that man will one day be master of it all! Everything
that grows . . . becomes more complex. People are always
raising their expectations – of life, and of themselves. Once
upon a time, an insignificant, formless piece of albuminic
acid, probed by a ray of the sun, suddenly burst into life!
and multiplied, and went on to make an eagle . . . a lion
. . . a man! And the time will come when from us, from
ordinary people like us – from *all* the people – a perfect
organism will spring into life – humanity itself! Humanity
yes! And then every single cell of humanity will have a past
full of the great conquests of rational thought – yes, our
work! The present is . . . the freedom to work together,
united in the pleasure of work . . . and the future – I can see
it, I can feel it – is beautiful! Mankind, growing and
maturing – that is life, that's its meaning!

LISA (*distressed*). If only I could believe that . . . if only I had
your faith!

LISA *takes a small book from her pocket, and rapidly writes in
it,* MELANYA *gazes at* PROTASSOV, *almost as if she were
praying. The effect is rather comic.* ELYENA'*s face, at first
rather severe, breaks into a sad smile.* VAGUIN *listens,
animated.* CHEPURNOY *has bowed low over the table so that
his face is not visible.*

VAGUIN. The role of poet suits you.

PROTASSOV. The fear of death – that's what stops people being bold, beautiful and free! It hangs over us like a black cloud, covering the earth with shadows. From it, phantoms are born. It makes people wander away from the straight path to freedom, the rational highroad of experiment. It drives them to make hasty, ugly guesses about the meaning of life. It frightens off reason so that thinking goes wrong. But we are people of the sun, children of the sun, of the radiant source of all life. Born of the sun, we can conquer that dark fear of death! We *are* the children of the sun! It's the sun which burns in our blood, which gives birth to our proud, fiery thoughts, which lights up the shadowy corners of our dark confusion . . . It's . . . an ocean of energy . . . of beauty and joy, that . . . intoxicates the soul!

LISA (*jumping up*). Oh, yes, Pavel, that's so – so *good*! Children of the sun . . . So . . . and me too? Me too? Quickly, Pavel – yes? Me too?

PROTASSOV. Yes, yes, of course! Everybody!

LISA. Really? Oh, that's wonderful! I can't tell you how wonderful it is! Children of the sun . . . is that right? Oh, but I'm cut in two, my soul's torn apart! Here, listen.

She recites with her eyes closed, then reads.

On powerful wings the eagle sails,
I long to join him in the sky.
I try, but all my trying fails.
A daughter of sad earth am I.

Bold is your logic, bright your dreams.
I love them, but can not forget
Dark burrows where the blind crowd teems.
The sun's rays have not reached them yet.

Oppressed by poverty, they need
Our love and care; they stand between
Your dream and mine, an alien breed,
A screen through which no light is seen.

Half way between the burrow and the bird,
How can I draw them skyward with a word?

All look at her for a few moments in silence. VAGUIN *doesn't like her excitement.*

PROTASSOV. Lisa, that's really amazing! I didn't know you wrote poetry?

ELYENA. You recited that very nicely, Lisa. And I understood every word . . .

VAGUIN. Please, everybody, listen to me – Elizaveta Fyodorovna, I know another poem about eagles. I think it might answer your question . . .

LISA. Say it, then!

VAGUIN. Like sparks that fret a cloud of smoke
We all are separate and lonely.
Each has a fire within us, only
The future is the fire we stoke.

For beauty, truth and freedom we
Serve in the sunset of today
That in tomorrow's sunrise may
The blind mole a proud eagle be.

PROTASSOV. Oh, well done, Dmitri! Splendid!

MELANYA (*delighted*). Heavens, how . . . perfect! Elyena Nikolaevna, you know . . . I understand her . . . I do understand . . . (*She weeps.*)

ELYENA. Do calm down . . . Don't cry.

LISA (*sadly*). There you all are, rejoicing . . . but it makes me sad, it's sad the way so many good thoughts flicker up and then disappear, like sparks in the night, not lighting up the road for anyone . . . It makes me sad.

MELANYA (*kissing* PROTASSOV's *hand*). Oh thank you, thank you, my radiant soul!

PROTASSOV (*embarrassed*). What are you doing! My hands might be dirty . . .

MELANYA. They could never be unclean.

LISA. Boris Boris'ich . . . what's the matter?

CHEPURNOY. Nothing . . .

LISA. What I said was good, wasn't it?

CHEPURNOY. You had the truth on your side . . .

LISA. I did?

MELANYA (*to* ELYENA). I shall take myself away . . . dearest heart!

MELANYA *goes into the house*, ELYENA *follows her*.

CHEPURNOY. But the beauty is on his . . .

VAGUIN. And which is better?

CHEPURNOY. Well . . . beauty is better . . . but truth is necessary.

LISA. And you? Which do you prefer?

CHEPURNOY. Oh . . . I don't know . . . perhaps a bit of both . . . in moderation . . .

ELYENA *comes out of the house*.

ELYENA. Pavel, Melanya Borisovna wants to say goodbye to you.

PROTASSOV. Lyena, why did she have to go and kiss my hand? It's stupid and unpleasant!

ELYENA (*with a smile*). You'll have to put up with it.

PROTASSOV (*going out*). She's got sloppy lips . . . What does she want?

PROTASSOV *goes into the house. A hysterical cry from* AVDOTIA *is heard from behind the corner of the terrace*.

AVDOTIA (*off*). You're lying, you bastard!

LISA (*shuddering*). What's that? Who is it?

AVDOTIA *runs into the yard*.

AVDOTIA. Missed, y' old devil!

YEGOR *comes in, carrying a heavy birch stick*.

YEGOR. Come here, I tell ya!

LISA. Oh my God, hide her, hide her!

AVDOTIA *runs up on the terrace*.

AVDOTIA. Oh good ladies, good sirs! at's after killing me!

ELYENA. Come in here – quickly!

AVDOTIA (*to* YEGOR). What's biting you, man?

AVDOTIA *goes into the house with* ELYENA.

CHEPURNOY. Och, it's that drunk again . . . (*To* LISA.) Why don't you go in?

LISA. For God's sake . . . for God's sake, stop him!

TROSHIN *comes round the corner.*

TROSHIN (*to* YEGOR). Yegor! Careful!

CHEPURNOY (*to* YEGOR). Get away from here!

VAGUIN. Yes, get rid of him!

PROTASSOV *comes running out of the house, followed by* MELANYA.

PROTASSOV. Yegor! You again . . .

YEGOR (*to* CHEPURNOY). You go to the devil yourself! At's my wife I want, give 'er back!

PROTASSOV. You're not in your right mind, Yegor . . .

TROSHIN. My dear sir, a wife belongs – er – quite simply – to her husband!

YEGOR. You can't hide 'er! I'll go and get 'er!

ROMAN *appears, looking sleepy. He stops behind* YEGOR.

ROMAN. Yegor. Stop your brawling.

CHEPURNOY. Away you go now.

LISA. Boris Boris'ich, he's got a club . . .

CHEPURNOY. Don't worry. You go in.

PROTASSOV. Yes, go on, Lisa.

YEGOR. You give 'er me! What you think you're doing? At's not your business!

MELANYA (*to* ROMAN). You – yardman, – call the police!

ROMAN. Yegor. I'm to call the police . . .

YEGOR. Master, listen here, I had a visitor . . .

TROSHIN. Er – quite simply – me!

YEGOR. A lettered man, a man with a soul . . .

TROSHIN. Absolutely true!

YEGOR. And the cow slapped him across the kisser with a wet rag!

TROSHIN. It's a fact. But not the kisser, Yegor – across the face.

PROTASSOV. My dear good fellow, come on – remember you're a human being!

YEGOR. Give 'er here!

VAGUIN. God, what a face!

MELANYA (*to* ROMAN). You, I told you, the police! Get hold of him, grab him!

ROMAN. Yegor, damn you, I shall have to . . .

YEGOR *comes up on to the terrace.*

YEGOR. Well, if you don't understand words . . .

LISA. Quick, run, he's coming! He'll kill her!

CHEPURNOY *goes to meet* YEGOR. *He speaks through his teeth.*

CHEPURNOY. Och, well, all right then. Hit me.

PROTASSOV. Lisa, go in . . .

PROTASSOV *forces* LISA *into the house.* MELANYA *follows.*

YEGOR. Get away, you.

YEGOR *raises his stick.* CHEPURNOY *looks straight into his eyes.*

CHEPURNOY. Go on, then.

YEGOR. I'll knock you down . . .

CHEPURNOY (*quietly*). No you won't, you dog.

YEGOR. Don't you get across me, sir!

CHEPURNOY. Use it, then. Go on.

YEGOR. You use it! (*He throws the stick down.*) There!

CHEPURNOY. Now, get out.

TROSHIN (*despairingly*). Yegor! Back off!

YEGOR (*retreating from the terrace*). You're a devil, sir!

CHEPURNOY (*contemptuously*). You're an animal.

TROSHIN (*to* VAGUIN). Bong shvoir, mongshieur! But the family hearth, sir, must always be inviolable . . .

VAGUIN. Beat it.

CHEPURNOY *goes down from the terrace, advancing on YEGOR.*

CHEPURNOY. Get . . . out! If there were no women here I'd have the pair of you . . .

TROSHIN *follows* YEGOR *off.*

TROSHIN. I submit to – er, quite simply – submit to coercion.

TROSHIN *disappears round the corner.* CHEPURNOY *comes back on to the terrace.*

CHEPURNOY. What a brute.

VAGUIN. Your own face was a study. I was lost in contemplation of it. Very expressive!

PROTASSOV (*coming out*). Have they gone? Have you seen them off?

LISA (*hurrying out*). He didn't hit you? Didn't touch you?

CHEPURNOY. Och, that's not so easy.

MELANYA *and* ELYENA *come out on to the terrace.*

PROTASSOV. God knows what we do now . . . I certainly shan't give him any more work . . . Look, Lyena, my hands are trembling . . .

VAGUIN. He might kill someone . . .

CHEPURNOY (*with a laugh*). Well, professor, what about brutes like that, then – are they children of the sun too?

LISA (*suddenly*). You were lying, Pavel! There isn't going to be anything like that . . . Life's full of horrible animals . . . Why do you talk about the joys of the future? Why? Why deceive us – yourself, everyone? You've left the real world so far behind you . . . you're out on your own, small and unhappy . . . Why can't you understand the real horror of life? You're surrounded by enemies, there are brutes on all sides . . . We must get rid of cruelty! We must get rid of hatred! Please, please, try to understand me, you must understand!

She is overcome by hysterics.

CURTAIN

Act Three

The setting is the same as for Act One. An overcast day. ELYENA *is sitting in an armchair by the window.* LISA *is walking about the room in agitation.*

ELYENA. You shouldn't excite yourself so.

LISA. I'm ill, I know, but my thoughts are healthy.

ELYENA. Did anyone say they were not?

LISA. I know what I say is ordinary and depressing. It bores you. You don't want to hear the truth . . . the tragic truth about life.

ELYENA. You exaggerate a great deal . . .

LISA. I don't! Look at the gulf that separates you from your cook . . .

ELYENA. Do you think it will go away if I stand on the edge and weep?

LISA. But how can you live calmly when there are people around you who don't understand you at all? I can't live like that . . . I'm afraid of people who don't understand me, that's what makes me ill . . . Elyena, sacrifices are needed! Do you understand? We must sacrifice ourselves . . .

ELYENA. All right, but freely, joyfully, in ecstasy and delight! But not by doing violence to oneself, Lisa! That's unworthy of a human being.

ANTONOVNA *enters from the dining room.*

ANTONOVNA. Elyena Nikolaevna . . .

LISA (*vexed*). What is it, Nanny?

ANTONOVNA. Now, now, it's not for you . . . The landlord's out there . . .

LISA. Oh well, let him wait . . . Go along, Nanny.

ANTONOVNA *exits.*

So I'm wrong?

ELYENA. I didn't say that . . .

LISA. Can't you see how lonely everyone is?

ELYENA. No . . . I don't feel that.

LISA. You just don't want to talk to me . . . Everyone's tired of me. You just want to enjoy life and close your eyes to anything nasty or frightening.

ELYENA. One can't force oneself to feel a certain way.

LISA. But you *do*! – life isn't good for you either, only you're too proud to admit it . . . even to yourself! I can see how things are between you and Pavel, you know.

ELYENA. We'll leave that, please.

LISA (*joyfully*). Ah! You see? It's too painful, isn't it?

ELYENA. No, but it's . . . distasteful.

LISA. It hurts, and you should let it hurt! It would revive you, wake you up a bit! You're lonely, Elyena, you're unhappy . . .

ELYENA. And you're delighted, aren't you? But there's something nasty in your delight, Lisa. What is it you want?

LISA. What do I want? (*Pause, fearfully.*) I don't know . . . I don't know . . . I'd like to have a real life, but I don't know how to . . . I can't! I don't feel I've got the right to live the way I'd like to . . . I would love to have someone who . . . to have a kindred soul . . . a soul. . . . mate. I need rest from my fears, and there's no one . . . no one . . .

ELYENA (*taking* LISA's *hand*). Forgive me . . . but surely . . . Boris . . .?

LISA. What right have I to . . .? I'm ill, aren't I? You all tell me so . . . you tell me so often, much too often! Let me go . . . I can't . . . about that . . . No, go away, let me go!

LISA *goes quickly to the door to her own room, and exits.* ELYENA, *with a deep sigh, walks about the room with her hands behind her head. Stops in front of her husband's portrait, gazes at it, biting her lip. Her hands drop.*

ELYENA (*in a half whisper*). Goodbye . . .

ANTONOVNA *enters.*

ANTONOVNA. Would it be all right now for the landlord . . .?

ELYENA. Oh . . . yes, all right.

ANTONOVNA (*exiting*). Go in, Nazar Avdeyich . . .

ANTONOVNA *exits and* NAZAR *enters.*

NAZAR. Goodly health to you, ma'am!

ELYENA (*nods*). What can I do for you?

NAZAR (*smirking, self-consciously*). Matter o' fact, ma'am, at's Pavel Fyodor'ich . . .

ELYENA. He's busy.

NAZAR. Ah, well, don't rightly know as I can put it to you . . .

ELYENA. Say what you have to say, and I'll tell him.

NAZAR. At's not a good subject for polite conversation . . .

ELYENA. As you like.

NAZAR. We-e-ell, at's all a same. Police do come, do you see, 'bout the smell . . . 'bout the cesspits and the like . . .

ELYENA (*frowning*). What's that got to do with my husband?

NAZAR. 'Course he's no worse than other folk . . . all sin alike . . . Still, on account of the cholera creeping, police do say there must be no smells, them not having looked into the fact that what is meant to have a smell will sure as God loves us *smell* . . . and they do talk of a fine, three hundred roubles, no less . . .

ELYENA (*with revulsion*). What is it you want?

NAZAR. A bit of advice, I thought, about maybe spraying some sort of chemistry against the smell.

ELYENA (*indignantly*). Oh, really, what do you . . . (*Controlling herself.*) Yes, well, I'll tell him . . . goodbye!

NAZAR. Straightway? Will you tell him straightway?

ELYENA (*going*). Nanny will give you his answer.

ELYENA *exits.* NAZAR *looks after her.*

NAZAR. Offended in her sensitivities, she is . . . High and mighty, aren't we? You wait, lady – I'll twist your tail!

NAZAR *exits.* PROTASSOV *and* ELYENA *appear from behind the portière.*

PROTASSOV. Oh, and Lyena, would you send for Yegor . . .

ELYENA. Yegor again?

PROTASSOV. How could we do without him, Lyena? He's so handy, and quick on the uptake. You should see the brazier he made me – it's a work of art! A really beautiful object . . . What a dull day. No sitting for you today?

ELYENA. No . . . When can I talk to you?

PROTASSOV. Please – not until this evening – but I'll be free this evening . . . Are you bored? Where's Dmitri?

ELYENA. No doubt he has other things to do besides entertaining your wife.

PROTASSOV (*missing her point*). M'm, yes, probably . . . You know, looking at you, recently, I've felt there's something different about you, something significant . . .

ELYENA. Really?

PROTASSOV. Yes, really . . . Well – now I must vanish in a puff of smoke . . .

PROTASSOV *exits to his rooms.* FIMA *enters.*

FIMA. Madam, please – will you let me go?

ELYENA. In the middle of the afternoon? But who'll serve tea?

FIMA. I mean, let me go for good . . . give me my cards.

ELYENA. Oh . . . very well, but first, would you please call Yegor?

FIMA. I won't go to Yegor's, Ma'am.

ELYENA. Why not?

FIMA. Because I won't, Ma'am.

ELYENA. Call Nanny.

FIMA. Can't. Nanny's gone for a walk. In the cemetery, she is.

ELYENA. I'll let you go when she comes back. Send me Roman . . . could you do that?

FIMA. Ah, that I could do, Ma'am. And you'll let me go today?

FIMA *exits.*

ELYENA. Very well.

CHEPURNOY *appears in the terrace doorway.*

CHEPURNOY. Why aren't your doors closed? Good afternoon!

ELYENA (*shaking hands*). I don't know . . . the servants seem to be . . . erratic today.

CHEPURNOY. Afraid of the cholera.

ELYENA. It seems to be spreading?

CHEPURNOY. It's running its course. Is Elizaveta Fyodorovna at home?

ELYENA. In her room.

CHEPURNOY. Ah yes? And how is she?

ELYENA. Well enough. Not up to much. As usual.

CHEPURNOY (*anxious*). Yes, yes. A tragic soul.

ELYENA. Boris Boris'ich . . . forgive me, I know it's nothing to do with me, but . . . do you mind . . . it's very important . . .

CHEPURNOY. Oh yes . . . What?

ELYENA. She told me you'd proposed to her . . .

CHEPURNOY (*quickly*). How? How did she tell you?

ELYENA. What do you mean – how?

CHEPURNOY. I mean – how did she look? Did she pull a face? Was she laughing at me?

ELYENA (*surprised*). How could you think that? She told me with joy.

CHEPURNOY. No. Is that true?

ELYENA. Certainly. With quiet joy. And strength.

ROMAN *appears in the terrace door.*

CHEPURNOY. I'm a fool. You know that? I'm a real ass!

ROMAN. Someone asking for me?

CHEPURNOY. No, not you, lad – it was myself I was scolding.

ELYENA. I sent for him . . . Roman, call the blacksmith, will you?

ROMAN. Yegor?

ELYENA. Yes.

ROMAN. Straightway?

ELYENA. Yes, yes.

ROMAN. All right.

ROMAN *exits.* CHEPURNOY *takes* ELYENA's *hand.*

CHEPURNOY (*joyfully*). Give me your hand, and let me . . .
there! . . . kiss it. You've given me a present. Joys as well as
sorrows come when least expected.

ELYENA. I'm sorry, I don't understand.

CHEPURNOY. Oh my God, don't you see? She told you with
joy that I'd asked her to marry me – with joy!

ELYENA. Yes, she did, I assure you.

CHEPURNOY (*triumphantly*). And yet she refused me!

ELYENA (*with a smile*). I'm sorry – it sounds so comic!

CHEPURNOY. Of course it's comic! You know, it's as I
thought – she won't marry me, not because she finds me
repulsive, but because she's afraid of her illness.

ELYENA. That's right, yes.

CHEPURNOY. Now I know what to do. I'll go to her like a
snowball rolling downhill . . . Well! What a piece of luck!
Luck is a great thing, you know!

ELYENA. You should take your tie off. She doesn't like
anything red.

CHEPURNOY (*smiling*). I put it on deliberately to tease her!
Doesn't matter now whether it's red or green . . . it no
longer matters! Can't go to her without a tie anyway . . .
(*Leaving.*) Thank you!

CHEPURNOY *exits.* YEGOR *appears in the dining room door,
bewildered, dishevelled.*

CHEPURNOY (*leaving*). Och, an old acquaintance! Here, give
me your hand! Peace, eh? That's the way! Oh, you Samson,
you!

CHEPURNOY *leaves.*

ELYENA. Just a moment. I ought to tell you . . .

YEGOR (*in a muffled voice*). Ma'am, wait . . .

ELYENA. What is it?

YEGOR. The wife. She's ill . . .

ELYENA. What's the matter with her?

YEGOR. Sicking up . . .

ELYENA (*anxiously*). How long for?

YEGOR. Since this morning, ma'am. She keeps calling for you.

Go fetch the lady, she do say, else I'll peg out.

ELYENA. Oh, why didn't you call me, you . . .

YEGOR. Account I was ashamed, Ma'am, after I be brawling here . . .

ELYENA. Oh, what nonsense . . . I'll go to her . . .

YEGOR. Wait, Ma'am . . . I'm afraid.

ELYENA. Why? What?

YEGOR. At could be the cholera.

ELYENA. Rubbish! There's nothing to be afraid of.

YEGOR (*asking, but almost demanding*). Elyena Nikolaevna – you'll cure her!

ELYENA. We must get the doctor . . . You go on now . . .

YEGOR. No doctor . . . don't believe in doctors! You, yourself, Ma'am . . .

PROTASSOV *enters.*

PROTASSOV. Aha, the gladiator's come, has he?

ELYENA (*quickly*). Pavel, his wife's sick . . .

PROTASSOV. There you are, you see, if you will beat her . . .

ELYENA. He thinks it's the cholera. I'll go to her, and you . . .

PROTASSOV (*anxiously*). You go . . .? No, Lyena, please . . . Why?

ELYENA. But why not?

PROTASSOV. But, Elyena, if it really is cholera, people can . . .

YEGOR *gives a muffled moan.*

YEGOR. Die of it. That right? So we're not people, then?

ELYENA. Stop it, Yegor . . . Pavel, you're being clumsy.

PROTASSOV. But you don't know anything about it, Lyena, you're not a doctor . . . It's no joke, cholera, it's dangerous!

YEGOR (*angrily*). And for them as are like to die, at's not dangerous?

PROTASSOV. Don't shout at me, Yegor!

ELYENA (*reproachfully*). Pavel! Come on, Yegor . . .

PROTASSOV. I'm coming too . . . You're being reckless, Lyena . . .

All three, led by YEGOR, *go into the dining room. Their voices can be heard.*

ELYENA. No, Pavel, go back and telephone for the trap, she may have to be moved.

PROTASSOV. It's the doctor that's needed down there, not you! What can you do?

He comes back, upset.

What can she do, in a case like this? Nanny! Wouldn't let me go with her, dammit! . . . Fima! Or Nanny! Are you all dead! Fima!

FIMA *comes running in.*

Here I am bawling my head off, while you're preening yourself in front of a mirror . . .

FIMA (*offended*). At's not true! I was cleaning the knives . . .

PROTASSOV. Well, leave the knives, I want you to go over to Yegor's . . .

FIMA (*decisively*). I'm not going down there.

PROTASSOV. Why not? Madam's gone there.

FIMA. All the same, sir!

PROTASSOV. But why?

FIMA. The cholera, sir!

PROTASSOV (*mimicking her*). Oh, the cholera, sir! But my wife's gone there, sir!

The door bell rings.

FIMA. The door bell, sir!

PROTASSOV. Yes, sir! Answer it, sir!

FIMA *runs off.*

S-s-s-s-s . . . hissing like a snake! Oh yes, dammit, the telephone . . .

Enter MELANYA.

PROTASSOV. Oh, hello, it's you. Have you heard the news? We've got cholera across the yard. Charming, isn't it? And

Elyena's gone down there to nurse them, how do you like that?

MELANYA. Oh dear, how awful, you've got it too! You know, my neighbour, the colonel – they took his cook away yesterday . . . And Elyena Nikolaevna's gone over there? Why ever did she do that?

PROTASSOV. Verily, verily, that is the mystery!

MELANYA. Why did you let her go?

PROTASSOV. Why? Don't know! . . . Oh, I've got to telephone!

PROTASSOV *runs into his own room.* FIMA *calls from the dining room.*

FIMA. Afternoon, Melanya Borisovna!

MELANYA (*disapprovingly*). Oh . . . hello, you beauty.

FIMA. There's a big favour I want to ask . . .

MELANYA. What's that?

FIMA. I'm getting married . . .

MELANYA. And so . . .?

FIMA. To a respectable man – a very respectable man!

MELANYA. Who is it?

FIMA. Your neighbour.

MELANYA (*starting in astonishment*). Not the colonel?

FIMA (*modestly*). No, Ma'am, how could I? It's Vassily Vassil'ich.

MELANYA. Oh no, not that old brute? Ugh! Why, he's nearly sixty, and all rheumatism! How can you, Efimia? On the other hand . . . a wee bit of treasure? Oh, I feel sorry for you, lass. Let him be, him and his money!

FIMA. I've already decided, M'm. It's all arranged.

MELANYA. Really? That's a pity. What do you want from me?

FIMA. I'm an orphan, M'm. Could you ever stand in as me mother, M'm?

MELANYA '*shows her a kukish*' – *a clenched fist with the thumb sticking up between the index and middle fingers.*

MELANYA. There you are – bite on that! How much did you

sell me to Elyena Nikolaevna for?

FIMA (*at a loss*). Me, M'm?

MELANYA. Yes, M'm, you, M'm! Well?

FIMA (*recovering her composure*). At's a pity. I thought seeing as how you once sold yourself to an older man . . .

MELANYA (*crushed*). What? What did you . . .

FIMA. . . . you might've helped me do that too . . .

MELANYA (*in a muffled voice*). Don't you dare . . .

FIMA (*calmly and brusquely*). After all, at's better to set yourself up like that than go on the streets, en't it? Least it's only with the one, not a hundred.

MELANYA (*horrified, quietly*). Go away . . . go on . . . I'll give . . . give you . . . give you some money . . . Go on, go away! I'll give you some . . .

FIMA. Thank you kindly, M'm! When? When will you give it me?

MELANYA. Go away now! I've none on me . . .

FIMA. I'll come and see you this evening. Don't let me down.

MELANYA. I won't, no. Now go on, for Christ's sake!

> FIMA *walks from the room without hurrying.* MELANYA *slumps into an armchair and weeps, moaning as if in pain.* PROTASSOV *enters from his room.*

PROTASSOV. She isn't back yet, is she? What are you doing, what's wrong with you?

MELANYA (*kneeling in front of him*). God's best angel! Save me, your slave!

PROTASSOV (*amazed*). What was that? Oh, do get up! What are you doing?

MELANYA (*embracing his legs*). I'm drowning in filth . . . drowning in my own rottenness . . . please, please, stretch out a hand to me . . . There's no one on earth better than you!

PROTASSOV. Excuse me, but if you don't stop . . . I shall fall over . . . and . . . don't kiss my trousers! What's the matter?

MELANYA. I've sullied my soul! Please, please – cleanse it! Who but you could do that?

PROTASSOV (*trying to understand*). Now look here, sit down
. . . No, I mean, stand up . . . Now sit down . . . there. All
right. What do you want?

MELANYA. Take me to yourself! Let me live here with you, let
me see you every day . . . see you, hear you . . . I'm rich,
take it all, all of it! Build yourself a temple for your science
. . . Build a tower! Climb to the top, live and work, and I'll
stand down below at the door, guarding the door day and
night . . . I shan't let anyone come up to you! Sell all my
houses, sell the land, take it all, Pavel, take it all!

PROTASSOV (*smiling*). Now hold on – that's quite an idea, you
know! What a laboratory I could build!

MELANYA (*happily*). Yes, yes . . . and take me too, so that I
can always see you . . . No need to talk to me, just look at
me sometimes, smile at me . . . if you had a dog you'd smile
at her occasionally, wouldn't you, pat her head? That's how
I'll be . . . like a dog!

PROTASSOV (*perplexed*). Wait, though . . . why do you say
that? It's all very strange . . . No, don't! I'm amazed, you
know, utterly amazed . . . I didn't realise you were so
enthusiastic . . .

MELANYA (*not listening*). I know I'm stupid, I'm a complete
blockhead! I don't understand any of your books, of course
– did you imagine I'd read them?

PROTASSOV (*at a loss*). Haven't you? Then what . . .?

MELANYA. Dearest. I've *kissed* your books . . . I look inside
them, and they're full of words nobody but you could
understand, and so . . . I kiss them.

PROTASSOV (*confused*). So that's why the covers are all
stained . . . But why kiss books? That's almost . . .
fetishism!

MELANYA. Don't you understand? I adore you! It's wonderful
just to be near you . . . so pure and clear . . . God's best
angel . . . I adore you, Pavel.

PROTASSOV (*in a low voice, amazed*). I beg your pardon . . . I
mean . . . In what way . . .?

MELANYA. Like a dog! I can't express myself . . . but I can be
silent! And I've been silent, for years and years . . . while

the skin was being torn from my soul . . .

PROTASSOV (*in the hope that he is mistaken*). I'm sorry, but I
 don't quite grasp the essential thought behind all this . . .
 Perhaps . . . perhaps you'd better talk it over with Elyena?

MELANYA. I have. She is quite beautiful. She understands
 that you don't love her . . .

PROTASSOV (*jumping up*). What's that? I don't love her?
 What are you talking about?

MELANYA. She knows it all, feels it all. She is a good person.
 But why have two fires in one room? She's a proud woman
 and . . .

PROTASSOV (*at a loss*). You know, this is all very confusing! I
 mean . . . I've never felt so ridiculous . . .

MELANYA. And when at last I'm with you, when you're
 mine . . .

PROTASSOV (*rather annoyed*). Mine? Mine? What do you
 mean, mine?

He looks at her, and then speaks quietly, almost fearfully.

Melanya Borisovna, let us try to be clear about this.
Forgive me if I put it bluntly, but . . . have you by any
chance fallen in love with me?

 MELANYA *gazes at him for some moments, then speaks in a
 low voice.*

MELANYA. Yes, my darling – that is what I've been talking
 about.

PROTASSOV. Yes . . . I see . . . I'm sorry . . . I thought . . . I
 thought you couldn't really . . .

MELANYA (*quietly*). Of course. That's why I . . . went too far
 . . . just now.

PROTASSOV. I'm very grateful, of course, and very touched
 . . . Unfortunately, you know . . . I'm married . . . Oh, no,
 that's not it! But don't you see . . . this isn't something that
 can be sorted out straight away . . . not at all! Lyena
 mustn't know about this, somehow we must work it out
 ourselves . . .

MELANYA. But Lyena does know.

PROTASSOV (*almost in despair*). Knows what?

> CHEPURNOY *and* LISA *come down the stairs. They walk in silence across the room and on to the terrace.* CHEPURNOY *is grimly calm,* LISA *excited.*

MELANYA (*quietly*). Hush, there's someone coming . . . Oh, it's my brother.

PROTASSOV (*to* LISA). Ah . . . M'm . . . You're – er – going out?

CHEPURNOY (*in a muffled voice*). We are.

> *They do. There's a pause. Then* PROTASSOV *speaks to* MELANYA *very sincerely and simply.*

PROTASSOV. Melanya Borisovna, this is a very extraordinary situation, I'm sure you'll agree . . . I dare say you find my reaction comic and . . . offensive . . . But my dear, it's all so strange to me, so unnecessary!

MELANYA. Unnecessary?

PROTASSOV. No, I'm sorry . . . I mean . . . I shall have to talk to Lyena about all this and . . . And then . . . I'm going . . . she's still down there, I'm worried about her . . . And I can't not tell her . . . don't be angry . . .

> PROTASSOV *goes to his rooms,* MELANYA *follows him quietly, then returns, bewildered and pathetic, muttering to herself.*

MELANYA. He didn't take it in . . . Oh, how humiliating!

> *Enter* ELYENA *from the terrace door.*

Oh my dear, take pity on a complete fool!

ELYENA. What is it? Did you . . . tell Pavel?

MELANYA. Everything. I told him everything.

ELYENA. And what did he say?

MELANYA. All my words . . . all my love . . . it all fell like dust on to water . . .

ELYENA (*simply, sincerely*). I feel for you . . . What did he say?

MELANYA. I don't know . . . Nothing got through to him, nothing reached his heart! Obviously nothing can soil fire

. . . I knelt to him . . . he didn't understand . . .

ELYENA. I told you to wait. You should have let me talk to
him first.

MELANYA. But I kept thinking you might be fooling me . . . I
offered him everything, all my money . . . the price of my
desecrated soul . . . but he didn't accept it! Who else would
have refused it? Only he . . .

PROTASSOV *enters with his hat in his hand.*

PROTASSOV. Elyena – a bath! At once! And everything off
you and into the stove with it. Fima! The bath! That Fima,
damn her – she's more of a myth than a maid . . .

ELYENA. Don't fuss so. The bath's ready, and I'll do
everything that's needed.

PROTASSOV. Go on, quickly, please! Cholera's no joke . . .

ELYENA. I'm going, I'm going . . .

PROTASSOV *sees his wife out, glancing anxiously, surrepti-*
tiously, at MELANYA. *She is sitting, as if guilty, with her*
head bowed low.

PROTASSOV (*re-entering*). Erm . . . er . . . yes . . . what a dull
. . . er . . . altogether unpleasant day it is.

MELANYA (*in a low voice*). Yes . . .

PROTASSOV. Yes, and this cholera . . . just at the wrong
time.

MELANYA. Quite . . . and so unexpected . . .

PROTASSOV. And on top of everything else, my refrigerator's
broken down . . .

MELANYA. Pavel Fyodorich, forgive me . . .

PROTASSOV (*apprehensively*). Of course . . . that is . . . er,
what? What do you actually mean?

MELANYA. Forget all that . . . all I said to you . . . forget it.

PROTASSOV (*delighted*). No, really?

MELANYA. Truly. I was stupid . . . and shameless . . .

PROTASSOV. Melanya Borisovna! I'm very fond of you – that
is, I mean, I respect you enormously. You're a wonderfully
spontaneous, warm-hearted person! You take such a lively
interest in everything . . . But – my dear friend – it would be

inappropriate . . . I mean . . . what you were saying . . . it's unnecessary . . . Let's be good friends, just good friends! Everybody should be friends . . . shouldn't they?

MELANYA. I'm ashamed to look at you.

PROTASSOV. No, stop . . . here, give me your hand! There, that's splendid! How good people are at heart, really, aren't they? How much simplicity there is in them! Their minds have this delightful capacity for understanding each other . . . I really love people – amazingly interesting things, people!

MELANYA (*smiling*). I never saw any people, not real people. I lived among tradesmen – my husband sold meat . . . It was only in this house that I realised that people – real people like you – exist at all . . . and straight away I tried to buy one.

PROTASSOV. What's that?

MELANYA. Nothing . . . don't listen to me . . . I was just . . .

PROTASSOV (*animated*). Look, why don't we have some tea?

MELANYA. Very well. I'll just go through to Elyena Niko-laevna . . . the least I can do is tidy myself up . . .

PROTASSOV. And I'll resolve the question of tea! You know, my refrigerator's broken down, dammit and Yegor's wife is ill so there's nobody to mend it and I can't do any work today . . .

PROTASSOV *goes into his own room, laughing.* MELANYA *looks after him and murmurs with deep feeling:*

MELANYA. My dear little baby . . . my beautiful innocent little baby!

MELANYA *goes into* ELYENA's *room. Enter* ANTONOVNA *from the dining room, bad-tempered, grumbling.*

ANTONOVNA. You'd think a horde of Tartars had been through the place . . . just look at that! Everything thrown every which way . . . Can't leave them . . . Ah, at's only dead folk as gets any order in their lives . . . over in the cemetery, it's only over there there's any peace . . .

LISA *and* CHEPURNOY *enter by the terrace door.*

Lisanka – medicine, and milk!

LISA (*irritated*). Be quiet! Go away.

ANTONOVNA. Well, really!

ANTONOVNA *exits indignantly.*

CHEPURNOY. So it's finished?

LISA. Yes, Boris Boris'ich! Not another word about it – ever!

CHEPURNOY. I see. The reason I started talking about it again today was that I came to think that you might be mistaken . . .

LISA. No, it's nothing to do with my illness, that's not what stops me, I'm not afraid of that . . . But I can't . . . I don't want to have children . . . Nobody ever seems to ask themselves what people are born for. I have asked. There's no room on this earth for anyone who hasn't the strength to make all life on earth as much a part of their personal life as their own. So . . . you'll go away, will you?

CHEPURNOY (*calmly*). Very well.

Enter VAGUIN *from the terrace.*

LISA. It would be easier for you . . . and don't wear red ties – they're horrid! I'm really sorry that today of all days you're wearing red.

VAGUIN. What a day! Just like October . . .

CHEPURNOY. To be sure, it's turned out a nasty little day.

LISA. Where are you thinking of going?

CHEPURNOY (*calmly*). Me? To Sepulchrov Province . . .

LISA (*anxiously*). Why . . . why there?

CHEPURNOY. I have a lot of friends there.

VAGUIN. 'He's gone to Sepulchrov Province' – that's how people sometimes speak of the departed . . . it's a pun.

LISA (*shuddering*). What are you saying? Ugh!

VAGUIN. Don't be silly. But you don't imagine Boris Boris'ich is about to die, do you? Unless of course he ups and shoots himself.

LISA (*reproachfully and anxiously*). Why do you talk like that?

VAGUIN. Let me hasten to reassure you – I don't know a single instance of a Ukrainian vet shooting himself . . .

ANTONOVNA (*from the dining room*). Lisanka, come and pour out the tea.

LISA *exits in silence.*

VAGUIN. I know it's sinful, but I love making her cross. She does make rather a display of her grief for the world's sorrows. These martyrs to the torments of living are remarkably tedious, don't you think? Anyway, I have an organic antipathy to anything sick.

CHEPURNOY. What about that picture – 'Heading for the Sun' or whatever it was – are you going to paint it?

VAGUIN. I certainly am. It's a magnificent subject, isn't it? By the way, I shall want to use you . . .

CHEPURNOY (*surprised*). Me? What possible place could I have in it? As a barnacle on the ship's bottom?

VAGUIN (*looking closely at him*). You have a remarkably stubborn line just above your eyes – full of character. Would you mind if I tried to catch it here and now?

CHEPURNOY. Oh, catch away!

VAGUIN *takes out his sketch book.*

VAGUIN. What a luxury! It won't take long.

He draws.

CHEPURNOY. Do you like funny stories?

VAGUIN. Very much, as long as they're not stupid.

CHEPURNOY. Right. Then I'll tell you one.

VAGUIN. Go ahead. Only I don't talk while I'm drawing.

CHEPURNOY. So I can hear. Well, here's how it was. There was once an English diplomatic mission on its way across the Channel, from Dover to Calais. There was a Frenchman on board. They got to boasting about who was better, the English or the French. 'Our people are everywhere!' said the English. 'Not so!' said the Frenchman. 'Why, many a French diplomat has been drowned in these straits, but not a single English one.' Whereupon a young Englishman, one of the diplomats, jumped overboard – plop! – and was drowned.

VAGUIN (*after a pause*). Then what?

CHEPURNOY. That's it.

VAGUIN. The whole story?

CHEPURNOY. Yes. What more do you want? A man wanted to uphold the honour of his country, and so drowned.

VAGUIN. Your funny story may not be stupid, but it's certainly not amusing.

CHEPURNOY. You tie your tie very well.

VAGUIN. You like it? A lady taught me.

CHEPURNOY. It's a good colour, too.

PROTASSOV *enters.*

PROTASSOV. Ah, some drawing going on in here? Hasn't Lyena come out yet? You know what, Dmitri – she's been busying herself with a cholera patient today!

VAGUIN. What?

PROTASSOV. It's true. With the blacksmith's wife. What do you think of that?

VAGUIN. Imprudent, to say the least.

ELYENA *enters from her room.*

VAGUIN. How could you allow that?

ELYENA. I surely don't have to be 'allowed' to do what I want, do I?

VAGUIN. But . . . it's not your business.

ELYENA. Why not? If I want to make it my business, it is.

VAGUIN. And you went and . . . God knows what!

PROTASSOV. No, she did very well! I admit I was alarmed for her, though . . . You've taken those drops, haven't you?

VAGUIN *closes his sketchbook.*

VAGUIN. Thank you . . . that's all. It's an interesting feature, that line of yours, that . . .

CHEPURNOY. I'm so glad.

LISA (*from the dining room*). Come and have tea!

VAGUIN. Coming!

VAGUIN *takes* CHEPURNOY *by the arm as they go in.*

PROTASSOV (*in a low voice*). Lyena, there's something I must tell you . . .

ELYENA. Now, straight away?

PROTASSOV (*hurriedly*). Well, you see, something quite absurd has happened. Melanya Borisovna – has she gone?

ELYENA (*smiling*). She's gone.

PROTASSOV. Now you mustn't laugh. Listen. You know – she seems to have fallen in love with me! Just – er – simply . . . in love! How d'you like that? God knows I've never given her the slightest encouragement, Lyena! What are you laughing about? – this is no laughing matter, if only you knew, it's really awful! Here she was, on her knees, crying, kissing my trousers . . . and my hand . . . this one . . .

ELYENA (*laughing*). Stop it, Pavel . . .

PROTASSOV (*rather cross*). I'm surprised at you, Lyena, I tell you she was serious! She offered me all her money . . . I want to live with you, dearest, she said – do you realise, she called me 'dearest' and 'Pavel' – and you must believe me, I hadn't given her a scrap of encouragement . . . For some reason she smells of saltpetre . . . What's the matter?

ELYENA. I can't help it! . . . it's so funny . . . you're so funny!

PROTASSOV (*rather offended*). Why? It's upsetting, and not at all funny . . . it's absurd! I was flabbergasted . . . I managed to say something or other to her, but everything in my head was all topsy-turvy . . . Mind you, she was absolutely serious! Oh yes, and she told me you knew everything, only I couldn't make out what actually it was you knew . . . and at first I didn't want to tell you about all this . . .

ELYENA (*gently*). You are a dear – but I knew it all . . .

PROTASSOV. You knew? But how . . . why didn't you warn me?

ELYENA (*as if remembering something; coldly*). Let's leave it all till this evening, shall we?

PROTASSOV. Oh, yes, let's . . . I want some tea, anyway . . . But if you really knew all about it, that's a relief. And you'll sort it all out, won't you?

LISA (*from the dining room*). Lyena, can you come here?

ELYENA. Coming . . .

PROTASSOV. You will see to it then, won't you?

ELYENA. All right, don't worry. Come on.

They walk to the door.

PROTASSOV. You know, when I lifted her up, to stop her kneeling, her armpits . . .

He finishes in a whisper.

ELYENA. Ugh, Pavel, you are revolting . . .

The stage is empty for a few moments. Sounds of conversation and clatter of china from the dining room. Enter CHEPUR-NOY.

CHEPURNOY. Ah . . . well, I can have a smoke out here . . .

He goes over to the window and puts his hands behind his back. Takes his cigarette from his mouth, looks at it, and sings softly:

'All night a golden cloud had stayed at rest . . .'

His voice trembles and breaks off.

VAGUIN (*entering*). 'In a deep crevice of the huge crag's breast . . .' I've been banished too – not allowed to smoke inside.

CHEPURNOY. So you like your stories funny, do you?

VAGUIN. Funnier than the last one, anyway.

CHEPURNOY. I'll invent one for you. But now – I'm away off home.

VAGUIN. When do we get the funny story then?

CHEPURNOY. Tomorrow. It's raining. (*In broad accent.*) To have my umbrella, or not to have it, as Hamlet used to say – Danish prince, you know. Well – goodbye!

VAGUIN (*holding him back by the arm*). I gather you're going away somewhere?

CHEPURNOY (*smiling*). Yes, I'm going away . . . have to go.

VAGUIN (*also smiling*). Well, bon voyage! For some reason . . . I like you very much today!

CHEPURNOY. Thank you.

CHEPURNOY. Thank you.

VAGUIN. You look like a lover . . . Tell me, have you ever been in love?

CHEPURNOY. Ah, well . . . when I was a student I did rather fancy my landlady . . . I even made her a declaration . . .

VAGUIN. Was she very beautiful?

CHEPURNOY. Hard to tell . . . she was all of fifty at the time . . . And when I made my proposition, she put the rent up by three roubles a month.

VAGUIN (*laughing*). Really?

CHEPURNOY. Oh, indeed, yes. Well . . . goodbye to you!

> CHEPURNOY *goes laughing into the dining room.* VAGUIN *looks after him thoughtfully, then walks about the room, smoking, humming softly, and shaking his head slightly.* ANTONOVNA *enters from* ELYENA'S *room.*

ANTONOVNA (*grumbling*). Oh, I thought it was that other one mooching about . . .

VAGUIN. Which other one?

ANTONOVNA. At Ukrainian. Where is he?

VAGUIN. Gone home.

ANTONOVNA. At's all he ever does. Turns up, has is tea, goes off. And there's the girl worn out with it . . . can't sleep nights . . . Why couldn't he at least tell her . . .?

VAGUIN. What girl? Why doesn't she sleep? What should she be told?

ANTONOVNA. Get away, sir! There's only the one girl in this house . . . getting older ivry day . . . Why get her all worked up for nothing? Sick enough as it is, she is . . . And you folk just walk about the place, making conversation, and at's nothing to anyone there's a person here with enough troubles to carry her off.

> ANTONOVNA *exits into the dining room.* VAGUIN *rubs his forehead hard, deep in thought, then shakes his head as if he has reached some decision.*

VAGUIN. Pavel!

> PROTASSOV *comes in with a book in his hand.*

PROTASSOV. Here I am!

VAGUIN (*with distaste*). How self-satisfied you look.

PROTASSOV (*surprised*). Is that what you called me in to tell me?

VAGUIN. I must have a talk with you.

PROTASSOV (*yawning*). Aaaah . . . Everyone wants to have a talk with me today . . . I've heard a lot of unusual things already, but not a word of it was constructive.

VAGUIN. Well, I'm going to say something constructive . . .

PROTASSOV (*looking at his book*). I shouldn't be so sure . . .

VAGUIN. Put your book down.

PROTASSOV. Where? I mean, why?

VAGUIN. Anywhere. The thing is this – I love Elyena Nikolaevna . . .

PROTASSOV (*calmly*). How could anyone not love her?

VAGUIN. I'm in love with her, don't you understand! – I love her as a woman!

PROTASSOV. Yes . . . er . . . well? (*Jumps up with sudden realisation.*) And . . . and . . . what about her? Does she know? Have you told her? What does she say?

VAGUIN. Yes, she knows.

PROTASSOV (*alarmed*). Well? Did she give you an answer?

VAGUIN (*embarrassed*). Nothing definite . . . yet.

PROTASSOV (*pleased*). Well, of course not! I knew she wouldn't . . . naturally she wouldn't . . .

VAGUIN (*with reserve*). Wait a moment . . . The thing is . . . actually . . . you don't treat her at all well.

PROTASSOV (*amazed*). Me? How? When?

VAGUIN. You pay no attention to her. You've killed her love for you.

PROTASSOV (*frightened*). Is that . . . what she said?

VAGUIN. It's what I say.

PROTASSOV (*offended*). Now look here, has everyone gone crazy today? Someone tells me I don't love Lyena, someone else says she doesn't love me . . . What is this? You're all quite unbelievable, you'll end up driving me mad! And Lyena, she's silent, she doesn't say a word! What's your part in this? Oh, I don't understand a thing!

VAGUIN. Pavel, you and I have been friends since childhood
. . . I'm very fond of you . . .

PROTASSOV. Then why not try adding a little tact to your
affection, if you can manage it, allow a man to speak for
himself, to stand up for his own freedom, his own dignity
. . . When he can do that, he'll do it better than you . . .

VAGUIN. And if he can't?

PROTASSOV. To hell with him then – he's not a man, is he?

VAGUIN. And if he doesn't want to?

PROTASSOV. It's impossible not to want to . . . I'm sorry,
Dmitri, but like all artists you're not really serious . . . you
haven't said a word until today, and now, suddenly – 'I love
her' . . .

VAGUIN. Oh, it's impossible to talk to you . . . Anyway, I've
said everything I wanted to say . . . I'm going . . .

PROTASSOV. No, hold on, I'll call Lyena . . . Lyena!

VAGUIN (alarmed). What's this? Why?

PROTASSOV. Why? (Calls.) Lyena! I want her to tell me all
about it in front of you. (Impatiently.) Oh – Lyena!

ELYENA enters.

Oh, there you are! Apparently Dmitri's in love too, just like
Melanya! Only in his case – it's with you.

ELYENA looks severely, and inquiringly, at VAGUIN.

VAGUIN (excited). Well, yes . . . why not? I told him that I'm
in love with you . . . and that you're unhappy with him . . .

ELYENA. Thank you. How very gallant.

VAGUIN (offended). I don't deserve your sarcasm. Perhaps I
have been tactless . . . rude, even . . . But I was governed
by my affection for Pavel . . . and gave in to an impulse . . .
something the nanny said to me . . . I suddenly felt I
wanted . . . something good to happen for you, Elyena
Nikolaevna . . . and that, between people like ourselves,
everything should be simple and straightforward.

ELYENA. Thank you.

PROTASSOV. I didn't say anything to offend you, Dmitri,
did I?

VAGUIN. No. But I must go – goodbye!

ELYENA. You'll come tomorrow, won't you?

VAGUIN. Yes . . . probably . . .

VAGUIN *exits.* PROTASSOV *looks questioningly at his wife.*

PROTASSOV. Well, Lyena? Where do you stand in all this?

ELYENA. What about you?

PROTASSOV. Well, I'm glad you're so calm . . . Oof! what a day! Did he make you a declaration?

ELYENA. Yes, he did.

PROTASSOV. Told you he loved you and so on?

ELYENA. Particularly the so on . . .

PROTASSOV. There's an . . . artist for you! And so what did you say?

ELYENA. Lots of things . . . a variety of things . . .

PROTASSOV. But you told him that you love me?

ELYENA. No, I didn't.

PROTASSOV. That's a pity. You should have told him that, you should have said straight away – I love Pavel . . . that is, I love my husband! Then he'd naturally have had to . . . mm . . . m'yes . . . er . . . well, I'm not quite sure how he'd have acted then . . . and anyway it's not important!

ELYENA. What is important then, in your view?

PROTASSOV. That such an event shouldn't be repeated.

ELYENA. Pavel! You talk about him, you even try to decide how he might or might not act . . . you express a wish on your own behalf . . . that you shouldn't be bothered by anything like this again . . . And where does that leave me?

PROTASSOV (*anxiously*). What do you mean? What are you trying to say?

ELYENA. Very little. I feel you don't really need me. I've never played any part in your life. You're at a great distance from me . . . a stranger. And what am I to you? You've never asked what ideas I live by, what I think . . .

PROTASSOV. Never asked? But . . . I don't have time to make conversation, Lyena! And . . . anyway . . . why didn't you say something yourself?

ELYENA (*proudly*). I'm not going to come to you like a beggar, asking for what should be mine by right, both as a human being and as your wife . . . I couldn't ask, and I would never demand – there's no value in something achieved by force.

PROTASSOV (*despairing*). Oh my God, what a nuisance it all is! I hate being at cross-purposes, having these endless scenes, it's all so unnecessary!

ELYENA. Now calm down. You see, I've decided to leave you, I've made my decision. In my mind I've already gone.

PROTASSOV (*amazed*). Lyena – no! Where – where would you go? And why? To Dmitri? You . . . you love Dmitri? Is that it? Is it?

ELYENA. I don't want to be his wife, if that's what you mean.

PROTASSOV. That's wonderful, anyway! But all the same . . . you don't love me any more? Tell me, Lyena, quickly!

ELYENA. Why should you care?

PROTASSOV (*openly*). Because I love you . . .

ELYENA. Oh, really, Pavel . . .!

PROTASSOV (*with conviction*). It's true, Lyena! It's just that I'm always so short of time . . . Listen, this can't be anything serious! I understand you've been hurt, but you must forgive me, forgive and forget! Because if you really went away I'd spend my entire time wondering – where are you? What's happening to you? . . . and then where would my work be? You'd be . . . crippling me, Lyena! What about my work?

ELYENA (*bitterly*). Take a close look at your own words – not one of them was about me . . . not a single word.

PROTASSOV *goes down on his knees.*

PROTASSOV. What do you mean, not one word? I'm telling you, I can't live without you . . . All right, Lyena, I admit it – I'm guilty – can't you forgive me? Don't stop me from living, life's so short, and there's so much fascinating work to be done!

ELYENA. And for me? What does life hold for me?

She stops and listens.

Wait . . .

> *There are rapid, loud footsteps on the stairs.* PROTASSOV
> *jumps up fearfully.* LISA *comes running down, her eyes wide
> open, full of terror. Her lips move, she makes signs with her
> hands, but she can't speak.*

PROTASSOV. Lisa, what is it?

ELYENA. Water, give her some water!

LISA. No, listen. Something terrible has just happened.
Believe me, I know . . . Such pain all of a sudden . . . as if
my heart stopped beating! Somewhere, something terrible's
happened . . . to someone close to us . . .

ELYENA. Come on now, calm yourself . . . It's your imagination . . .

LISA (*screaming*). No . . . believe me! believe me!

> *She falls into* PROTASSOV's *arms.*

CURTAIN

Act Four

The same scene as in the second act Midday. Lunch is over, and coffee served. ROMAN, *wearing a red shirt, is mending the garden fence.* LUSHA *is standing by the terrace watching him.* PROTASSOV *can be heard laughing indoors.*

LUSHA. Where are you from?

ROMAN. Ryazan.

LUSHA. I'm a Kalugan, I am.

ROMAN. There's nothing to that.

LUSHA. You're terrible frightening, you are.

ROMAN (*smirking*). Frightening? Why? At's the beard, then? There's nothing to that. A widower, I am . . . ought to get married again.

    LUSHA *comes closer to him.*

LUSHA. They were saying in the shop as how the master's a sorcerer. Is that true?

ROMAN. Could be he is. Proper clever they are, the gentry.

LUSHA. They scare me . . . Awful . . . caressing they all are.

ROMAN. And then there's those as makes false money . . .

LUSHA. What!

ROMAN. Ah, there's nothing to that . . . they do go for hard labour for it though, if'n they'm caught, same as anyone else.

    Enter PROTASSOV *and* LISA *from the house.*

PROTASSOV. Well, that's splendid! Drink up your milk, Lisa.

LISA (*wearily, with a grimace*). Why's that peasant wearing red?

PROTASSOV. Must like it . . . You know, Lyena's a lovely woman, she's so clever!

LISA (*stirring her milk with a spoon*). Oh, yes?

PROTASSOV (*walking about the terrace*). Yes, Lisa, yes, yes, yes, believe me . . . Ah, so here's the new maid . . . so that's what she looks like! What's your name?

LUSHA (*shyly*). Me? Lukeria.

PROTASSOV. Aha! – er – Lukeria, eh? . . . M'm . . . Well, er . . . can you read?

LUSHA. No . . . but I know my prayers.

PROTASSOV. And . . . um . . . are you . . . um . . . married?

LUSHA. Not yet, sir. I'm only a girl, sir.

PROTASSOV. You're fresh from the – er – from your village, then, are you?

LUSHA. Straight from there, sir.

PROTASSOV. Well – er – good! Well then, you'll – um – live here with us and . . . We're simple people, you know . . . here . . . it's good fun, you know, living in our house! Go on in, then.

LUSHA *goes into the house.*

LISA (*smiling*). How funny you always are, Pavel!

PROTASSOV. Funny? Funny. Ah, yes, well . . . you know, Lisa, Lyena says the same thing . . . I suppose you're right, really. But in fact, you know, we're all a long way away from the ordinary peope, and we really ought to do something about it . . . they ought to come closer to us . . . Elyena was speaking beautifully about that last night, so simply and convincingly . . . I'm really astonished to find that – er – that such a treasury of mind and heart was . . . right here beside me! And I didn't know! I didn't appreciate how useful it could be. Obviously there's something stupid in me, something . . . limited.

LISA. You simply don't notice people, that's all.

PROTASSOV. Yes – um – yes . . . there may be something in that. Last night, you know, after we'd seen you to bed, Lyena and I were talking in there for about three hours . . . Then we – um – sent for Dmitri and – um – you know he . . . oh, well, of course, that's not – er – not a thing to talk about . . .

LISA. What isn't?

PROTASSOV. This – er – well . . . apparently Dmitri's fallen
in love with Elyena . . . I mean, he says he has, himself,
. . . mind you, I don't believe him . . . nor does she, really
. . . And she was quite splendid the way she talked to him,
you know, like a . . . clever and loving mother . . . it was
really touching . . . we all wept buckets, it was wonderful!
You know, Lisa, living is so easy and pleasant if people will
only understand and respect one another! We shall all three
be friends . . .

LISA (*bitterly*). All three? And me?

PROTASSOV. And you too, of course, naturally! Naturally
you too! We shall all be friends, Lisa . . . we shall work,
we'll build up – for everyone – such a treasury of feelings
and thoughts, so much . . . and then, yes . . . proud in the
knowledge that we – yes, we! – have done so much for
people that it was important and necessary to do . . . we
can go out of this life pleasantly tired . . . fulfilled . . . calm
. . . accepting the inevitability of departure . . . How
perfect that is, Lisa, so clear and simple!

LISA. I love it when you talk like that. I love you, and feel that
life is the way you say it is, simple and beautiful . . . But
when I'm alone . . . and I'm usually alone . . .

PROTASSOV. Don't be sad, Lisa . . . M'm? Come on.
Yesterday you were imagining all kinds of things . . . and it
was all just your poor jangled nerves . . .

LISA (*fearfully*). Don't talk about nerves . . . sickness . . .
don't talk about it! Let me forget . . . I must forget . . . it's
vital to me! That's enough. I want to live as well . . . I've
got a right to live!

PROTASSOV. Don't get excited, please . . . and look, here's
Lyena . . .

ELYENA *enters.*

here's my good Lyena, my good, kind, slightly . . . severe
. . . strict friend.

ELYENA. Oh, come now! Don't.

She indicates LISA *with her eyes.*

LISA (*nervously*). Elyena . . . you do love him . . . don't you?

ELYENA (*embarrassed*). Yes, of course I do.

LISA. I'm so glad . . . I thought . . .

ELYENA. It's been very hard for me at times . . . horribly hard. This gentleman here, you know – without wanting to, without even being aware of it at all – can wound one very deeply . . .

LISA (*with animation*). Yes, wait, I know, I too . . . I love Boris Boris'ich . . . and yesterday . . . I refused him . . . refused him completely, finally! And then in the evening . . . I suddenly had this terrible feeling . . . that an accident . . . something terrible had happened to him! He's closer to me than anyone else . . . closer than any of you . . . and yesterday I discovered that I love him . . . I need him . . . I can't go on without him.

NAZAR *shouts from somewhere outside.*

NAZAR. Roman! Roman . . .

ROMAN (*quietly*). What?

LISA. He's so stubborn! But he's nice, isn't he?

ELYENA (*kissing her*). Dear Lisa! I wish you . . . happiness. A little happiness . . . is something we could all do with.

LISA. How hot your lips are!

PROTASSOV. Well, I – um – I – er – congratulate you! Just you see, it'll have a marvellous effect on you! Oh yes! A normal life! It's very important, you know! Yes. And Chepurnoy – well, I like him! I do! Anyway, he's incomparably more intelligent than that sister of his . . .

NAZAR (*off, shouting*). Roman! Where the devil are you?

ROMAN. I said – what?

LISA. I feel peaceful now. We'll go away into the steppes together . . . he loves the steppes . . . and we'll be alone, just him and me . . . quite alone . . . walking across the green wilderness . . . and all around us . . . as far as we can see . . . everything can be seen . . . everything and nothing!

NAZAR *appears around the corner of the house.*

NAZAR. Roman! Was I calling you or was I not?

ROMAN. I heard you. What you want?

NAZAR. You oaf! Go and shut the main gates. And the wicket, too. Ah, deepest respects, Pavel Fyodor'ich, how are you, sir?

PROTASSOV. Splendid, thank you. Why are you locking up?

NAZAR. En't you heard then? Disturbance there is, walking abroad, unrest . . . on account of the sickness, you see . . . The way people see it is, there en't really any sickness at all, save what the gentlemen doctors do spread about, on account of plumping up their turnover . . .

PROTASSOV. What barbaric nonsense!

NAZAR. Ah, well, sir, yes, of course, sir, we all know about the people, don't we? At's why they're known as the vulgar herd, an't it? Think up anything, they will, in their vulgarness . . . There'm too many of them doctors, they say, an not enough work for 'm, so they go an . . . like that . . . and so just in case, for the preservation of peace and property, like, I've give orders for the gates to be locked . . .

PROTASSOV. Oh, really, it's so absurd . . . It could only happen in this country!

NAZAR. Ah, don't even say it, sir! Just yesterday, seems they worked over a doctor a bit . . .

LISA. Who? Which doctor? Do you know the name?

NAZAR. Don't know, miss.

ELYENA. Lisa, what do you mean? Boris Boris'ich isn't a doctor . . .

LISA. No . . . he's not a doctor.

ELYENA. Let's go in.

ELYENA *takes* LISA *into the house.*

NAZAR. Scared the young lady a bit then, did I? Pavel Fyodor'ich – didn't Mr. Chepurnoy have a word with you?

MISHA *appears from around the corner.*

MISHA. Guv'nor! The contractor's out there . . . (*To* PROTASSOV.) Allow me to wish you good day, sir!

PROTASSOV. How do you do?

NAZAR. And let me say – goodbye until I have the honour again!

NAZAR *leaves*.

MISHA. A pleasant day, sir. Not too hot . . . .

PROTASSOV. Ah, yes – er – pleasant, that's it!

MISHA. May I take the liberty of asking, sir – that girl who was working for you, Fima – has she left?

PROTASSOV. What? Oh – er – yes – yes, she's left.

MISHA. They do say she's getting married? To a rich man, that would be, eh?

PROTASSOV. Er . . . er . . . I don't know. How would I know?

MISHA. No. And was she honest, this girl?

PROTASSOV. I'm sure she was. But clumsy. She – er – broke a lot of china.

MISHA. H'mm . . . well . . . fancy that! I see. Well, now, Pavel Fyodor'ich, did the Guv'nor say anything to you about a chemical factory?

PROTASSOV (*surprised*). A chemical factory? No! Er – what – er – factory, actually?

MISHA. Now, you see, sir, our idea is, we build a chemical factory, and we set you up as the manager . . .

PROTASSOV. I beg your pardon? Set me up? What am I? A tent? You have a rather strange way of expressing yourself.

MISHA. Pardongey moy! But the matter, sir, isn't just a matter of words, no, it goes . . . deeper than that. We – that is, the Guv'nor and me – we got great respect for you personally . . .

PROTASSOV (*coldly*). Very touched, I'm sure.

MISHA. We are apprised of your means, sir, and know that you will, in the near future, in all probableness, be obliged, sir, to find a post for yourself, sir, in the service, the which, sir, is very hard . . . all the more so for the likes of you.

PROTASSOV. H'm . . . yes . . . well, of course, you may be right.

MISHA. The Guv'nor and me, then, being fully cognisative of your capacities and knowledge, and recognising that you are a suitable man to serve a company in a capacity, have decided to make you the following offer – you draw up an estimate for us, for the equipping of a factory . . .

PROTASSOV. No, look, I'm sorry, but I'm – er – quite

incapable of – er – drawing up an estimate! I've never done
such a thing in my life! Anyway, I'm not interested in – er–
industrial chemistry – technology . . . Most grateful to you
for your . . .

MISHA. You're not interested in technoogy?

PROTASSOV. No. Oh no, it's very boring. Not for me at all!

MISHA (*looking at him pityingly*). You serious?

PROTASSOV. Absolutely. Completely – um – serious.

MISHA. Pity. At's really a . . . pity. Because you know, as I
see it . . . you're going to have to change your mind, sir.
Goodbye . . . for the moment!

    MISHA *exits.* ELYENA *appears from the house.*

ELYENA (*alarmed*). Pavel . . .

PROTASSOV. What?

ELYENA. Lisa seems to be seriously ill . . .

PROTASSOV. Ah, she's always like that after an attack . . .
It's nothing, really. Listen, I've just been talking to –
whatsit – the landlord's son . . . such an unattractive young
man, but you know he showed a quite touching concern for
me . . . expressed it very crudely of course . . . but all the
same . . . he was suggesting I should draw up some sort of
estimate, I don't know . . . some . . . anyway . . .

ELYENA. Anyway he'd like to make use of you, as a tool for
his own enrichment . . . yes. I know about their intentions.
The old man spoke to me . . . What's the matter, are you
cold?

PROTASSOV. Me? No. Not in the least. Why?

ELYENA. Why are you wearing your galoshes, then?

PROTASSOV (*looking at this feet*). Galoshes? Good Lord, so I
am! I wonder when I put them on? I really don't know . . .

ELYENA. Perhaps the new maid put them out for you, and
you didn't think . . .

PROTASSOV. Yes . . . Look – don't let that girl come near me!
She frightens me, she's – you know – untamed – wild – she
could easily break all my equipment, or spill something over
herself . . . I found her this morning putting hydrogen
peroxide on her hair, she must have thought it was eau-de-

cologne . . . (*He takes her hand.*) My darling Lyenka . . .
How you tortured me yesterday!

ELYENA. In a few minutes? You tortured me for months . . .
for years.

PROTASSOV. Oh, come on now, don't . . .

ELYENA. I wish you knew how humiliating it is to love
someone, and never feel the love being returned! You turned
me into a beggar, sitting around waiting for you to notice
me . . . waiting for your love . . . waiting . . . to be
touched! You don't know how humiliating that is – to have
to wait for love. Your soul is so full of light . . . your dear
head ponders so much about important matters, but very
little about the most important of all – people . . .

PROTASSOV. But that's all over, Lyena, it's all over! The only
thing is . . . um . . . Dmitri . . . Well . . . I do feel sorry for
him . . . Why on earth is someone ringing the bell? Oh, of
course, the gate's locked! It's probably Dmitri . . . though
I'd like it to be Chepurnoy . . . for Lisa's sake, of course.

ELYENA (*mischievously*). For Lisa's sake? Really?

PROTASSOV. Now, Lyena, surely you don't suspect me of
being jealous and . . . and all that . . .

ELYENA (*solemnly*). Oh no, certainly not. You – jealous? You,
for whom only science . . .

PROTASSOV. Lyena, how about me putting you over my
knee?

> *He is about to kiss her, then sees* MELANYA *approaching the*
> *terrace and is embarrasssed. Talks in a preoccupied voice.*

Ah, there you are, Lyena . . . you've got some fluff or
something on your shoulder . . .

MELANYA (*with a guilty smile*). Good afternoon.

PROTASSOV (*with exaggerated delight*). Melanya Borisovna!
You – er – we haven't seen you for such a long time!

MELANYA. A long time? But I was here yesterday . . . have
you forgotten all about it?

PROTASSOV. Ah! No . . . yes! No, indeed I remember.

MELANYA. I thought you were laughing about me, because of
yesterday . . .

PROTASSOV (*hurriedly*). Oh now, how could you imagine . . .! That was – er – nothing . . . a trifle . . . (*Suddenly realises what he's saying.*) That is, I mean – um – it could happen to anyone . . . (*He gives up.*)

ELYENA. You'd better just stay silent, Pavel.

MELANYA (*lovingly and sadly*). Oh, you . . .

PROTASSOV. Y-er-yes! I won't say a word more. I'll – er – yes, I'll go and take off my galoshes . . . God knows what they're doing there.

MELANYA (*with a sad smile*). There he goes – it was nothing, he says, a trifle . . . I bare my entire soul to him and he says – it could happen to anyone . . . as if I'd stepped on his corn!

ELYENA. Don't take offence, Melanya Borisovna!

MELANYA. Oh my dear, it's not for me to be offended by him, is it? I didn't sleep the whole night long, I kept walking and walking about the house, thinking – how could I have dared to talk to him? And do you know what it was? – I still had this idea that I could attract him with money, nobody can resist a really big sum of money, I thought . . . But he wasn't tempted . . .

ELYENA. Forget about all that . . .

Enter LISA, *slowly.*

LISA (*unhappily*). No Boris Boris'ich?

ELYENA. No, not yet . . . he hasn't come . . .

LISA *goes out.*

MELANYA. She didn't say hello . . . She looks terribly pale!

ELYENA. She had an attack yesterday.

MELANYA. Again? Poor thing . . . You say I should forget it all, but – no, I shan't forget! I daren't forget, because if I do some stupidity like that might spill out again. Oh my dearest, what a horrible old hussy I am! Shameless, mildewed . . . I don't have many thoughts, and none of those I do have are straight – they're like worms, wriggling in every direction . . . And I don't want to have thoughts like that, I don't want them! I want to be straight and

honest . . . I *must* be honest . . . or else I could do so much
harm . . .

ELYENA. If you want to, then you will be! You've had a hard,
ugly life. You ought to rest now, and forget all about the
past . . .

MELANYA. Yes, I've been through some hard times. My God,
yes, I've had it hard! I've been kicked and beaten . . .
shouted at . . . cursed . . . but it isn't my ears or my back
I'm sorry for, it's my soul! My soul's been twisted out of
shape, my heart's been dirtied . . . soiled . . . It's difficult
for me now, to believe in anything good. And what's the
point of life, if you can't believe? Boris – well, Boris of
course, he just laughs at everything, believes in nothing . . .
And look at him. He's like a stray dog. But you know . . .
when I spoke to you . . . you believed me straight away! I
was amazed! I thought you must be fooling me, but then
. . . you were so gentle and truthful with me . . . you
explained me to myself . . .

ELYENA. That's enough, my dear.

MELANYA. . . . and you did it so well, so simply . . . and it's
true, what you said – it isn't me, a female who loves – it's
me, a human being . . . I hadn't felt the human being in me
before, I didn't believe in the idea . . .

ELYENA. I'm so glad you understood.

MELANYA. I understood immediately. But even so, I thought,
let's try anyway, I thought, maybe I can buy this funny
gentleman, as my next husband. That's how low I am.

ELYENA. You shouldn't talk about yourself like that . . . You
must respect yourself, otherwise life's impossible . . . I feel
like hugging you . . .

MELANYA. Yes, yes, please, do hug me! Give alms for the love
of Christ to the rich tradeswoman . . .

ELYENA. You mustn't go on like that, you mustn't! And don't
cry . . .

MELANYA. Never mind . . . let me wash myself out with tears
. . . Elyena Nikolaevna, take me in . . . teach me something . . . something fine, something good . . . You're so
clever, you can . . .

Enter LISA.

Lizaveta Fyodorovna, good afternoon!

LISA *shakes hands with her silently.*

LISA. Has he still not come, Elyena?

ELYENA. No. What's the matter?

LISA. No?

ELYENA. Are you unwell?

LISA. No . . . just wretched . . . No!

LISA *exits into the garden.*

MELANYA. Who is she expecting?

ELYENA. Boris Boris'ich . . . Did you know, they're engaged?

MELANYA. They're –? No! Good heavens! So I shall be related to Pavel Fyodorich? And to you? Oh, Boris . . . and Lisa . . . My dear, I'm going to her – may I?

ELYENA. Of course.

MELANYA (*animated, joyful*). Just look how it's all working out! It's so lovely – here, let me kiss you . . .

Enter ANTONOVNA.

I'll go and see her in the garden . . . Good afternoon, Nanny, how are you, dear . . .?

Exits.

ANTONOVNA. Afternoon. That donkey, the new girl – why don't she clear the table? Taking on a maid through an agency – you got to engage a maid yourself, not through an office!

ELYENA (*taking her by the shoulders*). Stop grumbling, Nanny, it's such a lovely day.

ANTONOVNA. An so there should be warm days – at's summer, en't it? And any season's the time for a bit of order . . . When at sat down for at's tea, there, the new girl, didn't she go and swill down a whole samovar full, all by herself . . . just like a little horse!

Enter VAGUIN.

ELYENA. Do you begrudge her the water?

ANTONOVNA. At's not the water I mind about . . . but she gobbles sugar like it was turnips, an there you are!

ANTONOVNA *grabs something from the table and goes inside.*

ELYENA. Good afternoon, Chevalier.

VAGUIN (*embarrassed*). Well then – may I kiss your hand?

ELYENA. Why shouldn't you?

VAGUIN (*sighing*). Oh . . . just . . . because . . .

ELYENA. What a sigh, you poor unhappy martyr!

VAGUIN (*offended*). Looking at you now, do you know what occurs to me?

ELYENA. What?

VAGUIN. That you made use of me, in order to make Pavel grant you a little of his gracious attention. A sharp tactic.

ELYENA. Chevalier! What chivalry! – 'you made use of me' – what sort of talk is that? – 'a sharp tactic' – really!

VAGUIN (*bitterly*). You taught me a lesson, just as if I was a small boy . . .

ELYENA (*earnestly*). Dmitri Sergei'ich, I dislike listening to nonsense . . .

VAGUIN (*thoughtfully, simply*). I feel I've been playing a part, not too clever a part . . . and that offends me. In fact I don't feel too good altogether after yesterday's conversation . . . my head's in a muddle, somehow . . . Elyena Nikolaevna, tell me the truth . . .

ELYENA. Do you have to ask?

VAGUIN. Were you never attracted to me?

ELYENA. As a man, never. As a human being, profoundly.

VAGUIN (*with a laugh*). Presumably I'm supposed to feel flattered by that. I don't understand people, I really don't! I love the whole of you . . . all of you at once! Yesterday it struck me – and I understood – that the woman and the human being are so totally fused in one beautiful, rounded, unified individual . . . that I felt at once ashamed and . . . sorry for myself. Yesterday I fell in love with you.

ELYENA (*crossly*). Oh, not again . . . Why?

VAGUIN (*simply and insistently*). Yes, I fell in love with you.

For good. I don't want anything from you. I shall probably go off and get married and all that, make a suitable marriage, but I shall still love you, I shall always love you . . . And that's enough about that. You're tired of me, aren't you?

ELYENA *holds out her hand to him.*

ELYENA. I believe you. I think you're telling the truth now.

VAGUIN. And before . . . you never felt any truth in what I said? Is that it?

ELYENA. No, never. And how do you suppose that happened? I let myself go with you once, I couldn't stop myself, and confessed how lonely I felt. You were so lovely with me – so simple and direct and understanding – that I began to feel intensely warm and grateful to you . . . and it was then – only then, mark you – that you started to talk about love . . .

VAGUIN (*considering her words*). Only then? Did that offend you?

ELYENA (*smiling*). I don't know . . . A little, perhaps . . .

VAGUIN (*sadly, with vexation*). No . . . I see . . . I'm not much of a genius, am I? To put it mildly. Stupid. Don't understand people.

ELYENA. Let's leave it . . . m'm? And stay good friends?

VAGUIN (*with a short laugh*). Let's shake hands on that. Why not?

ELYENA (*kissing his forehead*). There. Be free. For an artist, freedom's as essential as talent or brains. Try to be truthful . . . and don't take such a poor view of women . . .

VAGUIN (*touched, but restrained*). Ah, that's unfair, my dear! But thank you. What you say is true – an artist should be alone. Freedom and loneliness go together, don't they?

ELYENA. Yes, my friend, probably they do.

VAGUIN. Pavel's coming. I can hear his clumsy tread . . .

Enter PROTASSOV.

Ah, my rival!

PROTASSOV. Has Melanya Borisovna gone?

ELYENA. She's in the garden with Lisa – shall I call her?

PROTASSOV. Don't tease, Lyenka! Have a peek in there – the new maid's eating the soap. I asked her to unwrap a new bar. First she hid the paper away in her pocket and then she started to lick the soap . . .

ELYENA. Oh, really . . .!

ELYENA *goes into the house.*

VAGUIN. Let her be! Why shouldn't we all enjoy ourselves as best we can? . . . I, for instance, have just been declaring my love to Elyena Nikolaevna all over again.

PROTASSOV (*anxiously*). Really? Well – h'm – I think . . . um . . . I think you ought to go away, Dmitri. Go away, and you'll soon get over it.

VAGUIN. I intend to go away. But I shan't get over it, that I do know. However, there's no need for you to worry.

PROTASSOV. Oh, no, no I . . . that's all right, it's just . . . a bit awkward, you know.

VAGUIN. A bit awkward, being happy? No, no, your sentiment's probably very creditable. It's also very silly.

PROTASSOV. Don't be angry with me, Dmitri . . . it's not my fault . . . it's Lyena, really . . . just that she loves me and not you . . .

VAGUIN (*with a short laugh*). How charming!

PROTASSOV. But, you know, Dmitri, I felt quite depressed after our talk yesterday . . . You're better than me – yes, you are, really! I'm like a planet with an undefined orbit . . . I revolve around my own axis, floating away somewhere or other and . . . that's all! But you revolve around the sun . . . in harmony with the whole system . . .

LISA *enters from the garden, followed by* MELANYA. ELYENA *appears from the house.*

VAGUIN. Well, I've no idea what I'm revolving about, but I advise you to start revolving around your wife . . . don't let her out of your sight . . .

PROTASSOV. Still, people are wonderful really, aren't they?

LISA (*to* ELYENA, *distressed*). No?

ELYENA. No, my dear . . . should we send for him?
LISA. No . . . don't . . .

LISA goes indoors.

MELANYA (*quietly, anxiously*). She seems to be wandering . . .
keeps on talking about the steppes . . . the wilderness . . .
LISA (*from the house*). Melanya Borisovna . . . where are you?
MELANYA (*running out*). Coming, I'm coming . . .
ELYENA. Pavel, I'm getting seriously worried about her . . .
We ought to call the doctor.
PROTASSOV. Well, I'll go for him then . . .

ANTONOVNA enters with a letter.

ANTONOVNA. Dmitri Sergey'ich – a letter for you.
VAGUIN. Where from?
ANTONOVNA. From the flat . . . urgent, they said . . .

ANTONOVNA exits.

VAGUIN. What on earth is this? (*Tears open the envelope and
reads, imitating CHEPURNOY's voice to begin with, but then
dropping back into his own and finishing very quietly.*) 'And
here is another funny story for you – the vet who hanged
himself. Like that English diplomat, he wanted to uphold
the honour of the company. Thank you for drawing that
stubborn line of mine. I'm sure you know how pleasant it is
to feel that some wee wrinkle of oneself has been preserved
somewhere. Pay more attention to the beauty of your tie.
This is important. Chepurnoy.' Oh my God!
PROTASSOV. But there's nothing terrible about that.
ELYENA. Quietly! What story? Who . . .? Perhaps it's a joke?
VAGUIN. No . . . hardly a joke . . . and yet . . . he was
laughing, dammit!

LISA comes in quickly and looks round at everyone.

LISA. He's come, where is he?
ELYENA. No, dear, he hasn't come . . .
LISA. But the voice . . . his voice? I heard him talking just
now. Why is everyone silent? Where is he?

VAGUIN. It was me . . . I was talking.

LISA. No. No! It was his voice . . .

VAGUIN. I was imitating him . . . mimicking him.

LISA. What for?

VAGUIN. Oh, just . . .

PROTASSOV. You see, we were just having a chat here, and then . . .

LISA. What? Then what?

ELYENA. You must calm down, Lisa . . .

VAGUIN. I was talking about his manner of speech, and said a few words in his voice . . .

LISA. Really? Are you telling the truth? Why are they silent, then? Pavel, what about you? Something's happened, hasn't it? Dearest Pavel, you're not capable of telling a lie are you? What is it?

VAGUIN *slips indoors unnoticed.*

PROTASSOV. No, Lisa . . . um . . . the thing is, you see. . . . um . . . it's true . . . I mean, what Dmitri said, he . . .

ELYENA. Listen, Lisa, my dear . . .

LISA. Don't touch me, Elyena! Pavel . . . Pavel, you must tell me . . .

PROTASSOV. I don't know anything . . .

LISA. Then there is something to know? Elyena, send for him, send for Boris . . . straight away!

ELYENA. Yes, yes, of course, at once . . . but do calm yourself!

LISA. No. You're lying about something. And where's Vaguin gone? Oh, he's in there . . . talking to Boris's sister and . . . her face . . . her face . . .

PROTASSOV (*quietly to his wife*). What shall we do?

ELYENA (*quietly*). Get the doctor, quickly.

PROTASSOV *goes into the house.*

LISA. I'm going to fall . . . Oh Elyena, hold me, I shall fall . . . What were you whispering about?

ELYENA. What can we do to calm you? . . . Pavel . . .

LISA. He's run off now – where? Elyena, for God's sake, look me in the eyes, you mustn't lie to me, Elyena, I beg you . . .

MELANYA *comes out of the house, followed by* VAGUIN.

Where are you going? Where's your brother, where's Boris?

MELANYA. I don't know . . .

LISA. Oh, tell me, quickly quickly . . . straight away . . . is he dead?

MELANYA. I don't know . . . I don't know . . .

MELANYA *goes towards the gates, and off.*

LISA. No! No! You must! Say something to me, please! Oh, my heart's being torn apart! Because if he's dead . . . it was me who did it, me! me! I killed him . . . Oh, no!

VAGUIN. Oh come on, now, what a silly idea . . .

MISHA *runs up to the terrace shouting with an animation close to delight.*

MISHA. Ladies! Sir! Have you heard? That vet, Chepurnoy . . .

VAGUIN (*shaking his fist at him*). Shut up, man!

MISHA. . . . he's hanged himself!

LISA (*tearing herself away from* ELYENA; *calmly and clearly*). Yesterday evening, about nine.

MISHA. Yes, yes . . . on the willow tree by the stream . . . I didn't think you knew . . .

MISHA *runs off.* LISA, *her eyes wide open, gazes at them all and speaks in a low, strangely significant voice.*

LISA. I knew it . . . do you remember, Elyena . . . I felt it. (*Quietly, with horror.*) No! It wasn't me . . . tell me it wasn't me who killed him . . . no! (*Shouts.*) I didn't want to . . . no!

VAGUIN *and* ELYENA *lift her and carry her into the house. She struggles, repeating the one word 'No!' faster and faster.* ROMAN *comes slowly round the corner and peers into the house, from which* LUSHA, *frightened, comes running.*

LUSHA. Listen . . . what are you called? – from Ryazan . . . what are they doing?

ROMAN. What, then?

LUSHA. Dragging the young lady along, that's what, and her screaming No! no!

ROMAN. At was her screaming here?

LUSHA. At was her . . . an they dragging her off . . . I'm scared!

ROMAN (*philosophically*). What she shout for then?

LUSHA. Don't know, do I? At what they're like, the gentry?

ROMAN. Maybe she didn't ought to be screaming. At's not right.

MISHA *comes hurrying round the corner.*

MISHA. Who was shouting?

ROMAN (*nodding towards* LUSHA). Her lot.

LUSHA (*waving him away*). Don't you go looking at me, it was the gentry!

MISHA (*severely*). Who was it?

LUSHA. At young lady.

MISHA (*having a good look at her*). Why?

LUSHA. They was a dragging her . . .

MISHA. Who were?

LUSHA. Them . . . that lot . . . in there . . .

MISHA *claps her on the shoulder.*

MISHA. Oh you, you're . . . thick as a butcher's block, aren't you?

MISHA *goes up on to the terrace.* ANTONOVNA *appears.*

What's going on here, Nanny?

ANTONOVNA. Young lady's had an attack.

MISHA (*to* ROMAN *and* LUSHA). There you are you see – boobies!

ROMAN *goes slowly to the garden fence and starts work again.*

What did that come from then, Nanny?

ANTONOVNA. From the Lord . . . everything come from Him!

MISHA (*with a crafty smile*). Or maybe from the vet?

> *He exits, satisfied.* ANTONOVNA *looks after him reproachfully, and sighs. She speaks regretfully.*

ANTONOVNA. Cheeky donkey . . . Lukeria, what are you doing out here? Go into the house.

LUSHA. Nyanka, what kind of attack would at be? Would at be the falling sickness?

ANTONOVNA. Yes, yes! In you go now . . .

LUSHA (*going off*). Ah, now, the falling sickness, at's nothing, I seen at. Wasn't half scared though when they was a dragging the young lady long there . . .

> ROMAN *grunting.* VAGUIN *comes out, looks hard at* ROMAN. *Takes out his album and a pencil.* ANTONOVNA *follows* LUSHA *in.*

VAGUIN. Hey, old fellow.

ROMAN. That me?

VAGUIN. Yes, you. Stay like that . . .

ROMAN. What for?

VAGUIN (*drawing*). I'm going to draw you . . . there . . .

ROMAN. How 'bout that then! Can't do me no harm, can it?

VAGUIN. It'll do you twenty kopecks of good.

ROMAN. At's all right then.

VAGUIN. Raise your head a bit.

ROMAN (*lifting his head*). I can do that.

VAGUIN. Not so high as that . . . where do you think you're going?

ROMAN. Look good to you, do I?

VAGUIN. Not bad . . .

> *Pause. An occasional groan can be heard from the house. Somewhere far away in the streets, a vague commotion. Enter* MELANYA.

VAGUIN. Well?

MELANYA (*thickly*). I saw him . . . terrible . . . blue . . . tongue stuck out . . . as if it was on purpose . . . terrible! How is Lisa?

VAGUIN (*grimly*). There, you can hear.

MELANYA. Why did this start? It was all going so well . . .

VAGUIN. What do you mean, start?

MELANYA. I don't know . . . Oh, I don't understand
anything! Only . . . it's so terrible and . . . you're drawing?
How can you?

VAGUIN (*quite kindly*). And you're breathing? You can't not
breathe, can you? All right, old fellow . . . here's your
twenty!

He throws the coin at ROMAN's *feet.*

MELANYA. Is Elyena Nikolaevna alone in there? I'll go in,
perhaps I'll be needed. Oh God, Boris will have to be buried
and everything . . . I didn't stop to make any arrange-
ments, just glanced at him and . . . came on here . . . Out
in the streets there people are making a noise about
something, running about, getting agitated . . . and I don't
understand any of it . . . I've got his blue face swaying in
front of my eyes, he's sticking his tongue out at me,
laughing and laughing . . .

She weeps, and goes into the house.

ROMAN (*with relish*). Look, the lady there – she's crying.
What'll be the matter with her?

VAGUIN. Her brother's dead.

ROMAN. Aha! Well, then, at's all right, at's reason enough,
en't it? Only you know women cry a lot for nothing, don't
they? Give her a clout across the head an she'll howl.

*A noise in the street. It grows louder. Muffled shouts.
Somewhere in the yard a frightened cry from* MISHA:
'Roman!'

You can wait. (*He listens.*) At could be a fire . . . or maybe
someone getting a beating . . . a thief at would be . . . A
thief can have a hard time of it, too. I'll go have a look.

ROMAN *goes off.* ELYENA *enters from the house.* VAGUIN
looks at her enquiringly.

ELYENA (*very upset*). I don't think she'll recover.

VAGUIN. Oh, surely she will! It isn't the first time she's been like this?

ELYENA. Yes it is. Like this. The first time. It happened so suddenly. She's become . . . cunning . . . like someone really . . . insane. At first she was asking for poison . . . bring me some poison she was screaming . . . and then, all at once . . . it was strange . . . frightening . . . she went very quiet, and calm, and her eyes . . . her eyes took on a cunning glint like . . . like a wild animal . . .

VAGUIN. Are you all right? Shall I get you some water?

ELYENA. No, no thank you. She lay down on the bed . . . told me my presence was irritating her, so I went into the next room . . . I listened . . . heard her getting up, very quietly, very, very quietly and carefully. I went in. She was over by Pavel's table, and there was his revolver lying in the drawer . . . here it is . . . and we . . . we fought for it . . . she was like a wild animal . . . scratched my hands . . . like a wild animal . . .

VAGUIN. Oh my God! Why didn't you call me? You could have shouted . . .

ELYENA. I don't understand – honestly, Dmitri, I really don't know how we managed not to shoot each other! She's lying down again now . . . tied down . . . the new maid helped me . . . Nanny just stood there, watching and crying, begging me not to touch Lisa, because she's the general's daughter . . . What an awful noise, why are they making such a noise? It sounds awfully close.

VAGUIN. The yardman went to find out.

ELYENA. And Pavel's still not back? Oh, what's happening?

Commotion outside the gates. Shouts of 'Grab him!' 'Aaaah!' 'Over the fence' 'Look out!' 'Get your stick!' 'Hit him!'

ELYENA. My God! Come on, quickly, over here . . .

VAGUIN. I'll go by myself.

The DOCTOR *rushes round the corner, dishevelled and without a hat.*

DOCTOR. Quick! hide me! Lock the doors!

ELYENA. Doctor! What is it? What's the matter?

DOCTOR. They're rioting . . . smashed up the hospital . . . caught me by the gates . . . they'll kill me . . .

> VAGUIN *rushes to the gates.*

ELYENA. Here, take the gun . . .

DOCTOR. They'll break in and I'll . . .

ELYENA (*taking him into the house*). Come in here . . . quickly . . . quickly . . . Nanny! Nanny!

> *By the gates, a loud crash of a broken board, the wicker gate bangs, crash of broken glass.* PROTASSOV *comes bounding in, followed by some ten men, whom he brushes away with his hat and his handkerchief. This amuses them, and some of them laugh.*

PROTASSOV. Get off, you chumps! Idiots . . . get away!

FIRST MAN (*from the crowd*). Hey, you hit me with your handkerchief!

SECOND. Go on, sir! Give him at again with your hat!

THIRD (*angry*). I'll teach you name calling if at's what you want?

SECOND. Where's at doctor? Let's find'm!

THIRD. At one's a doctor too, stands to reason . . .

VAGUIN (*off, somewhere behind the corner*). Lock the gates . . . Roman, get rid of them!

PROTASSOV. Don't you dare push me, you fathead!

VAGUIN. Pavel! Pavel! Hold on! I'll give them a thrashing . . . go on, get out, all of you, out, out, out!

> *Enter* YEGOR *and* TROSHIN. YEGOR *slightly drunk,* TROSHIN *thoroughly so.* YEGOR *throws himself at* PROTASSOV *and grabs him by the collar.*

YEGOR. Ahaa! my little chemist! Been caught, have you?

PROTASSOV (*trying to struggle free*). Don't you dare . . .

YEGOR. Look at this one, now! At's the biggest 'sterminator of them all! Makes medicines, he do!

PROTASSOV. Rubbish! You silly chump, I don't make

anything at all . . . Here, help!
VOICE FROM THE CROWD. Louder! Can't hear you!

> ELYENA *runs out on to the terrace, sees the mob, seizes the revolver and dashes over to her husband.*

ELYENA. Let go, Yegor! Let go! Get away, Yegor!
PROTASSOV. Lyena, Lyena . . .
YEGOR. Remember? Cholera – a person can die of that . . . remember? You . . .
ELYENA. I'll kill you, Yegor.

> ELYENA'S *appearance has provoked various loud exclamations in the crowd:*

VOICES. Look what's popped up!
  Hey, lady, you with the gun!
  Give it to her, Yegor!
  Go on, get her!
  At's a real woman!
YEGOR. Ma'am, I'm a widower now . . .
ELYENA. I'm going to shoot . . .
YEGOR. An you'll be a widow . . . I'll strangle 'im!

> ELYENA *shoots. Just before this,* ROMAN *has appeared behind the crowd. He has a large length of plank in his hands. Without hurrying, he raises it and proceeds to bang people over the head. He does so in silence, with concentration, with no sign of annoyance. At the moment when* ELYENA *shoots at* YEGOR, ROMAN *hits him, and* YEGOR *falls to the ground with a groan, dragging* PROTASSOV *down with him.*

> ELYENA *advances on the crowd, brandishing her revolver. Her shot leads to a sharp change of mood on the part of the crowd. Someone cries, in surprise, and not loudly:*

VOICE. She fired that . . .! Look at that, Yegor's down! Murdering cow!

> *Someone runs from the yard, shouting:*

VOICE. Watch out, now, they're killing us!

Another hurries after him, calling:

VOICE. Don't be so yellow, what you scared on? Only a woman, en't it?

Nearly all of them retreat.

ELYENA (*carried away*). Get out, go on! I'll shoot! Dmitri – where are you? Roman, help my husband. Out, you brutes, out, out!

ROMAN *goes up to* TROSHIN, *who is sitting on the ground beside* YEGOR, *pushes* YEGOR *aside.* ROMAN *mutters something, and hits* TROSHIN *with the plank. He moans and falls down.* VAGUIN *comes running round the corner, very dishevelled, in time to see* ROMAN *gallantly fighting.* VAGUIN *has a brick in his hand.*

VAGUIN. What the hell are you doing?
ROMAN. You what?
VAGUIN (*turning away*). Elyena . . . where's Pavel?

ROMAN *drops his plank and squats down beside* PROTASSOV.

ELYENA (*coming down to earth*). He was . . . he . . . he fell . . . (*Shouting.*) He's been killed!
VAGUIN. Oh, surely not . . .

MELANYA *runs in, hears* ELYENA'S *words.*

MELANYA. Who's been killed? Oh no . . . no . . . I don't believe it . . .!

ELYENA *points her revolver at* YEGOR.

ELYENA. It was him . . . Yegor . . . I'll . . .
VAGUIN. What do you think you're doing! Stop!

He knocks the gun from her hand.

Come to your senses!
MELANYA (*beside* PROTASSOV). He's alive! . . . Pavel Fyodorich!
ELYENA. Water . . . give him some water!

VAGUIN (*to* MELANYA). Yes, go on, go for some water . . .
Elyena, you must calm yourself!

MELANYA *runs indoors.*

ROMAN. At's all right . . . ivyr one of 'em's alive, see, all of
'em moving now . . . Folk get beat on more than that and
stay live yet.

VAGUIN *and* ELYENA *lift* PROTASSOV *up. He is in a faint.*
ROMAN *gives* MELANYA *a shove.*

ELYENA (*fearfully*). Pavel . . . Pavel!
VAGUIN. He's only fainted.
ROMAN (*to* TROSHIN). Go on, get up . . . don't fool now, or
I'll give you more o' that . . .

ANTONOVNA *runs in.*

ANTONOVNA. Pashenka! Where's Pashenka!
VAGUIN. Don't shout, Nanny.
PROTASSOV (*half coming round*). Lyena . . . that you? Have
they gone! Aah . . .
ANTONOVNA (*to* ELYENA). They gone and killed him, and
you . . . you wasn't looking after him . . . eh?
ELYENA (*to her husband*). Does it hurt? Where does it hurt?

YEGOR *regains consciousness, lifts his head, groans.*

ANTONOVNA. Take him in, carry him in . . .

MELANYA *comes back with water.*

MELANYA. Oh, God, thank God! he's come round! Here . . .
drink . . . drink this . . .
ELYENA. Tell me – where does it hurt? Were you hit hard?
PROTASSOV. Doesn't hurt . . . doesn't hurt anywhere . . . He
was strangling me . . . that one, Yegor . . . (*Fully recovering.*) Oh, Lyena, Lyena! Are you all right? I thought
someone was going to hit you . . . with some sort of
plank . . .
ELYENA. No, no, I wasn't hit, don't worry.
VAGUIN. Were you, Pavel?

PROTASSOV. No, not badly. For some reason they went for my stomach, damn them . . . What about that doctor, is he alive?

MELANYA. Yes, yes, he's alive . . . he's on the sofa in the drawing room. He's crying.

ELYENA (*noticing* ANTONOVNA, *fearfully*). And Lisa . . . Nanny, what about Lisa?

ANTONOVNA. I untied her. I dursn't see her like that.

ELYENA. Where is she?

ANTONOVNA (*weeping*). In there . . . her dress was all torn . . . I changed her . . .

VAGUIN. What's she doing?

ANTONOVNA. Looking at that one's photograph . . .

ELYENA. Go in to her, Nanny, please! Go on!

ANTONOVNA. Pashenka should be put to 's bed.

She exits, looking back. PROTASSOV *calls after her.*

PROTASSOV. It's nothing, Nanny – I just had a fright . . .

MELANYA. My darling . . . was it awful?

YEGOR, TROSHIN *and* ROMAN *are in a separate group.* ROMAN *is slightly more animated and active than usual.*

PROTASSOV. For me? Not at all, I was frightened for her . . . I thought someone fired and then . . . hit her over the head with a . . . a stick or . . . or a plank . . .

ELYENA (*with pride*). Nobody touched me. Come on, let's go indoors.

PROTASSOV. I defended myself most – er – most successfully, yes. What a pity you didn't see me! And you know, Lyena – I shouldn't have taken off my galoshes, I could have gone for them with my galoshes!

VAGUIN (*smiling at* LYENA). There, you see, Pavel is himself again!

PROTASSOV (*working himself up*). Yes, could have chucked my galoshes straight in their stupid mugs . . . (*To* YEGOR.) And as for you, sir . . .

MELANYA. Oh, what's the point of talking to him? Come indoors, you must lie down . . .

PROTASSOV. Let me tell him . . .

ELYENA. Wait . . . Yegor, did I hit you?

YEGOR (*thickly*). No, M'm . . . You missed. Someone whacked me on the head . . .

ROMAN (*proudly*). That was me!

ELYENA *gazes intently at* YEGOR *and the others.*

VAGUIN. Yes, you should have seen how this sinister machine was functioning . . . terrifying!

TROSHIN. Gentlemen! I too have received contusion of the head!

ROMAN. That was me, too.

TROSHIN. Gentlemen, kindly make a note of that.

YEGOR *goes up to him and with a smile takes a bottle from his pocket.* ELYENA *stares hard into* YEGOR's *face.*

ELYENA. Yegor, do you want some water?

YEGOR. Vodka'll do.

PROTASSOV (*to* YEGOR). You . . . you're amazingly stupid, sir.

ELYENA. Don't Pavel . . .

PROTASSOV. I. Don't. Make. Any. Medicines. Damn you!

VAGUIN. Oh, do stop it, Pavel!

PROTASSOV (*tearfully*). No . . . wait . . . please. I've got to know why he fell on me like that! What have I ever done to you, Yegor? Eh? What?

YEGOR (*thickly*). Nothing. Don't know.

MELANYA. You'll find out all right at the trial, my friend . . . that's where you'll hear it!

PROTASSOV (*with distaste*). Oh, don't . . . really! What trial? Yegor . . . I had such a high opinion of you . . . you're a wonderful worker, you know . . . Surely I paid you well enough, didn't I? So why did you have to . . .

YEGOR (*gets up, speaks thickly and angrily*). Don't touch me, master.

ELYENA (*firmly, with insistence*). Leave him in peace, Pavel.

VAGUIN (*to* YEGOR). You'd better go.

YEGOR (*rudely*). I know that. I'm going.

YEGOR *goes off, walking uncertainly.* ROMAN *and* TROSHIN *are already over by the garden hedge, sitting on the ground drinking vodka brought by* ROMAN. YEGOR *goes silently over to them, sits down and offers his hand to* ROMAN.

MELANYA. Look at that! What an ape!

ELYENA. Oh, do leave him alone . . . Come on, Pavel . . .

PROTASSOV (*agitated*). He really made me very cross . . . there's something . . . untouchable about him . . . People ought to be bright . . . radiant . . . like the sun . . . not . . .

LISA *comes out on the terrace. She is wearing a white frock. Her hair is dressed strangely beautifully. She walks slowly, with a kind of solemn gait, a vague, enigmatic smile fixed on her face.* ANTONOVNA *follows her.*

LISA. Goodbye! No, don't say anything . . . I've decided . . . I'm going away! No, no objections, you mustn't make objections . . . I'm going far, far away, for a long time, a very long time . . . for ever. You know? Listen.

She stops, and in a low voice, smiling, reads from the back of CHEPURNOY'S *photograph.*

My dear one through the desert strides
Through red and burning seas of sand.
I know that in the distance hides
A hollow land, an empty land.

The sun, like summer's evil eye,
Hangs in the sky, its face ablaze.
I'll go to him and help defy
His arid days, his lonely days.

She sings, quietly and strangely.

Strong is my dear one, fair am I,
Two little flowers, dropped from the sky,
Alone on the vast red sands we lie.

Pause. Then, with a sigh, she reads again.

We shall walk out there, hand in hand,

Embraced by the burning wilderness,
To bury, far out in the sand,
His wasted dreams, my mute distress.

> LISA *looks at them all thoughtfully. Smiles.*

That's all. I made it for Boris. Boris . . . Do you know him?
No? (*She goes off towards the garden.*) I am so sorry for you
. . . I'm so sorry . . .

> ANTONOVNA, *with a hostile look at* ELYENA, *follows her.*

ELYENA (*quietly, distressed*). Pavel . . . Pavel . . . do you
understand?

PROTASSOV. You said that beautifully, Lisa! Dmitri, you
understood, didn't you? Isn't it wonderful!

VAGUIN (*cruelly*). Pavel. Can't you see – she's gone mad.

PROTASSOV (*incredulous*). Surely not? Lyena?

ELYENA (*in a low voice*). Let's go . . . let's go after her . . .

> *All three go into the garden.* YEGOR *sits by the hedge and
> glares at them with grim hatred in his eyes.* TROSHIN *mutters
> something unintelligible, feeling his head and shoulder with a
> shaking hand.*

ROMAN. There's nothing to that. I been beaten harder than
that, an look on me! Noo shut te up! Alive, en't te? At's
good enough. Keep your silence, at's the way. Alive, an
that's fine.

VAGUIN (*thoughtfully*).
Two little flowers, dropped from the sky,
Alone on the vast red sands we lie . . .

CURTAIN

BARBARIANS

Characters

YEGOR PETROVICH CHERKOON, an engineer, aged 32

ANNA FYODOROVNA, his wife, aged 23

SERGEI NIKOLAYICH TSYGANOV, an engineer, aged 45

TATIANA NIKOLAEVNA BOGAYEVSKAYA, an upper-class landlady, aged 55

LYDIA PAVLOVNA, Tatiana's niece, aged 28

VASSILY IVANICH REDOZUBOV, mayor of the town, aged 60

GRISHA, Redozubov's son, aged 20

KATYA, Redozubov's daughter, aged 18

ARKHIP FOMICH PRITYKIN, a timber merchant, aged 35

PELAGEYA IVANOVA, Pritykin's wife, aged 45

MAVRIKY OSSIPOVICH MONAKHOV, an excise supervisor, aged 40

NADIEZHDA POLIKARPOVNA, Monakhov's wife, aged 28

PAVLIN SAVELICH GOLOVASTIKOV, a lower middle-class philosopher, aged 60

DROBYAZGIN, of the Treasury department, aged 25

DOCTOR MAKAROV, aged 40

VESYOLKINA, daughter of the Postmaster, aged 22

POLICE SUPERINTENDANT, aged 45

IVAKIN, gardener and bee-keeper, aged 50

STEPAN LUKIN, Ivakin's nephew, a student, aged 25

DUNYA'S HUSBAND, an indefinite character, aged about 40

MATVEY GOGIN, a village lad, aged 23

STYOPA, the Cherkoons' maid, aged 20

YEFIM, Ivakin's assistant, aged 40

Act One

A meadow on the bank of a river. Beyond the river can be seen a small provincial town, gently wrapped around by the green of the gardens. Nearer the audience is an orchard, with apple trees, cherry trees, rowans and limes, a few bee-hives, a round table dug into the ground, benches. Around the orchard is a dilapidated wattle fence, with old boots, an old jacket, a red shirt hung on the stakes. A road runs beside the fence, from the ferry to the posting station. In the orchard to the right can be seen the corner of a little old house with a lean-to covering a stall that sells bread, rolls, sunflower seeds and home-brewed beer. On the left, beside the fence, is a thatched building; the orchard continues beyond this.

A hot summer's afternoon. In the distance can be heard a corncrake, and, scarcely audible, the doleful note of a reed-pipe. In the orchard, on the earth bank below his window, sits IVAKIN, *clean-shaven and bald, with a kindly, comical face, he is playing with concentration on a guitar. Beside him is* PAVLIN, *a clean, neat little old man in a light, tight-fitting coat and a warm peaked cap. On the window-sill are a red jug of beer and some mugs.* MATVEY, *a village lad, is sitting on the ground by the fence, slowly chewing bread. From the right, from the direction of the station, comes the lazy voice of an ill woman.*

WOMAN (*off*). Yefim!

> *Silence.* DUNYA'S HUSBAND *appears on the road to the left, a man of indefinite age, tattered and timid. Again comes the cry.*

WOMAN (*off*). Yefim!
IVAKIN. Hey, Yefim!

> YEFIM *enters, coming along inside the fence.*

YEFIM. I heard. (*To* MATVEY.) What you think you're doing in here?

MATVEY. Nothing. Just . . . sitting.

A third cry from the woman, this time with irritation.

WOMAN (*off*). Yefim!!

IVAKIN. Yefim! What's up with you, man?

YEFIM (*calling*). Be right there! (*To* MATVEY.) You get along out of here.

> YEFIM *takes his shirt off the fence.* DUNYA'S HUSBAND *coughs and bows to him.*

Ah, you're here, are you? What you want?

DUNYA'S HUSBAND. I'm back from the monastery, Yefim Mitrich . . .

YEFIM (*walking on*). Turned you out, did they? Bunch of parasites. Smelly devils.

IVAKIN. When you're called, man, you should go. (*To* PAVLIN.) Little man likes to give orders.

> YEFIM *has gone.*

PAVLIN. All sizes want to do that.

IVAKIN. But people don't like it . . . they don't want to be yelled at for nothing. No.

PAVLIN. Doesn't matter what you do, people won't approve. All the same, everyone needs a bit of discipline.

IVAKIN. Now this little waltz, you can play this in a completely different style . . . like this. (*He plays.*)

DUNYA'S HUSBAND. Lord, how the man damned them, seen and unseen . . . And what for, eh?

MATVEY. It's hot.

DUNYA'S HUSBAND. I'm hot too, but I bear it in silence. Fact is, a man who's had even just a bite to eat, already he thinks he's someone's boss. Good bread?

MATVEY. Good, and mine.

DUNYA'S HUSBAND. Country stuff, eh? Yes, they bake good bread in the villages.

MATVEY. When there's flour to be had they do. But I bought this from Ivakin.

DUNYA'S HUSBAND. Really? Still, it smells just like the

country stuff to me. Would you — er — let me have a little
bit . . . just to try?

MATVEY. Not enough here for me.

DUNYA'S HUSBAND sighs, moves his lips.

IVAKIN. There, see. And you can play it even slower.

PAVLIN. You say it's called 'The Waltz of the Crazy Priest'?

IVAKIN. Just that.

PAVLIN. Why call it that? Don't I detect a certain yielding to
temptation there? A touch of disrespect for the clerical
status?

IVAKIN. Oh, there he goes, off being clever-clever again.
You're too damn pernickity, Pavlin!

PAVLIN. It's no good trying to get at me. Everyone knows that
humility is the essence of my soul. But I have a restless
mind.

IVAKIN. The fact is, my friend, you don't dispose people to
like you.

PAVLIN. Because above all things I love the truth. I murmur
not when the mob persecutes me. Resolute in my intentions,
I pursue only the truth, the whole truth, and nothing but the
truth.

IVAKIN. Of course. What else? Got yourself a nice little
house, nice little bit of land, nice little bit of money . . .

Voices can be heard, left. IVAKIN looks in that direction.

Here comes that girl, postmaster's daughter. Where would
she be going?

PAVLIN. Wagging her tail. A young woman of infernal
habits.

Enter DROBYAZGIN and VESYOLKINA.

VESYOLKINA. I tell you she was married to an engineer!

DROBYAZGIN. Maria Ivanovna, really! Why do you refuse to
believe in facts?

VESYOLKINA. I believe what I see, no more and no less.

DROBYAZGIN (*almost in despair*). But pessimism like that is
utterly out of keeping with your appearance. I tell you,

Lydia Ivanovna's husband was the director of a liquorice factory, and she didn't chuck him at all, he simply died of choking on a fish-bone.

VESYOLKINA. She chucked him, I tell you.

DROBYAZGIN. Maria Ivanovna, in the Department of Finance we know everything — everything!

VESYOLKINA. We know much more than you do in the Post Office, much much more! He stole some money and now he's being prosecuted . . . and she's mixed up in it too somehow. Oh yes!

DROBYAZGIN. Lydia Ivanovna? Oh, really! Why, Tatiana Nikolaevna herself told me . . .

VESYOLKINA. And as for arguing, you'd do better to treat me to some beer.

>IVAKIN *gets up and goes round the corner of the house.* PAVLIN *picks up* IVAKIN's *guitar, looks inside it, touches the strings.*

DROBYAZGIN. Yes of course, but . . . but all the same, you know, she's a widow!

VESYOLKINA. Is she really? All right, you'll see . . .

>*They exit towards the right.*

DUNYA'S HUSBAND (*softly*). Listen . . . listen . . . for the love of Christ . . . give me a — a bit!

MATVEY. Why didn't you come straight out with it? You asked to try it — who eats bread just to try it?

DUNYA'S HUSBAND. Straight out . . . it's so shameful . . . Thanks.

IVAKIN. Pavlin. Look — the town! Beautiful, eh? Like eggs in a frying-pan. Eh?

PAVLIN. They'll bring that railway through and it'll soon be ruined.

IVAKIN. Ruined? Why? Bellyaching again!

PAVLIN. An invasion of alien hordes . . .

>*Enter* VESYOLKINA *and* DROBYAZGIN. *They sit down at the table, drink beer, and talk in low voices.* IVAKIN *and* PAVLIN *move off behind the corner of the house.*

MATVEY. Who would you be, then?

DUNYA'S HUSBAND. From the town . . . I was.

MATVEY. Your townsfolk, now, they're rich . . . and what are you?

DUNYA'S HUSBAND. Ruined. I've lost my strength, lost everything. My wife was the ruin of me . . . my wife . . . yes. She was all right at first . . . we lived peacefully enough. She's pretty and lively, you know. Then suddenly — I'm bored, she says. She started to drink. I went along with that.

MATVEY. You drank too?

DUNYA'S HUSBAND. Oh yes, me too. What can you do? Then she went in for all sorts of debauchery, and of course I beat her for that . . . yes. So she — ran away. I had a little daughter . . . she ran away too when she was fourteen.

He is silent, thinking.

DROBYAZGIN (*loudly*). That's not true, Maria Ivanovna! The doctor and Nadiezhda Polikarpovna — they're both like people in a novel — you know, *romantic* people.

VESYOLKINA. Ssh! Not so loud!

MATVEY. Is she a loose woman too?

DUNYA'S HUSBAND. Who?

MATVEY. Your daughter.

DUNYA'S HUSBAND. No . . . I don't know. No idea where she is. Then someone beat me up when I was drunk — kicked me in the guts — and I haven't been well since . . . No good for work . . . don't know how to do anything anyway.

MATVEY. Fine sight you are too. How do you manage?

DUNYA'S HUSBAND. Just . . . day by day.

DROBYAZGIN (*jumping up*). Maria Ivanovna! It's amazing . . in fact it's terrible! You simply will not believe in anything bright and noble . . .

VESYOLKINA. Don't shout! You're crazy, you know.

DROBYAZGIN. No! To say that Lydia Ivanovna . . . and the police superintendant . . . no.

VESYOLKINA. Sit down.

DUNYA'S HUSBAND. The engineers are coming today.

MATVEY. To build the railway?

DUNYA'S HUSBAND. Yes . . . They build their iron roads, but there's nowhere for a man to go . . .

MATVEY. Still, there'll be some work, eh? A bit of work for a while, think of that!

PAVLIN appears in the orchard, goes towards the table. VESYOLKINA sees him coming.

VESYOLKINA. Here comes Pavlin Savel'ich . . .

DROBYAZGIN. Well, venerable sage, what have you got to say to us?

PAVLIN. Good health to you both.

DROBYAZGIN. Thank you.

PAVLIN. The mayor has just crossed the river. He's on his way here.

VESYOLKINA. Wants to meet the engineers — imagine, that proud old man!

Enter IVAKIN, panting.

DROBYAZGIN. Yes . . . Well, Ivan Ivanich — hot, eh?

IVAKIN gazes into the distance, left.

IVAKIN. Ye-es.

PAVLIN. Impatience, that's what intensifies the heat. Look at me, I'm not expecting anyone, so I don't feel the heat.

IVAKIN. The doctor's coming . . . and that Excise officer . . .

VESYOLKINA. Who are we expecting, then? We're not expecting anyone either.

PAVLIN. I wasn't talking about you — it's him, he's expecting his nephew.

DROBYAZGIN. The student?

IVAKIN. Yes . . . That timber merchant, Pritykin, he's coming too.

VESYOLKINA. The town's very first student — that's interesting, isn't it?

DROBYAZGIN. Ah, but not the first, though, Maria Ivanovna! That statistician who went and shot himself . . .

VESYOLKINA. Doesn't count. He hadn't finished his studies . . .

PAVLIN. That's right, he was thrown out for blatant political behaviour . . .

IVAKIN (*brusquely*). And he shot himself because you wrote a denunciation of him. Why you had to go and do a thing like that . . . only another dirty dog would know.

IVAKIN moves away. PAVLIN calls after him

PAVLIN. I shall always denounce the deleterious when I see it! (*To the others.*) Ivan Ivanich is a man with an extremely coarse nature. Furthermore, he's unfair. I know for sure that our statistician friend shot himself because of his hopeless love for Nadiezhda Polikarpovna.

DROBYAZGIN. How do you know that?

PAVLIN. Because I pay attention.

Along the road from the left come the DOCTOR, MONAKHOV and PRITYKIN. DUNYA'S HUSBAND slips away unnoticed. MATVEY stands up and bows.

PRITYKIN. No, doctor, I'm sorry, but I can't understand what possible pleasure there can be in catching fish.

DOCTOR (*morosely*). At least a fish doesn't talk.

MONAKHOV. What do you understand about anything, anyway, nuncle? Very little indeed. Your bath in the summer and your steam-box in the winter — that's the sum of your spiritual pleasures.

PAVLIN goes over to the bank and sits down by the fence.

PRITYKIN. The human body likes to be clean.

DROBYAZGIN (*shouts*). We're here already!

The DOCTOR stops by the fence.

DOCTOR. Order us some beer, Drobyazgin.

DROBYAZGIN (*shouts*). Ivakin! Fetch us some beer — good and cold, and plenty of it.

PRITYKIN. When you're playing cards, it's good to catch a man revoking.

MONAKHOV. I won't argue with that.

PRITYKIN. And then there's music. When the trumpeters get going I feel like a guardsman.

DOCTOR (*smiling grimly at* MONAKHOV). Now he's flattering you.

> DROBYAZGIN *goes to the fence and stands listening. It's clear he wants to join in the conversation, but he can't manage it.* VESYOLKINA *goes further into the orchard, gazes at the town, and sighs softly.*

PRITYKIN. How would that help me? But there you are — now he's taught the whole fire brigade to be musicians Mavriky Ossipovich has earned everlasting fame in the eyes of the entire town.

MONAKHOV. We-ell, I don't know about that. But I'll tell you this — I had to work damned hard on them. They're not men, they're walrusses.

PRITYKIN. Mavriky Ossipovich, even when I look at a samovar these days, I think of you.

DOCTOR (*unsmiling*). Does he look like a samovar?

> DROBYAZGIN *laughs.*

PRITYKIN. Not at all. I only meant — brass in any shape or form reminds me of you.

DOCTOR. He's going to pulverise you with flattery.

PRITYKIN. Reminds me of your musical work, that is.

MONAKHOV. What are you up to, nuncle, singing sweetly like this?

PRITYKIN. If I do sing, I sing like a lark, without any ulterior motive . . . And as for the sneering of this doctor here, he's a man of an altogether morose character. He doesn't like anything at all — except perhaps fish.

> MONAKHOV *looks off to one side.*

MONAKHOV. Our ladies seem to be tired. Look, they're barely moving.

DROBYAZGIN. It's hardest for Tatiana Nikolaevna, with all that weight and all those years.

IVAKIN. Here's the beer.

DOCTOR. Well, I'm not going to walk round . . .

The DOCTOR *steps over the fence.*

MONAKHOV. And her niece doesn't seem to be interested in our company.

DROBYAZGIN. Lydia Pavlovna sees herself as a lady of high society. She has haughty way with her.

PRITYKIN. She sits a horse well.

MONAKHOV. Ay, she does that well enough, nuncle.

PRITYKIN. There we were, talking about what's pleasant in life, and forgot all about the female sex — and what could be pleasanter? Mind you, I'm not talking about my wife, of course.

MONAKHOV (*laughing*). Come on, Fomich, let's drink our beer.

They walk along the fence.

PRITYKIN. But time's passing, the mail-coach should be here by now. Let's see what they look like, these constructors.

MONAKHOV. M'm, yes — interesting to see. They'll play cards, that's certain.

PRITYKIN. And take a little drink too I should think, eh?

They exit. Enter DUNYA'S HUSBAND.

MATVEY. Everyone getting ready to meet these engineers, are they?

DUNYA'S HUSBAND. They've gone on down to the village, to the fair, for . . . for a walk. But there you are — people get hold of some money and everyone wants to know them.

Enter LYDIA IVANOVNA *from the right. She is dressed in a riding habit, with a whip.*

LYDIA. Look, be an angel and hold my horse for a while. I'll pay.

MATVEY. I can do that.

LYDIA. Please do.

LYDIA *exits right.*

MATVEY. Ah, there's something!

DUNYA'S HUSBAND (*enviously and anxiously*). There, you see, if you hadn't been here she'd have had to ask me to look after her horse . . . aarch! Listen, if she gives you a big tip, let me have just . . . just five copeks? Will you, Matvey?

MATVEY. She may only give me five.

> *Both exit right. The* DOCTOR *and* VESYOLKINA *are talking in the orchard.*

DOCTOR (*morosely*). When people are young they write all kinds of stuff.

PAVLIN (*getting up*). May I point out that the holy fathers also wrote when they were at an advanced age.

DOCTOR. So what?

PAVLIN. Nothing. Just that.

> *Enter* PELAGEYA, PRITYKIN *and* NADIEZHDA, *the latter a very beautiful woman, tall with enormous, motionless eyes.* BOGAYEVSKAYA *is behind her.*

NADIEZHDA. And then he says to her, 'Alissa, my love for you will never die until I die myself, as long as I live I am yours alone!'

PELAGEYA. Just imagine! And our men couldn't even put words like that together!

> NADIEZHDA *sits down on a log.*

NADIEZHDA. A Frenchman, now, he may be unfaithful but he's a noble and passionate lover. A Spaniard loves fiercely, even ferociously, and an Italian in love will always play his guitar every night below the window of the woman he loves.

BOGAYEVSKAYA. They taught you to read, Nadiezhda, but it was all for nothing.

NADIEZHDA. Tatiana Nikolaevna, you're of an age when all this is no longer of any interest to you, but I . . .

BOGAYEVSKAYA. But you . . . do nothing but wag your tongue.

PELAGEYA. I envy you, though, my dear. You know so many love stories, and they're all such good stories, just like the dreams of a young girl! Where's that Arkhip of mine?

BOGAYEVSKAYA. That's Lidochka's horse over there.

NADIEZHDA. Do introduce me . . .

BOGAYEVSKAYA. To the horse?

NADIEZHDA *(seriously)*. No, to Lydia Pavlovna.

BOGAYEVSKAYA. There you are, darling girl — you've read a thousand novels but you can't even ask a simple question properly . . . it makes you look quite ridiculous.

NADIEZHDA *(calmly)*. Never mind. Nobody can get everything right.

BOGAYEVSKAYA *walks off to the right, calling.*

BOGAYEVSKAYA. Lidusha!

PELAGEYA *(softly)*. Dear oh Lord, she's so rude to you!

NADIEZHDA *(calmly)*. The gentry always talk like that to ordinary folk. Even in novels, where everything's much better than in real life, the gentry are always impertinent. Oh, look — isn't she beautiful!

BOGAYEVSKAYA *enters, followed by* LYDIA.

BOGAYEVSKAYA. Here she is — Lidushka, Nadiezhda Polikarpovna was asking to be introduced to you.

NADIEZHDA *curtseys.*

BOGAYEVSKAYA. You see, she even knows how to curtsey.

The DOCTOR *comes up to them.*

NADIEZHDA. I know you by sight. Every day you go cantering past our house on your horse and I look out and admire you — you look just like a — a countess, or a marquise! It's so lovely.

LYDIA. I often see your face at the window, and admire it too.

NADIEZHDA. Thank you. It's pleasant to hear one's beauty praised, even by a woman.

BOGAYEVSKAYA. Just listen to that!

DOCTOR *(gloomily)*. Is it more pleasant to hear it from a woman or from a man?

NADIEZHDA. An appropriate appreciation of beauty can

only of course come from a man.

LYDIA. How confidently you said that . . .

PRITYKIN (*shouting*). Listen, everyone! They're coming! Listen.

They all listen. The sound of bells.

NADIEZHDA (*to* LYDIA). Aren't you fascinated to see what they're like?

LYDIA. Who? Aunt, it's time we were going.

NADIEZHDA. The engineers.

PRITYKIN *comes running in.*

PRITYKIN. They're just coming!

LYDIA (*to* NADIEZHDA). No.

BOGAYEVSKAYA. I'm tired, Lidushka. Wait a minute.

PELAGEYA. What about if they're old?

LYDIA (*softly, to her aunt*). It's like a reception ceremony — quite ridiculous.

BOGAYEVSKAYA. Let's go into the orchard . . . I'll just get something to drink . . . Come on . . .

She starts to move off. They all follow her slowly.

PRITYKIN. So they've arrived, eh, Doctor? Interesting, isn't it?

DOCTOR (*morosely*). Why? If they'd walked all the way — well, that might be something.

NADIEZHDA. Oh, rubbish!

BOGAYEVSKAYA. She'd like to see them arriving on horseback, in armour, with great billowing cloaks.

They all exit right, their slow conversation drowned in the sound of the bells. From the right appears REDOZUBOV, *the mayor, walking slowly, his hands behind his back. He is a grey-haired, severe old man with black rugged eyebrows. He stops, listening to the noise from the posting station. Enter* PAVLIN, *taking off his cap well before they meet.*

REDOZUBOV. Afternoon. You well?

PAVLIN. Thank you, thank you, and what wonderful news

am I going to hear about your own precious health?

REDOZUBOV. Ask the doctor. Arrived, have they?

PAVLIN. Absolutely — our long expected construction
  engineers! One is middle-aged, with a moustache, already a
  bit intoxicated it seems . . . the other's rather younger and
  amazingly red-headed. There's a young lady with them,
  very beautiful, and her maid, all dolled up . . . They came
  in two carriages and there's a third with all their things and
  that student, Ivakin's nephew.

REDOZUBOV. What's he doing with them?

PAVLIN. Evidently due to his poverty-stricken condition he
  has had to adapt himself to the usages of charity . . .

REDOZUBOV. Is that Madam Bogayevskaya's horse?

PAVLIN. Hers, yes. She went for a drive to Fokina, and now
  she's tidying herself up at Daria Ivakina's — Daria was her
  maid for a long time, you know, living in . . . and now her
  mother's the housekeeper there . . .

REDOZUBOV (*with a gloomy laugh*). What do you know about
  the grandmother?

PAVLIN. The grandmother? Ah, I don't quite remember . . .

  Enter PRITYKIN.

PRITYKIN. Good afternoon, Vassily Ivanich.

REDOZUBOV (*not shaking hands*). Afternoon.

PRITYKIN. Have you come to meet our guests?

REDOZUBOV. They mean nothing to me.

PRITYKIN. Oh, but — just in general — they're useful people
  for the town.

REDOZUBOV. Well, let the town meet them then.

  He walks off towards the station.

PRITYKIN (*softly*). He can't mean that?

PAVLIN. Of course not. He's just longing to get a contract for
  the railway sleepers.

PRITYKIN. Sly old devil. Pavlin — you see if you can get to
  know their maid and find out — you know, generally —
  what's what? Know what I mean?

PAVLIN. I know.

They exit towards the station. Enter IVAKIN, *looking happy,
with* STEPAN LUKIN.

STEPAN. Well, how's life with you?

IVAKIN. As you can see, I'm fit — what else does a man
    need? But you're looking a bit yellow round the gills — in
    fact you look completely washed up. Why d'you have to go
    and get yourself chucked into prison?

STEPAN. Impossible not to. It's become a universal obligation
    now, brother, like military service . . . anyway, it's not
    important. But don't you go talking about it, brother, will
    you? Understand?

IVAKIN. Brother, indeed! I'm not your brother, I'm your
    uncle.

STEPAN. Ah, come on, what sort of uncle are you? You're just
    a friend from my childhood, that's all. Look, I've got a bit
    of a beard on me and you haven't lost your hair yet . . .

IVAKIN. That's enough of that. Come and have a beer, and
    show some respect for your elders.

PRITYKIN *comes running in and looks around.*

IVAKIN. What is it, Arkhip Fomich?

PRITYKIN. Oh, it's just . . . (*Calls off.*) Hey, lad, come here.

MATVEY *enters.*

You know who I am? Right. Run into town, to my place,
and tell them to have horses ready at the ferry, with a cab,
and a cart for the luggage. Got all that? Off you go then!

MATVEY *runs off, calling as he goes.*

MATVEY. Hey, keep an eye on the horse, will you?

IVAKIN. The town of Verkhopolye has started spinning like a
    top.

STEPAN. What's wrong with your bridge?

IVAKIN. Collapsed in the floods. Of course the mayor's in no
    hurry to get it mended — he runs the ferry, doesn't he?
    D'you know these engineers?

STEPAN. I'm going to work for them. How are all your
    beehives? And your guitar? And the fishing?

IVAKIN. All in order.

> *Enter the* DOCTOR, MONAKHOV, DROBYAZGIN,
> VESYOLKINA. IVAKIN *and* STEPAN *leave the orchard.*
> PAVLIN *appears in their place, stands there for a moment,
> and then vanishes, to reappear in the course of the conversa-
> tion between* TSYGANOV *and* DUNYA'S HUSBAND.

MONAKHOV (*enviously*). That Pritykin didn't waste any time
  making their acquaintance, the little rat!

VESYOLKINA. Doctor, have you noticed that young man —
  his hair? Just like a blazing torch!

DOCTOR. When have you ever seen a blazing torch?

VESYOLKINA. What about funerals? — remember when
  Prince whatsisname was buried . . .?

DROBYAZGIN. What marvellous eyes she has! Mavriky
  Ossipovich, did you notice?

VESYOLKINA. Nonsense! Perfectly ordinary eyes . . .

DROBYAZGIN. They are not! They're poetic eyes, remarkably
  poetic . . .

MONAKHOV. Anyway it's not polite to talk about the beauty
  of one lady in front of another.

DOCTOR. It's revolting — everyone rushing about like — like
  maybugs around a fire . . .

PRITYKIN (*off, shouting*). Doctor! Can you come here please?

DOCTOR. What for?

PRITYKIN. You're needed . . . professionally.

DOCTOR. Oh, rubbish.

> *He exits.*

MONAKHOV (*enviously*). So you're going to make their
  acquaintance too, nuncle.

> VESYOLKINA *goes out after the* DOCTOR. TSYGANOV
> *meets her as she exits, an elegantly dressed gentleman, slightly
> tight. She is embarrassed and for some reason turns abruptly
> away from him.* TSYGANOV *looks askance, raising his
> eyebrows.* DROBYAZGIN *bows to him.*

TSYGANOV (*touching his hat*). Good afternoon. Who do I have the honour to be . . .?

DROBYAZGIN (*embarrassed*). Er . . . um . . . Porfiry . . . that
is . . . um . . . Department of Finance Clerk Porfiry
Drobyazgin . . . an . . . um . . . official.

TSYGANOV. Aha! Delighted! Tell me, is there an hotel in this
town?

DROBYAZGIN. Oh indeed, yes! With — with a billiard room!
And there's a high school . . . for girls.

TSYGANOV. Really? Thank you very much. I don't think I
have any special need for a girls' high school . . . Are there
any cabs?

DROBYAZGIN. Oh yes — three! They wait by the church.

TSYGANOV (*looking towards the town*). If one were to call, they
wouldn't hear, would they?

DROBYAZGIN (*smiling*). How could they, sir? It's a long
way . . .

Enter DUNYA'S HUSBAND *from the left.*

DUNYA'S HUSBAND. Your excellency, sir, help a sick,
unfortunate man . . .

TSYGANOV (*finding a coin*). Certainly — here — you're
welcome.

DUNYA'S HUSBAND *shudders with delight.*

DUNYA'S HUSBAND. Lord grant you . . . bless you . . . may
you . . .

He gulps, and exits.

TSYGANOV. A drinker?

DROBYAZGIN. No. He really is unfortunate . . . always
ill . . . and his wife ran off and left him . . . and altogether
he's . . .

MONAKHOV *comes up, interrupting.*

MONAKHOV. Excuse me, sir, if I may make so bold . . .

TSYGANOV. Please . . .

MONAKHOV. Mavriky Ossipovich Monakhov, Excise Supervisor . . .

TSYGANOV. Most honoured . . . Sergei Nikolayich Tsyganov.

MONAKHOV. Allow me to inform you, sir, that the hotel is dirty and full of bed-bugs . . .

DROBYAZGIN. Indubitable bed-bugs, and vast in number.

MONAKHOV. You should rent Madam Bogayevskaya's house, it's the best house in town, a real gentleman's residence, you know! As a matter of fact, I think she's still here, I'll go and arrange it at once . . .

He goes out quickly. ANNA FYODOROVNA *and* STYOPA *are entering.*

TSYGANOV. Wait a minute though — it's very kind of you but . . . listen!

DROBYAZGIN (*dashing off*). I'll bring him back immediately . . .

TSYGANOV. No, no . . . Oh, it's absurd! He's run off now!

ANNA. What's the matter?

TSYGANOV. They're very amiable here — just like real savages. Let me congratulate you — there are no hotels in the town . . . or rather, there is an hotel — just one — but it's full of bedbugs.

ANNA. It seems to be difficult to reach the town, too — something's happened to the ferry.

TSYGANOV *beckons, off.*

TSYGANOV. Hey, listen, you — come over here.

DUNYA'S HUSBAND *enters.*

TSYGANOV. Tell me now . . . in this town of yours, is there anything . . . remarkable?

DUNYA'S HUSBAND. Crayfish, sir! Supergigantical crayfish!

STYOPA *is looking at* DUNYA'S HUSBAND *intently.*

TSYGANOV. H'm, well, that's something, I suppose . . . from time to time, anyway. But they probably live in the river, don't they, not in the town?

DUNYA'S HUSBAND. Yes, yes, in the river . . . they're . . .

they live . . . you know . . . in the water.

STYOPA (*softly, of* DUNYA'S HUSBAND). Anna Fyodorovna . . . it's him!

ANNA. Who?

STYOPA. Father . . . my father! What'll I do?

TSYGANOV. And what is there in the town?

DUNYA'S HUSBAND. The fire brigade. They play trumpets.
Brass trumpets. The Excise man taught them.

ANNA. Be quiet. Stand behind me.

TSYGANOV. Do they play loudly?

DUNYA'S HUSBAND. Absolutely full blast!

STYOPA. I'll go over there . . . towards the station . . . he
hasn't seen me.

TSYGANOV. That's no comfort at all, I must say. Well,
thanks . . . here, that's for your trouble.

DUNYA'S HUSBAND. Oh, your excellency!

He tries to kiss TSYGANOV's *hand.*

TSYGANOV (*with revulsion*). No, please, no need for that . . .
Off you go now!

DUNYA'S HUSBAND *exits:* STYOPA *gazes after him.*

STYOPA. A beggar . . . my father's a beggar. I told you I'd be
bound to meet him. I told you I mustn't come here . . . I
told you!

ANNA. Don't fuss. I'll keep him away from you.

STYOPA. I'm scared. He drove my mother into the
ground . . . A beggar!

TSYGANOV. May one ask what's going on?

ANNA. That's her father.

TSYGANOV. Aha! How amusing.

ANNA. Is that all you can say? Go on, Styopa, go along to the
station.

TSYGANOV. We'll look after you, don't worry.

CHERKOON *shouts from offstage.*

CHERKOON. Anna! Anna, come here!

TSYGANOV *looks in the direction of the shout.*

TSYGANOV. Who's that he's talking to? Hold on . . . no, dammit, I don't believe it . . .

ANNA *calls back to* CHERKOON.

ANNA. Yes, what is it?

TSYGANOV, *delighted,* stretches out his arms towards LYDIA, *who is approaching.*

TSYGANOV. Lydia Pavlovna, is it really you? It is, it is!

LYDIA *comes up to him.*

LYDIA. Sergey, my dear.

TSYGANOV. You, here in Tierra del Fuego among the savages! Why?

VESYOLKINA *appears in the orchard. She is walking along, fanning her face with some flowers.* DROBYAZGIN *appears, and they walk side by side, listening to the conversation.*

LYDIA. I came to stay with my aunt. It's good to see you. But as usual you seem to be . . .

TSYGANOV. Embroiled with business. That's my fate. My first acquaintance on this alien soil turns out to be the Excise man.

LYDIA. And is that your wife?

TSYGANOV. Mine? I never have had, and never will have, such a property. And where is your esteemed husband?

LYDIA. Frankly, I don't know. And nothing could interest me less.

TSYGANOV. Do I understand from that . . .? Well, bravo! So you've split up at last, have you?

VESYOLKINA (*hearing* TSYGANOV's *words*). Well? Who was right, eh?

DROBYAZGIN *hunches his shoulders in embarrassment.*

LYDIA. Don't shout it about.

TSYGANOV. I think you've met my partner already? Georges, come here . . .

CHERKOON *approaches.*

Here is a man whose nerve is as bold as his hair is red . . .
You know who this is, Georges? You remember how much
and how often I've talked about a certain young lady . . .

CHERKOON. I do remember, indeed . . . In fact he's talked a
great deal about you.

LYDIA. I'm touched.

CHERKOON. . . . but I never expected I'd meet you . . . and
certainly not in a gloomy dump like this.

LYDIA. You don't like the town?

CHERKOON. I don't like pastoral scenes.

TSYGANOV. He only likes scandalous scenes.

NADIEZHDA *enters, stands and stares at* CHERKOON. *She
is motionless as a statue, her face like stone.*

CHERKOON. All these little houses hiding themselves in the
trees like birds' nests . . . it's sickeningly peaceful, repul-
sively 'nice' . . . makes one feel like tearing the whole idyllic
scene to pieces.

TSYGANOV. Introduce her to your wife.

CHERKOON. Oh, yes, may I?

LYDIA. Please do. But you're very harsh about our poor little
town.

TSYGANOV. I can see that at last you're going to start
appreciating the tenderness of my soul and all my other
worthy qualities.

CHERKOON. Whatever I see, I always like it or dislike it on
the spot.

TSYGANOV. He is, as you see, a man without qualities.

LYDIA. A person with nothing but faults? At least that's
something definite.

TSYGANOV *notices* NADIEZHDA.

TSYGANOV. H'm. Georges, go on — introduce her to your
wife.

CHERKOON (*calling*). Anna! She'll probably love this sweet
little scene, she's a dreamer, a great one for peace and
quiet.

LYDIA. A lot of people find a scene like that poetic.

CHERKOON. Cowards, wasters, people who are tired of life . . .

TSYGANOV. Who is that dignified lady coming towards us with your wife?

LYDIA. That's my aunt.

Enter ANNA, *with* BOGAYEVSKAYA.

CHERKOON. Anna, you must meet Lydia Pavlovna, this lady's niece . . .

BOGAYEVSKAYA. Let me introduce you, Lidusha . . . (*introductions.*) They're renting my big house.

ANNA. I'm so glad everything's been arranged so quickly and neatly.

TSYGANOV. Long live the architect of this triumph, the great and good Supervisor of Excise.

LYDIA. Shush — his wife is in the orchard.

TSYGANOV. That's his wife? H'm.

TSYGANOV *stares at* NADIEZHDA.

ANNA. But I'm tired now. I'd like to get there as soon as possible.

BOGAYEVSKAYA. They'll be bringing the ferry across in a moment.

NADIEZHDA *walks off slowly.*

CHERKOON. And there are horses waiting for us on the other bank already. That timber merchant arranged it — what's his name?

BOGAYEVSKAYA. Pritykin. Lidusha, I'll go over in the boat and get things ready, see to whatever they need.

ANNA. Oh, don't worry about us.

CHERKOON. We're not helpless.

LYDIA (*To* BOGAYEVSKAYA). Wait a minute. (*To* ANNA.) Do you ride?

ANNA. Oh no!

LYDIA. That's a pity. I was going to offer you my horse — there's a ford a little way upstream.

ANNA. Thank you. But I'm afraid of horses — I once saw a

boy being killed by a horse and ever since I've always felt
that every horse is going to kill someone.

LYDIA (*smiling*). But you'll travel in a carriage? You're not
afraid of that?

ANNA. No, that's not the same. There's a coachman in front
of me, or a cabby.

CHERKOON. All that may be very touching, Anna, but God
knows, it's not amusing!

ANNA. I wasn't trying to be amusing.

TSYGANOV (*To* LYDIA). And so we meet again!

CHERKOON (*to* ANNA). You might occasionally make the
effort.

TSYGANOV. Something of a miracle, isn't it?

LYDIA. Perhaps it just shows what a cramped little world it is.

BOGAYEVSKAYA (*to* ANNA). Come over here and see how
pretty and neat the little town looks.

She takes ANNA *over to the fence.*

TSYGANOV. You're more beautiful than ever . . . And there's
something new in your eyes.

LYDIA. Probably boredom.

CHERKOON. Are you bored?

LYDIA. Life in general doesn't seem to me particularly
cheerful.

REDOZUBOV *appears from the direction of the station. He
comes up, stops, coughs. No-one notices. He raises his hand to
his cap and drops it again hurriedly as if the gesture might
have been noticed.*

CHERKOON. I didn't expect you to say that.

LYDIA. Why not?

CHERKOON. I don't know. I suppose I thought you'd have a
different view of life from that.

LYDIA. Well, what is life? Just people. I've seen plenty of
people. They get monotonous.

REDOZUBOV. I am the local mayor. Vassily Ivanov Redozubov. The mayor.

CHERKOON (*coldly*). What do you want?

REDOZUBOV. I want to speak to the chief engineer. Are you in charge?

TSYGANOV. We're both in charge. Can you conceive such an idea?

REDOZUBOV. It's all the same to me. Will you be needing timber for sleepers?

CHERKOON (*coldly*). My dear man, I shall start discussing business in a week's time, not before.

Pause.

REDOZUBOV (*surprised*). You — er — perhaps you didn't . . .

CHERKOON. Didn't what?

REDOZUBOV. I said . . . I'm the mayor of this town, I said.

CHERKOON. I heard you. So what?

REDOZUBOV (*containing his anger*). I am a man of sixty-three, the senior church elder . . . the whole town is run by me . . .

CHERKOON. Why do you imagine I need to know all that?

TSYGANOV. Most respected Mister Mayor, as soon as we've had time to settle ourselves in a bit we'll certainly be taking account of all your rare qualities.

CHERKOON. But for the moment leave us in peace. When we want you, we'll send for you.

REDOZUBOV *measures* CHERKOON *with an an angry look and walks away in silence.*

ANNA. Why did you have to be so offensive, Yegor? He is old, after all.

CHERKOON. An old ruffian. I know his sort. He's not a mayor, he's a horse — a stupid, greedy, cocky old cart-horse.

TSYGANOV (*to* LYDIA). What do you think of this red-headed bruiser?

LYDIA (*coldly*). Not much, to be honest.

BOGAYEVSKAYA. Lida, we must go.

ANNA. My husband always sounds abrupt, but really . . .

CHERKOON. He's gentle and kind — is that what you were going to say? Don't listen to her. I am exactly what I seem to be.

LYDIA. Goodbye. Oh, look! That man's got no idea how to handle a horse!

She walks quickly off, right, followed by BOGAYEVSKAYA.

BOGAYEVSKAYA. So — we'll be expecting you.

TSYGANOV. We're very grateful. We shan't be long.

ANNA. Where's that student of ours?

CHERKOON *gazes at the town.*

CHERKOON. Don't know.

ANNA. Do you think we can ask him to look after our things? We can't leave Styopa alone.

CHERKOON. He's not a footman.

TSYGANOV. Georges! You're looking at that town like Attila in front of Rome . . . How little everything in the world has become!

CHERKOON. Repulsive little place . . . Has that woman had lovers?

TSYGANOV. Now look here, brother Georges — what a question!

ANNA. Yegor! Really!

CHERKOON. What? You shocked? Didn't you know that lots of women have lovers?

ANNA. But people don't talk about it like that.

CHERKOON. People don't. I do. Is it immoral?

ANNA. It's improper. And coarse.

CHERKOON. Really? I thought it was immoral. Has she, Sergey?

TSYGANOV. I don't know. I refuse to contemplate it. And if anyone came and told me anything . . . like that . . . about her, I'd refuse to believe them.

Enter PRITYKIN *and* DUNYA'S HUSBAND.

PRITYKIN. Everything's ready, if you'd be so good as to come! Your luggage is on the ferry already.

TSYGANOV. Thank you. You have been busy, haven't you?

PRITYKIN. Not at all, it's nothing, nothing . . . the duties of hospitality, you know . . .

TSYGANOV. You're a most amiable man, to be sure! Tell me now — what do people drink round here.

PRITYKIN. Oh, everything, everything!

TSYGANOV. But what do they prefer?

PRITYKIN. Vodka.

TSYGANOV. A coarse taste, but a healthy one.

They exit together.

CHERKOON (*to* ANNA). Come on.

ANNA *takes* CHERKOON'*s arm.*

ANNA. Yegor, tell me — why have you suddenly got so . . . gloomy?

CHERKOON. I'm tired.

ANNA. That's not true. You're never tired.

CHERKOON. Well then, I'm in love.

ANNA (*softly*). Why are you being so coarse, Yegor? Why?

DUNYA'S HUSBAND *comes up to them.*

DUNYA'S HUSBAND. Your excellency . . .

CHERKOON. Go away.

ANNA *gives him a coin.*

ANNA. Here.

ANNA *and* CHERKOON *exit.* MATVEY *jumps on.*

MATVEY. How much did she give you?

DUNYA'S HUSBAND. Twenty copeks. But altogether, a rouble twenty came my way.

MATVEY. You lucky dog! I only got two fives!

PRITYKIN (*shouting, off*). Hey! You, boy!

MATVEY. Coming!

MATVEY *runs off.* PAVLIN *steps over the fence.*

PAVLIN. Did you say, a rouble twenty?

DUNYA'S HUSBAND (*timidly*). Yes, a rouble twenty.

PAVLIN. Show me . . . H'm yes, that's right. And what for, eh? Eh? Ah, you mangy old rat, you, get along with

you . . . No, wait, there's a little item I could tell you . . .
d'you want to hear?

DUNYA'S HUSBAND. Yes please, Pavlin Savelich . . .

Enter REDOZUBOV.

PAVLIN (*severely*). Go on, go on, what are you doing, hanging
about here!

DUNYA'S HUSBAND *leaves*.

REDOZUBOV. Have they gone?

PAVLIN. Yes.

REDOZUBOV. What were you talking to their maid about?

PAVLIN. All sorts of things . . . everything . . . but I couldn't
do anything with her. I even gave her a rouble . . .

REDOZUBOV. Why did you do that? She might say you tried
to bribe her.

PAVLIN. Ah, well, now, Vassily Ivanich, I didn't *really* — I
gave it to her *in my mind*, if you follow, I just thought to
myself, what if I give her a rouble? And then I thought, no,
it won't help, she's too spoilt, this girl.

REDOZUBOV *stares at the town, not listening*.

Vassily Ivanich! You know she's a runaway? She's the
daughter of Dunya's husband . . . she admitted it!

REDOZUBOV (*abruptly, severely*). And do you know, Pavlin
Savelich, that the Governor himself shakes hands with me?

PAVLIN (*reverentially*). Of course I know! Everyone knows
that!

Pause. STEPAN's *voice comes from the window*.

REDOZUBOV (*softly*). Who's that talking?

PAVLIN. Ivakin's nephew. The student.

REDOZUBOV (*softly*). Quiet.

*They listen. A dog is howling unhappily in the distance; the
call of a corncrake.*

STEPAN (*off*). We're going to build a new railroad through
here and destroy this old life of yours completely.

STEPAN *laughs.*

REDOZUBOV (*softly*). You hear?
PAVLIN (*with conviction*). He's talking nonsense.
REDOZUBOV. Don't forget.

He exits, followed by PAVLIN.

CURTAIN

Act Two

The garden of BOGAYEVSKAYA'*s house. A canvas awning is stretched out between the trees, over a very large, simple, unpainted table. At the table is* CHERKOON, *in front of him a pile of papers, maps, plans. The house is on the left; a wide path leads up to it. At the end of the garden, a fence. Under the trees to the left sits* ANNA, *in a wicker chair, with a book in her hands. She stretches.*

ANNA. Are you hot?

CHERKOON. Of course.

ANNA. Still no sign of Sergey Nikolayich. You always do far more than he does, yet you always choose to work with him. Why?

CHERKOON (*without looking up*). He's got far more experience than I have.

ANNA. But he's so . . . dissipated.

CHERKOON. Knowledge is more valuable than morals.

Pause.

ANNA. They're all so inquisitive here . . . always watching us, following our movements . . . Naive people.

CHERKOON. To put it simply — idiots.

ANNA. Right now there's someone in the next door garden peeking through the fence. I can see their eyes glinting.

CHERKOON. To hell with them. Let them glint.

Enter STEPAN.

STEPAN. Well, I've taken on that boy, Matvey Gogin. Here are his cards.

ANNA. Give them to me.

CHERKOON. No, don't give them to her, she'll stuff them away somewhere or other and then forget where she put them. I tell you, it's no joke . . .

STEPAN. My god, the people here! It's like a zoo. When you

look at them you start to have doubts about the future of Russia. And when you think of the thousands of towns and villages there are out there, all populated by characters like these — it's enough to swamp your soul in one-hundred-degree proof pessimism.

CHERKOON. For a working man pessimism's about as useful as white gloves. Well, what's this Matvey like?

STEPAN. Doesn't seem too stupid. Anyway, here he comes . . . You don't need me here?

Enter MATVEY, *dressed more tidily than in Act One.*

CHERKOON. No. (STEPAN *exits. To* MATVEY.) Well, what have you got to say for yourself?

MATVEY. Well, I'd like to thank you for hiring me, your excellency . . .

CHERKOON. My name is Yegor Petrovich, and like you I'm a peasant, not some kind of nob. We've got nothing to thank each other for. You're going to do some work for me, I'm going to pay you some money. If you slack I'll fire you, and if you try to swindle me I'll have you run in. That clear?

MATVEY. Yes, sir. I'll try my best for you . . .

CHERKOON. We'll see. Off you go now.

MATVEY *hesitates, thinking.*

MATVEY. Thank you kindly, sir . . .

CHERKOON (*glancing up*). Still here?

MATVEY. Sir?

CHERKOON. Nothing. Go on.

MATVEY *exits. Pause.*

ANNA. You're always so demanding with people, Yegor.

CHERKOON. That's how they were with me.

Pause.

ANNA. Do you like Tatiana Nikolaevna?

CHERKOON. Yes. I like her niece even more.

ANNA. Why do you tease me?

CHERKOON. Why do you allow me to? Protest.

GRISHA REDOZUBOV's *head appears over the fence.*

ANNA (*alarmed*). Look, Yegor, look!

CHERKOON (*surprised*). What do you want?

GRISHA. Grisha Redozubov. The mayor's son. We're your neighbours.

ANNA. He's got such an amiable smile, Yegor — invite him over.

CHERKOON. Well, come on over and see us, let's get to know each other.

GRISHA. I can't climb over this. I'm too fat.

ANNA (*laughing*). Come through the gate, then.

GRISHA. Round by the street, you mean? All right.

GRISHA *vanishes. Enter* TSYGANOV.

ANNA. Isn't he funny!

CHERKOON. Some entertainment for you.

TSYGANOV. I was hoping to go to sleep but I couldn't, dammit! Hordes of provincial flies on the wing — bzz-bzz! — smacking full tilt into the window panes — bang! smack! — landing on my nose, tickling my ears . . .

CHERKOON. On top of which, after last night, you've probably got a headache.

TSYGANOV. Ye-e-es . . . You know, a provincial town's cordial reception for two engineers didn't pass off entirely satisfactorily for one of them . . . What the hell is it they drink here?

CHERKOON. Pritykin calls it Dragon's Breath.

TSYGANOV. High-powered stuff . . . You know, Georges, it's odd, but I seem to have caught some sort of mental dyspepsia or something — suddenly today I caught myself thinking about that . . . what was her name? . . . little brunette, used to sing in the chorus at the operetta . . . drowned herself in the Moika in the end . . . did you know her?

CHERKOON. No.

TSYGANOV (*thoughtfully*). Small . . . nice eyes . . . and just now, when I was burning the wings off this fly with my cigarette, it reminded me of her. What *was* her name?

ANNA, *looking towards the house, starts.*

ANNA. What on earth's that? Oh, look, look!

TSYGANOV. Hallucinations now?

CHERKOON. My God, what an idiot!

GRISHA *enters, wearing a heavy fur coat.*

GRISHA. Here I am. Oof! It's hot!

CHERKOON. Listen, you nut — what have you got yourself done up like that for?

GRISHA (*smiling*). In a fur coat, you mean? That's my father — steaming the fat off me. I'm supposed to join the army in the autumn, so he's steaming me to make me thinner.

TSYGANOV. Brilliant.

CHERKOON. And you allow him to make a fool of you like that?

GRISHA. What can you do? You can't argue with him — he gets fighting mad in five seconds flat. Anyway, maybe if I get really thin they won't take me in the army at all.

CHERKOON. Well, for the moment anyway take off your coat, it's disgusting to look at you. You ought to be ashamed of yourself. I bet the girls all laugh at you — think about that! It's an abomination! You tell your father that you're no longer going to wear a fur coat in a heat wave. Understand.

GRISHA. Oh, yes, sure — you tell him! Just try!

TSYGANOV. Listen, laddie — what if your father decides to ride you like a horse, and makes you carry him to church on Sunday?

GRISHA. Oh, he'd never make a fool of himself — he's too proud for that!

CHERKOON (*insistently*). Take off that coat.

GRISHA *takes off his fur coat.*

GRISHA. Oh, all right . . . just as long as he doesn't see.

ANNA. You must love him very much?

GRISHA (*after a pause*). He's old, you know. He'll be dead before long. Then I'll be my own boss.

CHERKOON. Go home and send him here to me.

GRISHA (*amazed*). Who? My father? Send him? Send my father?

CHERKOON. Yes. He's at home, isn't he?

GRISHA (*lost*). Yes, but . . . how can I tell him? You're a . . . Send, indeed. *Send*! He's the first man of the town!

> CHERKOON *jumps up and goes to the fence.*

CHERKOON. To hell with it.

GRISHA (*alarmed*). What are you doing? Madam, what's he going to do? Hey, I'm off! To hell with all of you! What a trouble-maker!

CHERKOON. Don't let him go, Sergey. (*He shouts over the fence.*) Hey, you! Anybody there? Hey!

ANNA (*laughing*). Yegor, really, you're going too far . . .

GRISHA. Yes, madam, it's wicked, it'll just make trouble. I was lured in here and suddenly . . . No, I'm off . . . What the hell's going on?

TSYGANOV. Be a hero, laddie, be a hero! All you have to do is wait, and be quiet. Sit down.

CHERKOON (*across the fence*). Are you there? Ah. Come over here, will you? What? Yes, straight away.

REDOZUBOV (*behind the fence*). Grigory! Grishka!

GRISHA (*terrified*). He's calling me . . . Oh my God!

CHERKOON. He's over here with me.

TSYGANOV. Here comes another species of the local fauna.

GRISHA (*fearfully*). Oh help! It's Pelageya Pritykina! Well I'm damned!

TSYGANOV. You know what, laddie — you need a drink to keep your courage up. It does help.

GRISHA. Oh yes please, give me one, quick! Oh dear, I don't know . . .

ANNA (*laughing loudly*). Oh come on, that'll do! What a funny boy you are! (*Calls.*) Styopa!

> *Enter* PELAGEYA.

PELAGEYA. Good morning.

TSYGANOV (*bowing*). What can we do for you?

PELAGEYA. Is Tatiana Nikolaevna at home?

TSYGANOV. Unhappily, I don't know.

Enter STYOPA.

PELAGEYA. Ah, Grisha — good morning!

GRISHA (*muttering*). Here we go.

CHERKOON. You're being greeted by a lady and you just sit there . . .

ANNA (*to* STYOPA). Bring some port, and some liqueurs.

TSYGANOV. And brandy and vodka.

GRISHA. But I know her.

PELAGEYA. Yes, of course, we know each other! And is this your wife? How beautiful!

CHERKOON. She doesn't know where Tatiana Nikolaevna is either.

STYOPA *comes in with a trayful of bottles, glasses.*

PELAGEYA. I don't mind about that. To tell you the truth, I didn't really come to see her, I can see her any time — but it's a real honour for me to make your acquaintance.

CHERKOON. Anna, I think that's addressed to you.

TSYGANOV (*to* ANNA). Yes, must be you. Well, laddie, what can I give you?

GRISHA. Whatever bites hardest.

PELAGEYA. No, really, I meant everybody . . . Oh yes, your wife, of course, from the point of view of admiring la grande twoylettey, but you too, gentlemen, you're very interesting as well!

GRISHA (*drinking*). Oooh, it's sweet! Lovely!

TSYGANOV (*bowing to* PELAGEYA). Most gratified, Ma'am. (*To* GRISHA.) Kindly remember, laddie, that the liquid you're drinking is called *chartreuse*.

ANNA (*to* PELAGEYA.) Do sit down.

PELAGEYA. Merci! You know I kept saying to Arkhip, that's my husband, you rotten swine, I said, why can't you introduce me to those engineers, and he tried to scare me off of you, Ooh, he says, they're too upitty for the likes of you, he says, but of course you're not upitty at all, I knew you wouldn't be, of course you're educated and so you're proud and why not, everybody needs to have something to be proud about, we're proud of our money and you're proud of your book-learning, anyone who hasn't got something to be proud of, he's like a — what's he like? — like a baby that lived but a year and then died so there's nothing to be said about him, I know because I bore one of that sort once . . .

ANNA *gets up hurriedly.*

ANNA. Perhaps you'd like to walk over to the verandah with me?

PELAGEYA. I'll come with pleasure, my dear! Ooh, aren't you warm, aren't you nice . . . I'm so glad you've come here, you know, terribly glad! Our little town is nice, isn't it, and all the ongvirongs, the woody ongvirongs and the meadowy ones and the marshy ones and ooh! all the blackberries, you've never seen so many blackberries . . .

TSYGANOV (*looking after the ladies*). Quite amusing, Georges, eh? An interesting woman.

GRISHA (*suddenly laughing*). She's a fool of a woman.

CHERKOON. What?

GRISHA. She's a fool, I said. She's old, and she goes and marries a young man. She's rich, and he takes the lot off her. And of course he plays around. He's no fool . . . Ooh, my father's coming! I need another drink! Where can I hide?

TSYGANOV stands in front of GRISHA, *who pours himself a large liqueur, swallows it quickly, rolls his eyes wildly. Enter* REDOZUBOV, *looking furtively at* CHERKOON. *He is followed by* PAVLIN, *carrying a large exercise book under his arm.*

REDOZUBOV (*without bowing*). Grisha! What are you doing here?

GRISHA (*smirking*). Just . . . er . . . nothing.

CHERKOON. I invited him over.

REDOZUBOV. Why?

CHERKOON. I wanted to.

REDOZUBOV. And did you think he'd asked me if he could come?

CHERKOON. Why should he?

They look at each other.

REDOZUBOV. I'm his father.

CHERKOON. Well, sir, I've no time for a long conversation with you now. Your son must stop wearing that idiotic coat. It's ridiculous.

REDOZUBOV (*amazed*). What? What's this you're saying?

PAVLIN *moves carefully away from* REDOZUBOV.

CHERKOON. If he goes on wearing that fur coat I shall write to the military authorities and tell them that you're forcing your son to evade his military service. Is that clear?

GRISHA (*suddenly*). Papa! I want to go for a soldier! Honestly!

CHERKOON. Do you understand? It's an indictable offence . . .

REDOZUBOV (*lost*). Hold on . . . What right have you got to . . . ? Pavlin, you'll be a witness . . . Grisha, go home.

GRISHA. Papa! I can't get any thinner — I just can't!

PRITYKIN *appears on the left and stands behind the trees.*

REDOZUBOV (*more calmly*). You, mister, came here to build a railroad. Go on and build it. I'm not interfering with you, and don't you go interfering with other people. Right? And . . . stop goggling those green eyes of yours at me! Grigory! Home! . . . I'll be speaking to the Governor about you!

TSYGANOV (*smiling gently*). You'll be speaking from the dock, I'm afraid. Such a shame! Sixty years old, mayor of the town, church elder, godfather to the son of the Chief of the Fire Brigade . . . and so on and so forth . . . Such a brilliant career, and such a dismal end! Imagine it!

REDOZUBOV. Grigory! Go home! Don't you listen to them! Don't even look at them!

GRISHA (*weeping drunkenly*). They'll send you to prison! And me too, we'll both go to prison!

REDOZUBOV *grabs* GRISHA *by the hand.*

REDOZUBOV. Come on, you puppy . . .

> *They exit quickly, followed by* CHERKOON.

CHERKOON (*calmly*). Let me point out that if you beat that boy I shall make you pay for it.

PRITYKIN (*amazed*). He was scared! Vassily Redozubov — scared!

TSYGANOV. Likes to be treated respectfully, does he?

PRITYKIN. He has a passion for it. If he saw someone being buried with respect he'd be envious enough to take the corpse's place. You know those two huge pillars in front of his house? He was determined to have an entrance porch as big as the Prince's even if it meant blocking the street completely. He was told he mustn't but he did it anyway — the case has been going on for over six years. He won't give in. He's never given in over anything to anybody.

> PAVLIN *steps forward and makes his statement counting off the charges on his fingers.*

PAVLIN. Allow me to add, sir, that he is also a very cruel man. He beat one wife into her grave, the other one ran off to a convent, one of his sons is a buffoon and the other's disappeared without trace.

TSYGANOV. And who or what are you?

PAVLIN. Me, sir? Everyone here knows me, sir.

PRITYKIN. He's a friend of Redozubov — another back-biter.

PAVLIN. I like to be on friendly terms with everybody.

TSYGANOV. Did you want to ask me something?

PAVLIN. Exactly that, sir. Here (*holds out the exercise book.*) is a work written by me. You are a learned man, sir, and I would very much like to hear your views on it if you'd be so good. The book's entitled 'Some Considerations of Words, Compiled for the Purpose of Laying Bare Lies, by a disinterested lover of the truth.' I spent nine years writing it.

TSYGANOV (*taking the book*). And what is the focus of your argument?

PAVLIN. I am against new words. The actions of men have

remained immutable since the beginning of time, but different names keep being given to them. That is what I am speaking out against. In general . . . I am against all new words.

TSYGANOV. What sort of new words?

PAVLIN. For example, people used to talk about 'slander' but now they're talking about 'correspondence'.

PRITYKIN. What he's on about is how he was exposed in the newspaper after he'd written a denunciation of the school-master . . . I bet you've never spoken out against Mayor Redozubov over anything . . .

PAVLIN. Arkhip Fomich, a bush can't overshadow a tree! The Mayor is of higher significance than I am in this town. What is above me is also beyond me.

TSYGANOV. All right, I'll read your manuscript.

PAVLIN. I am unspeakably grateful.

TSYGANOV. Call round some time . . .

PAVLIN. I shall make it my duty . . .

All three exit. Above REDOZUBOV's *fence his daughter* KATYA's *head appears. She gazes intently round the garden.* CHERKOON's *voice can be heard, and* KATYA *vanishes. Enter* CHERKOON *and* ANNA.

ANNA. You shouldn't make fun of people like that just because they're stupid.

CHERKOON. They're wicked.

ANNA. But it's only from stupidity.

CHERKOON. Oh God — I always know what you're going to say.

ANNA. Everything's always so difficult with you, Yegor.

CHERKOON. You find it difficult? I just find it boring.

He sits down at the table.

Those . . . guests are waiting for you out there.

ANNA. I know. I'm going. You — er — don't want to give me a kiss?

CHERKOON. No.

ANNA *turns quickly and goes out.* CHERKOON *works.*

KATYA *appears again over the fence, and throws a stone at*
CHERKOON. *Then a stick. She vanishes.*

CHERKOON (*towards the fence*). Hey! You! Savages! I'm not
putting up with that sort of joke.
KATYA. I don't give a damn about you!

CHERKOON *stands up.*

CHERKOON. Are you a woman?
KATYA. None of your business . . . carrot-top!
CHERKOON. Whatever you are, it's stupid and insulting to
throw stones.
KATYA. Well, you insult people.
CHERKOON. What people?
KATYA. Ha! What people! My father and my brother . . .
CHERKOON. Ah, so that's it. All the same, it's not fair to
chuck things from round a corner. You might at least show
yourself.

Enter STEPAN, *who looks at* CHERKOON *in surprise.*

KATYA. Think I'm afraid of you, do you?
CHERKOON. I might. But it's much more likely that you're
just very ugly.
STEPAN. Who are you talking to, boss?
CHERKOON. A lady.
STEPAN (*looking round*). Where is she?
CHERKOON. Over there.
STEPAN. What's going on? — I don't understand a thing.
Boss, the police superintendant wants to see you.
CHERKOON. Why? What is it.
STEPAN. Don't know. I'm going to have a look at this lady.
KATYA. You just try!
CHERKOON (*exiting*). Be careful. She throws sticks and stones
at men.
KATYA. Only at redheads.
STEPAN. You're not going to whack me with a stick, then?
KATYA. Come over and see.
STEPAN. H'm . . . terrifying. All the same I think I'll come
over.

KATYA *immediately appears at the fence.*

KATYA. No, no, you mustn't! My father won't half give it to you if he sees you. What do you want?

STEPAN. Nothing. What about you?

KATYA. When that redhead comes back I'm going to get him on the nose with a stone.

STEPAN. Oho, are you! What for?

KATYA. I know what for. Listen, that beautiful lady — is she the redhead's wife?

STEPAN. Why do you have to know that?

KATYA. Because I have to. Does he love her?

STEPAN. You'd better ask him that. Or her.

KATYA. As if you didn't know.

STEPAN. I'm not an expert on the subject.

KATYA. Oh go on, you needn't pretend. All students are depraved. They don't believe in God and they read forbidden books — I know all about it. Do you read forbidden books too?

STEPAN. I'm afraid so. Sinful, isn't it?

Enter TSYGANOV. *He listens to them, smiling.*

KATYA. Quite shameless, aren't you? Why do you do it?

STEPAN. Oh, you know — just habit.

KATYA (*quietly*). Lend me one . . . an interesting one, mind you . . . Will you? I love reading . . . Oh!

KATYA *disappears.* STEPAN *looks round.*

TSYGANOV. Admirable, young man.

STEPAN (*embarrassed*). What? Oh . . . that . . . It was nothing special . . . she was just asking for some books . . . across the fence of course . . . Well, anyway, what about it?

TSYGANOV. I didn't say anything.

STEPAN. No but . . . you're smiling.

TSYGANOV. You're not making flowery speeches so you can't be in love yet.

STEPAN. Oh, come on! — love — that's silly.

TSYGANOV. So I've often told myself, young man, but that

didn't help me, I still fell in love. She's pretty too — like a dishevelled little demon. I wish you luck.

TSYGANOV *goes out again, taking a bundle of maps from the table.* STEPAN *looks over the fence, then makes as if to climb over it. Enter* BOGAYEVSKAYA *and* NADIEZHDA.

BOGAYEVSKAYA. What are you doing, young man? — is something driving you up the wall?

STEPAN. My cap . . . I hung my cap on the fence . . . it fell down the other side . . .

BOGAYEVSKAYA. But your cap's on your head.

STEPAN. Not this cap . . . a . . . a different one.

BOGAYEVSKAYA. You seem to have lost your head, not your cap. Nadiezhda Polikarpovna, let me introduce Stepan Danilich Lukin.

NADIEZHDA *looks at him intently.*

NADIEZHDA. Just a baby still.

BOGAYEVSKAYA. So let's leave him to play at climbing fences. Oh, here they all come. You know, Nadiezhda, if only you didn't talk so much you might seem a lot more clever.

STYOPA *enters with a basketful of crockery, bottles of lemonade, liqueurs; she collects up the papers on the table and spreads a cloth. Shortly after the* DOCTOR, TSYGANOV *and* ANNA *appear.*

NADIEZHDA (*calmly*). I have a very good mind.

BOGAYEVSKAYA. Don't talk nonsense. Apart from all that stuff of yours about love you can't talk about anything at all, do you realise that?

NADIEZHDA. Oh yes, I don't talk about anything else.

TSYGANOV (*to* DOCTOR). Let's start with a drink, doctor, shall we?

DOCTOR. And go on with a drink.

TSYGANOV. That goes without saying. Everything here, Styopa? Now then . . .

TSYGANOV *busies himself with the bottles. The* DOCTOR

stares at NADIEZHDA *with a sombre, unflinching gaze.*
ANNA *comes and sits down next to her.*

ANNA. It must be dull for you, living here?

NADIEZHDA. Some people complain that it's dull, but not me. I read books all the time, or just sit and think.

ANNA. What sort of books? Romances?

NADIEZHDA. Of course. What else can you read? There was once a man here who worked for the local council . . . he shot himself in the end . . .

ANNA. Shot himself? Why?

DOCTOR (*darkly and angrily*). Because he loved her.

BOGAYEVSKAYA. Now then, doctor . . .

NADIEZHDA (*calmly*). . . . and he used to give me some other sorts of books to read, not romances — not novels at all. But they were boring, I couldn't read them at all.

TSYGANOV. What about here, in the town — do you get any real life romances here?

NADIEZHDA. Well of course we do! Even here people fall in love.

ANNA. Love among the locals must be pathetic.

NADIEZHDA. Love is the same everywhere, if it's true love.

TSYGANOV. What is true love?

NADIEZHDA. One that can never change and never die.

TSYGANOV. H'm, yes, I see. You have read a lot of novels. I dare say you often receive declarations of love yourself?

NADIEZHDA. No, not very often. That man with the council, the one who shot himself, he used to write me long letters, and before him there was the council chairman, he used to talk about love a lot but then he'd go off hunting and one day he caught a cold when he was drunk out there in the woods, and three days later he died.

The DOCTOR *walks slowly away during the course of this. At the end of it* ANNA *shudders.*

ANNA. Died?

NADIEZHDA. Yes. I didn't like him, he drank a lot and made horrible noises in his nose and his face was always red . . . And now the doctor, here, says he's in love with me.

BOGAYEVSKAYA. Really, my dear — do try to keep your mouth shut!

She gets up and walks into the house. The DOCTOR *is standing under the trees, gazing at* NADIEZHDA, *motionless.*

ANNA. You tell us all that so . . . simply.

TSYGANOV. And what do you feel about him?

NADIEZHDA. Nothing. He's just like my husband.

TSYGANOV. Oh come on, they're not a bit alike!

NADIEZHDA. Oh yes they are. Not to look at, no, but their souls come from the same mould. They both like fishing, and anyone who likes fishing is already half dead. They sit there hunched over the water as if they're waiting for death.

TSYGANOV (*to* ANNA). There's something in that.

ANNA. Yegor would like that.

NADIEZHDA. Oh, your husband! — what fascinating eyes he's got! And his hair, just like fire! He's a marvellous man — once seen, never forgotten! In this place all the men have exactly the same sort of eyes, in fact it's just as if they don't have any eyes at all.

ANNA (*softly*). How . . . strange you are.

TSYGANOV (*slowly*). Ye-e-es . . . and even . . . strangely frightening.

NADIEZHDA (*smiling for the first time*). Are you serious?

TSYGANOV. Cross my heart.

NADIEZHDA. The doctor says the same.

ANNA (*quietly*). Poor man . . .

MONAKHOV's *voice can be heard. He is laughing. Enter* CHERKOON, *the police* SUPERINTENDANT (YAKOV ALEKSEYICH), MONAKHOV, LYDIA *and* BOGAYEVS-KAYA.

CHERKOON. Anna! Yakov Alekseyich is leaving.

He remains on one side, with LYDIA.

ANNA. Wouldn't you like to sit out here for a little while?

SUPERINTENDANT. Thank you very much, Ma'am, but that's enough for a first visit. You know what, Sergey

Nikolayich — somehow or other I've finished off all the sherry! Never even noticed! Devilish stuff!

TSYGANOV. I'll be getting some more of the same soon.

SUPERINTENDANT. Can't wait for it, can't wait!

The SUPERINTENDANT *laughs loudly.* MONAKHOV *goes up to the* DOCTOR.

MONAKHOV. Well, nuncle, what's up?

DOCTOR. Nothing. I need some beer.

MONAKHOV. That's right! You have a drink and it'll all pass.

SUPERINTENDANT. So, it's an outing on the river tomorrow, then? I'll send the Fire Brigade's horses for you at five o'clock, all right? And would you like some music?

BOGAYEVSKAYA. Oh, spare us, for pity's sake! What's the fun in having one's ear-drums burst? Anyway, there might be a fire, the firemen might be needed in town.

SUPERINTENDANT. Don't even speak of it! I don't like fires — don't like it when things get too hot in general! (*He laughs loudly.*) Well, goodbye, everyone! Damn glad to have people like you living in my town you know and all the rest of it . . . I'm no good at making speeches . . .

NADIEZHDA. Did you bring your trap?

SUPERINTENDANT. Abso-defino-lutely. Shall I run you home? Do me that honour!

TSYGANOV. Where are you going, Nadiezhda Polikarpovna? Won't you stay a bit longer?

NADIEZHDA. No, it's time I was going . . . Goodbye. Mavriky, I'm going home. Goodbye, Anna Fyodorovna.

MONAKHOV. Home? Oh, that's wonderful, Nadya.

ANNA. I shall always be delighted to see you.

TSYGANOV. So shall I.

SUPERINTENDANT. Yes, it's a pleasure to see her, isn't it? Your arm, Ma'am! Anna Fyodorovna — the best of everything to you! Sergey Nikolayich — I look forward to . . . a certain something! Respected Tatiana Nikolaevna — goodnight!

BOGAYEVSKAYA. It's a bit early to be wishing me that,

Superintendant. Very generous, though, I'm sure.

SUPERINTENDANT. I can begrudge you nothing, Ma'am. You know, I'm really grateful to the mayor, peevish peasant that he is — if he hadn't complained about you how would I ever have made your acquaintance? Blessings to all!

He exits with NADIEZHDA *on his arm.* ANNA *goes up to the* DOCTOR.

ANNA. Doctor, would you care for a stroll in the garden?

DOCTOR. All right. Come on.

ANNA. You might at least say . . . with pleasure.

DOCTOR. I've forgotten how to speak like a human being . . .

They go out, talking.

CHERKOON *and* LYDIA, *talking in low voices, both serious, come up to the table.* TSYGANOV *gazes intently after* NADIEZHDA, *pours himself out a large glass of something, and drinks.* MONAKHOV, *standing beside the table, makes approving noises with his tongue.*

CHERKOON. Watch it, Sergey. You're drinking yourself to death.

TSYGANOV. Why don't you learn a little urbanity from the superintendant, Georges?

CHERKOON (*to* LYDIA). Excuse me . . . (*to* TSYGANOV.) Listen, Sergey . . . that ghastly female — the wife of the excise man — she looks at me with such greedy eyes all the time . . .

TSYGANOV. You're stupid, Georges . . . that's very pleasant for me.

CHERKOON. No, but seriously . . . it's embarrassing, you know.

TSYGANOV. Go along now — you're being waited for.

CHERKOON *shrugs and goes back to* LYDIA.

TSYGANOV. Mavricky Ossipich — a drink?

MONAKHOV. I shan't say no to pleasure even at the hour of death.

TSYGANOV. Quite right too. Cigar? Do you play cards?

MONAKHOV. Why else would nature have given me hands?

TSYGANOV. Ah, so you're a wit as well? Not only the possessor of such a beautiful woman, (MONAKHOV *laughs*.) but with a nice line in repartee too.

MONAKHOV (*abruptly*). Do you want to take a bet?

TSYGANOV. What bet?

MONAKHOV. I'll lay you a hundred silver roubles to your fifty that you'll fall in love with my wife. Is it on?

TSYGANOV (*looking at him attentively, with the elegant impudence of a gentleman*). You've got no objections?

MONAKHOV *draws a nought in the air with his finger.*

MONAKHOV. Zero. I give it my blessing.

TSYGANOV (*more emphatically*). And if — try to imagine an exceptional case — if she falls in love with me?

MONAKHOV. I'll lay five hundred to a hundred that she won't.

TSYGANOV (*laughing*). What a delightful fellow you are! But let's leave it at that for the moment shall we, and go and have a game of cards? Call the doctor. Pritykin's in there, going over his invoices with that student of ours — let's go and take him. It won't be long before he finds a way of robbing us, will it?

They go towards the house. Indoors ANNA *is playing a sad tune.*

MONAKHOV. Of course not.

TSYGANOV. Most people seem to be getting smaller — only the crooks get bigger.

MONAKHOV *laughs loudly.* CHERKOON *and* LYDIA *appear from among the trees. They walk slowly, stop beside the table, and continue talking without sitting down.*

CHERKOON. Will you be staying here for long?

LYDIA. I don't know. Probably about a month.

CHERKOON. I'm stuck here almost until winter — till late autumn at least.

LYDIA. I don't like small towns. They're always full of insignificant people. When I'm among them I ask myself why it is that there are any people at all.

CHERKOON. Yes, I know. Energy freezes solid among them. In big cities energy's on the boil day and night, there's a constant interaction of conflicting forces, the fight for life never ceases. Lights burn. Music plays. There's everything that makes life beautiful.

LYDIA. A big city's like a symphony . . . like a magician's enchanted house where everything's to be found and everything can be taken. One really wants to live, in a big city.

CHERKOON. To live, that's it! I want to do a lot of living — I want to live greedily . . . Everything that's bad, I've seen it, everything that's harsh, I've experienced it . . . There was a time, you know, when people would make me feel small simply because I was hungry . . . and it's humiliating for a man to know that his clothes aren't clean and his nails haven't been cut . . .

LYDIA. I can see you've had some hard times.

CHERKOON. I have. It's essential for me to get even with people for what's happened to me in the past — really essential! There's no pity in me, not a scrap of indulgence towards those greedy, stupid animals who are in charge of society, and for the feebleness of those who submit to them — it just enrages me.

LYDIA. Even now life isn't easy for you, is it?

CHERKOON. Now? No, not even now.

LYDIA (*making a wide circle with her arm*). This isn't what you need — you need a really broad field of battle . . . It seems to me that you're capable of doing something big, something important . . . You're so . . . direct. But can you put a proper value on yourself? It isn't a mistake, you know, to put too high a value on oneself — one can push oneself up, jump up to reach it . . . but to lower one's price, that's like bending over so that others can jump over your head.

CHERKOON. I understand all that.

LYDIA. It seems to me that a man shouldn't have too much of

anything, but what he does have should be first class. We shouldn't be greedy, cluttering up our lives with cheap, unimportant things . . . Life will only be beautiful when people start wanting nothing but the rare and the excellent.

CHERKOON. You're a romantic.

LYDIA. Is that bad? If that's the way things should be? Who's that?

> *Enter* DUNYA'S HUSBAND. *He's more tattered than in Act One — drunk, walking boldly.*

CHERKOON. What do you want?

DUNYA'S HUSBAND (*with inspiration*). Let me tell you, sir — I am a father!

CHERKOON. Whose father?

DUNYA'S HUSBAND. Hers . . . the girl you have as your maid . . . Stepanida. She's a runaway . . . she ran away from me. And so I demand . . . because . . . I am her father. So . . . what are you going to do? Because . . . I can demand.

CHERKOON (*to* LYDIA). My father was like that, almost.

LYDIA. Send him away. He's revolting.

CHERKOON. What are you demanding?

DUNYA'S HUSBAND. Her wages. Whose daughter is she? Mine. And so her wages are mine. And so I demand them. Otherwise I'll take her away, that daughter of mine. Pavlin says, nobody can hold on to someone else's daughter, if she's a runaway . . . And the father can always demand the wages, Pavlin says. Always.

CHERKOON. You're not a father. It's a long way from fathering a child to being its father. A father is a man, and what sort of man are you?

LYDIA (*with a laugh*). How young you are! He won't understand, why do you bother?

CHERKOON. No, of course he won't understand. Go on, you — go away.

DUNYA'S HUSBAND (*retreating*). But . . . Stepanida's wages?

CHERKOON. Get away with you!

DUNYA'S HUSBAND (*scared, and sobering up slightly*). All

right, all right, I'll go . . . only . . . you could at least let me have fifty copeks . . .

LYDIA (*throwing a coin*). There. Go on.

CHERKOON. Beat it, smartly! Well?

> DUNYA'S HUSBAND *vanishes, without looking round.* ANNA *looks on from the bushes.*

LYDIA (*smiling*). How simple! Just barters his daughter for a small piece of adulterated silver. And we're told we must pity people like that, even love them . . . how do you like that? Pity can't help them, and it's surely not possible to love them? Ah, here's Anna Fyodorovna. Have your guests tired you out?

ANNA (*coldly*). No, I'm all right. They're playing cards. I came out to have a look.

CHERKOON (*suspiciously*). Have a look at what?

ANNA. I saw that pitiful creature coming into the garden.

LYDIA. Well, I'm off home. We'll be seeing each other this evening, so I won't say goodbye.

CHERKOON. Yes, we'll see you again soon.

> *Exit* LYDIA. CHERKOON *looks after her.* ANNA *watches him, biting her lip.* STYOPA *rushes in to her.*

STYOPA. Did he come for me . . . for me?

ANNA. No, Styopa . . . he just came, that's all. There's nothing to be afraid of.

STYOPA. For the love of God don't give me away to him!

ANNA. Of course we won't. Now stop worrying . . . go along in.

STYOPA. I'll go to the convent! I will! They won't let him in the convent . . . they won't, will they?

CHERKOON. Run along, Styopa. It's all nonsense. He can't do anything to you.

ANNA. We shan't let him have you, Styopa.

STYOPA (*exiting*). Oh God . . .

ANNA. Yegor, I think we must somehow do something about that man . . .

CHERKOON (*brusquely*). Nothing must be done 'somehow'.

ANNA (*gently*). You're vexed . . .

CHERKOON. No. But I want to tell you — you make your dislike of Lydia Pavlovna all too clear.

ANNA. Now wait a minute, Yegor — what gave you that idea?

CHERKOON. Dishonesty is always superfluous, Anna, particularly between you and me. I like her. She's interesting. You see that, and you're scared.

ANNA (*anxiously*). Scared? What am I scared of? I . . . I'm not scared. No.

CHERKOON. Anna, I can see.

ANNA. What? What can you see? Tell me . . . quickly . . . No, don't say it, you mustn't!

CHERKOON (*fiercely*). Quietly, Anna!

ANNA. Don't say anything. Please. Let me get used to the idea.

CHERKOON. The idea's been around in your head for a long time — and you're not used to it yet?

ANNA. But I can't accept it, I can't! I love you, you know that I love you. I forgive you everything.

CHERKOON. I don't need your forgiveness.

ANNA. Of course I know I'm an ordinary, dull sort of person, but I do love you . . . and I can't be without you. I can't . . . surely you don't have to despise me for that? You couldn't be so cruel . . .

CHERKOON. I don't despise you — that's not true. But I don't love you any more — that is true.

ANNA. But you did love me . . . No, wait . . . you're wrong, it can't be true.

CHERKOON. It's burned out. Gone. And only lechers and cheats live with their wives when they don't love them.

ANNA. Oh no, wait, wait, please! Give me time . . . I'll try . . . perhaps . . . I can be . . . different. Perhaps I could be not so uninteresting.

CHERKOON. Oh Anna, you should be ashamed of yourself. How can you renounce your own self?

ANNA. Oh but my darling, my beloved . . . I can't live without you!

CHERKOON (*firmly*). Nor I with you.

> *He goes into the house.* ANNA, *crushed, sits slowly down at the table. A noise; someone can be heard climbing over the fence.* ANNA *doesn't hear.* KATYA *comes running out from under the trees, runs up to* ANNA *and hugs her.*

KATYA. Oh my dear sweet lovely, don't you cry, he's a swine, that one!

ANNA (*jumping up*). Go away! Who are you?

KATYA. He's a fool too! How can he talk like that to you, how could anyone not love you?

ANNA. Who are you? How did you . . . ?

KATYA. I'm Katya, the mayor's daughter, Katya Redozubov! You must chuck him out, leave him . . . you're young, you'll find love again, you'll find someone good and kind to love! As for him — I'll slap his chops for him!

ANNA. Why were you listening? Oh my God . . .

KATYA. Oh, I know everything that goes on here! I watch you all through the cracks in the fence all day long . . . and I love you so, so much!

ANNA (*recovering slightly*). You know, it's not right to eavesdrop.

KATYA. Why isn't it? It must be right to see everything you can, it's all so interesting. And if I hadn't seen and come over you'd be sitting here crying all on your own. But now I'm here to comfort you.

> *Enter* STEPAN.

ANNA (*to* KATYA). Don't say anything . . . just be quiet . . . you don't know anything, you didn't hear anything . . . please!

KATYA (*importantly*). I quite understand. Oh, it's . . . that one.

> STEPAN *takes off his cap and bows.*

STEPAN. That very one. May I ask if you did us the honour of climbing over the fence?

KATYA. What's it got to do with you? I suppose you think that

if I came over the fence I must be a little fool, eh? Well, I'm
no stupider than you, so there! Remove yourself!

STEPAN. Good heavens! What on earth have I done to annoy
you?

KATYA (*stamps her foot*). Be quiet! One doesn't have conversations with you. (*To* ANNA, *taking her arm.*) Come along!

ANNA. I'm sorry . . . I can't . . . I haven't got time . . .

KATYA. I understand. I'll just stay with you. Come along.

> *She takes* ANNA *towards the end of the garden.* STEPAN *is
> bewildered. Enter* REDOZUBOV *and* PAVLIN. *REDOZU-
> BOV is dishevelled and excited.*

REDOZUBOV. Pavlin, you be a witness . . . Earlier on they
lured my son over here and made him drunk, and now it's
my daughter . . . (*To* STEPAN.) Who are you? You work
for them? Go and call them. Now Pavlin, you watch.

STEPAN. You're making a mistake, sir.

REDOZUBOV. It's all the same to me! It's a den of rogues,
this, oh yes! A lodge of mazons, aren't you? Go on, call
them!

STEPAN. I don't want to.

REDOZUBOV. Wha-a-at? Listen, I'm telling you, and you'd
better.

> *Enter* CHERKOON.

PAVLIN. The young man's a student, not a . . .

REDOZUBOV. Aha, there you are! One of the same order!

CHERKOON (*calmly*). What is it? What's the matter?

REDOZUBOV. Where's my daughter?

CHERKOON. I don't know.

REDOZUBOV. You're lying, you mazon!

CHERKOON (*to* STEPAN). What's a mazon!

STEPAN. First I've heard of it.

REDOZUBOV. No joking, now! Where's my daughter.

PAVLIN. You'd call them freemasons, but the learned way is
to say 'franc-mazon'.

CHERKOON. Listen, grandad — apart from the fact that a
while ago she was throwing stones at me, I know nothing at

all about your daughter. That clear?

KATYA *comes running in.*

REDOZUBOV. What's this, then? Katya, who told you you could . . .

KATYA. Don't start shouting now. Come here to me! Come on, come on, don't be scared, he won't come after you . . .

REDOZUBOV. Little one! This is no place for you.

KATYA (*to* CHERKOON). Don't you move an inch! You hear? Yes, you! You're a monster!

She exits, taking her father after her. STEPAN *laughs.* CHERKOON *looks at him, smiling.* PAVLIN *observes, thin-lipped.*

CHERKOON. How absurd . . . but very nice, really. Quite a girl — comes in, hands out her orders . . . H'm.

STEPAN (*laughing*). Dammit, it was neatly done, wasn't it?

CHERKOON. I must have a word with the old man some time.

GRISHA'S *head appears over the fence. He looks alarmed.*

PAVLIN. If I may say so, sir, you shocked and disturbed him thoroughly.

CHERKOON (*to* STEPAN). Who's this?

STEPAN (*with a laugh*). The local sage . . . and all things to all men, as required.

GRISHA. Hey, boss!

CHERKOON. Well?

GRISHA. He didn't beat me! Honest he didn't!

KATYA *runs in.*

KATYA. Hey, you! Listen! My father's asking for you! Come on! Well, what are you grinning about? Oh, I know all about you, carrot-top! Ooooh yes!

She sticks out her tongue at him and runs off. STEPAN *bursts out laughing.* PAVLIN *doesn't know how to react.* CHER-KOON *smiles, and follows* KATYA *out.* GRISHA *watches him apprehensively.*

CURTAIN

Act Three

(*Two months later.*) *The same garden. The sun is setting. Multicoloured lights are hanging in the trees. Wine and snacks are set out on the table.* MATVEY, *dressed very tidily, is opening beer bottles under the trees.* PRITYKIN *stands at the end of the garden. Beside him,* MONAKHOV *is softly playing a clarinet. A lot of noise in the house. Someone is playing 'Siskin' with one finger on the piano, and keeps going wrong. The* SUPERINTENDANT *can be heard laughing loudly.* STYOPA *is busy arranging the things on the table.*

MATVEY. I've saved up nearly three hundred roubles already.

STYOPA. So what?

MATVEY. Shows I'm not a fool.

STYOPA. I never said you was a fool. But you're greedy enough, I know that alright . . . always talking about money, like all you yokels . . .

MATVEY. Yokels is nothing to do with me.

> CHERKOON *enters and moves over to the table, followed by* NADIEZHDA.

CHERKOON. Styopa, give me some Seltzer water. (*To* NADIEZHDA.) You had to come out for a breath of fresh air too, did you? Stuffy in there, isn't it?

NADIEZHDA. Oh, it's . . . not too bad.

CHERKOON. Why are you looking at me so . . . strangely.

NADIEZHDA (*softly*). What's so strange?

CHERKOON (*with a laugh*). Can I get you a cold drink . . . a Seltzer or something?

NADIEZHDA. No. I don't want anything.

CHERKOON. Well then, I'll go and finish the game.

> CHERKOON *goes back towards the house.* NADIEZHDA *follows him slowly.*

MATVEY (*obstinately*). Whether I'm a yokel or not doesn't mean a thing. That Stepan Danilich, he's a student and he knows everything, and he says as how at first everyone in the world was just hicks and yokels, but then the ones that were a bit cleverer than the others, they got to be the bosses and the toffs, that's all.

STYOPA. Ah, leave off. I don't go for all that stuff.

MATVEY. We get wed and you'll go for something else. I'm a strong lad, I am . . .

STYOPA (*as if to herself*). I shall go off to the convent.

Enter the SUPERINTENDANT *and* TSYGANOV, *both drunk.*

MATVEY (*laughing*). Oh don't talk rubbish! To the convent . . . that's stupid.

SUPERINTENDANT (*by the table*). Everything's splendid here . . . but it's a long way to come for the snacks and the snifters.

TSYGANOV (*pouring out wine*). She is an epic woman.

SUPERINTENDANT. Still on about her, are you? Ye-e-es . . . an untamed little animal! I've been courting her for over two years . . . I'm no monster, as you can see, military type and all that . . . But no, you're not a hero, she tells me . . . Well, why aren't I a hero? Who can tell? And anyway, what is a hero? Stuck away in a little provincial town and suddenly she wants . . . a hero? It's ridiculous!

MONAKHOV and PRITYKIN come to the table. BOGAYEVSKAYA shouts from the house.

BOGAYEVSKAYA. Yakov Alekseyich! It's your deal!

The SUPERINTENDANT *walks off with something to eat in his hands.*

SUPERINTENDANT. On my way!

TSYGANOV (*to* MONAKHOV). You know, we keep talking about your wife all the time.

MONAKHOV. That's good to hear. And what are you actually saying, if that's not a secret?

TSYGANOV. We're trying to understand what makes her tick. And we don't understand.

PRITYKIN. It's very hard to understand a woman.

MONAKHOV. Are you talking about your wife?

PRITYKIN (*tugging at his sleeve*). No, no . . . in general. There's not many men who understand women.

MONAKHOV. What's necessary to understand, nuncle, I've understood. And what isn't necessary, I don't need to understand.

PRITYKIN. Well of course it's more peaceful that way . . . And then again — you'll never understand everything.

TSYGANOV. And where did you acquire her, exactly?

MONAKHOV. I noticed her during a service at the parish school.

PRITYKIN. Here she comes now . . . and the doctor's with her . . .

He laughs. MONAKHOV *echoes him quietly.* TSYGANOV *looks at them and his moustache twitches with contempt.*

MONAKHOV (*to* TSYGANOV). She doesn't approve of that Maupassant of yours, you know. It's boring, she says, and the pieces are all too short. I like him, though! Some of his little touches — whew!

TSYGANOV. Nadiezhda Polikarpovna, would you like some more champagne!

NADIEZHDA. Please. It's delicious.

MONAKHOV. Careful, Nadeizhda. You'll get drunk.

NADIEZHDA. You do say such coarse things! People might think I'd been drunk in the past. Why are you walking around with that stick?

MONAKHOV. Because I intend to play it shortly.

PRITYKIN (*taking* MONAKHOV *by the arm*). Come on, let's go and watch the superintendant coming up trumps.

They exit: MONAKHOV *unwillingly.*

TSYGANOV (*handing* NADIEZHDA *a glass*). Don't you like the clarinet?

NADIEZHDA. I like the guitar. It can be played very

movingly. But a clarinet always sounds as if it has a cold in its head. You drink an awful lot, doctor.

DOCTOR. My name is Pavel Ivanich.

TSYGANOV. You know, that's the first time I've heard your name. Isn't that odd?

DOCTOR. No one heeds a soul here, let alone a name.

TSYGANOV. How sombre you always are, my dear Pavel Ivanich.

DOCTOR. Not everybody can laugh in a morgue.

CHERKOON (off, calling). Sergey! Lydia Pavlovna's asking for you.

TSYGANOV. Excuse me . . . Coming!

DOCTOR (looking gloomily at NADIEZHDA). You like him . . . that one?

NADIEZHDA. He's very pleasant. Interesting to talk to. And he dresses nicely.

DOCTOR (in a quiet, muffled voice). He's a swine. He wants to seduce you . . . and he'll do it, the swine.

NADIEZHDA (calmly). You're always shouting abuse at everybody. You shouldn't. It shows off your rotten teeth.

DOCTOR (passionately and with pain). Nadiezhda! I can't bear to see you among these people! It'll kill me! With all my heart and soul I beg you . . . go away! They're gluttons, they're insatiable, nothing's too much for them, Nadiezhda, they'll gobble up everything in sight, everything!

NADIEZHDA (standing up). Why are you being so familiar? It's not at all polite.

DOCTOR. Don't go! Please! Listen, Nadiezhda . . . you're like the earth itself, rich with life-giving power . . . buried inside you there are . . . hidden oceans of love! Give me a tiny fraction of it, a fraction! I'm broken . . . crushed by passion . . . but I could love you like fire, and forever!

NADIEZHDA. Good heavens! But . . . but if I don't happen to find you attractive at all? I mean, just look at yourself — what sort of lover could you be? It's too ridiculous.

DOCTOR. Well just you watch out. I shall lie across your path. You'll see. You've already killed one man, and I shall be the second. The moment I see that that villain has taken possession of you . . .

NADIEZHDA (*with slight irritation*). Really, you're being very stupid! How could he possibly take possession of me when I don't want him to? Anyway, none of this is any of your business. How tiresome you are . . . quite insufferable, in fact.

VESYOLKINA *comes running in.*

VESYOLKINA. Have you heard what's happened? Really unexpected news! Anna Fydorovna's arrived — suddenly — just like that! I don't understand it at all! They can't have separated, then? Or perhaps they've come together again? And in that case, what about Lydia Favlovna? Because of course he's in love with her . . .

The DOCTOR *walks away from the table and glowers at* NADIEZHDA.

NADIEZHDA (*slowly*). How interesting . . . only I don't believe . . . that he's in love with Lydia Pavlovna.

VESYOLKINA. Oh come on, the whole town knows that!

NADIEZHDA. It's not possible to know that, my dear, because it's in the heart.

VESYOLKINA. And in the eyes, and in the voice.

NADIEZHDA (*thoughtfully*). But why has she come — his wife — what for? Even if she isn't a dangerous rival . . .

DOCTOR. Who for?

NADIEZHDA (*after a pause; slowly*). What's that got to do with you?

VESYOLKINA. Aren't you well? You look . . .

DOCTOR (*softly, like an echo*). What's that got to do with you?

VESYOLKINA. Oh really, how rude! Come along, my dear, let's go and see what's what.

She and NADIEZHDA *exit.* MONAKHOV *appears from among the trees, and goes up to the* DOCTOR *with a smile.*

MONAKHOV. Well, nuncle, eh?

DOCTOR. I've heard that brilliant question of yours a hundred times. What do you want to know? Well?

MONAKHOV. Ssh! You are fierce, aren't you? I don't want to know anything. I know everything it's necessary to know.

DOCTOR (*spitefully*). Do you know that I . . . love your wife?

MONAKHOV (*quietly, mockingly*). Who doesn't know that, nuncle?

DOCTOR (*about to leave*). Well . . . go to hell, then.

MONAKHOV (*grabbing his sleeve*). Now, now, why start swearing? We were not born to sue, as the poet says . . . anyway, I don't like anything melodramatic.

DOCTOR (*abruptly, quietly*). What do you want?

MONAKHOV (*mysteriously*). For her to know unhappiness . . . to receive a blow . . . but not from me! And not from you either, nuncle. For you . . . I just feel sorry . . . I've got a kind heart, after all, and I can see . . . I can see everything. A blow will make her softer, unhappiness . . . softens people. Do you understand, nuncle?

DOCTOR. Are you drunk? Or . . . ?

MONAKHOV. I've been drinking, yes . . . everyone's been drinking . . . Pleasant, isn't it? Very pleasant.

DOCTOR (*angrily*). You're just . . . a poisonous snake!

The DOCTOR *walks quickly away,* MONAKHOV *goes to the table, a pitiful, strange smile on his face. He drinks some wine, mutters.*

MONAKHOV. Yes . . . hurts, doesn't it . . . think it doesn't hurt me?

Enter PELAGEYA, *followed by* DROBYAZGIN, VESYOL-KINA.

PELAGEYA. Mavriky Ossipovich, have you heard?

MONAKHOV. What, precisely?

VESYOLKINA. Cherkoon's wife has come back.

MONAKHOV. Back already? Oh yes. And how is one supposed to react to this event?

PELAGEYA. Can't you see how things are for yourself?

VESYOLKINA. He's fallen in love with Lydia Pavlovna.

DROBYAZGIN. I think they're very well suited to each other.

MONAKHOV. Good. That's fine, then.

PELAGEYA. What's fine about it?

DROBYAZGIN glances round, takes a pear from the table, and eats it surreptitiously.

MONAKHOV. Everything. They are well suited. She has come back. You are all beautiful people. And I am a good man. The main thing is, we must all try not to trip over each other.

He laughs and exits.

PELAGEYA. It's true, he is a good man. Only he doesn't understand very much.

VESYOLKINA. He hasn't any time for understanding, he has to watch his wife.

DROBYAZGIN. Nadiezhda Polikarpovna is a virtuous woman.

VESYOLKINA. You always think you know everything. All she's waiting for is to find someone to fall in love with.

DROBYAZGIN. Everybody wants that. Even the chickens.

PELAGEYA (*sighing*). It's true, everybody wants that.

VESYOLKINA. Pelageya Ivanovna, do you love your husband?

PELAGEYA. Very much. But he doesn't much love me. It's my own fault. Forty shouldn't wed twenty. Oh look, here comes the mayor . . . and our hostess . . . such a nice woman she is . . .

Enter BOGAYEVSKAYA, REDOZUBOV, GRISHA *and* PAVLIN. DROBYAZGIN *draws himself up and adopts an air of modesty.* GRISHA *makes faces at him, amicably.* VESYOLKINA *notices, and laughs.*

PAVLIN. So I said to her, the convent, I said, there's nothing difficult about that, my girl, but you take on that awful father of yours, and bring some warmth to him, now that'd be a real task, I said, that'd be a proper cross to carry.

REDOZUBOV. You hear that, Grisha?

GRISHA. I heard. But I don't want to go to a convent . . . what do you mean?

REDOZUBOV. Ah, you fool!

PELAGEYA. It's always so good at your place, Tatiana Nikolaevna! And it's such a lovely birthday party — did I congratulate you? — plenty of everything and all of it so delicious, all sorts of rare things . . . Oh my dear, it really is so nice to be here!

BOGAYEVSKAYA. Well, if I've given some pleasure, I'm glad. But it's awfully hot.

PELAGEYA. Have some lemonade and brandy . . . Sergey Nikolayich taught me to drink lemonade and brandy, it's really refreshing!

REDOZUBOV (*unhappily*). Tatiana Nikolaevna, why did you go and invite me? I could have been sitting at home . . . Pavlin there came for me, it's like Balthazar's feast over there, he said . . .

BOGAYEVSKAYA. If you don't like it, leave your children here and go home. And Pavlin talks rubbish, even though he's old enough to know better.

REDOZUBOV (*thoughtfully*). I've been swallowed by that man . . . swallowed . . . I do everything Cherkoon wants me to . . . Is this really me?

BOGAYEVSKAYA. All the same, you don't do so many stupid things as you used to. You should have been reined in long ago.

REDOZUBOV. I've broken up those pillars of mine . . . Clung on to them for seven years, drowned all that money in the courts . . .

PAVLIN. Such a shame about the pillars. They were a great embellishment for our little town.

BOGAYEVSKAYA. Don't talk nonsense.

PELAGEYA. Of course it did make driving difficult . . . but nothing else really. And after all everybody who saw them asked 'Whose are those pillars?' and after that they'd all know that the mayor of Verkhopolye is Redozubov.

REDOZUBOV. Grisha! What are you ogling those bottles for?

GRISHA. Just looking, papa . . . there's a terrible lot of them . . .

BOGAYEVSKAYA. Why do you yell at him? Turns the lad into

a fool and then yells at him for being foolish.

REDOZUBOV. You think I don't know what's happening here? Those damned mazons . . . they're barbarians, destroyers! They overturn everything, everything's collapsing, and all because of them!

BOGAYEVSKAYA (*yawning*). Obviously everything was badly built.

REDOZUBOV. You're a lady, none of it matters to you. You upper crust people, anything you made you used other people's hands for, that's why you don't care. But we humped it, every inch. Oh yes.

BOGAYEVSKAYA. Oh yes. But we weren't money-grubbers. Anything good we made is still there, and still good. But when you die, my good man, all that will be left on the spot where you lived will be pillaged land and plundered earth.

REDOZUBOV (*angrily*). Grisha! Get off, go away! Where's Katerina? . . .

Enter the SUPERINTENDANT *and* PRITYKIN.

Go and tell her to come home . . . Go on! Here comes Pritykin — in what way is he better than me, eh? And yet the way they treat him . . .

He exits, with PAVLIN.

BOGAYEVSKAYA. Perhaps I shouldn't have needled the old man so much. I'm a fool.

PELAGEYA. But my dear, the way he was going on . . .

SUPERINTENDANT. Your house, Tatiana Nikolaevna, is Eden, and you yourself are . . . a goddess!

BOGAYEVSKAYA. Oh yes. A close resemblance.

SUPERINTENDANT. And so I wish you, dear goddess, at least another fifty happy returns!

BOGAYEVSKAYA. Rather too many, isn't it?

PRITYKIN. Honestly, Tatiana Nikolaevna, it's true — anywhere else Redozubov would have been barking at me like a dog, but in your house he can't. Everyone respects you, so nobody can behave badly.

BOGAYEVSKAYA (*calmly*). They know I can turn them out.

SUPERINTENDANT. Well said!

PRITYKIN (*enthusiastically*). Yes, they know!

PELAGEYA (*sighing*). Yes, it's good when someone feels he can be turned out.

PRITYKIN (*to his wife, provocatively and with meaning*). Who exactly do you have in mind?

PELAGEYA. Oh just — in general! You didn't think I meant you?

PRITYKIN. You just watch it.

SUPERINTENDANT. At ease, men! Now then . . . we've had some food, we've had some drink — what now?

PRITYKIN. Snap?

PELAGEYA. Even I can play snap.

SUPERINTENDANT. Excuse me . . .

BOGAYEVSKAYA. Go on, go on, please.

> *All go out, except* BOGAYEVSKAYA, *who sits in a chair and fans herself with a handkerchief.* MATVEY *is hanging up the lanterns and adjusting them.* STEPAN *and* KATYA *appear together.* STEPAN, *as usual, is talking abruptly, and apparently mocking.*

STEPAN. There, the great fire of reason is burning. And all clever and honest people can see by its light how squalidly and messily life is arranged.

KATYA (*softly*). And are there many clever and honest people there?

STEPAN (*with a laugh*). Well — not very many.

> BOGAYEVSKAYA *laughs softly.*

That's why I'm telling you to go there. Give up two or three years of your youth to dreaming about a new kind of life, and to fighting for those dreams. Throw a little portion of your heart into the general bonfire of protest against petty-mindedness and lies.

KATYA (*simply*). I'll go.

STEPAN. It may scare you. Maybe you'll come running back to this dump, but at least you'll have something to remember your youth by . . . and that'll be reward enough for anything you can give.

KATYA. I shan't come back.

STEPAN. Not a whisper of what's going on there reaches this godforsaken corner of nowhere. Just look at them — look at how blind, deaf and stupid they all are.

KATYA (*with a shudder*). Monakhov and the doctor . . . they look like frogs.

STEPAN. Yes. And what could you do here? Marry some merchant, someone like your brother . . .

He sees BOGAYEVSKAYA, *is slightly embarrassed, straightens his cap.* BOGAYEVSKAYA *smiles.*

BOGAYEVSKAYA. What is it, my dear? Don't be embarrassed. He's talking well, Katyusha, talking honestly, not promising anything . . . that's good. When he starts making promises, don't believe him.

STEPAN (*not polite, and very sincere*). You're lovely, you know, you really are!

BOGAYEVSKAYA. Now then, off you go . . . go and get on with it.

Exit STEPAN *and* KATYA.

BOGAYEVSKAYA. Ooooh! . . . my little people!

LYDIA enters, reading a note, moving her eyebrows in agitation.

Lidusha!

LYDIA. Oh, you're here, are you? Fed up with all those people?

BOGAYEVSKAYA. At my age one gets fed up with people pretty quickly. Listen . . . sit down . . . there's something I want to tell you. You know, I've been living here for thirteen years now, never poking my nose out into the world, and I've gone native — there's all sorts of things I no longer understand, so you must forgive me if I say something I shouldn't . . .

LYDIA puts her hand on BOGAYEVSKAYA's *shoulder.*

LYDIA. You don't have to. You mean . . . Cherkoon and me, don't you?

BOGAYEVSKAYA. Yes, that. You know . . . everyone here's nodding and winking . . .

LYDIA. What's that to us?

BOGAYEVSKAYA. No, not worth talking about, I suppose.

LYDIA (*thoughtfully*). Here . . . if you're interested . . . his wife sent me a note . . . telling me she feels no hostility towards me . . . something like that . . . People are really pitiful, aren't they?

BOGAYEVSKAYA. People? . . . maybe. But I do feel sorry for her.

LYDIA (*smiling*). You don't think I'd take away a beggar's last scrap, I hope?

BOGAYEVSKAYA. Oh, really, Lidochka! You're a Bogayevskaya — you must know your own worth. Well, I've had a bit of a rest, I must go back to them now. Tell me this — does he please you at all?

LYDIA. Not much. But compared to all the others . . .

BOGAYEVSKAYA. Yes . . . but he's brusque . . . and crude. Still, God send you some happiness.

LYDIA. Oh aunt, if it's there, I'll take it if I want it.

BOGAYEVSKAYA (*quietly*). Here they come.

LYDIA. Why whisper?

Enter ANNA, NADIEZHDA, CHERKOON.

BOGAYEVSKAYA. Good evening, Anna Fyodor'na, how nice to see you. It's my birthday, and here you are.

ANNA (*nervously excited*). Many happy returns . . . Good evening, Lydia Pavlovna.

LYDIA *shakes hands and smiles.*

ANNA. It's really strange . . . I've been living in the depths of the country for the past two months, almost completely alone, tucked away in a quiet corner . . . and now suddenly here I am . . . back among the noise . . . it makes me feel giddy.

CHERKOON (*frowning*). You should have a rest.

ANNA. Later . . . Where's Katya?

NADIEZHDA (*to* LYDIA). How pretty Anna Fyodor'na's become!

LYDIA. I always thought she was beautiful.

KATYA (*running in*). You're here! Oh, how lovely! Oh, I'm so glad, it's so good you've come! Look at you, you're thinner! And your eyes . . . !

> *They embrace.* CHERKOON *frowns.* NADIEZHDA *is watching him and* LYDIA. VESYOLKINA *and* MONAKHOV *are in the bushes.*

ANNA. What about them?

KATYA. They're . . . serious . . . restless.

ANNA. But you . . . how are things with you?

KATYA. Fine . . . very interesting. I'm still walking out with Stepan . . . my father goes on about it — Ooh! doesn't he just! Stepan's clever, but he will talk to me as if I was a little girl . . . he's much better when he's talking to the workers . . . Shall we go for a walk?

ANNA. He comes from them.

> *They go out together,* TSYGANOV *enters.* CHERKOON *follows his wife with his eyes.* MONAKHOV's *face is grinning at him from the bushes. The* DOCTOR *is standing in the background.* LYDIA *peels a pear, humming.*

CHERKOON. Why have you left the other guests?

TSYGANOV. Nadiezhda Polikarpovna disappeared . . . and I don't feel myself to be in my proper place away from her.

NADIEZHDA. You pay compliments very nicely. One can't even understand them straight away.

TSYGANOV. Thank you for the compliment.

NADIEZHDA. Yegor Petrovich, now — he never says nice things.

> LYDIA *goes into the house.*

TSYGANOV. He's a savage. No manners at all.

NADIEZHDA. Mavricky! What's that you've found?

MONAKHOV. A spider.

NADIEZHDA. How revolting!

MONAKHOV. I enjoy observing. It's an instructive occupation.

NADIEZHDA. What instruction will you receive from a spider?

MONAKHOV. He's caught an insect, not very big, but he's even smaller — he can't cope with it. He fussed around it for a while, then went running to a neighbour. Help me kill it, he says, and you can eat some yourself.

The DOCTOR *speaks from a distance, sharply and without expression.*

DOCTOR. He's behaving like you, Monakhov. Just like you.

The DOCTOR *walks away.*

TSYGANOV. What was that?

NADIEZHDA. Oh dear . . . he scared me.

MONAKHOV. Been drinking. Lots of people start philosophising when they're drunk.

He walks away.

CHERKOON. That doctor really is an amazingly crude creature.

TSYGANOV. You hear what the red-headed gentleman says?

NADIEZHDA. He's speaking the truth, and that's good. Yegor Petrovich always speaks beautifully.

TSYGANOV. Georges, you and I are going to have to fight a duel. I can feel it coming on. My goddess, let us move away from him. He has a bad effect on my nerves. Let us walk in the garden and talk about love.

They move off together.

NADIEZHDA. Yegor Petrovich won't ever talk about it.

TSYGANOV. A passionless character.

NADIEZHDA. Now there you must let me differ . . . What a good name you have for him — Georges.

They exit. CHERKOON *drums his fingers in a worried way on the table, and whistles sharply. Enter* ANNA, KATYA *and*

STEPAN. *From the house comes the triumphant voice of*
PELAGEYA. *By the time* ANNA *starts talking about children,
the* SUPERINTENDENT *and* PRITYKIN *have arrived at the
table.* GRISHA, *his lips moving, is reading the labels on the
bottles with concentration.*

PRITYKIN. I said a few things to that old devil, the mayor, I
can tell you. Oh yes, he won't forget me in a hurry. He's
afraid of me here because I'm my own man in this place.
(*He laughs loudly*).

ANNA. It's only two months since I left, but really it feels like
years. Everything's so frightening.

STEPAN. Yes. Life's a serious business.

ANNA. You know, Katya, there are men who actually take
pleasure in beating a woman . . . They'll hit her straight in
the eyes with their fist . . . hit her face till it bleeds . . . kick
her, even . . . do you understand?

KATYA (*softly, after a pause*). I know. My father used to beat
mama . . . and he beats Grisha.

ANNA (*with pain*). Oh God . . . Oh my dear child.

CHERKOON. Sit down. Don't excite yourself.

STEPAN. It's funny . . . watching you now . . . it's as if you'd
only gained your sight yesterday.

ANNA. It's terrifying to look at some of those children!
They're infected, diseased . . . Their eyes are mournful,
fearful . . . wavering like candles at a funeral . . . And the
mothers beat and curse their children for having been born
sick. Oh, if only everybody knew the sort of things their lives
are built on!

PRITYKIN. We do know. It may all be weird and wonderful
to you, but it's nothing new to us. The common people are
just brutes, and getting worse all the time. The women are
docile enough, but the men are prison fodder one and all.

MONAKHOV. Oh, but the women are too! Who carries on the
illicit vodka trade?

SUPERINTENDENT. Well of course! And do you know how
the women poison their husbands? A wife'll bake a lovely
cabbage pie with arsenic in it, you know, and serve that up.
Oh yes!

KATYA (*heatedly*). What else can they do if they're always getting beaten? It just becomes necessary.

PELAGEYA (*timidly*). Ooh my dear, whatever is she saying now?

SUPERINTENDANT (*jocularly*). Now then young lady, for a speech like that I could have you . . .

KATYA. Don't breathe all over me . . . ugh!

ANNA (*bewildered*). But surely, if you already knew all that . . .

CHERKOON. Don't be naive, Anna.

STEPAN (*with a smile*). Which of the company here did you expect to surprise?

KATYA. I do dislike the way you smile — what are you laughing at all the time?

STEPAN. Life is full of crimes for which there are no names. The criminals go unpunished because they are the ones who are always in command. And you . . . all you do is make exclamations.

The SUPERINTENDANT *takes* PRITYKIN *by the arm and they go out together.*

KATYA. Well, what is to be done?

ANNA. Yes, what?

GRISHA *looks round, takes a bottle from the table and walks off with it.*

STEPAN. Open the eyes of the congenitally blind. There's nothing else you can do. Nothing.

CHERKOON. We must build new railroads . . . iron roads. Iron is the only power that can destroy this stupid, wooden life of ours.

STEPAN. People themselves will have to be made of iron if they want to rebuild our life. We shan't do it. We can't even destroy what's obsolete or help what's already dead to decompose. It's all too close to us, too dear and familiar. Obviously it won't be us who'll create a new world. No, not us. That needs to be understood. It puts each of us in his right place straight away.

MONAKHOV (*to* KATYA). Your little brother's made off with a
bottle of Chartreuse . . . Look, he's drinking it, over there.

KATYA (*running off*). Oh, the wretch!

MONAKHOV. A powerful potion, that stuff.

GRISHA (*off*). What's it got to do with you? Get off, it's not
yours, get away from me, I'm not going to let you have
it . . .

    STEPAN *goes off towards the noise.*

STEPAN. He's quite capable of giving her a thump.

ANNA. Is Sergey Nikolayich still trying to educate him? That
could have serious results.

CHERKOON. Well, Sergey's unlikely to have taught him to
pinch bottles.

ANNA. But what about drinking . . . ?

    She looks round, then talks fast and nervously.

Yegor, just so you'll understand straight away, I came back
here to you . . .

CHERKOON. Let's leave all that until later.

ANNA. No, please, wait. I've resigned myself to the idea that
you and I are strangers . . . anyway that I'm a stranger to
you . . .

CHERKOON (*quietly, mocking*). A stranger? Why, was it only
kisses that brought you close to me and nothing else?

ANNA (*with pain*). No . . . Oh, I don't know! But I can tell
you one thing — it's hideously hard for me without you. I'm
so stupid, so useless! I don't know anything and I don't
know how to do anything . . .

CHERKOON. Look, tell me straight out — what is it you
want?

ANNA. Don't be cruel to me. I didn't come here to ask for your
charity . . . I love you, yes, I do love you very deeply,
Yegor, but I know, if you've decided . . . I know it's useless
if you've decided . . .

CHERKOON (*in a hollow voice*). Why just scratch at each
other's nerves, Anna?

ANNA. I know my love is a small thing, Yegor, but it tortures me . . . No, don't go, please! I'm ashamed that my love is as it is . . . I was hurt and offended at first, and when I went away . . . I thought of death.

CHERKOON (*gloomily*). What can I say to you? I don't understand you.

ANNA (*with fear, begging*). I'm so helpless on my own, so insignificant, and everything's so frightening . . . When I'm alone it's quite unbearable just to catch sight of a sick, beaten child who's afraid even to cry . . .

CHERKOON (*firmly*). Anna, I must know what you want.

ANNA. Oh . . . I want . . . to be near you . . . just a little longer . . . just a little. I won't get in your way . . . live just as you want! But it's essential for me . . .

CHERKOON (*morosely*). It'll be painful for you, I warn you.

Enter KATYA.

ANNA (*with a pale smile*). Then I shall go away again. I will go. But don't you see — I understand nothing about life, I never thought seriously about anything until now . . . You'll have to teach me . . .

KATYA. What are you talking about?

ANNA. About life, my dear. (*To* CHERKOON.) You'll have to give me something in exchange for what you've taken.

CHERKOON. I don't know . . . how I can do that. I don't know, Anna. It's so awkward for me.

KATYA (*grumpily*). Oh, so it's awkward, is it? Oh yes! (*Stamping her foot.*) Aaargh! I — hate — men! One day I'm going to give that Stepan Lukin a lesson he'll never forget!

ANNA (*smiling*). But I feel awkward too, you know . . . and bad about being the way I am. But where could I go? With my family, everything's just as it always was, everyone thinking they're in the right, everyone angry all the time, taking offence at everything. Same old furniture, same old books, same old tastes . . . everything cold and dead. Sometimes they'll suddenly take fright and start fussing pettishly about how life these days is ruined . . . and then once again, as if they were wallowing in drink, they'll turn over their memories of the good old days . . .

TSYGANOV and NADIEZHDA come to the table. TSYGANOV pours himself some wine.

And I've grown away from them all. They're quite incomprehensible to me.

TSYGANOV. Being with you, my dear, is both pleasant and frightening. Like standing on the edge of a cliff.

NADIEZHDA. What a lot you drink.

KATYA. Have you two made it up?

CHERKOON. Don't tell her, Anna. Let her die of curiosity.

KATYA. I can see for myself, anyway. Oh, if you were my husband I'd . . . get hold of you like that! (*She clenches her fist.*).

CHERKOON. Stop terrifying me like that.

ANNA. Dear Katya.

MONAKHOV appears in the trees.

TSYGANOV. It makes me furious that you're so immune to the poison I'd like to inject you with. It's such a pity.

ANNA (*quickly*). Let's go away from here, Katya.

She takes KATYA by the arm.

KATYA. Not into the house, though. Let's go to the summerhouse.

They exit. CHERKOON heads for the house.

CHERKOON (*with a laugh*). You do your business too openly, Sergey.

TSYGANOV. The world can look on, rapt in admiration, if it wants to, Georges.

NADIEZHDA (*thoughtfully*). Georges . . . nice name! Mavricky what are you doing there?

MONAKHOV enters, nods towards the table.

MONAKHOV. Just . . . on my way to the . . .

NADIEZHDA. It's just horrible the way you snoop about in front of everyone.

MONAKHOV (*brusquely*). What are you grousing about? Got stomach ache again? Or is it your corns?

NADIEZHDA (*to* TSYGANOV). You see? He deliberately says coarse, horrible things, just to put men off me.

TSYGANOV. Really? What a curious method.

NADIEZHDA (*sincerely and simply*). Oh, if you only knew how beastly he is! If he's not saying that my breath smells he's . . .

MONAKHOV (*alarmed*). What! What do you mean, Nadya, who did I say that to?

NADIEZHDA (*goes up to him*). You need reminding? Oh, I can remind you alright!

MONAKHOV (*stepping back*). Oh come on, Nadya, what's all this? I was joking . . .

> *They disappear into the bushes.* TSYGANOV *sits down wearily in an armchair. His face is sad.* DROBYAZGIN *and* GRISHA *come up to the table.*

DROBYAZGIN. Sergey Nikolayich, may I ask you something? What are 'secret vices'?

TSYGANOV. I shan't tell you, my friend. I prefer you the way you are — blatantly vicious. It's aesthetically more satisfying.

DROBYAZGIN. Well, are there such things as secret virtues?

TSYGANOV. Surely they must all be secret — I've never seen a blatant virtue.

GRISHA. What's its name again? — that thick green stuff you gave me the first time? Do you remember?

TSYGANOV. Chartreuse, laddie.

> GRISHA *repeats the name in a low voice, and smiles.* MATVEY *lights lanterns in the garden.*

DROBYAZGIN. Sergey Nikolayich — who is the wisest of all wise men?

TSYGANOV. The history of philosophy provides a story on that subject. Once upon a time there were three wise men. The first held that the world consists only of thought. The second maintained exactly the opposite view — whatever that might be, I've forgotten. But what I do know is that the third wise man seduced the wife of the first, stole a manuscript from the second, published it under his own name, and was crowned with laurels.

GRISHA (*delighted*). Pretty smart!

DROBYAZGIN (*doubtfully*). H'm, yes, bit of a swindle, that.

TSYGANOV. Not to say a downright diddle. And now — a drink to youth! A man understands too late in life how wonderful it is to be a young lad like Grisha!

> LYDIA *stands with a flower in her hands and looks on with distaste as the men drink.*

DROBYAZGIN. Sergey Nikolayich, I suppose there will always be thieving and robbery?

TSYGANOV. Undoubtedly, my friend. At least until the day comes when someone steals everything — you understand, everything there is! Then there'll be nothing left to steal, and, like it or not, people will become honest.

GRISHA (*laughing*). And then everyone will go round naked! But you know, when the great thief Yemelka Pugachov tried to steal everything in the world they boiled him alive — heated up a great cauldron of silver and shoved him in head first! He kicked the bucket in a flash! (*He laughs.*)

LYDIA. Uncle Serge.

TSYGANOV. What can I do for you, my dear?

> DROBYAZGIN *and* GRISHA *make way respectfully, then exit.*

LYDIA. Why do you go on with them like that?

TSYGANOV. It's amusing, you know, corrupting those two little piglets a bit. Perhaps a touch of vice will make them faintly resemble human beings.

LYDIA. Serge Tsyganov, epicure and lion, drinking with . . . well, with what?

TSYGANOV. And in love with the wife of an exciseman . . . Yes, the world is turning out badly. Something must have gone wrong with the harmony of the universe.

LYDIA. But seriously — what is wrong with you?

TSYGANOV (*softly*). That woman, dammit . . . what a woman!

LYDIA. Are you fooling?

TSYGANOV. No.

BOGAYEVSKAYA (*shouting, off*). Sergey Nikolayich!

TSYGANOV. Coming. You know what, my dear — I may possibly propose to her that she should enter into lawful matrimony with me . . . As shop-assistants say, it's time I was taken down off the shelf . . . Are you coming?

LYDIA. No . . . It's depressing, watching you lot. It makes me want to leave this place.

TSYGANOV. Because someone has unexpectedly returned to it?

LYDIA. Must you be vulgar with me too?

> TSYGANOV *shrugs and goes out.* LYDIA *goes towards the exit, right, humming softly.* ANNA *comes to meet her, walking quickly.*

ANNA. Did you get my note?

LYDIA. Why did you go and write that?

ANNA. Did it offend you?

LYDIA. It seems to me you're just humiliating yourself.

ANNA. Oh, but surely, if you love someone, that's not important!

LYDIA. Is there something you want to tell me?

ANNA (*anxiously, with pain*). Yes. Yes . . . Please don't despise me . . . I'm loathsome to myself at the moment. I've no other place but with him – do you understand? No other place. Life is so . . . vast. I can only live when I'm near him.

LYDIA (*coldly*). Why is it necessary for me to know that?

ANNA. Don't talk like that. The strong ought to be kind. I want to ask you but I can't seem to . . . You know what I want to ask you?

LYDIA. Yes.. Perhaps I do. Do I love your husband — is that it? No. I don't.

> GRISHA *comes carefully to the table, takes a bottle of wine and disappears.*

ANNA. Is that true? (*She seizes* LYDIA's *hand.*) And him —

does he love you? Tell me, please!

LYDIA. I don't know. I don't think so.

ANNA (*with pain*). It's not possible — you must know!

LYDIA. He and I are friends. We talk . . . about all sorts of things.

ANNA (*with pride*). Ah, and I can talk about lots of things myself now!

LYDIA (*smiling*). Well, that's splendid.

ANNA. I'm a woman. I love him, and I want to be with him.

LYDIA. May I go?

ANNA (*with sincerity*). You find me repulsive, don't you? You must understand — I can't live any other way.

LYDIA. I'm sorry but . . . it seems to me . . . your sort of love is . . . hard for him to bear.

ANNA. He's strong. He's very strong!

LYDIA. Goodbye.

She exits.

ANNA. Don't despise me . . . Oh well, what does it matter anyway . . . Oh dear Lord . . . help me . . . help me!

Enter the SUPERINTENDANT *and* PRITYKIN, *both very drunk.* ANNA *sees them and hurries off.*

SUPERINTENDANT. Just imagine for a moment, Arkhip, that you're the Superintendant of Police, and that you really must get married . . . But who to, eh? That's the question — who to?

PRITYKIN. Whatever my circumstances, I would marry someone rich.

SUPERINTENDANT. Of course. Goes without saying. Yes. But what if they're both rich — Nadiezhda Monakhova and Lydia Pavlovna — what would you do then?

PRITYKIN. I'd take Lydia Pavlovna.

SUPERINTENDANT. H'm yes, maybe . . . But why?

PRITYKIN. Because Monakhova's married. Anyway, listen, you know that student, I've got something to tell you . . .

SUPERINTENDANT. Ah, to hell with the student! Young puppy! Yes, Monakhova's married . . . h'm . . . true enough. But then she could become a widow . . .

PRITYKIN. Any woman could be a widow.

SUPERINTENDANT (*astonished*). Absolutely . . . precisely . . . *any* woman! And — whew! — you see what that means? We shall all die! Do you understand.

PRITYKIN. That's the general lay-out.

SUPERINTENDANT. Lay-out is right! Well said, you swine. They'll lay you out and you'll stay laid out!

PRITYKIN. My, my, the things he says!

SUPERINTENDANT (*thoughtfully*). Some people go off hunting, or play cards, but you . . . just lie where you've been lain.

PRITYKIN. You should pay more attention. That young puppy as you call him, he says — the people's blood is up . . .

SUPERINTENDANT. Oh rubbish!

Enter DROBYAZGIN, *running*.

PRITYKIN. No, really. He's a poisonous menace.

DROBYAZGIN. Yakov Alexeyich, you must come, quickly! The doctor has given Monakhov a clout on the head!

SUPERINTENDANT. What's that? Why?

DROBYAZGIN. Don't know.

The three of them go into the house. DUNYA'S HUSBAND *appears behind the trees, wildly drunk, in tatters.* CHERKOON *leads the* DOCTOR *in by the arm, followed by* NADIEZHDA *and then* STYOPA.

CHERKOON. You'd better leave straight away.

DOCTOR (*roaring*). Who the hell are you? You're the ones who've corrupted everyone here . . .

CHERKOON (*softly*). Be quiet, damn you! You should be ashamed of yourself.

DOCTOR. A pair of vultures, that's what you are! Well, I'm not your stinking meat, you won't peck me to pieces the way you have old Redozubov! Who do you think you are, that's what I want to know?

CHERKOON. Come along now, get a move on . . .

He takes the DOCTOR *to the end of the garden.*

NADIEZHDA (*joyfully, to* STYOPA). Did you see that? The way he dealt with him? What a fine, brave man! It was so simple — just took him by the arm and led him away.

She follows CHERKOON *out.*

STYOPA (*shouts*). Yegor Petrovich!

She has seen her father, is frightened and angry.

STYOPA. It's you again! What are you here for? What do you want?

DUNYA'S HUSBAND. Stepanida! I am your father — aren't I? So . . . come with me.

STYOPA. I don't want to! I won't! Go away! I won't go with you!

DUNYA'S HUSBAND. Then I'll have the police bring you to me.

STYOPA. I'd rather go to my grave . . .

Enter CHERKOON, NADIEZHDA, ANNA, LYDIA, TSY-GANOV.

You hear that? You're no father to me, you're just a disease.

CHERKOON. Oh, it's you again. What do you want?

DUNYA'S HUSBAND. Her. I've come for this one.

STYOPA. He's come to lay hands on my soul.

ANNA. Go inside, Styopa.

CHERKOON. Get off with you, at once.

DUNYA'S HUSBAND. If you're stealing my daughter, at least give me a rouble.

STYOPA *grabs some money out of her pocket, throws the coins down, and runs away.*

STYOPA. There! Hope it chokes you! There!

CHERKOON. Listen, you, if you . . .

NADIEZHDA. Oh, why bother to talk to him?

CHERKOON. I beg your pardon, Nadiezhda Polikar-povna . . .

NADIEZHDA. You mustn't ever talk to his sort. (*To* DUNYA'S

HUSBAND.) Here, you. Go away. Tomorrow I'll be telling
the Superintendant to deal with you.

DUNYA'S HUSBAND. I can't be dealt with. I'm not scared of
anything.

TSYGANOV. There's a man for you. Growing every day.

LYDIA. He senses his own strength — the power of his
weakness.

ANNA. But, Sergey Nikolayich, you're always giving him . . .

TSYGANOV. Don't worry. It's not going to break me.

NADIEZHDA (*To* CHERKOON). What a hard day you've had
— nothing but unpleasantness.

ANNA (*involuntarily, like an echo*). Hard . . . Are you tired,
Yegor?

CHERKOON. It's just . . . I don't know what to do about that
man, to make him leave Styopa in peace. It's making me
angry.

NADIEZHDA. You don't need to do anything. I'll see to it.
Don't upset yourself.

TSYGANOV. My dear — I think your husband's the one who's
upset.

NADIEZHDA (*in surprise*). My husband?

CHERKOON (*in a sudden rage*). He's like a muddy puddle that
someone's stepped into — that's your husband.

ANNA (*stunned, quietly*). Yegor, really!

TSYGANOV (*with a laugh*). You exaggerate, Georges.

CHERKOON (*to* NADIEZHDA). I'm amazed you're not ashamed of yourself for letting such a . . . a mediocrity come
anywhere near you.

NADIEZHDA (*breathless with delight*). Oh . . . the way you said
that! Truthful . . . uncompromising! (*To* TSYGANOV.)
This is the one who's really frightening . . . this one here.

ANNA (*anxiously, to* LYDIA). My God, how . . . strange she is!
Isn't she strange? Do you see what I mean?

LYDIA. Yes, I do see. Come on.

NADIEZHDA. I'm not strange. I love manliness, that's all.

CHERKOON (*embarrassed*). Well, that's . . . er . . . something . . . I know nothing about. I'm going for a stroll.

NADIEZHDA. Me too. I'm coming with you.

They exit.

ANNA (*anxiously, to* TSYGANOV). She's funny, isn't she? She's
nice, I can see that, but . . . badly brought up.

TSYGANOV (*to* ANNA). You must have a rest, after your
journey. It's noisy here, and confusing.

ANNA. Yes, I'll go and . . . No, but she's so . . . I don't
know . . .

> *She goes out quickly.* TSYGANOV *smokes and smiles.*
> *Drunken laughter and talk can be heard; and in come*
> MONAKHOV, DROBYAZGIN, GRISHA.

LYDIA (*with distaste*). Oh, it's all so revolting! And that
woman . . . well, both of them, really . . . they're so
pathetic. What are you laughing about?

TSYGANOV. How about if she's finally found her hero, eh?

LYDIA (*after a pause*). No. It's unbelievable, Uncle Serge.

TSYGANOV (*laughing*). What's unbelievable about it?

MONAKHOV. So he hit me. Alright, fine, let him! I'm alive,
aren't I? And he'll soon be dead.

LYDIA. The drunks are coming. I'm off.

TSYGANOV. Come on then.

GRISHA. I can bash someone's face in too — pow!

LYDIA. But why is he involving himself in all that . . . filth?

TSYGANOV. It's elemental. It attracts . . . like a magnet.
Naked instinct, my dear, barely made decent by an old rag
of romanticism.

> *They go out.* MONAKHOV *winks at his companions and*
> *makes a threatening gesture with his finger in the direction of*
> TSYGANOV.

DROBYAZGIN. Why? My God, he's brainy, that one!

MONAKHOV. What's a brain?

> *He laughs loudly.* DROBYAZGIN *and* GRISHA *follow suit.*

CURTAIN

Act Four

A large, cosy room. In the wall, left, is a door into an entrance hall, and two windows; to the right, the door into ANNA's room and another into CHERKOON's. Straight ahead are large double doors into the drawing-room, the corner of which protrudes into this room. Between the corner and the Russian stove in the right hand corner is a recess with a wide sofa on which TSYGANOV is lounging, smoking. To the right, between the doors, an upright piano. ANNA is playing, barely touching the keys. BOGAYEVSKAYA is sitting at a table in the middle of the room laying out a game of patience. In CHERKOON's room STEPAN is quietly flicking an abacus. CHERKOON is walking about the room absorbed in thought. He stops in front of the window and gazes out into the darkness. Evening. The lamps are lit.

BOGAYEVSKAYA. It's getting chilly.

ANNA. Shall I get your shawl?

BOGAYEVSKAYA. Lidusha's gone for it.

TSYGANOV. Can't you stop clicking that thing, young man?

STEPAN. I'll stop as soon as I catch him.

BOGAYEVSKAYA. Who are you chasing?

STEPAN. The timber merchant, Pritykin.

BOGAYEVSKAYA. Surely he hasn't been fiddling the books?

STEPAN. Fairly assiduously.

BOGAYEVSKAYA. Yes, there's a tradesman for you. Even when he's in love he still cheats.

TSYGANOV. It's a characteristic common to people of all sorts and conditions. Actually I'm against the exposure of swindlers. It only makes them refine their techniques. Why do you keep walking about, Yegor? Who are you expecting?

CHERKOON (*after a pause*). So I'm walking about. What's that to you?

TSYGANOV. I've no further questions . . . as counsel for the prosecution would say. What ridiculous weather!

ANNA. He was upset by that argument.

CHERKOON (*coldly*). What do you know about it?

ANNA. It seems to me . . . when people can't agree with each other . . . it's irritating for everyone.

CHERKOON (*sarcastically*). Really? Well, I do congratulate you. Such an original observation.

BOGAYEVSKAYA. I thought it was really interesting, the tussle they had. Not that I understood anything, but it was interesting.

CHERKOON. Lydia Pavlovna is too outspoken.

TSYGANOV. From you, that's rich.

BOGAYEVSKAYA. I'm going to miss you when you leave . . . miss you a lot.

TSYGANOV. Come with us. Surely there's nothing for you to do here?

BOGAYEVSKAYA. And there? There's nothing for me to do anywhere, my dear. I've been doing nothing all my life.

TSYGANOV. And doing nothing wrong?

BOGAYEVSKAYA (*mixing the cards together*). No, not a single thing wrong. It's no good, Anna Fyodorovna, it won't come out.

ANNA (*sadly*). No? What a pity. I did so want it to come out.

BOGAYEVSKAYA. We'll just ask fate once more.

STEPAN (*in mock solemn tones*). Fate cannot be forced.

CHERKOON (*softly*). It's fate that does the forcing.

STEPAN. Particularly with the greedy.

BOGAYEVSKAYA. On you go, clickety-click.

LYDIA *comes in with the shawl.*

TSYGANOV. Until fate snaps you up too.

BOGAYEVSKAYA. Ah, thank you, Lidusha. Did you hear about Arkhip Pritikin? — he's having a romantic affair with Maria Vesyolkina.

LYDIA. How extremely interesting, aunt.

BOGAYEVSKAYA. Still, it is amusing, isn't it?

TSYGANOV. Nothing interests you, my dear, apart from your riding. Strange, the way you live — riding horses across

fields in all weathers, and nothing else! It's amazing how
you've changed.

LYDIA. For the worse?

TSYGANOV. Of course. From childhood on we all go in that
direction.

LYDIA. Then what are you amazed about?

TSYGANOV. I expected you to be a beautiful, poisonous
flower flourishing in the field of vice. Instead you are . . .
well, what are you? What are you looking for? What do you
want?

LYDIA. When I find it, you'll soon hear.

STEPAN. You're looking in the wrong place. The wrong place.

BOGAYEVSKAYA. Now then, my dear, perhaps I'm putting a
restraint on your eloquence?

TSYGANOV. Not at all. Why?

BOGAYEVSKAYA. Well, there, it's just that some people do
restrain themselves from uttering vulgarities in front of a
dignified old woman like me . . . and so on . . .

LYDIA. You're too proper, aunt. In the circles I've moved in
they say much worse things than that.

BOGAYEVSKAYA. Worse? In that case, I apologise. I told you
I'd gone native.

TSYGANOV. Oh, come on!

KATYA *comes running in.* STEPAN *jumps up.*

STEPAN. Well? What's happening?

KATYA. Yes . . . I'll go.

STEPAN (*approvingly*). Oh well done! Good girl!

KATYA *goes up to* ANNA.

KATYA. It's difficult, you know. He's crying! He's a pitiful
sight!

STEPAN. The world's revenge. He's been crushing people all
his life.

KATYA (*stamping her foot*). Don't you dare say that! It's none
of your business.

ANNA. Don't get upset, now, it's all right.

TSYGANOV. Of course it's his business. He's the one who

dragged you away.

KATYA. Nobody dragged me away. I dragged myself. Don't talk rubbish. But I'm really sorry for father . . . I love him . . . Oh, I know, he's rough, and he's cruel . . . but so are they all. They're all rough and cruel. And you too, Stepan Danilich, you too.

STEPAN (*flares up; then laughs*). Maybe . . . Oh well . . . but you know, life is arranged in such a way that cruelty's inevitable.

KATYA. I hate that smirk of yours. Be quiet.

ANNA. Now do calm down . . . Let's go into my room.

ANNA leads KATYA into her room.

CHERKOON (*smiling*). Nice little monkey.

TSYGANOV. And you, young man, are going to have a scold for a wife.

Enter STYOPA.

STYOPA. Stepan Danilich . . .

STEPAN (*with distaste*). Do you have to be vulgar all the time?

CHERKOON (*grimacing*). Gentlemen, please!

STYOPA. Stepan Danilich . . . Matvey Goggin's asking for you.

STEPAN turns abruptly and goes out into the hall, followed by STYOPA.

TSYGANOV. A spirited young man. What are you smiling at, Lydia Pavlovna?

LYDIA. They make a good couple.

CHERKOON. Yes. A fine pair.

LYDIA. They've got a splendid life ahead of them.

TSYGANOV. But probably a hungry one.

LYDIA. I like that Lukin — there's something . . . significant about him.

TSYGANOV. That smile of his contradicts you.

LYDIA. It contradicts everything.

STEPAN comes in from the hall, smiling slightly, followed by

MATVEY, *dressed in a good new coat. He hesitates, and whispers something in* STEPAN's *ear.*

STEPAN. Oh no, signor. You say it yourself.

CHERKOON. What is it? What do you want, Goggin?

MATVEY (*embarrassed*). It's like this, sir . . . I want to get married.

TSYGANOV. How original! How on earth did you think that up?

MATVEY. Well sir, it's just . . . time I did. I'm twenty-three . . .

CHERKOON. And so?

MATVEY. The thing is, Yegor Petrovich — I need your help! I can earn it! I'm from the common people myself, so I know all their bad ways, and I shan't let them . . .

STEPAN. You have raised up a man . . . who is ready to serve his country.

Enter KATYA *and* ANNA *who stand by the piano.*

CHERKOON (*frowning*). Help you how?

MATVEY. Well you see, sir, it's Stepanida I've chosen, and she doesn't want to. I won't, she says, and that's that. But she's such a modest girl, she'd never misbehave if we was married, she'd be afraid to . . . So you see I wanted to ask you and the lady to . . . well, just scare her a bit!

CHERKOON. What on earth for?

MATVEY. Why, to make her marry me! You marry him, you tell her, else we'll send you packing to that father of yours! And she's dead scared of him! I've already given him fifty copeks, you know, to make him push her in my direction.

KATYA (*in amazement*). Oh, what a swine!

MATVEY (*startled*). Eh?

CHERKOON (*coldly, to* STEPAN). Give him his cards.

MATVEY (*stunned*). Cards? Me? What . . . what for?

STEPAN. Think hard. What could it be for?

CHERKOON. Off you go.

MATVEY (*kneeling*). Yegor Petrovich . . .

CHERKOON (*sharply*). Get up!

MATVEY (*jumping up*). But . . . Sergey Nikolayich — what for?

KATYA (*triumphantly*). Aha!

MATVEY (*querulously*). But what have I done wrong? Oh, Stepan Danilich, you got me into this . . .

TSYGANOV. Go on, now. Later, maybe . . .

CHERKOON (*calmly*). Nothing, maybe.

MATVEY (*going out with* STEPAN). Oh, sir, it's not right, you can't do this, suddenly, for no reason, surely? Eh?

TSYGANOV (*to* CHERKOON). I don't think you acted with the wisdom of Solomon there . . . No, not at all. The boy's already pinched his fill, why go and kick him out now? He's not stupid, he'll grab all he can anyway. Smart lads are all swindlers.

STYOPA *runs in and throws herself at* CHERKOON's *feet.*

STYOPA. Yegor Petrovich, God bless you!

CHERKOON. Hell's bells! Get up at once, girl!

STYOPA. I was afraid . . . I was all of a tremble . . . I thought, they're going to give me to him, they're bound to . . .

KATYA. Silly girl . . .

ANNA. Styopa, listen! Nobody can touch you.

STYOPA (*fearfully*). But I'm alone, I'm all alone! Anyone can do anything to me . . . they'll come and take me, my father and him . . . they'll just take me!

ANNA (*going up to her*). That's enough, Styopa.

STYOPA. I'll go away to the convent . . . I will! They won't get me out of there. They couldn't, could they?

ANNA. Come into my room.

ANNA *takes* STYOPA *into her room.*

KATYA (*to* CHERKOON). You did well just then. Just what he needed. One, two — a bump on the head and no joy.

CHERKOON. At last I've been favoured with your praise.

TSYGANOV (*yawning*). For which you had waited so anxiously and so long.

CHERKOON. But when I taught your papa like that — one, two . . .

KATYA. Oh, you . . . ! That was . . . my father!

> KATYA *runs into* ANNA'S *room.* ANNA *comes in past her, pours out a glass of water, and turns to go out again.*

ANNA. Yegor. You did exactly the right thing.

CHERKOON (*frowning*). Oh, Anna, stop it.

TSYGANOV. That's it, Georges. Modesty befitting to a hero.

LYDIA. But Uncle Serge, how quickly the reward follows on the exploit.

ANNA (*as she goes out*). How is it you don't all get tired of laughing at everything in the world?

CHERKOON (*gloomily*). You think I'm not capable of seeing all this for what it is?

LYDIA (*listening*). Was that the bell?

CHERKOON (*quickly*). Yes. I'll go . . .

> *He exits.*

TSYGANOV. And I know who he's hoping to see.

LYDIA. Why are you so quiet, aunt?

BOGAYEVSKAYA. Can't think and talk at the same time . . . I have a problem here.

TSYGANOV. And I know who he's expecting.

BOGAYEVSKAYA. A fifth queen's suddenly appeared from somewhere. And there's no nine.

LYDIA. Here's the nine . . . And that's no lady, that's a jack.

BOGAYEVSKAYA. Verily, verily, so it is! Imagine! These eyes of mine . . . A jack, well, well!

TSYGANOV (*singing*). And I know, and I know . . .

LYDIA. Not witty at all, Uncle Serge. Aunt, aren't you going up soon? It's not good for you to sit up so long.

BOGAYEVSKAYA (*preoccupied*). Wait a minute . . . I'm just . . . Yes . . . very soon . . .

> *Enter* CHERKOON *and* SUPERINTENDANT.

CHERKOON. And you haven't found him yet?

SUPERINTENDANT (*gloomily*). No. God knows where he is.

But where can anyone run away to, from this place? Good evening Lydia Pavlovna. Good evening Tatiana Nikolaevna.

He shakes TSYGANOV's *hand in silence.*

BOGAYEVSKAYA (*without looking at him*). What about your clerk, then?

SUPERINTENDANT. Vanished, the villain. We're hunting high and low . . . my throat's like a desert.

TSYGANOV. There, I can help. (*He pours out wine.*) How much did he steal.

SUPERINTENDANT. Four hundred and sixty-three roubles and thirty-two copeks. What an idiot! Why not take the lot? There was about eight thousand there, but the fool just takes one packet. Anyway, so he's stolen that, well, so what? It's nothing marvellous, it's not murder. He could come and say, here I am . . . he'd get some mitigation for that, but no, he goes off and hides, if you please! And now there's nine people hunting for him.

CHERKOON. Poor little brute.

BOGAYEVSKAYA (*without looking up from her cards*). And he stole like a beggar, in copeks.

TSYGANOV. Well said, Tatiana Nikolaevna!

LYDIA *and* CHERKOON *laugh. The* SUPERINTENDANT *looks at his watch.*

SUPERINTENDANT. I came round, you see, Sergey Nikolayich, to tell you, and all that and so on and so forth, because you saw him on the day of the crime and you're going to have to . . . you know . . .

TSYGANOV (*seriously*). I understand. Suspicion of complicity will fall on me.

SUPERINTENDANT. Eh? What? Oh, you . . . (*He laughs loudly.*) Really, I wish I could sit about here with you much longer, but I must be off . . . Some fool over there's been beating his wife . . .

BOGAYEVSKAYA (*still not looking up*). To death?

SUPERINTENDANT. Seems like it. But where's Pritykin? He

came along here with me, we were thinking of getting up a hand of whist . . .

CHERKOON. He's busy with Stepan Lukin.

SUPERINTENDANT (*sadly*). . . . but on the way here one of my men reported the beating . . . And now there's your lad Lukin . . . You might tell him to restrain himself a bit. There's rumours going round . . . about him getting together with the factory workers . . . what does he have to go and do that for? You know, there's this very loyal and pious man here — Golovastikov — I tell you, vitriol! We're even afraid of him ourselves! He knows everything, even your dreams, he knows those too! And I wouldn't like to, you know, have recourse to certain measures . . . would I? I don't like unpleasantness.

TSYGANOV. That's all right, I'll see to it. And who takes pleasure in unpleasantness?

SUPERINTENDANT. Exactly! Well . . . respects all round . . . Oh, Sergey Nikolayich, you're a delightful man . . .

TSYGANOV (*seeing him out*). Despite the suspicion hanging over me of complicity in the theft, by Porfiry Drobyazgin, of thirty-two copeks, the property of the exchequer of this town?

The SUPERINTENDANT *roars with laughter.* PELAGEYA's *sugary voice can be heard in the hall, and caustic replies from* STEPAN.

CHERKOON (*quietly, to* LYDIA). How do you like that, eh?

LYDIA. You mean about Lukin's activities?

CHERKOON. No, no, that's quite natural. But that little clerk, Drobyazgin . . . dammit, what can we do for him, that's the thing. Because, you see, to tell the truth . . . it was Sergey. Do you understand?

LYDIA (*smiling*). You're soon going to turn into a perfectly respectable man — you really are!

CHERKOON (*seriously*). It was Sergey who corrupted that boy . . . that's certain. What are you laughing about?

LYDIA. You remember how you once wanted to turn this town upside down?

CHERKOON. Did I? Well, all right, perhaps I did. What about it?

LYDIA. I was just reminding you. You said that by your will-power alone, new tastes and ideas would arrive here. And Uncle Serge said nothing, but just look at how many corpses are lying around thanks to him.

CHERKOON. Ah, I see your drift. Go on.

LYDIA. But I don't see that life here has improved thanks to you. And it seems to me that you yourself have lost some of your lustre.

STEPAN (*from the hall*). Yegor Petrovich! Could you come out here for a moment?

PRITYKIN (*querulously*). Please, Yegor Petrovich!

CHERKOON (*going out*). I'll give you your answer later.

LYDIA. Aunt, do give up! Let's go up now. Come on.

BOGAYEVSKAYA. But I feel quite at home down here. Wait a minute ... It's all so mixed up ... muddled up ... tangled up ... This is the hardest game of patience of them all, my dear. They call it 'Two Inevitabilities'.

LYDIA. I'm going.

> LYDIA *goes out into the hall and then up the stairs.*

BOGAYEVSKAYA (*bowed over the cards*). You're going ... you're going ... and what am I going to do now? Yes ... But now I don't know what I can do. (*She raises her head and looks around.*) Eh? All gone away ... and I'm on my own. Ah well, alone-alone-lone ... (*She looks at the cards and suddenly muddles them all up.*) Oh, Tatiana ... you'll soon be dead, Tatiana, you old fool, soon be dead ... Yes.

> She goes towards the hall. PELAGEYA *appears in the doorway, with a scarf on her head, pathetic, her face flabby, with none of her usual make-up.* BOGAYEVSKAYA *steps back before her.*

BOGAYEVSKAYA. What do you want? Who is it?

PELAGEYA (*softly*). It's me ...

BOGAYEVSKAYA. Pelageya — is it you?

PELAGEYA. Yes ... yes, it's me. Is my husband here?

BOGAYEVSKAYA. I think so, yes. Why?

PELAGEYA (*weeping quietly*). He's getting rid of me . . . deserting me . . . Spends his evenings sitting with Vesyolkina, they play cards together . . . and the daughter's all set to seduce him . . . Oh my dear!

BOGAYEVSKAYA. Now then, don't mess about, you're always talking such nonsense! Stop making a fool of yourself and come upstairs to my room.

PELAGEYA. Oh, my dear good friend, you don't know . . . He beats me! He does! You've made a shambles of my life, he says, you rotten old witch, he says, get out of here, he says . . . But where would I go? Everything of mine's been made over to him, all my property's in his hands . . . Oh, my dear, whatever shall I do?

BOGAYEVSKAYA (*walking on*). Come on upstairs . . . you can't go making that noise down here . . .

PELAGEYA (*following*). I'm coming, I'm coming . . . But you've got to tell me what I'm to do about him . . . What'll become of me? Oh, I can hear him coming! Let me go up in front of you, my dear . . .

> *They disappear. Almost at the same moment a door opens and is slammed shut and* PRITYKIN *appears from the hall, very agitated, followed by* CHERKOON *and* STEPAN.

PRITYKIN. No, my clever little student, you don't do that to me! I'm somebody in this town, I am, everybody knows me here, and one day I shall be mayor, yes, sir — mayor! And you, if I may say so, are just a young man still and nothing more.

CHERKOON. Now then, this isn't the place for shouting.

PRITYKIN. Well, is it the place for calling me a swindler? Eh? And just why am I a swindler anyway?

STEPAN (*mocking*). There are the figures.

PRITYKIN. Figures? You can write down figures any way you like. There's no argumentation in that. Oh no.

STEPAN. And you did write them down the way you liked, didn't you? Will you explain to me where that thirteen hundred roubles of yours came from?

PRITYKIN. Yegor Petrovich, forgive me if I don't go into explanations now ... Let's keep this just between ourselves, shall we? Sergey Nikolayich trusts me ... As for Mr Lukin there, what he wants I don't know.

STEPAN. To catch you out cheating.

PRITYKIN. Cheating? No, really, I cannot take that from ...

CHERKOON. Let's leave it until tomorrow.

PRITYKIN. No, sir, I can't do that! I'm an honest man, Sergey Nikolayich knows that ... I calculated correctly, sir, you ask him, sir, he knows.

CHERKOON (*quietly, angrily*). Quiet. Come in here. Well?

PRITYKIN. Now hold on ... I can't be pushed around ...

> CHERKOON *pushes him through the door of his room and slams it shut.* STEPAN *throws the accounts on the table, thrusts his hands in his pockets and goes out, muttering through his teeth.*

STEPAN. Argh ... fiddling away ...

> STYOPA *comes out of* ANNA's *room with a book in her hands and goes through into the drawing-room.* ANNA's *voice can be heard, reading. Footsteps and noise in the hall. Enter* TSYGANOV *and* NADIEZHDA.

TSYGANOV. ... and went out to stand in the porch on my own. It's good to look at the sky sometimes — especially in autumn.

NADIEZHDA. Where is everyone, though?

TSYGANOV (*with a slight smile*). The one you want will appear when he hears your voice ... But you won't get anything out of him ... The clouds move across the sky so fast in autumn ... heavy black clouds ...

NADIEZHDA. I don't like black. The most important and impressive colour is red. Queens parade about in red, and various other aristocratic dames.

TSYGANOV. I've never seen them, but I can imagine how beautiful that would be. We-ell ... I shall be leaving soon, my dear.

NADIEZHDA (*on the sofa*). You won't be leaving alone.

TSYGANOV. Not alone? How am I to take that? Have you made a decision?

NADIEZHDA. Made what decision?

TSYGANOV (*quietly*). Are you coming with me? To Paris? Just imagine — Paris! Marquises, barons, counts . . . and all in red . . . and you'll have everything you want, I'll give you everything.

NADIEZHDA (*calmly*). Sergey Nikolayich, now you are actually being improper. As if I were some . . . some sort of . . .

TSYGANOV. What you are is wonderful, you're amazing, terrifying! And I love you. Believe me, I love you like a young boy! You are . . . power! Oh, there's so much happiness, so much sheer enjoyment in store for you . . .

NADIEZHDA. Sergey Nikolayich, why say all that? How can you love like a young boy when you're nearly fifty already and in a couple of years' time you'll be completely bald? What's the good of all that, Parising here and Parising there, if I can't love you? You're a very interesting man, but you're getting on in years and no sort of match for me. If you'll excuse me saying so, it's even a bit insulting, those ideas of yours.

TSYGANOV (*almost groaning*). Oh . . . hell! Well all right . . . would you like it if we got married? I could arrange a divorce for you and . . .

NADIEZHDA. Makes no difference to me, does it? It's the man that's important, not anything else . . . No, you'd better leave it, please. You've taught me a lot, I'm cleverer than I was, now, and braver . . .

TSYGANOV (*coming to himself*). Very well, then. Let's bury it, shall we? Honestly, that's my last attempt. There's no time left for me . . . or strength. No, no strength either.

NADIEZHDA. There you are, you see. You're a clever man. You understand that strength can't be bought in the market.

TSYGANOV. Yes, you're quite right. It's rather like horse-sense — not sold even in department stores.

NADIEZHDA. There you are!

Enter REDOZUBOV *and* PAVLIN. REDOZUBOV *is much aged.*

REDOZUBOV. Evening. Is my daughter here?

TSYGANOV. I think so.

He knocks on ANNA's *door.*

REDOZUBOV (*to* PAVLIN). You see? All in pairs. Oh yes.

ANNA *appears in her doorway.*

ANNA. Ah, good evening, Vassily Ivanich . . . Katya!

NADIEZHDA. Good evening, Anna Fyodorovna.

ANNA (*starting*). Oh, it's you!

NADIEZHDA. Yes.

KATYA (*to her father*). Why have you dragged yourself round here?

PAVLIN (*quietly*). He was miserable.

ANNA (*calling*). Styopa! (*To* NADIEZHDA.) Will you have some tea?

NADIEZHDA. I won't say no.

Enter STYOPA.

ANNA. Some tea, please, Styopa . . . I'll be back in a moment.

TSYGANOV. And some brandy, Styopa, and some brandy.

He goes to NADIEZHDA *and says something to her softly.*

REDOZUBOV. Who have you been with? Just her?

KATYA. Be quiet! Don't talk nonsense!

REDOZUBOV. Come home now . . . Eh? Won't you? It's the last few days . . . you might stay at home just for them . . . Eh?

KATYA. All right. Wait here. I'm just coming.

She goes quickly into ANNA's *room.*

REDOZUBOV (*to* PAVLIN). You see? Grown right away from me, she has. They've nudged my daughter away, turned my son into a drunk . . . destroyed my whole life. And it's all nothing to them.

PAVLIN (*quietly*). Don't fret. Just wait.

REDOZUBOV. Wait? Wait for what? Who can I complain to?

PAVLIN. They've bought the Superintendant, but no one can buy the Lord. Do you understand?

REDOZUBOV. They've made a fuss of that Pritykin and beaten me into the ground. And now my daughter — she may be in there with that student, and here am I, waiting! Me, waiting!

He suddenly stands up and shouts in a rage.

Kat'ka!

NADIEZHDA. Oh! What is it?

TSYGANOV. My dear man, what on earth's the matter?

Enter CHERKOON, *followed by* PRITYKIN *looking as if he has toothache.* KATYA *and* ANNA *come running in.*

KATYA. What are you shouting for?

REDOZUBOV. Katya — home!

CHERKOON. Look here, this isn't a flea-market, you know.

REDOZUBOV (*moaning*). That's right, go on, go on, finish me off! Knock me down, you robber, beat me to the ground!

KATYA. Father! Oh God . . .

CHERKOON. Now look here, grandad . . .

REDOZUBOV. Silence! Don't you speak to me, you mazon, you! Katerina — home at once! Well, Arkhip? Eh? Happy, are you? Jackal!

PRITYKIN. Oh, but Vassily Ivanich, it's not my fault . . .

REDOZUBOV. Ha! Marries a rich old woman, grabs all her property . . . going in for mistresses now, fancying yourself as mayor . . . Ah, you backscratching little toady!

CHERKOON. Look here, go and have your row somewhere else, will you . . .

KATYA (*shouting*). Go on, before they turn you out! I'd be so hurt and ashamed if they did that, how could I ever come here again? Then I'd start to hate you . . .

REDOZUBOV. What?

ANNA. Listen — she loves you, honestly . . . she was so sorry for you she was crying . . . I tell you, she loves you!

REDOZUBOV. Then why is she leaving me, if she loves me?

KATYA. Come on . . . Let's go, for God's sake.

KATYA leads her father into the hall. PAVLIN *prevaricates, strangely, and stops by the door.*

CHERKOON. You go too, Arkhip Fomich. There's nothing more for us to talk about.

PRITYKIN (*sighing*). All right . . . I'll go. But I can promise I shan't forgive young Lukin's part in all this. He's a local, and so am I. Yes, sir.

PRITYKIN exits.

ANNA. My God, how . . . how strange it all is.

NADIEZHDA *has been watching* CHERKOON *all the time from the corner, smiling. Her smile is strange, fixed.* TSYGANOV *smokes hard at his cigar and looks at everyone, twitching his moustache.* STYOPA *prepares the tea and glances furtively, with hatred, at* PAVLIN. ANNA *looks at* NADIEZHDA, *shudders, makes a movement towards her, then quickly turns round and goes into her room.*

TSYGANOV (*to* CHERKOON). Have you . . . settled things with him?

CHERKOON. Yes. You and I will have to have a talk. Oh, Nadiezhda Polikarpovna, you're here? I didn't see you. Good evening. Terrible weather, isn't it?

TSYGANOV. We're obviously not going to have our talk now.

CHERKOON. No, of course not. (*To* NADIEZHDA.) What are you doing over there in the dark? Let's go into the drawing-room.

NADIEZHDA. With pleasure. I was just waiting to see when you'd notice me.

They go into the drawing-room. Their low voices can be heard in conversation.

TSYGANOV (*to* PAVLIN). H'm, yes, you're still here, eh? Well, what have you got to say for yourself?

PAVLIN. The old man — the mayor — he's destroyed completely now. For him to allow that he could have been turned out of here . . . well. And after a thing like that it would be quite inappropriate for Katerina to come here again.

STYOPA (*involuntarily, softly*). Ooooh! Snake-in-the-grass!

TSYGANOV *is deep in thought, not listening to* PAVLIN.

TSYGANOV. Ah, yes . . . Well?

PAVLIN. Then everyone would see the way things are. May I make so bold as to ask, sir . . . what do you think of my work? Have you had an opportunity to look through it?

TSYGANOV *looks at him in silence.* PAVLIN *backs away.*

PAVLIN. The little exercise book, the manuscript of my work? — I said, have you been good enough to read it?

TSYGANOV. What? Oh, that, yes. (*Brusquely.*) It's rubbish, grandad.

PAVLIN (*incredulously*). My work . . . nine years of work . . . rubbish?

TSYGANOV (*carelessly*). I'll just go and get that philosophical work of yours . . . Hold on . . . (*To* STYOPA, *as he goes towards the drawing-room.*) Warm me up a bottle of the red, Styopa . . .

TSYGANOV *exits.*

PAVLIN. I saw your papa again today, young lady.

STYOPA *leans her hands on the table and stares at him.*

PAVLIN. It's windy out, with a cold drizzle of rain . . . and there's your father, a bit drunk, walking along . . . all naked and . . . and weeping . . . weeping bitterly.

STYOPA (*in a muffled voice*). You're lying! Why are you always getting at me? (*She throws the lid of the samovar at him.*) There! You old devil! Horrible old witch-doctor!

ANNA *runs in from her room.*

ANNA. What was that?

PAVLIN *picks up the lid.*

PAVLIN. The snuffer . . . it fell down . . . by accident.
STYOPA. Send him away!

TSYGANOV *comes in with* PAVLIN's *exercise book.*

TSYGANOV. Here you are . . .
STYOPA. Drive him off!
PAVLIN. Drive me, young lady? I'm leaving by my own desire.

ANNA *goes up to* STYOPA *and asks something in a low voice.* STYOPA *exits into* ANNA's *room.* ANNA *stands by the table, hears the conversation in the drawing-room. Her face shows pain and revulsion.*

And so, sir, you are pleased to tell me — rubbish!
TSYGANOV. Yes, yes.
PAVLIN. Meaning that I was reasoning erroneously for nine years? Thank you most kindly, my dear sir. And on your part there can of course be no error? Goodbye.

PAVLIN *exits.*

TSYGANOV. The Superintendant was right — vitriol indeed. Are you unwell?
ANNA (*whispering*). What's she saying? Listen.
TSYGANOV (*softly*). In circumstances like this I don't allow myself to hear anything.
ANNA. Oh, what does she think she's doing?
TSYGANOV (*loudly*). Why aren't you all coming? Tea's ready!
CHERKOON. Just coming.
ANNA (*softly, with pain*). You thought I was . . . I was eavesdropping, didn't you? Aren't you ashamed of yourself?
TSYGANOV. No, of course not. (*Calling.*) Yegor, here a moment.

ANNA *runs off into her room.* CHERKOON *appears in the doorway.*

CHERKOON. Yes. What?

TSYGANOV (*quietly*). Come here. Your wife heard something just now which upset her very much.

CHERKOON (*grimacing*). Oh, it's the same old story. Nadiezhda Polikarpovna's up to her usual tricks, that's all. Telling me how different kinds of people are supposed to declare their love. It's very amusing, really.

> *He goes out quickly.* TSYGANOV *shrugs his shoulders, twiddles his moustache. He pours out a large brandy and drinks it down. Picks up his hat, goes into the hall.* MONAKHOV *comes to meet him, docile and sad.*

MONAKHOV. (*softly*). Good evening.

TSYGANOV. Oh, hullo. Have some brandy?

MONAKHOV. May I? Please. It's cold out. I hope my Nadiezhda's here?

TSYGANOV (*pouring*). More?

> MONAKHOV *nods in silence.* TSYGANOV *whistles a tune.*

MONAKHOV (*softly*). I . . . er . . . came for her.

TSYGANOV (*smiling*). Shall I call her?

MONAKHOV. No . . . don't . . . I'd better have some more to drink first.

TSYGANOV (*smiling*). Are you sure it's better?

MONAKHOV. Don't laugh . . . why are you laughing?

TSYGANOV. Do you remember our bet?

MONAKHOV. Yes, of course. You lost.

TSYGANOV. Doesn't that please you? Hey, what's wrong? Don't!

MONAKHOV (*weeping*). I'm sorry . . . I'm so miserable . . . what'll I do, what'll I do? How can I . . . Apart from her, I've got nothing, nothing!

> TSYGANOV *tries to conceal his distaste.*

TSYGANOV. Oh, come on . . . come to my room . . . or come out into the fresh air if you like . . . Suffer, if you must, but never be ugly or ridiculous about it . . .

They go into the hall. The room is quiet. From the drawing-room come the low purring tones of NADIEZHDA.

NADIEZHDA. True love regrets nothing. True love is afraid of nothing.

CHERKOON (*laughing*). Oh, let's leave it . . . They way you're talking today . . .

CHERKOON *appears in the drawing-room doorway. He is excited.*

NADIEZHDA (*behind him*). There's nothing else to be said about love. What I was talking about was how different kinds of heroes make their declarations of love. But loving itself . . . that must happen in silence.

CHERKOON (*muttering*). In silence, eh? Well . . . let's have some tea, shall we?

NADIEZHDA (*softly*). Are you afraid?

CHERKOON. Me? Afraid? Of what?

NADIEZHDA. Of me. I never would have thought . . .

CHERKOON. No, really, that's enough.

NADIEZHDA. I'd never have thought that you could be afraid.

CHERKOON (*standing close to her*). Watch out. Be careful.

NADIEZHDA. What must I be careful about?

CHERKOON *puts his hands on her shoulders.*

CHERKOON. You . . . love me, don't you? Say it. Do you love me?

NADIEZHDA (*quietly, firmly*). Yes. As soon as I saw you. Straight away. My — Georges! You are . . . my Georges, aren't you?

She embraces him. He makes a movement to free himself. ANNA *enters. She has been crying, has a handkerchief in her hands. Seeing her husband and* NADIEZHDA, *she draws herself up, taut as a bowstring.*

ANNA (*quietly*). That's . . . disgusting!

CHERKOON (*with a drunken smile*). Don't rush to conclusions,

Anna . . . Although . . . I suppose it's all the same . . .

NADIEZHDA (*calmly*). Yes. Now. It is all the same.

ANNA (*with revulsion*). Oh . . . you are foul! You're a foul beast!

NADIEZHDA (*calmly*). Because I've fallen in love?

CHERKOON (*as if just waking up*). Wait, Anna. Be quiet.

ANNA. Be quiet? How low can you fall? If it wasn't this thing . . . if it was anyone else . . . but this thing . . . this animal . . . !

NADIEZHDA (*to* CHERKOON). Come along, Georges . . .

CHERKOON. Nadiezhda Polikarpovna, listen . . .

Noise in the hall. TSYGANOV *comes running in, followed by the* DOCTOR *and* MONAKHOV.

TSYGANOV. Grab hold of this maniac!

The DOCTOR *has a large, old-fashioned revolver in his hand. He steadies himself with one hand on the door hinge and aims at* TSYGANOV.

DOCTOR. I'll kill you. I'm going to kill you.

He fires, and misses.

TSYGANOV. You fool! Can't even shoot straight!

CHERKOON *dashes to the* DOCTOR.

CHERKOON. Stop! Stop it!

ANNA & NADIEZHDA (*together*). Get away, he'll kill you!

The DOCTOR *turns the revolver chamber with his fingers.*

DOCTOR. Oh, hell! Damn the thing!

NADIEZHDA *grabs the gun from him.*

NADIEZHDA. Oh, you . . . stupid ass!

CHERKOON. Are you crazy?

MONAKHOV. Nadya! Put that gun down.

LYDIA *runs in.*

LYDIA. What's happening?

TSYGANOV (*excited*). I've quite enough sins of my own, I don't fancy paying for someone else's . . .

ANNA (*to* LYDIA). He was kissing her . . . kissing *that*! That! (*To* MONAKHOV.) Take away that . . . (*To* LYDIA.) They were kissing.

LYDIA *leads* ANNA *into her room.*

LYDIA. Styopa — ask my aunt to come down, will you?

STYOPA *runs out of* ANNA's *room and across into the hall, disappears upstairs.*

DOCTOR (*in a muffled voice, to* CHERKOON). Kissing? You were?

CHERKOON. Get out.

TSYGANOV *is wrapping a handkerchief round his hand.*

TSYGANOV. Ah, the chump's woken up.
DOCTOR (*miserably*). Nadiezhda! Who have you chosen?

NADIEZHDA *has been staring at the* DOCTOR *all this time with a satisfied smile.*

NADIEZHDA. Don't be so familiar. You're not entitled.
DOCTOR. Who have you chosen?
NADIEZHDA (*pointing with pride at* CHERKOON). Him!
MONAKHOV (*groaning*). Nadya . . . Nadya . . . Why? . . . Nadiusha!

BOGAYEVSKAYA, *followed by* STYOPA, *enters.*

BOGAYEVSKAYA. Scandals and ructions now, is it? We've come to that.

She and STYOPA *go through into* ANNA's *room.*

DOCTOR (*to* TSYGANOV). So you are . . . an honourable man. I'm sorry. Turns out he's the one I should have . . . Never mind, it's all the same, you're both predators . . . I'm sorry I didn't kill you . . . yes, sorry . . .
NADIEZHDA (*sympathetically*). What can you do now? Oh, you . . .

DOCTOR. Right. There's nothing for me to do. I'm all burnt up.

CHERKOON. I tell you, that's enough now.

MONAKHOV. Nadya, let's go home.

NADIEZHDA (*firmly*). My home is there — where he is. That's my home.

DOCTOR. For four long years my heart was on fire, and now . . . what?

TSYGANOV. Yegor! What's he spouting about now? He tore my nail off!

CHERKOON (*to* DOCTOR). Yes, you're getting off lightly for that little caper. Away you go now, that's enough.

DOCTOR (*coming to himself; with simplicity*). Goodbye, Nadiezhda. Forgive me . . . for everything. Goodbye. With them, you'll soon perish. Yes, you'll perish. Goodbye. Goodbye, you two vultures.

The DOCTOR *exits.*

TSYGANOV (*to* NADIEZHDA). Well? Satisfied at last? It's just like all the best novels — one happy love story, three or four unhappy ones . . . a revolver shot . . . attempted murder . . . blood . . . (*He shows his bandaged finger.*) . . . all right?

NADIEZHDA (*stupidly*). What's he going to do now — go off and shoot himself?

TSYGANOV. I would. From shame.

MONAKHOV (*quietly, to* CHERKOON). Give me back my wife! Give her back. I've got nothing else — she's everything to me, everything! I've given her my whole life, took a whole life and gave it to her . . .

CHERKOON. Go on. Take her. Please.

NADIEZHDA (*amazed, to* CHERKOON). What? What did you say? Take her? Yes?

CHERKOON (*firmly*). Yes. Look, Nadiezdha Polikarpovna — I can only ask you, please, forgive me.

NADIEZHDA. What for?

CHERKOON. You must not attach any importance to . . . what I did. It was a . . . momentary flare-up . . . which you provoked yourself. That's not love.

NADIEZHDA (*muffled*). Say it more simply . . . so that I understand faster.

CHERKOON. I don't love you. No.

NADIEZHDA (*incredulous*). But . . . no, it's not true! You kissed me! Nobody's ever kissed me! Only you.

MONAKHOV (*meekly*). What about me, Nadiezhda? . . . Me?

NADIEZHDA (*heavily*). Quiet, zombie.

CHERKOON. Let's put an end to this. Do you understand now? Forgive me . . . if you can.

He wants to go out.

NADIEZHDA (*with a strange sadness*). No . . . no. Look, I'll sit down. Georges . . . come and sit beside me? Yegor Petrovich . . .

CHERKOON. I don't love you. I do not!

CHERKOON *goes to his room.* NADIEZHDA *sits down on the sofa. She is stunned.* TSYGANOV *is amazed and delighted. His moustache is twitching.* MONAKHOV *stands by the door, looking lopsided, broken.*

TSYGANOV (*cheerfully*). What a ridiculous town! Everything here's upside down. The doctor ought to be curing people, but he goes round wounding them . . .

MONAKHOV. Nadya!

NADIEZHDA. H'm?

MONAKHOV. Let's go home.

NADIEZHDA (*calmly, softly*). Go by yourself, zombie. Go on.

MONAKHOV, *with a sigh, goes into the hall.*

TSYGANOV (*quietly*). Come to Paris then, my dear. Will you?

NADIEZHDA. So . . . he doesn't love me. Is that true?

TSYGANOV. Of course. Anyone who loved would surely . . .

NADIEZHDA. Don't. I know.

TSYGANOV. Well, there you are, my treasure, you see . . .

NADIEZHDA (*unhappily*). Maybe . . . maybe he's just afraid?

TSYGANOV (*sighing*). What could he possibly be afraid of?

NADIEZHDA. And the doctor . . . Will he kill himself?

TSYGANOV. I doubt it. But if he does, well — so what? We're all quite used to it. Today, the doctor, tomorrow, probably . . . me.

NADIEZHDA (*shaking her head*). How could he, anyway . . . The revolver is here, look.

TSYGANOV. He could buy another.

NADIEZHDA. They don't sell them in this town. Oh, it's so stuffy in here! Let's go . . . at least as far as the porch . . . we could stand there for a while . . . come on.

TSYGANOV. With you, I'll go anywhere — up on the roof if you like. I love you . . . I love you!

NADIEZHDA (*with deep conviction*). No, don't, please! How can you love me, if he can't? He was afraid, yes, even he was afraid! No one can love me, no one. No one can love me.

> *They go out.* STYOPA *comes running out of* ANNA's *room, followed by* LYDIA. STYOPA *takes something from a cupboard.* CHERKOON *comes in, glowering, crushed.*

LYDIA. Fifteen drops, Styopa.

STYOPA. Lordy, it's all so strange . . . What sort of life are we . . .

LYDIA. Go on, go on, hurry.

> STYOPA *exits into* ANNA's *room.*

CHERKOON. How's Anna?

LYDIA (*shrugs*). All right. What do you expect me to say?

CHERKOON. I . . . I mean, she . . . it'll be awkward for her to see me.

LYDIA. What do you want with her?

CHERKOON. Please, would you tell her . . . Nadiezhda Polikarpovna has gone. I explained to her what happened . . . and asked her to forgive me. She's gone. She won't come back.

LYDIA. I don't really understand.

CHERKOON. She . . . aroused me . . . she did it herself . . . so, well I . . . I kissed her. I couldn't stop myself. She's powerful, that woman.

LYDIA (*ironically*). Ah, I see! She's to blame, is she? She seduced you? You poor thing.

CHERKOON (*quietly*). Are you . . . Do you find me loathsome, now?

LYDIA (*quietly, emphatically, vengefully*). Oh yes. Yes, I find you loathsome all right! I despise you.

CHERKOON. No! How can you say that? When you saw I was falling . . .

LYDIA. I don't go in for rescuing people who are falling. If they're weak enough to fall, let them fall, let them drown! It will freshen things up, get rid of everything superfluous, and only what's superfluous.

CHERKOON. I felt you were looking for something in me . . . I admired you a lot and . . . but now, I don't dare tell you . . .

LYDIA. No, don't you dare! No! I was looking . . . I thought I'd found a firm, resolute man, a man I could respect. For a long time now I've been looking for someone I could bow to and still walk proudly beside him . . . Maybe it's a dream . . . but I shall go on looking.

CHERKOON (*quietly*). Someone . . . you could bow to . . .

LYDIA. And walk beside. I can't believe that there aren't — somewhere on earth — some choice spirits, heroic people, people who see life as a great creative work . . . Surely there must be people like that?

CHERKOON (*in a muffled, despairing voice*). It's impossible to preserve one's true self, you must understand that . . . It's impossible. Life's too powerful, the filth is too powerful . . .

LYDIA (*angrily*). Everywhere you go there are pitiful, greedy people . . .

A shot is heard outside.

CHERKOON (*miserably*). Oh God, what now, what is it now!

ANNA *dashes in from her room.*

ANNA. Yegor! Where . . . Oh my God!

She collapses on to the sofa.

LYDIA. I'll go and see.

> LYDIA *exits.* BOGAYEVSKAYA *appears from* ANNA's *room.*

BOGAYEVSKAYA. I was just about to go up to bed, and then . . .

TSYGANOV (*in the hall*). Don't go out.

CHERKOON. Who fired?

> TSYGANOV *comes in. He is pale, his moustache drooping.*

TSYGANOV. She did. Nadiezhda Polikarpovna.

CHERKOON. But who at?

TSYGANOV (*shuddering*). Herself. Right there in front of me . . . in front of her husband too . . . So calmly and simply . . . Oh, hell and damnation!

> BOGAYEVSKAYA *goes into the hall.*

BOGAYEVSKAYA. Fool of a woman! Who ever would have thought it?

> ANNA *rushes to her husband.*

ANNA. Yegor . . . it's not your fault! It isn't!

CHERKOON. Where's that damned doctor?

MONAKHOV (*entering*). No need for a doctor . . . No need for anything. Well, gentlemen — between you, you've killed a human being. Why?

ANNA. Oh, Yegor, it wasn't you, it wasn't you!

MONAKHOV (*quietly, horrified*). What have you done? Eh? What have you done?

> *All are silent. The wind can be heard howling outside.*

CURTAIN

ENEMIES

The British première of Enemies *was given by the Royal Shakespeare Company on 22nd July, 1971 at the Aldwych Theatre with the following cast:*

The Bardin Household

ZAKHAR BARDIN	Philip Locke
PAULINA, *his wife*	Brenda Bruce
YAKOV BARDIN, *his brother*	John Wood
TATIANA, *Yakov's wife*	Helen Mirren
NADYA, *Paulina's niece*	Mary Rutherford
GENERAL PECHENEGOV, *retired, the Bardin's uncle*	Sebastian Shaw
KON, *his batman*	Reg Lye
MIKHAIL SKROBOTOV, *Zakhar's business partner*	Patrick Stewart
KLEOPATRA, *Mikhail's wife*	Sara Kestelman
NIKOLAI SKROBOTOV, *his brother, assistant public prosecutor*	Alan Howard
AGRAFENA, *the housekeeper*	Lila Kaye
POLOGGY, *a clerk*	Phillip Manikum
SINTSOV, *a clerk*	Ben Kingsley
GREKOV	Glynne Lewis
LEVSHIN	David Waller
YAGODIN	Hugh Keays Byrne
RYABTSOV	Paul Alexander
YAKIMOV	Terence Taplin
FIRST WORKER	Patrick Godfrey
SECOND WORKER	Ronald Forfar
VYRIPAEV	John Kane
PEASANT WOMEN	Mary Allen
	Holly Wilson
CAPTAIN BOBOYEDOV, *Intelligence Corps*	Barry Stanton
KVACH, *his corporal*	Ralph Cotterill

LIEUTENANT STREPETOV, *Infantry Corps*   John York
DISTRICT POLICE INSPECTOR   Clement McCallin
POLICEMAN   Edward Phillips
SOLDIERS   Colin Edwynn
     Michael Egan

Directed by David Jones
Designed by Timothy O'Brien
Costumes by Tazeena Firth and Timothy O'Brien

Act One

A garden. Tall, ancient lime trees. Beneath them, upstage, a white army tent. Right, under the trees, a wide couch made of turf with a table in front of it. Left, in the shade of the lime trees, a long table set for breakfast. A small samovar is boiling. Round the table are wicker chairs and armchairs. AGRAFENA is making coffee. KON is standing under a tree, smoking his pipe. POLOGGY is in front of him.

POLOGGY (*gesturing absurdly*). Of course, you know best. I am what you might call a small man, my life is totally insignificant it's true, but all the same every one of those cucumbers was grown by me with my own two hands and I simply cannot permit them to be picked without my getting some remuneration.

KON (*gloomily*). Nobody's asking your permission. They pick them, they'll go on picking them.

POLOGGY (*hands pressed to heart*). Oh, but look here, surely if one's property is being violated one has the right to ask for the protection of the law?

KON. You can ask. Today they're lopping cucumbers, tomorrow they'll be lopping heads. That's your law for you.

POLOGGY. Well, indeed, that's a peculiar thing to hear, coming from you, in fact a very dangerous thing! How can you, an ex-soldier, with medals on your chest, speak disrespectfully about the law?

KON. There isn't any law. There's only orders. Left turn! By the right, quick march! And away you go. When they shout Halt! – you stop.

AGRAFENA. Kon, I wish you wouldn't smoke that shag around here, it's enough to burn the leaves off the trees.

POLOGGY. If they only did it from hunger, I could understand, hunger can explain practically anything, in fact you might

even say that all wicked actions are committed to satisfy hunger.
When a person simply has to have food, then of course . . .

KON. Angels don't eat, but that didn't stop Satan setting himself
against God.

POLOGGY (*delighted*). Now that's what I call real insolence!

> *Enter* YAKOV BARDIN. *He always has a guilty smile; his
> movements are apathetic and slow; his eyes sick and dull. He
> talks quietly, and as if he were listening closely to his own words.*
> POLOGGY *bows to him.* KON *straightens up and salutes
> smartly.*

YAKOV. Well? What?

POLOGGY. I've come to see Zakhar Ivanovich with a humble
request . . .

AGRAFENA. He's come complaining. Some lads from the factory
have been stealing his cucumbers.

YAKOV. Ah. Well, you'll have to tell my brother, not me.

POLOGGY. Perfectly correct. And I am in point of fact on my way
to him this very moment . . .

KON (*irritably*). You're not on your way anywhere, you're just
standing on one spot and whining.

POLOGGY. I fail to see how I am being a nuisance to you, Kon.
If you'd been reading a newspaper, of course, something of that
sort, then perhaps you might have been able to accuse me of . . .

YAKOV. Kon – here a moment.

KON (*crossing to* YAKOV). You're an old blabbermouth, Pologgy,
always full of stupid complaints.

POLOGGY. You've absolutely no right to say things like that!
What were we given tongues for, if not for submitting complaints?

AGRAFENA. Oh, do stop, Pologgy. You're more like a mosquito
than a man.

YAKOV (*to* KON). What's he here for? Why can't he go away?

POLOGGY (*to* AGRAFENA). If my words offend your ear and fail
to reach your heart, I shall be silent.

POLOGGY *saunters off, and as he goes along the path he feels the trees with his hand.*

YAKOV (*embarrassed*). Well, Kon? It seems I . . . offended someone again yesterday?

KON (*grinning wryly*). Does seem that way.

YAKOV (*walking up and down*). Hm. Extraordinary. Why am I always rude when I'm drunk?

KON. It's often the way . . . But some people are better drunk than sober. [We had a corporal in our company, he was a real creep when he was sober, a bully he was, and a squealer, but when he was drunk he'd cry like a baby. Brothers, he'd say, I'm only a man, same as you lot – come on, spit in my face. Some of them would, too.]

YAKOV. Who did I talk to yesterday?

KON. The prosecutor. You told him he had a mouth like a mousetrap . . .* Oh, but first off you got Zakhar Ivanich embarrassed...

YAKOV (*thoughtfully*). I always start on my brother first.

KON. Then it was the prosecutor. You told him the managing director's wife has a string of lovers.

YAKOV. Ah yes, I see. What's it to me, all that?

KON. Don't know, sir. And then you told . . .

YAKOV. All right, all right, Kon, that'll do. [I don't want to find I insulted everybody.] Ah, it's a dreadful thing, this vodka . . .

He goes over to the table, looks at the bottles, pours out a large glass of drink, sips it. AGRAFENA *glances sideways at him, sighs.*

I'm talking about my illness, Agrafena [Ivanovna]. You feel rather sorry for me, don't you?

AGRAFENA. Very sorry, Yakov Ivanich. You're so straight with everyone, just as if you weren't a gentleman at all.

YAKOV. But Kon here isn't sorry for anyone. He is a philosopher.

---

* Lit. Rus: '. . . a wooden tongue . . .'

It's people who've taken a beating who develop a philosophy.
For a soldier to start thinking, he's got to have taken many a
good beating – right, Kon?

> The GENERAL *calls from the tent* – 'Hi! Kon!'.

You've been given a rough time, that's why you're so clever.
KON (*walking off*). One glimpse of the general, though, and I turn
  into a fool again.
GENERAL (*emerging from the tent*). Kon! Swimming! At the
  double, now!
> *They disappear down the garden.* YAKOV *sits down and rocks
> on the chair.*

YAKOV. Is my wife still asleep?
AGRAFENA. Madame's up and has had a bathe.
YAKOV. So you feel sorry for me.
AGRAFENA. You should have treatment, sir.
YAKOV. Pour me a drop of brandy, then. I know there's some
  there.
AGRAFENA. You'd mebbe best not, Yakov Ivanich.
YAKOV. Why? One less drink isn't going to help, is it?

> AGRAFENA *sighs and pours out a large glass of brandy.*
> MIKHAIL SKROBOTOV *enters, walking quickly, agitated. He
> rubs his black, pointed beard irritably, and twiddles his hat in
> his hand.*

MIKHAIL. Is Zakhar Ivanich up yet? No? Of course not. Give
  me ... is there some cold milk? Thank you. Good morning,
  Yakov Ivanich. You want to hear the news? Those wretches are
  demanding that I sack Dichkov, the foreman ... *demanding*!
  They threaten to stop work if I don't, damn them!
YAKOV. Well, sack him then.
MIKHAIL. Oh yes, very simple – but that's not the point. The
  point is, Yakov Ivanich, that concessions are bad for discipline.
  Today it's only sacking the foreman, tomorrow they'll be
  wanting my head on a plate.

YAKOV (*gently*). You think they'll wait for tomorrow.

MIKHAIL. Very funny, I'm sure. But just you try dealing with those grubby gentlemen, all two thousand of them, with their heads turned by your brother, will all his liberal nonsense, as well as by all kinds of idiots with their stupid leaflets.... (*Looks at his watch.*) Nearly ten o'clock, and they're promising to start their nonsense after lunch ... I must say, Yakov Ivanich, your dear brother has certainly ruined the factory for me while I've been away, the men have been completely corrupted by his lack of firmness.

YAKOV. You must tell him that.

MIKHAIL. I've told him once and I shall tell him again.

AGRAFENA. Here comes Paulina Dmitrevna.

YAKOV. That means they'll all appear.

> Enter SINTSOV, *right. He is about thirty, looks wary, often smiles. In his bearing and face there is something calm and distinctive.*

SINTSOV. Mikhail Vassilich, there are some workers' representatives in the office. They're demanding to see the managing director.

MIKHAIL. Demanding, are they? Tell them to go to hell.

> PAULINA *has entered, right.*

I beg your pardon, Paulina Dmitrevna.

PAULINA (*amiably*). You're always swearing. What is it this time?

MIKHAIL. What is it? It's your 'proletariat', as usual! Now they come *demanding*! They used to come begging for things, humbly. But now it's 'demand'!

PAULINA. You're very hard with the men, I must say.

MIKHAIL (*raising his arms and then letting them drop in a despairing gesture*). Well, really!

SINTSOV. What am I to tell the men in the office?

MIKHAIL. Tell them to wait. Go on, then.

SINTSOV *walks off, without hurrying.*

PAULINA. He has an interesting face, that clerk. Has he been with us long?

MIKHAIL. About a year.

PAULINA. He gives the impression of being a superior type [of person]. Who is he?

MIKHAIL (*shrugs*). [A clerk. Not a bad worker.] Earns forty roubles a month. (*He looks at his watch, sighs, looks round, sees* POLOGGY *under the tree.*) Well? What is it?

POLOGGY. I've come to see Zakhar Ivanovich, sir.

MIKHAIL. What for?

POLOGGY. On account, sir, of an infringement of the laws of property.

MIKHAIL (*to* PAULINA). Allow me to introduce another of our new clerks, a man of remarkable gifts – he has a passion for growing vegetables. He also harbours a deep conviction that everything on earth was created expressly to infringe his interests. Everything's against him – the sun, England, new machinery, the frogs . . .

POLOGGY (*smiling*). If I may make so bold, sir, when the frogs start up their croaking they bother everybody.

MIKHAIL. Get on back to the office! What do you think you're doing, dropping your work all the time to come up here complaining? I don't like it – go on, away with you!

POLOGGY *bows and goes off.* PAULINA *watches him through her lorgnette, smiling.*

PAULINA. There, you see how strict you are. And he's quite amusing, really. You know, I'm sure Russians are much more diverse than people abroad.

MIKHAIL. If you said, much more perverse, I'd agree with you. I've been in management for fifteen years now, and I assure you I know all there is to know about your noble Russian working man. Just to think of them makes my head spin and my stomach heave. Oh, what's keeping Zakhar Ivanich!

PAULINA (*to* AGRAFENA). Grusha, go and call my husband. (*To* MIKHAIL.) You know what he's doing? He's finishing off yesterday's game of chess with your brother.

MIKHAIL. Naturally. And meanwhile the workers are planning to go on strike after lunch. I tell you, Russia will never come to any good. It's a fact. This is a country of anarchists. Work-shy anarchists. There's an ingrown revulsion for work . . . an utter incapacity for order . . . total lack of respect for the law.

PAULINA. But of course! How can there be respect for the law in a country that has no laws? I mean, between you and me, our government . . .

MIKHAIL. Oh, I'm not trying to justify anyone! The government's as riddled with anarchy as anyone else. Now the Anglo-Saxon – he's the law's punch-bag.

Enter, behind, ZAKHAR BARDIN *and* NIKOLAI SKROBOTOV.

There's no better material for building a state. Your Englishman dances along in front of the law like a circus horse on its hind legs, he's got respect for the law built into his very bone and muscle . . . Ah, here they are. Good morning, Zakhar Ivanich. Morning, Nikolai. (*To* ZAKHAR.) May I tell you the latest result of your liberal policies with the workers? They're demanding I sack Dichkov immediately. If I don't, they stop work. So – how about that?

ZAKHAR (*rubbing his forehead*). Hm . . . Yes . . . Dichkov? Isn't he the one who's always fighting? Some story about girls, too? Yes, yes, I know him. Well, yes, by all means dismiss him, it would only be just.

MIKHAIL (*agitated*). Oh, really, Zakhar Ivanich! With all due respect to you as my partner and colleague, can't we talk seriously? It's a question of good business practice, not of justice – justice is Nikolai's affair, not ours. And I'm sorry but I must tell you again that your idea of justice is the ruination of good business.

ZAKHAR. Oh, come now, you're talking in paradoxes!

MIKHAIL. The paradox is the idea of justice in industry, can't you understand?

NIKOLAI. You're shouting, Mikhail.

PAULINA. Talking business in front of me, and so early in the morning! It's not very polite.

MIKHAIL. I'm sorry, Paulina Dmitrevna, but I have to. It seems to me absolutely vital to make this clear. Until I went away on leave I held the factory like *that* – (*He holds up a clenched fist.*) – and no one dared let out so much as a squeak. As you know, I considered all these Sunday classes – reading circles and so on – unwise in the kind of situation we have here. When the raw Russian brain is touched with the spark of knowledge it doesn't burst into the light of reason, it simply smoulders and stinks and . . . I'm sorry, I seem to be digressing.

NIKOLAI. You should talk a little more quietly.

MIKHAIL (*hardly able to control himself*). Thank you for the advice, Nikolai, no doubt it's very sound but it doesn't happen to suit me. In a mere six months, Zakhar Ivanich, your treatment of the workers has shaken and undermined the entire structure which it took me eight years of hard work to build! They respected me, they regarded me as the master. But now it's perfectly clear that there are two masters, one kind and one cruel. The kind one, of course, is you . . .

ZAKHAR (*embarrassed*). Oh, really, why talk like that?

PAULINA. You are saying some odd things, Mikhail Vassilich.

MIKHAIL. I've every reason to. I've been put in an idiotic position. Last time this came up I told the workers I'd close the factory rather than dismiss Dichkov. They realized I meant what I said, and calmed down. Then on Friday, Zakhar Ivanich, in the canteen, you told that man Grekov that Dichkov was a ruffian and that you intended to sack him.

ZAKHAR (*gently*). But my dear chap, if he goes around striking men on the jaw . . . and all that? Surely we can't allow that sort of thing? We're Europeans, we're civilized people.

MIKHAIL. First and foremost, we're factory owners. Every holiday the workers go around bashing each other on the jaw – what's it got to do with us? [Anyway, you'll have to put off teaching them good manners for the moment.] There's a deputation waiting for you in the office; they're going to demand the dismissal of Dichkov. What do you intend to do?

ZAKHAR. But surely Dichkov isn't all that valuable? I'm sure he's not, you know . . .

NIKOLAI (*coldly*). It seems to me it's not so much a question of the man, as of the principle.

MIKHAIL. Exactly. The question is, who are the masters in this factory – you and I, or the workers?

ZAKHAR (*at a loss*). I understand that, but . . .

MIKHAIL. If we give in to them on this, what will they demand next? They're brazen. Six months of Sunday reading circles and all the rest of the Europeanism have done their stuff – they glare at me like wolves. And then there's these leaflets going around . . . it all smacks of socialism to me, I don't mind saying.

PAULINA. Socialism! What, here, at the back of beyond? How comical!

MIKHAIL. Comical? Perhaps it is, to you. My dear Paulina Dmitrevna, all children are amusing while they're young and small. But bit by bit they grow up, until one day you find yourself facing full-grown scoundrels.

ZAKHAR. What do you want to do, then?

MIKHAIL. Close down the factory. Let them go hungry for a bit – that'll cool them down.

YAKOV *gets up, goes over to the table, has a drink, and walks slowly off, left.*

[Closing the factory will involve the women. They'll start weeping. Women's tears act like smelling salts on men drunk with dreams. They soon sober up.]

PAULINA. You're talking very ruthlessly, Mikhail Vassilich.

MIKHAIL. Certainly. Life demands it.

ZAKHAR. But, look, are you sure this is . . . is it really unavoidable? I mean, it seems so . . .

MIKHAIL. Have you something else to suggest?

ZAKHAR. Well – I could go and talk to them, couldn't I?

MIKHAIL. You'd only give in to them, and make my position even more impossible. No, I'm sorry, but I find you and your promises offensive as well as harmful.

ZAKHAR (*hurriedly*). Oh, I'm not arguing, my dear chap! I'm just wondering what's for the best. I'm more of a country gentleman than an industrialist, you know, and all this is new to me, and very difficult. I want to see justice done, but. . . . You know, the peasants are so much more gentle and good-natured than the workers, I've always got on splendidly with them. . . . Of course, there are some interesting characters among the workers, but on the whole I agree – they *are* awfully unruly . . .

MIKHAIL. [Particularly since you started handing out promises all round . . .

ZAKHAR. But don't you see, as soon as you left they started to get restless . . . I mean, there were agitations and . . . Well, perhaps I did behave unwisely, but I had to calm them down somehow, didn't I? We were being written about in the newspapers – written about critically, I mean . . .]

MIKHAIL (*impatiently*). It's now seventeen minutes past ten. We have to make a decision. There are two possibilities. Either I close the factory down – or I go. Closing the factory will cost us nothing, I've seen to that. The urgent orders are all ready, and there are reserves in the warehouses.

ZAKHAR. Hm, yes. I see. We have to decide, do we? Yes, yes, of course. Nikolai Vassilich, what do you think?

NIKOLAI. I can only talk about it in the abstract, but from that point of view, of course, my brother's right. If civilization means anything to us, we must stand firmly by our principles. A factory is a state in miniature.

MIKHAIL (*with a disparaging gesture*). You'll get yourself into trouble with that analogy.

NIKOLAI. Not at all. Every state has to have a governing body which can bind together the conflicting interests of its component parts with hoops of steel . . .

MIKHAIL. Is that out of a book?

NIKOLAI. . . . don't be so testy . . . and a body in power is only firmly in power when it holds its subjects strictly within the framework it has drawn up for them.

ZAKHAR. In other words, you agree we should close down? Oh dear . . . Mikhail Vassilich, don't be angry . . . I'll give you my answer in . . . ten minutes? All right?

MIKHAIL. Certainly.

ZAKHAR (*walking quickly off left*). Paulina, come with me, will you?

PAULINA (*following him*). Oh God, this is all so disturbing!

MIKHAIL (*through his teeth*). Spineless jellyfish!

NIKOLAI. Calm down, Mikhail. No need to lose all control.

MIKHAIL. Can't you understand? My nerves are completely shattered! I go down to the factory and – look! (*He takes a revolver out of his pocket.*) I'm not blind, and I'm not a fool. They hate me, thanks to that – imbecile! And I can't just abandon the business, you'd be the first to blame me if I did. Our entire capital is tied up in it. And if I pull out, that balding ditherer will ruin everything!

NIKOLAI (*calmly*). Hm, that's bad. Unless you're exaggerating.

SINTSOV (*entering*). The men are asking for you.

MIKHAIL. For me? What is it now?

SINTSOV. There's a rumour the factory's going to be closed after dinner.

MIKHAIL (*to his brother*). How about that? Who could have told them?

NIKOLAI. Probably Yakov Ivanich.

MIKHAIL. Oh, hell! (*He looks at SINTSOV, unable to disguise his irritation*.) Well, what concern is it of yours, Mr Sintsov? Coming out here, asking .... Eh? What?

SINTSOV. The book-keeper asked me to come and fetch you.

MIKHAIL. He did, eh? And what's this habit you've got of leering and smirking like that, eh? What are you so happy about, then?

SINTSOV. I think that's my own business.

MIKHAIL. Well I don't. And I strongly advise you to watch your conduct when you're with me. ... Yes!

SINTSOV. May I go?

MIKHAIL. You may.

TATIANA *enters from the right*.

TATIANA. Aha, the managing director! In a hurry again? (*Calls out to* SINTSOV.) Good morning, Matvey Nikolaich.

SINTSOV (*warmly*). Good morning. How are you? I hope you're not too tired this morning!

TATIANA. Not at all. My arms ache a bit from all that rowing yesterday, that's all. You on your way to work? I'll come as far as the gate. Do you know what I want to say to you?

SINTSOV. How could I?

TATIANA (*walking beside* SINTSOV). There was a lot of sense in what you were saying yesterday, but the *way* you said it was too aggressive, too ... prejudiced. Some things are far more convincing if you say them without too much emotion ...

The rest of their conversation becomes inaudible.

MIKHAIL. Did you see that? Oh, it's impossible! One moment you're telling off an employee for being insolent, the next he's hobnobbing under your very eyes with the wife of your partner's brother. ... The brother's a drunkard, the wife's an actress, and what the hell they're doing here nobody has any idea.

NIKOLAI. She's an odd woman. Good looking, dresses well, most attractive in fact – and yet she seems bent on having an affair with a pauper. Original, perhaps, but foolish.

MIKHAIL (*ironically*). It's called being democratic. She's the daughter of a laundress, you see, so she claims to feel happier among the common people.

NIKOLAI. . . . I've a notion she's quite approachable, too – seems to be the sensual type . . . all right, you needn't gape like that!

MIKHAIL. What's happened to that liberal of ours? Gone back to sleep, I expect. . . . No, I tell you, what Russia lacks is vitality. The people are dazed, nobody knows his own place, they just wander about, dreaming and talking . . . the whole thing's falling apart, it's all cock-eyed; there are hardly any people of real talent about, and if there are any, they're all anarchists. [The government's just a gang of crazed, angry, stupid men, unable to understand anything, unable to do anything. Instead of a Russian history all we get is the endless Russian scandal.] Above all, nobody takes the slightest interest in their work . . .

NIKOLAI. You're talking the most extraordinary nonsense, you know.

MIKHAIL. What?

TATIANA (*returning*). Are you shouting too? Everyone's started to shout for some reason.

AGRAFENA. Mikhail Vassilich . . . Zakhar Ivanich is asking if you'd . . .

MIKHAIL. Ah, at last.

MIKHAIL *exits without letting* AGRAFENA *finish her sentence.* TATIANA *sits down at the table.*

TATIANA. What's he so excited about?

NIKOLAI. I doubt if you'd find it interesting.

TATIANA (*calmly*). Possibly. You know, he reminds me of a policeman I once knew. We used to have this policeman on duty in the theatre in Kostroma – a tall man, with protruding eyes . . .

NIKOLAI. I don't see the resemblance to my brother.

TATIANA. I'm not talking about physical resemblance. This policeman, he was always hurrying somewhere, too. He never walked, he ran. He didn't smoke, he practically asphyxiated himself. [He didn't seem to be living at all, he was so busy jumping and turning somersaults in an effort to attain something as quickly as possible – though he never knew what.

NIKOLAI. Are you sure he didn't?

TATIANA. Quite sure. Anyone with a clear purpose pursues it calmly. But he was in a perpetual hurry, and a very peculiar kind of hurry – it whipped him on from inside, so he ran and he ran and got in his own way and everyone else's too. He wasn't greedy, in the narrow sense, only greedily anxious to get all his duties behind him as quickly as possible, including the duty of taking bribes.] He didn't just take bribes, he snatched them, snatch and run off without even time to say thank you. In the end he was run over by some horses and killed.

NIKOLAI. Are you trying to say that my brother's efforts are all pointless?

TATIANA. Is that what it sounded like? I didn't mean that . . . it's just that he's like that policeman.

NIKOLAI. None of it very flattering to my brother.

TATIANA. I wasn't trying to flatter him.

NIKOLAI. You have a curious way of flirting.

TATIANA. Indeed?

NIKOLAI. It's rather depressing.

TATIANA (calmly). Don't some women find you depressing?

NIKOLAI. Ah-ha!

PAULINA (entering). Everything seems to be going wrong today, somehow. No one's had breakfast, they're all out of temper, you'd think they hadn't had enough sleep. Nadya went off into the woods early this morning, with Kleopatra Petrovna, to pick mushrooms – I told her not to only yesterday. Life is really getting too difficult!

TATIANA. You eat too much.

PAULINA. Really, Tanya, what's that tone for? Your attitude towards other people is quite abnormal.

TATIANA. Because it's calm?

PAULINA. Oh, it's easy enough to be calm when [you've got nothing, when] you're free of all responsibility! But when you've got thousands of people depending on you for food – I can tell you, it's no joke.

TATIANA. [Why not give it all up then? Stop feeding them, let them live how they like.] Give it all away, the factory, the land, everything. . . . And calm down.

PAULINA. How can you talk like that? You should see how upset Zakhar is. We've decided to close the factory for a while, until the workers have come to their senses. But don't you see how distressing it is? Hundreds of people will be out of work. A lot of them have children. It's terrible.

TATIANA. Don't do it then, if it's so terrible. Why cause yourself pain?

PAULINA. Oh, Tanya, you're maddening! If we don't close, the workers will strike, and that'll be even worse.

TATIANA. What will be worse?

PAULINA. Everything! We can't give in to their every demand, can we? Anyway, it's not their demands at all, it's those socialists, putting ideas in their heads and teaching them to shout. (*Vehemently – but obscurely : she has no idea what she's talking about.*) I can't understand it! Socialism abroad is perfectly appropriate, it makes life more various and it's all done out in the open. But here in Russia it gets whispered to the workers in holes and corners, regardless of the fact that in a monarchy it's quite out of place! What we need is a constitution, not that sort of thing. What do you think, Nikolai Vassilich?

NIKOLAI (*smiling*). A little differently. Socialism's a highly dangerous phenomenon. And in a country which has no philosophy of its own, no racial philosophy so to speak, where everyone grabs any ideas that are going around, it's bound to fall on fertile soil. We're a people of extremes. That's our sickness.

PAULINA. Oh, how true that is! Yes, we're a people of extremes.

TATIANA (*getting up*). Particularly you and your husband. Not to mention the assistant prosecutor here.

PAULINA. You don't know anything about it, Tanya. Zakhar is considered to be one of the reds of the province.

TATIANA (*walking up and down*). I should think he's only red with shame – and that not often.

PAULINA. Tanya! What *is* the matter with you, for God's sake?

TATIANA. Was that an insult? I didn't know. [To me, your life is like a play put on by amateurs. The parts have been wrongly cast, nobody's got a scrap of talent, everybody's acting abominably, so the play makes no sense at all.

NIKOLAI. There's something in that. . . . And everyone's complaining, 'Oh, what a boring play!'

TATIANA. That's right. We're ruining the play. And I think the extras and the stage hands are beginning to realize it. One day they'll just chase us off the stage . . .]

Enter the GENERAL *and* KON.

NIKOLAI. Now wait a minute! What are you getting at?

GENERAL. (*shouting as he approaches*). Paulina! Milk for the general! Ha! *Cold* milk! (*To* NIKOLAI.) Aha, the tombstone of the Law! (*To* TATIANA.) My excellent niece – your hand! (*To* KON.) Kon, question one: what is a soldier?

KON (*drearily*). Whatever those in command wish him to be, your excellency.

GENERAL. Can he be a fish?

KON. A soldier must be able to do anything that . . .

TATIANA. Uncle dear, you amused us with this little scene yesterday. Surely you don't play it every day?

PAULINA (*with a sigh*). Every day, after his swim.

GENERAL. Yes, every day! And every day different, that's how it has to be done! This old clown has to think up the questions as well as the answers.

TATIANA. Do you enjoy that, Kon?

KON. The General enjoys it.

TATIANA. What about you?

GENERAL. He does too.

KON. I don't, really. I'm a bit old for circus acts. But if you want to eat you have to put up with it.

GENERAL. Oho, you cunning old rascal. About turn! Quick march! Left, right, left, right . . .

TATIANA. Don't you get bored with making a fool of an old man?

GENERAL. I'm an old man myself. And you bore me. Actresses are supposed to amuse people. What are you doing about that?

PAULINA. Uncle, did you know . . .

GENERAL. I don't know anything.

PAULINA. We're closing the factory.

GENERAL. Ah! Good idea! It *hoots*! There you are, sound asleep in the early morning, and suddenly – hoo-oo-oo-oot! Close it down, by all means.

MIKHAIL *enters, walking fast.*

MIKHAIL. Nikolai, here a moment. Well, the factory's closed. But we'd better take some precautions, just in case. Get off a telegram to the vice-governor, tell him briefly how things stand, and ask for some troops. Put my name to it.

NIKOLAI. He's my friend, too.

MIKHAIL. I know. I'm off now to tell those damn delegates about the closure. Don't say a word about the telegram – I'll let them know myself when the moment comes, all right?

NIKOLAI. Yes.

MIKHAIL. You know, it really feels wonderful when you make a stand! It's a sign of youth. I may be older than you in years, Nikolai, but I'm younger in heart, eh?

NIKOLAI. I think it's less a question of youth than of being highly strung.

MIKHAIL (*ironically*). Oh yes, of course! Goodbye now. I'll show you who's highly strung, just you wait and see!

MIKHAIL *exits, laughing.*

PAULINA. So it's decided then, is it, Nikolai Vassilich?

NIKOLAI (*exiting*). So it seems.

PAULINA. Oh my God!

GENERAL. What's been decided?

PAULINA. To close down the factory.

GENERAL. Oh, that. You already told me. Tra-lala. Te-te-tum. It's boring.

TATIANA. I agree.

PAULINA. But it's all so worrying and awkward!

GENERAL. Kon!

KON. Sir!

GENERAL. Rods. Boat. All correct?

KON. Ready and correct, sir.

GENERAL. I'm going to converse with the fish, since I'm averse to humans. (*He roars with laughter.*) Ha! Nicely put, eh? (*Enter* NADYA, *running.*) Ah, my little butterfly! What's up?

NADYA (*joyfully*). We've had an adventure! (*She turns back, and calls.*) Come on, do! Grab his arm, Kleopatra Petrovna! (*To* PAULINA) We were just coming out of the woods, Aunt Paulina, and suddenly [there were] these three drunken workers . . . (came up to us.)

PAULINA. There you are! Haven't I always told you . . . (not to wander in the woods!)

KLEOPATRA *enters*, GREKOV *behind her.*

KLEOPATRA. Just think how disgusting!

NADYA. Why disgusting? It was just funny! Three workers, aunt, all smiling and saying, 'Dear ladies, dear ladies . . .'

KLEOPATRA. I shall certainly ask my husband to dismiss them.

GREKOV (*smiling*). What for?

GENERAL (*to* NADYA). Who is that, under all the dirt?

NADYA. He's the one who rescued us, Grandfather, don't you understand?

GENERAL. I don't understand a thing.

KLEOPATRA (*to* NADYA). Nobody could, the way you tell it.

NADYA. I'm telling it perfectly well.

PAULINA. But, Nadya, we don't understand any of it.

NADYA. That's because you all keep interrupting! They came up to us and they said, 'Dear ladies, dear young ladies, let's all sing a song together . . .'

PAULINA. Oh! What an impertinence!

NADYA. No, no, it wasn't, really! They said, 'We know you sing very well. Of course, we have taken a drink,' they said, 'but we're all the better for that.' And it's true, Aunt Paulina, when they're a bit drunk they aren't as sullen as usual.

KLEOPATRA. Fortunately for us this young man . . .

NADYA. I can tell it better than you. And then Kleopatra Petrovna started to scold them – you shouldn't have done that, I'm sure you shouldn't. And then one of them, a tall, thin man . . .

KLEOPATRA (*grimly*). I happen to know his name.

NADYA. . . . took her arm and said, sadly, somehow, 'You're such a beautiful, well-educated woman, it's a real pleasure to look at you, and yet here you are swearing at us. We haven't harmed you, have we?' He said that so nicely, you know, right from the heart. And then one of the others, he was, well, really rather . . . He said, 'Why talk to them? They don't know anything. They're just wild beasts.' Us! Wild beasts!

NADYA *laughs.*

TATIANA (*smiling*). You seem to like the label.

PAULINA. I warned you, Nadya. You're always running about all over the place . . .

GREKOV (*to* NADYA). May I go?

NADYA. Oh, no, please don't! Look, have some tea? Or some milk? Will you?

The GENERAL *laughs.* KLEOPATRA *shrugs.* TATIANA *watches* GREKOV, *humming to herself.* PAULINA *lowers her head and carefully wipes a spoon with a cloth.*

GREKOV (*smiling*). No thank you. I won't have anything.

NADYA (*persuading*). Please. Don't be shy. (He's just an old man.) They're all good, kind people, honestly!

PAULINA (*protesting*). Oh, Nadya!

NADYA [(*to* GREKOV). Don't go. I want to tell them the whole story . . .

KLEOPATRA (*irritably*). In a word, this young man made a timely appearance and persuaded his drunken friends to leave us in peace. I asked him to escort us home and that was it.

NADYA. Oh no, how can you say that? If all that happened was what you said, everyone would die of boredom!

GENERAL. By jove! Die of boredom, eh?]

NADYA (*to* GREKOV). Oh, do sit down! Aunt Paulina, ask him to sit down. Why are you all looking so sour? Are you too hot, or what?

PAULINA (*to* GREKOV). Thank you, young man.

GREKOV. It was nothing.

PAULINA (*more coldly*). It was good of you to defend these young women.

GREKOV (*quietly*). They didn't need defending. No one was harming them.

NADYA. Oh, Aunt Paulina! How can you speak in that tone?

PAULINA. Please don't teach me how to speak.

NADYA. [But don't you understand, it wasn't a question of defending! He just said, 'Leave off, lads! That's no way.' And they were delighted to see him! 'Grekov!' they said, 'come on then, you're a good lad!' And he really is good, Aunt Paulina, and clever. . . . I'm sorry, Grekov, but you are, you know.

GREKOV (*grinning*). You're putting me in an awkward spot.

NADYA. Am I? I didn't mean to. . . . It's not me, it's them, Grekov.

PAULINA. Nadya! I really don't understand these transports of delight. It's all too absurd. That's enough, now.

NADYA (*excited*). Laugh, then, if I'm funny! Don't just sit there like a lot of owls, go ahead and laugh!]

KLEOPATRA. Nadya has a way of turning every trifle into an

occasion for noisy ecstasies. And this is a fine time to choose, in front of a . . . stranger . . . who, as you see, is laughing at her.

NADYA (*to* GREKOV). Are you laughing at me?

GREKOV (*simply*). Not at all. I'm admiring you.

PAULINA (*astonished*). Oh, really! Uncle, please . . .

KLEOPATRA (*with a wry smile*). There you are, you see.

GENERAL. Now then, basta! The joke's gone far enough. Here, young man – here you are. Now be off with you.

GREKOV (*turning away*). Thank you. I don't want it.

NADYA (*covering her face*). Oh Grandfather! Why?

GENERAL (*stopping* GREKOV). Hold on! This is ten roubles!

GREKOV (*calmly*). What of it?

They are all silent for a moment.

GENERAL (*embarrassed*). Er . . . what, er . . . who are you?

GREKOV. A worker.

GENERAL. A blacksmith?

GREKOV. A fitter.

GENERAL (*severely*). Same thing. Why don't you take the money, eh?

GREKOV. I don't want to.

GENERAL (*irritated*). What are you playing at? What *do* you want?

GREKOV. Nothing.

GENERAL. Sure you don't want to ask for the young lady's hand, eh?

The GENERAL *roars with laughter; the others are embarrassed.*

NADYA. Oh! What are you *doing*!?

PAULINA. Uncle, please.

GREKOV (*calmly, to the* GENERAL). How old are you?

GENERAL (*surprised*). What? How old? Me?

GREKOV (*as before*). How old are you?

GENERAL (*glancing round*). What is this? Er, well – sixty-one. What of it?

GREKOV (*walking away*). At your age you should have more sense.

GENERAL. What's that? More sense? Me?

NADYA *runs after* GREKOV.

NADYA. Listen, please don't be angry. [He's an old man. They're all nice people, really.

GENERAL. What the devil . . . ?]

GREKOV. Don't worry yourself. It's all quite natural.

NADYA. [It's the heat, it puts them in a bad mood. And I didn't tell the story well at all . . .

GREKOV (*smiling*). However you told it, they wouldn't have understood, believe me.]

GREKOV *and* NADYA *exit together.*

GENERAL. How dare he talk to me like that!

TATIANA. You shouldn't have thrust your money at him.

PAULINA. Ah, Nadya! That Nadya!

KLEOPATRA. The nerve of it! Playing the proud spaniard like that! I shall certainly [see that] (ask) my husband . . . (to dismiss him!)

GENERAL. The young pup!

PAULINA. But, really, Nadya's impossible! And then to walk off with him! She really worries me.

KLEOPATRA. These 'Socialists' of yours get more impudent every day.

PAULINA. What makes you think he's a socialist?

KLEOPATRA. I can see it. All the superior workers are socialists!

GENERAL. I shall tell Zakhar. He can throw that young pup out of the factory on his neck.

TATIANA. The factory's closed.

GENERAL. Right out on his neck.

PAULINA. Tanya, call Nadya back, will you, dear? Tell her I'm – I'm deeply shocked.

TATIANA *goes out.*

GENERAL. The scoundrel. How old, eh?

KLEOPATRA. Those drunks *whistled* at us! (*To* PAULINA.) And you – you play along with them . . . All those reading circles . . . What's the point of it all?

PAULINA. Yes, yes . . . and on Thursday when I was driving through the village, imagine! Suddenly there was a whistle – they even whistle at me! Quite apart from the rudeness, they might have frightened the horses!

KLEOPATRA (*sententiously*). Zakhar Ivanich is much to blame. As my husband says, he doesn't keep a proper distance between himself and those people.

PAULINA. He's too gentle. He wants to be kind to everyone. He's convinced that a friendly relationship with the people is to the advantage of both sides, and certainly the peasants bear this out – they lease the land, pay their rents, and everything's fine. But these . . .

Enter TATIANA *and* NADYA.

Nadya, my dear! Don't you understand how improper . . .

NADYA (*passionately*). It's you, you who's improper! You're all out of your minds with the heat, you're vicious, and sick, and you don't understand anything! As for you, Grandfather – Oh, how *stupid* you are!

GENERAL (*furious*). Me? Stupid? How much more . . . ?

NADYA. Why did you have to say that . . . about asking for my hand? Aren't you ashamed of yourself?

GENERAL. Ashamed? No! No, basta! I've had enough for one day! (*He walks away and bellows.*) Kon! Where the devil are you? Got your feet stuck in the mud, have you? Idiot! Blockhead! (*He exits.*)

NADYA. And you, Aunt Paulina, you of all people! You've lived abroad, you talk about politics . . . not to invite him to sit down, not even to offer him a cup of tea – you . . . you grand lady, you!

PAULINA (*gets up and throws down the spoon*). No, this is frightful.

It's intolerable, [you don't know what you're saying.] (stop it at once.)

NADYA. And you too, Kleopatra Petrovna, you were polite as anything on the way back but as soon as we got here . . .

KLEOPATRA. Well, really, what was I supposed to do? Kiss him? I'm sorry, but his face was dirty. And I don't feel like listening to your reprimands, any more. . . . You see, Paulina Dmitrevna? There's your democracy for you – or – what d'you call it? – your humanism. For the moment my husband has to cope with it all, but you wait – it'll come back on you eventually.

PAULINA. Kleopatra Petrovna, I do apologize to you for Nadya . . .

KLEOPATRA (*leaving*). Quite unnecessary. It isn't only her. It's not just Nadya, you're all to blame . . .

KLEOPATRA *exits*.

PAULINA. Nadya – when your mother was dying and entrusted me with you and your upbringing . . .

NADYA. Leave Mama out of it! You get it all wrong when you talk about her!

PAULINA (*amazed*). Nadya! Are you ill? Pull yourself together. Your mother was my sister, I knew her better than you did.

NADYA (*in unrestrained tears*). You don't know anything! Poor people and rich people can never be sisters! My mother was poor, but she was good. You couldn't ever understand poor people, you don't even understand Aunt Tanya!

PAULINA. Nadya – I must ask you to leave us. Go along, please.

NADYA (*leaving*). Oh, I'll go. But I'm right all the same. It's me that's right, not you.

PAULINA. Good heavens! A perfectly healthy girl, and then suddenly she throws a fit like that! Almost hysterical. I'm sorry, Tanya, but I can see your influence at work here. It's true. [You talk to her about everything, just as if she was a grown-up. Taking her off to meet our employees, all those clerks – so-called working-class intellectuals – really, it's ludicrous! And taking her out boating with you . . .]

TATIANA. Oh, do calm down. Have a drink or something. You must agree your behaviour with that workman wasn't very sensible. Nothing would have happened to the chair if you'd asked him to sit on it.

PAULINA. No, you're wrong, you know. Nobody could say I treat the workers badly, but there's a limit to everything, my dear.

Enter YAKOV, *slowly, drunk.*

TATIANA. And whatever you say, I don't take her everywhere – she goes by herself. And I think she should be allowed to.

PAULINA. [She goes by herself! As if she understood where she's going!]

YAKOV (*sitting*). There's going to be a riot at the factory.

PAULINA (*wearily*). Oh, stop it, Yakov!

YAKOV. There is, you know. There'll be a riot. They'll burn the factory down and roast us all in the fire like – like rabbits.

TATIANA (*annoyed*). So you're drunk already.

YAKOV. By this time of day I'm always drunk already. I've just seen Kleopatra – she really is a worthless bitch. Not because she has all those lovers, but because there's a vicious old dog squatting where her heart should be.

PAULINA (*getting up*). Oh God. . . . Everything was going so smoothly, and then suddenly . . . (*She walks up and down the garden.*)

YAKOV. A very small dog. With a mangy coat. A small *greedy* dog . . . sitting there, baring its teeth . . . It's full up, it's eaten everything in sight, but it still wants something more . . . doesn't know what, so it gets in a state . . .

TATIANA. Be quiet, Yakov. Look, here comes your brother.

YAKOV. I don't want my brother. Tanya, I quite understand that it's no longer possible to love me, but, still, I don't like it. Don't like it, and don't stop loving you.

TATIANA. Why don't you freshen yourself up?

ZAKHAR (*coming up to them*). Well, have they announced that the factory's closing down yet?

TATIANA. I don't know.

YAKOV. It hasn't been announced, but the workers know.

ZAKHAR. Why? Who told them?

YAKOV. I did. I went and told them.

PAULINA (*comes up to him*). Whatever for?

YAKOV (*shrugs*). I just did. They're interested. I tell them everything – when they'll listen. I think they're quite fond of me. They like to see that the boss's brother is a drunkard, it makes them feel that all men are equals.

ZAKHAR. Hm. You go to the factory quite a lot, Yakov, and of course I've no objection. But Mikhail Vassilich says that when you're chatting to the workers you sometimes criticize the way the factory's managed.

YAKOV. He's lying. I don't know a thing about management. Or mismanagement.

ZAKHAR. He also says that you sometimes take vodka with you.

YAKOV. More lies. I don't take it with me, I send out for it. And not sometimes. Always. Don't you understand that I'm of no interest to them without my vodka.

ZAKHAR. But, Yakov, surely you can see – I mean, as the boss's brother . . .

YAKOV. That's not my only failing.

ZAKHAR (*offended*). Well, I'll say no more. I'll say no more. There's an atmosphere of hostility growing up around me which I just don't understand.

PAULINA. It's true. You should have heard what Nadya was saying a moment ago.

POLOGGY *enters, running.*

POLOGGY. Sir . . . may I tell you . . . it's the director . . . he's just – just been . . . shot, er, killed.

ZAKHAR. What?

PAULINA. You – What did you say?

POLOGGY. Killed outright ... fell down ...

ZAKHAR. Who ... who shot him?

POLOGGY. The workers.

PAULINA. Have they been arrested?

ZAKHAR. Is the doctor there?

POLOGGY. I don't know.

PAULINA. Yakov Ivanich, do go!

YAKOV (*gesturing helplessly*). Go where?

PAULINA. How did it happen?

POLOGGY. The director got ... in a state of ... some agitation ... and his foot ... hit the stomach ... of one of the workers.

YAKOV. They're coming now.

> *Noise.* MIKHAIL *is led in, supported on one side by* LEVSHIN, *a balding elderly worker, on the other by* NIKOLAI. *Various workers and clerks follow, and then a* POLICEMAN, KLEO-PATRA *and* NADYA.

MIKHAIL (*wearily*). Let me go. ... Put me down ...

NIKOLAI. Did you see who fired?

MIKHAIL. I'm tired. Oh, I'm so tired ...

NIKOLAI (*insistent*). Do you know who fired?

MIKHAIL. It hurts. ... A man with red hair. ... Put me down ...

> *They lay him on the lawn couch.*

NIKOLAI (*to the* POLICEMAN). You hear? A red-haired man.

POLICEMAN. Yes, sir.

MIKHAIL. It's not important ... now. ... He had green eyes.

LEVSHIN. You should leave him rest now, sir.

NIKOLAI. Hold your tongue. Where's the doctor? The doctor? I want to know where the doctor is!

> *Everyone fusses around, whispering.*

MIKHAIL. Don't shout ... it hurts ... do let me rest ...

LEVSHIN. Ay, you rest there, Mikhail Vassilich, and don't you

worry. Ah, human affairs, copeck affairs! We go down for a
copeck, it's mother to us and death to us.

NIKOLAI. Officer! Get rid of everyone who isn't needed here.

POLICEMAN (*quietly*). Off you go, lads. There's nothing to see
here.

ZAKHAR (*quietly*). Where's the doctor?

NIKOLAI. Misha! ... Misha! ... (*He bends over his brother;
others join him.*) I think ... he's gone. He has.

ZAKHAR. No, surely –

NIKOLAI (*slowly, quietly*). Yes. He's dead. Do you understand
what that means, Zakhar Ivanich?

ZAKHAR. [But ... couldn't you be mistaken?

NIKOLAI. No. And] it was you who put him in front of that
bullet. You!

TATIANA. How cruel ... and ... pointless.

NIKOLAI (*bearing down on* ZAKHAR). Yes, you!

The DISTRICT POLICE INSPECTOR *enters, running.*

INSPECTOR. Where's Mr Bardin? Is he badly wounded?

LEVSHIN. Gone. Finished. He chivvied them here and he chivvied
them there. And now, himself. There.

NIKOLAI (*to* INSPECTOR). He managed to say it was a man with
red hair who shot him.

INSPECTOR. A redhead, eh?

NIKOLAI. Yes. You should act on that at once.

INSPECTOR (*to* POLICEMAN). I want all red-headed men at the
factory rounded up at once.

POLICEMAN. Yes, sir.

INSPECTOR. And I mean all of them!

The POLICEMAN *exits.* KLEOPATRA *enters, running.*

KLEOPATRA. Where is he? Misha! What is it? Has he fainted?
Nikolai Vassilich, is he in a faint?

NIKOLAI *turns away.*

He's not dead, is he? Is he?

LEVSHIN. He's quiet now. . . . Wherever it was, he didn't get there.

NIKOLAI (*angrily, but quietly*). You. Get out. (*To the* POLICE INSPECTOR.) Get rid of him.

KLEOPATRA. The doctor . . . why isn't the doctor . . . ?

INSPECTOR (*to* LEVSHIN, *quietly*). Go on, clear off.

LEVSHIN (*quietly*). I'm going. No need to shove.

KLEOPATRA (*quietly*). Have they killed him?

PAULINA (*to* KLEOPATRA). My dear . . .

KLEOPATRA (*quietly, angrily*). Get away from me! This is your doing – yours!

ZAKHAR (*in a crushed voice*). I can understand . . . the shock . . . but why . . . why say such a thing?

PAULINA (*tearfully*). Oh, my dear, that's a terrible thing to say.

KLEOPATRA. Oh yes? Terrible, is it?

TATIANA (*to* PAULINA). You'd better go.

KLEOPATRA. You killed him. You, with your damned flabbiness.

NIKOLAI (*coldly*). That'll do, Kleopatra. Zakhar Ivanich can see for himself how guilty he is.

ZAKHAR. I don't understand . . . what are you saying? How can you accuse me like that?

PAULINA. How horrible! My God, it's so hard and unfeeling!

KLEOPATRA (*exalted*). Unfeeling, you say? You, who set the workers against him, you who destroyed his authority! They were afraid of him, they trembled under his eye, and now – there! There! They've killed him, and it's you – you who's to blame! His blood is on you!

NIKOLAI. That's enough. There's no need to shout.

KLEOPATRA (*to* PAULINA). Oh yes, you're weeping, are you? Then weep my husband's blood off your hands!

POLICEMAN (*entering*). Sir . . .

INSPECTOR. Quiet!

POLICEMAN (*whispers*). The red-headed men, sir – they're being rounded up now . . .

The GENERAL *appears at the end of the garden, pushing* KON *before him and roaring with laughter.*

NIKOLAI. Sh-sh-h, please!
KLEOPATRA. Well, murderers?

CURTAIN

Act Two

A moonlit night. Thick, heavy shadows on the ground. On the tables, untidily, are quantities of bread, cucumber, eggs, bottles of beer. Candles burning, with shades. AGRAFENA is washing plates. YAGODIN is sitting on a chair, holding a stick, and smoking. To the left stand TATIANA, NADYA and LEVSHIN. Everyone talks in hushed voices, as if listening to something. A general mood of unhappy, anxious expectancy.

LEVSHIN (*to* NADYA). Everything human is poisoned with copper on this earth, lass. That's why life can seem dreary, even to your young soul. The copper copeck shackles us all together. Maybe you're free, still, maybe you've not found your place in the human chain, but the copeck chimes its message to every living soul – love me, as you love your own self. Nay, but that's nought to you.

YAGODIN (*to* AGRAFENA). Efimich is on to teaching the gentry now. He's a queer one.

AGRAFENA. Why shouldn't he? It's only the truth he's saying. The gentry can do with a bit of the truth for once.

NADYA. Is yours a hard life, Levshin?

LEVSHIN. Mine isn't too hard. I've got no children. I've got a woman – the wife, that is – but they all died, did the children.

NADYA. Aunt Tanya, why does everyone talk quietly when there's a dead person in the house?

TATIANA. I don't know.

LEVSHIN (*smiling*). That's our guilt, lass, before the dead one. We're all guilty, all round.

NADYA. But, Levshin, dead people haven't always been – killed. And whenever someone's dead, people talk quietly.

LEVSHIN. Ay, my dear, for we kill every one of 'em. Bullets for some, words for others, but it's us as kills 'em with our goings-on.

We drive folk from this world, into the earth, and we don't see it, we don't feel it. It's only when we chuck a body to his death like that, do we get a glimmering of our own guilt. [We'll feel a bit sorry for the dead one, a bit ashamed when we think on him. And then afeared in our souls. For we're all being driven the same road, all being readied for the grave.]

NADYA. Yes . . . it's frightening.

LEVSHIN. Nay, it's nothing. Today it's frightening, mebbe, tomorrow we'll not think on't. And folk'll be back at their pushing again. [One of 'em who gets pushed'll fall down, and they'll all be quiet for a moment – uncomfortable, like. Then they'll give a bit of a sigh, and be right back at it again.] Back at the old game. Poor ignorant folk, there's but the one road for all . . . But you've not felt your own guilt yet, lass, the dead don't worry you, you can talk loud before them.

TATIANA. What must we do to . . . live differently? Do you know?

LEVSHIN (*mysteriously*). Do away with the copeck! Bury it! Once that's gone, what's to quarrel about, what's to push at each other for?

TATIANA. Is that all?

LEVSHIN. It'll do for a start.

TATIANA. Shall we take a turn in the garden, Nadya?

NADYA (*thoughtfully*). If you like . . .

The two of them walk down towards the rear of the garden. LEVSHIN goes over to the table. Outside the tent appear the GENERAL, KON and POLOGGY.

YAGODIN. So you'll even try sowing on stony ground, Efimich. You're an odd one.

LEVSHIN. Why?

YAGODIN. You're wasting your time. You think they'll ever understand? You might stir the soul of a worker, but never theirs. They need a different medicine.

LEVSHIN. The soul's another story, brother. At least these two are scratching the right itch.

AGRAFENA. Will you not have some more tea?

LEVSHIN. That I will.

They are silent. The hearty voice of the GENERAL *can be heard.* NADYA's *and* TATIANA's *white dresses are glimpsed among the trees.*

GENERAL. Or you can take a piece of string and stretch it across the road where it can't be seen. Someone comes along and suddenly – kerflop!

POLOGGY. It's a real pleasure to see a man fall down, Excellency!

YAGODIN. Hear that?

(GENERAL. Come on, I'll show you. Down to the fence, Kon!)

LEVSHIN. I heard.

KON. [There can be none of that tonight, with the dead in the house. You can't play jokes in front of dead people.

GENERAL. Don't try to teach me what I can do! When you die I shall dance the mazurka.]

TATIANA *and* NADYA *come up to the table.*

LEVSHIN. [The man's old.]

AGRAFENA (*going towards the house*). It's a terrible thing, him and his naughty ways.

TATIANA *sits down at the table.*

TATIANA. Tell me, Levshin. Are you a socialist?

LEVSHIN (*simply*). Me? No. Timofey and me are weavers, miss. We're weavers.

TATIANA. But you know some socialists? You've heard of them?

LEVSHIN. Ay, we've heard of them. As for knowing them, no, we don't know them. But we have heard of them.

TATIANA. Do you know Sintsov? In the office?

LEVSHIN. We do, that. We know all the clerks.

TATIANA. Have you spoken to him?

YAGODIN (*anxiously*). Why would we be speaking to him? Their place is up in the office, ours is down with the looms. When one of us goes up there, they give us the management's orders. That's all. That's our acquaintance.

NADYA. You seem to be scared of us, Levshin. Please don't be. We're very interested.

LEVSHIN. What's to be scared of? We've done no wrong. We were told to come here and keep guard, so we've come. There's some as are angry down there, saying, We'll burn down factory, burn down everything, leave nought but embers, but Timofey and me, we're against ugly deeds. Nothing must be burnt. [Why burn? Wasn't it us as built it all, us and our fathers, and our grandfathers? And then to go *burning* it?

TATIANA. You're not thinking there's anything harmful behind our questions?

YAGODIN. Why? We mean no harm to anyone.]

LEVSHIN. The way we look at it, what our hands have made together, is sacred. Men's labour must be valued justly, that's what. Burning don't help. But then, folk live in darkness. They like a fire. And they're angry now. The departed was a touch strict with us – may he not be remembered for it!

NADYA. What about my uncle? Is he better?

YAGODIN. Zakhar Ivanich?

NADYA. Yes. Is he any kinder? Or does he treat you badly too?

LEVSHIN. We don't say that.

YAGODIN (*grimly*). Strict or kind, they're all the same to us.

LEVSHIN (*explains gently*). The strict one's a boss, and the kind one's a boss. A disease don't pick and choose.

YAGODIN [(*bored*). Mind you, Zakhar Ivanich has a good heart . . .

NADYA. You mean, he's better than Skrobotov, then?

YAGODIN (*quietly*). The managing director is dead now.

LEVSHIN. Your uncle's a fine man, miss. But it isn't us as'll benefit from his beauty.]

TATIANA (*irritated*). Come on, Nadya. They don't want to understand us, you can see that.

NADYA (*quietly*). Yes.

They walk off silently. LEVSHIN *glances after them, then at*
YAGODIN. *Both smile.*

YAGODIN. How they do pluck at your soul!

LEVSHIN. It's all 'very interesting', for them.

YAGODIN. Or else they thought we'd maybe let something drop
. . . ?

LEVSHIN. That young one, now, she's a good little lass. A pity
she's rich!

YAGODIN. We'll have to tell Sintsov. Tell him the lady was
pumping us.

LEVSHIN. We'll do that.

YAGODIN. How about it, then? They'll have to give in, now.

LEVSHIN. Now he's not there, ay. What can they do?

YAGODIN (*yawning*). Ye-e-e-es. Ah, but I'm sleepy.

LEVSHIN. Bear up, brother. The General's coming.

The GENERAL *walks up towards the table. Beside him is*
POLOGGY, *walking respectfully, and behind him,* KON.
POLOGGY *suddenly seizes the* GENERAL's *arm.*

GENERAL. What? What?

POLOGGY. A hole, Excellency, a hole!

GENERAL. Ah. Hm. What's all this? This – mess on the table?
Been eating here, have you?

YAGODIN. Yes, sir. And the young ladies.

GENERAL. That's it, then. So you're on guard duty, eh?

YAGODIN. Yes, sir. Keeping watch.

GENERAL. Good men. I'll speak to the Governor about you. How
many of you here?

LEVSHIN. Two.

GENERAL. Idiot! I can count up to two! I mean, how many
altogether?

YAGODIN. About thirty.

GENERAL. You armed?

LEVSHIN (*to* YAGODIN). Timofey, where's that pistol you had?

YAGODIN (*points to table*). There.

GENERAL. Dammit, man, don't pick it up by the muzzle! Here, why is it dripping wet?

YAGODIN. They must have put too much oil on it . . .

GENERAL. That's milk, not oil! What are you doing, soaking the thing in milk? What a ragbag you are! Wipe it, Kon. And teach these idiots how to hold a gun. (*To* LEVSHIN.) You, have you got a revolver?

LEVSHIN *indicates his breast pocket.*

LEVSHIN. Here.

GENERAL. And if these – these rioters come. . . . Will you shoot?

LEVSHIN. They won't come, sir. It's just that they lost their tempers. It's done with now.

GENERAL. [But if they do come?

LEVSHIN. They took it badly, the closing of the factory. Some of them have children.]

GENERAL. What's this song and dance you're giving me? I'm asking you, will you shoot?

LEVSHIN. Well, sir, we're prepared to shoot. Why wouldn't we be? But we don't know how. If it was shotguns, now . . .

GENERAL. Kon! Go and teach them. Take them down to the river.

KON (*sullenly*). Allow me to report, Excellency, that it's the middle of the night. It'll cause a lot of excitement if we start shooting now, people will come and want to know what's happening. But it's all one to me, of course. Anything you say.

GENERAL. See to it tomorrow.

LEVSHIN. It'll be all quiet by tomorrow. They'll open the factory . . .

GENERAL. Who will?

LEVSHIN. Zakhar Ivanich. He's having a talk with the men now.

GENERAL. The devil he is! If I had my way I'd shut it once for all. No more hooting in the small hours!

YAGODIN. We wouldn't mind sleeping a bit later, too.

GENERAL. You! I'd starve the lot of you! That'd teach you to riot!

LEVSHIN. We're not rioting, are we?

GENERAL. Silence! What d'you think you're doing, standing there? You should be patrolling the fence. If anyone tries to climb over, shoot. I'll answer for it.

LEVSHIN. Come on, Timofey. Don't forget your pistol.

As they leave, the GENERAL *shouts after them.*

GENERAL. Pistol! Greenhorns! Can't even call a weapon by its proper name!

POLOGGY. Excellency, allow me to take the liberty of informing you that the masses, by and large, are coarse and brutish. To take an example from my very own experience, sir, I happen to have a vegetable garden, and with my own two hands, sir . . .

GENERAL. Yes, yes. Admirable.

POLOGGY. Working of course in the free time at my disposal . . .

GENERAL. Yes, yes, everyone should work.

Enter TATIANA *and* NADYA.

TATIANA (*from a distance*). Why are you shouting?

GENERAL. Because I'm annoyed. (*To* POLOGGY.) Well?

POLOGGY. But almost every night the workers descend on my labours . . .

GENERAL. Steal your vegetables, eh?

POLOGGY. Precisely. I of course seek the protection of the law, the which is represented here by his honour the commissary of district police, a personage entirely indifferent to the animadversions of the general population . . .

TATIANA. Why ever do you [talk in such a silly sort of language?] (use such extraordinary words?)

POLOGGY (*confused*). I? Forgive me . . . but I studied for three years at the business college and I read the paper every day . . .

TATIANA (*smiling*). That explains it.

NADYA. You're funny, Pologgy.

POLOGGY. I'm delighted if I make a pleasant spectacle for you. A person should try to give pleasure . . .

GENERAL. Pleasure, eh? Don't you love fishing?

POLOGGY. I've never tried, Excellency.

TATIANA. Which? – fishing or loving?

POLOGGY (*embarrassed*). The former.

TATIANA. And the latter?

POLOGGY. I have tried the – the latter.

TATIANA. Are you married?

POLOGGY. It is my dearest wish. But as I earn only thirty roubles a month . . .

Enter KLEOPATRA *and* NIKOLAI, *walking rapidly.*

. . . I cannot venture upon such an undertaking.

NIKOLAI (*agitated*). It's beyond belief! Utter chaos!

KLEOPATRA. How dare he! How could he!

GENERAL. What's going on?

KLEOPATRA (*shouting*). Your nephew is . . . completely, totally gutless! He's agreed to all the demands of the ruffians – my husband's murderers!

NADYA (*quietly*). They're surely not all murderers?

KLEOPATRA. Making a mockery of his corpse, and of me! To open the factory before there's even been time to bury the man who was murdered because he closed it!

NADYA. But Uncle was afraid they'd burn everything down . . .

KLEOPATRA. Be quiet. You're only a child.

NIKOLAI. And that young fitter's speech – a clear call for socialism!

KLEOPATRA. Some young clerk's ordering everyone around, advising everyone . . . He even dared to suggest that the crime was provoked by the victim himself!

NIKOLAI (*making a note in a notebook*). Very suspicious, that character. He's too clever by half for a clerk.

TATIANA. Do you mean Sintsov?

NIKOLAI. I do indeed.

KLEOPATRA. I feel as if someone had spat in my face.

POLOGGY. Allow me to remark, Excellency, that when Mr Sintsov reads the newspapers he makes numerous political comments which are far from impartial ...

TATIANA (*to* NIKOLAI). Does that interest you?

NIKOLAI (*defiantly*). Certainly! Did you think you'd embarrass me?

TATIANA. I think we can do without Mr Pologgy's presence.

POLOGGY. Excuse me. I'll go, of course ... (POLOGGY *exits quickly, left.*)

KLEOPATRA. He's coming here. No, I won't ... I can't see him ...

NADYA. What's happening?

GENERAL. I'm too old for all this to-do. Killing. Rioting. Zakhar should have foreseen all this when he invited me here for a rest. [I shall tell him that it doesn't suit me. Yes. That's what I'll do.]

> ZAKHAR *enters, excited but pleased. He sees* NIKOLAI *and stops in embarrassment, adjusts his spectacles.*

Listen, my dear chap ... er ... do you know what you've done?

ZAKHAR. Wait a minute, Uncle ... Nikolai Vassilich ...

NIKOLAI. Sir.

ZAKHAR. The workers were in such a state of excitement ... I was afraid they might destroy the whole factory ... so I – I agreed not to close down. I agreed to their demand about Dichkov too, but I made it a condition that they hand over the murderer. They're looking for him now.

NIKOLAI (*coldly*). They could save themselves the trouble. We shall find him without their help.

ZAKHAR. I feel it's better if they themselves. ... Yes. We've decided to open the factory as from noon tomorrow.

NIKOLAI. Who is 'we'?

ZAKHAR. I, er ...

NIKOLAI. Ah, yes. Thank you for the information. But it's clear

to me that on my brother's death his vote passed to me and to
his wife. If I'm not mistaken, you should have consulted us on
this question, not gone off and made a decision independently.

ZAKHAR. But I invited you to come! I sent Sintsov to fetch you,
and you refused!

NIKOLAI. Surely you can see that on the day of my brother's
death I can't be expected to attend to business?

ZAKHAR. But you were there, in the factory!

NIKOLAI. I was there, yes. I listened to some of their speeches.
What of it?

ZAKHAR. But don't you understand, something had to be done!
Your brother, it turns out, sent a telegram to the town asking
for troops. They'll be arriving by noon tomorrow.

GENERAL. Aha, troops! Now you're talking! Soldiers – that means
real business.

NIKOLAI. A very wise precaution.

ZAKHAR. I don't know. When they see the soldiers the workers'
mood is bound to deteriorate. God knows what might happen
if the factory remained closed. I think I did the right thing. I
think it will prevent a riot.

NIKOLAI. My conclusion is different. You should never have
given in to those ... creatures. If only out of respect for the
memory of my dead brother.

ZAKHAR. Oh, God. . . . But there was the possibility of another
tragedy!

NIKOLAI. That's nothing to do with me.

ZAKHAR. Possibly. But what about me? I'm the one who has to
live with the workers. And if it came to bloodshed ... and anyway, they might destroy the entire factory.

NIKOLAI. That I don't believe.

GENERAL. Nor do I.

ZAKHAR (crushed). So you condemn my action?

NIKOLAI. Yes, I do.

ZAKHAR (candidly). Why is there all this hostility? I want only
one thing – to avoid the disaster which could so easily happen.

I don't want any bloodshed! Surely it's not impossible to find some peaceful, reasonable way of living? But you look at me with hate in your eyes, the workers with distrust ... And all I want is what's right, what's right and good.

GENERAL. Good, good – what's that? Only a word – not even that – a bunch of letters! G for George, O for Oboe, D for Dog. ... Got nothing to do with getting on with the job. Eh? How's that?

NADYA (*with tears*). Stop it, grandfather! Uncle, don't worry, he doesn't understand. Oh, but Nikolai Vassilich, how is it that *you* can't understand? You're so clever, why can't you trust my uncle?

NIKOLAI. Excuse me, Zakhar Ivanich, I shall go. I cannot – I am not in the habit of discussing business with children. (*Exits.*)

ZAKHAR. You see how it is, Nadya ...

NADYA (*taking his hand*). It doesn't matter, it doesn't matter. The important thing is for the workers to be satisfied. There are so many of them, and so few of us, and ...

ZAKHAR. Just a minute, Nadya. I have to tell you that I'm very displeased with you. Very.

GENERAL. So am I.

ZAKHAR. You sympathize with the workers. It's only natural at your age. But you mustn't lose all sense of proportion, my dear. Look how you brought Grekov to the table this morning ... I know him, he's a very bright lad, but all the same you shouldn't have made a scene with your aunt on his account.

GENERAL. [That's the stuff to give her!

NADYA. But you don't even know what happened!

ZAKHAR. Believe me, I know more than you do.] Our people are coarse and uncultivated. If you offer them a finger they'll grab your whole arm.

TATIANA (*quietly*). As a drowning man grabs a straw.

ZAKHAR. There's a lot of sheer animal greed in them. They need to be trained, not spoilt. Yes, trained. Kindly give that some thought.

GENERAL. Now I've got something to say. You talk to me Devil only knows how, miss. Let me remind you that it'll take you forty years to reach my age. Then, perhaps, I'll allow you to talk to me as an equal, not before. D'you understand? (*Shouts.*) Kon!

KON (*from behind some trees*). Here, sir.

GENERAL. Where's that – what'sisname – Frog?

KON. What frog, sir?

GENERAL. You know, that – what'sisname – Cloggy . . . Floggy . . . Troggy . . .

KON. Pologgy? I don't know, sir.

GENERAL. Find him.

> *He goes into the tent.* ZAKHAR, *head bowed, walks back and forth, cleaning his spectacles with a handkerchief.* NADYA *sits thoughtfully on a chair.* TATIANA *stands watching them.* KON *exits.*

ZAKHAR. They say, we don't know who did it, but we'll find out. Of course they know! I think. . . . (*He glances round, lowers his voice.*) I think they're all in it. It's a plot. To be honest, he did madden them, he used to make fools of them. Mock them. It was almost an illness with him, his love of power. And they – you know, they're frightening, their simplicity is frightening! They've killed a man, and yet they can look at you with such clear eyes – as if they didn't realize a crime had been committed at all. That terrifying simplicity!

NADYA. Why don't you sit down?

ZAKHAR. [Why did he send for troops? Why? They found out about it, of course. They find out everything. It may even have helped to kill him. Of course I had to open the factory – otherwise my relations with them would have been ruined for ages.] At a moment like this they have to be treated with more consideration, more leniency, not less. Who knows how it will end? We must be ready for anything. Yes. In times like these a wise man sees that he has friends among the people. . . . (*Enter* LEVSHIN *backstage.*) Who's that?

LEVSHIN. It's us. We're keeping guard.

ZAKHAR. Well, Efimich, now that a man's been killed you're all quiet and humble, eh?

LEVSHIN. We're always that way, Zakhar Ivanich. Always humble.

ZAKHAR (*reproachfully*). Yes. You kill humbly, too, don't you? Incidentally, Levshin, what's all this you've been preaching? All these wild ideas – we must do away with money, and bosses, and all that? You'd better drop that, my friend. You won't do yourself any good with that sort of talk.

> TATIANA *and* NADIA *go off to the right, where the voices of* SINTSOV *and* YAKOV *can be heard.* YAGODIN *appears from behind the trees.*

LEVSHIN (*calmly*). Now what kind of talk would that be? I've been living a good while, thinking a good while, and, well, I have things to say.

ZAKHAR. Not all bosses are brutes – you must know that. You can see I'm not a vicious man, I'm always ready to help you. All I want is what's best . . .

LEVSHIN (*sighs*). Who wants the worst for himself?

ZAKHAR. Can't you understand, it's *you*, I want the best for *you*!

LEVSHIN. We do understand.

ZAKHAR (*looking at him*). No. No, you're wrong. You don't understand. You're strange people. Beasts one moment, children the next.

> ZAKHAR *walks off.* LEVSHIN *leans on his stick and gazes after him.*

YAGODIN. Preaching again?

LEVSHIN. He's a Chinaman, that one, a real Chinaman. What's he trying to say? He understands nobody but himself.

YAGODIN. He wants what's best. He told you.

LEVSHIN. That's right.

YAGODIN. Let's be off. Here they all come.

> LEVSHIN *and* YAGODIN *retreat as, back right,* TATIANA, YAKOV, NADYA *and* SINTSOV *appear.*

NADYA. We're all walking round and round. It's like a dream.

TATIANA. Would you like something to eat, Matvey Nikolaich?

SINTSOV. What I'd really like is a glass of tea. I've talked so much today my throat's sore.

NADYA. Aren't you afraid of anything?

SINTSOV (*sitting down*). Me? No, nothing.

NADYA. Well I am. Everything's suddenly got muddled, so I can't tell any more which are the good people and which are the bad.

SINTSOV (*smiling*). It'll unmuddle itself. The thing is not to be afraid to think. Think without fear, right through to the end. Anyway, there's nothing to be afraid of.

TATIANA. Do you suppose they've calmed down?

SINTSOV. Yes. Workers so seldom win, even a little victory gives them great satisfaction.

NADYA. Do you love them?

SINTSOV. That's not quite the word. I've been living with them a long time – I know them. I know their strength. I believe in their good sense.

TATIANA. And that the future belongs to them?

SINTSOV. That too.

NADYA. The future. I can't grasp that idea – 'the future'.

TATIANA [(*with a laugh*). They're a cagey lot, these proletarians of yours. Nadya and I tried to talk to them, but we got nowhere.

NADYA. It was horrid. The old man spoke as if we were some sort of – villains – spies, or something. There's another man, Grekov, he looks at people in a different way. But old Levshin keeps on smiling as if he pitied us – as if we were sick!]

TATIANA. Do stop drinking, Yakov. It's quite awful to look at you.

YAKOV. What else can I do? That's what I ask everyone.

SINTSOV. Surely you can find something?

YAKOV. Don't want to. I feel a revulsion, an unconquerable revulsion, for business and everything to do with it. You see, I belong to the third category.

SINTSOV. The what?

YAKOV. The third category. People fall into three categories. Some spend their whole lives working themselves to death, others sit back and rake in the profits, and the rest – the third category – won't work because it's stupid and pointless, can't rake in the profits because it's stupid and embarrassing. So you see, I belong to the third lot. It includes all the idlers, monks, spongers and other parasites in this world.

NADYA. Why do you say these tedious things, Uncle? You're not really like that at all. You're just kind and gentle . . .

YAKOV. In other words, a good-for-nothing. I understood that when I was still at school. People drop into their own category at an early age

TATIANA. Nadya's right, Yakov. It's tedious.

YAKOV. I agree. Matvey Nikolaich, what do you think – does life have a face?

SINTSOV. Possibly.

YAKOV. It has. And it's always young. Not so long ago life used to look at me with indifference. But now it looks at me sternly and asks . . . asks, Who are you? What are you? Where are you going?

He is scared by something, wants to smile, but his lips tremble, he can't control them, his face is distorted by a pathetic, terrible grimace.

TATIANA. Stop it, Yakov, please! Look, here comes the prosecutor. I don't want you to talk in front of him.

YAKOV. All right.

NADYA [(*softly*). Everyone's so sad. All waiting for something to happen, and scared of it. Why won't they let me make friends with the workers? It's stupid.]

NIKOLAI (*coming up*). May I have a glass of tea?

TATIANA. Of course.

For a few moments they all sit in silence. NIKOLAI *stands, holding his tea.*

NADYA. I wish I could understand why the workers don't trust Uncle Zakhar, and why . . .

NIKOLAI (*grimly*). They only trust people who exhort them with stuff like, Workers of the World, Unite! They trust that, all right.

NADYA (*quietly, hunching her shoulders*). When I hear those words – that challenge to the whole world . . . I feel we're all just in the way here – not needed on the earth.

NIKOLAI (*excited*). Exactly! That's just how any civilized person would feel! And before long there's going to be another cry echoing round the earth – Civilized People of the World, Unite! It's time to shout that, high time! The barbarian is coming, he's on his way, to trample underfoot the fruits of a thousand years of human endeavour. . . . He's on his way, driven by greed . . .

YAKOV. . . . and his soul is in his belly, in his hungry belly – and there's a thought to drive a man to drink. (*He pours more beer.*)

NIKOLAI. [The crowd is coming,] driven by greed . . . and 'organized' only by virtue of one desire – to grab and guzzle everything in sight!

TATIANA [(*thoughtfully*). The crowd . . . everywhere you go there are crowds . . . in theatres . . . churches . . . crowds of people. . . . But, I don't know, that's not quite right.

NIKOLAI. It is quite right.] What do these people contribute? Nothing but destruction! And please note that the destruction will be more appalling in this country than anywhere else.

TATIANA. It's always so odd to hear the workers spoken of as 'leading' something – it's not how I see them at all.

NIKOLAI. But you, Mr Sintsov – you, of course, don't agree with us?

SINTSOV (*calmly*). No.

NADYA (*quickly, quietly*). Aunt Tanya, remember how the old man talked about the 'copper copeck'? It's so simple.

NIKOLAI. And why do you not agree, Mr Sintsov?

SINTSOV. I have a different way of thinking.

NIKOLAI. A well-reasoned answer. But perhaps you'd deign to share your views with us?

SINTSOV. I'd rather not.

NIKOLAI. I'm extremely sorry. I shall console myself with the hope that next time we meet your attitude will have changed. Yakov Ivanich, may I ask you to be kind enough to see me to the house? My nerves are on edge . . .

YAKOV (*rises with difficulty*). Certainly, certainly . . .

> YAKOV *and* NIKOLAI *go out.*

TATIANA. The prosecutor's a repulsive character. I hate agreeing with him.

NADYA (*standing up*). Why agree with him, then?

SINTSOV (*laughing*). Yes, Tatiana Pavlovna, why indeed?

TATIANA. I feel the same way myself.

NADYA (*walking about*). He was rude to me earlier. He didn't bother to apologize. (*Exits.*)

SINTSOV (*to* TATIANA). You may *think* as he does, but you don't *feel* the same way. You want to understand, but not him – he feels no need to.

TATIANA. For some reason I feel sorry for him. He's probably a very cruel man.

SINTSOV. He is. He's in charge of all the political cases in the town. The way he treats the prisoners is disgusting.

TATIANA. I ought to tell you – he wrote something in his note-book about you.

SINTSOV (*smiling*). Very likely. He has long talks with Pologgy . . . Indeed, he works very hard at it. Tatiana Pavlovna – I've a favour to ask of you.

TATIANA. I'd be delighted to do anything I can, believe me.

SINTSOV. Thank you. I expect the troops have been sent for . . . ?

TATIANA. They have.

SINTSOV. They were bound to be. That means a search. Could you help me to hide something?

TATIANA. Do you think your house will be searched?

SINTSOV. Bound to be.

TATIANA. Might they arrest you?

SINTSOV. I doubt it. Why would they? For making speeches? Zakhar Ivanich knows that all my speeches tell the workers to keep calm.

TATIANA. And there's nothing against you in your past?

SINTSOV. I don't have a past. Well? Will you help me? I wouldn't have bothered you, only I'm afraid all the people who might have hidden these things are likely to have their own places searched tomorrow. Passions were running so high today that a lot of people made public speeches. (*He laughs softly.*)

TATIANA (*embarrassed*). I'll be frank. My position in this household doesn't allow me to treat my room as my own . . .

SINTSOV. So you can't. Ah, well . . .

TATIANA. Don't be angry with me.

SINTSOV. Oh, I'm not. It's quite understandable.

TATIANA. Wait, though. I'll have a word with Nadya.

> TATIANA *goes off.* SINTSOV *drums on the table with his fingers, looks after her. Cautious footsteps are heard.*

SINTSOV (*softly*). Who's that?

GREKOV. Me. Are you alone?

SINTSOV. Yes. But there's people about. How are things now?

GREKOV (*with a smile*). Nasty. Really nasty. You know they promised to find out who fired the shot. They've got an investigation going now. Some of them are shouting, 'It was the socialists killed him!' – same old dirty song.

SINTSOV. Do you know who it was?

GREKOV. Yakimov.

SINTSOV. Never! Ha – I didn't expect that! He's so quiet and sensible. . . . How strange!

GREKOV. He's got a temper. Now he's set on owning up. Got a wife and child, and another on the way. I've just been talking to Levshin – he's got some fantasy about replacing Yakimov with someone less important.

SINTSOV. He's a queer old bird! But it is sad. And depressing. (*Pause.*) Look, Alyosha, you'll have to bury that stuff. There's nowhere to hide it.

GREKOV. I've found somewhere. The telegraphist – he'll take it . . . Matvey Nikolaich, you ought to get away from here.

SINTSOV. No. I'm not leaving.

GREKOV. You'll be arrested.

SINTSOV. So what? If I went away now it would make a poor impression on the men. No, it's better to . . .

GREKOV. That's true. But I'm sorry about it.

SINTSOV. Yakimov's the one to feel sorry for.

GREKOV. Yes. And there's nothing to be done. He wants to give himself up. Well – goodbye. Funny to see you guarding the bosses' property.

SINTSOV (*smiling*). What can you do? [My platoon all seem to have gone to sleep.

GREKOV. No they haven't. They're round and about, in little groups. Discussing things. It's a lovely night. Well, goodbye for now.]

SINTSOV. I'd like to come too, but I'd better hang on here . . . You're sure to be arrested too, you know.

GREKOV. We'll be inside together then. I'm off.

GREKOV *exits.*

SINTSOV. Goodbye. (TATIANA *enters.*) Don't worry, Tatiana Pavlovna. It's all been fixed up now. Goodbye.

TATIANA. I really feel very bad about it . . .

SINTSOV (*briskly*). Goodnight.

SINTSOV *exits.* TATIANA *walks softly up and down.* YAKOV *enters.*

YAKOV. Why don't you go to bed?

TATIANA. I don't want to. I think I shall go away from here.

YAKOV. Yes. As for me, there's nowhere I can go. I've already gone round every continent and every island.

TATIANA. This place is oppressive. Everything's crumbling, it makes my head spin in the strangest way. One has to tell lies, and I don't like doing that.

YAKOV. Hm. No, you don't like doing that . . . unfortunately for me . . . unfortunately . . .

TATIANA (*to herself*). But I've just told a lie – I said I'd talk to Nadya about hiding something – she'd have agreed, too. But I've no right to start her on that road . . . those people do sometimes take liberties . . .

YAKOV. What are you talking about?

TATIANA. What? Oh – Sintsov. It's all so strange. Not long ago life was so clear and simple, one could see what one wanted . . .

YAKOV (*softly*). Talented drunks, handsome idlers, and other such specialists in gaiety, have ceased to command attention, alas! As long as we stood aside from the dreary hustle and bustle, we were admired. But the hustle and bustle is getting more and more dramatic. 'Hey, you comedians, you clowns – get off the stage!' they're shouting. But the stage is *your* element, Tanya.

TATIANA. My element? I did once think that on the stage my feet were planted in solid ground . . . that I might grow tall. . . . (*Emphatically, with distress.*) But now it's all so painful – I feel uncomfortable up there in front of those people, with their cold eyes saying, Oh, we know all that, it's old, it's boring! I feel weak and defenceless in front of them, I can't capture them, I can't excite them . . . I long to tremble in front of them with fear, with joy, to speak words full of fire and passion and anger, words that cut like knives, that burn like torches . . . I want to throw armfuls of words, throw them bounteously, abundantly, terrifyingly . . . so that people are set alight by them and, shout aloud, and turn to flee from them. . . . And then I'll stop them. Toss them different words. Words beautiful as flowers. Words full of hope, and joy, and love. And they'll all be weeping, and I'll weep too ... wonderful tears. They applaud. Smother me with flowers. Bear me up on their shoulders. For a moment – I hold sway over them all. ... Life is there, in that one moment, all of life, in a single moment.

YAKOV. Yes, I know. Living in moments is all we're capable of.

TATIANA. Everything that's best is always in a single moment. How I long for people to be different – more responsive, less careful – and for life to be different, not all hustle and bustle, a life in which art is needed, always, by everybody, all the time! So I could stop feeling ... totally superfluous ...

YAKOV *is staring into the darkness, his eyes open wide.*

What's wrong with you? Why do you drink so much? It's killing you. You used to be so beautiful, you had an inner beauty ...

YAKOV. Stop it.

TATIANA. Do you realize how my heart aches?

YAKOV (*with horror*). However drunk I am, I understand it all ... that's the terrible part. My brain's so damned persistent, it goes on working and working, every moment of the day. And always I can see this face, this broad, unwashed face, staring at me with enormous eyes which ask ... 'Well?' Do you understand? Just one word ... 'Well?'

PAULINA (*running on*). Tanya, Tanya, you go, please ... It's Kleopatra, she's gone crazy, she's insulting everyone ... You might be able to calm her down. I can't.

TATIANA (*wearily*). Leave me out of your squabbles, can't you? Get on and tear each other to pieces, and stop dashing about trampling on other people!

PAULINA (*alarmed*). Tanya! What do you mean? What's wrong with you?

TATIANA. I don't understand you. What is it you want, all of you, what's eating you?

PAULINA. Do go and see her, Tanya. ... Oh. Look. She's coming.

ZAKHAR (*off*). I'm asking you, will you please be quiet.

KLEOPATRA (*off*). It's you, you're the one to keep quiet!

PAULINA. She's going to come shouting out here, with all the men about. . . . Oh, this is awful . . . Tanya, please!

ZAKHAR *enters, with* KLEOPATRA *close behind him.*

ZAKHAR. For pity's sake – I shall go out of my mind!

KLEOPATRA. Don't try to run away from me. You're going to listen, I'll make you. . . . There you've been, currying favour with the workers, you just had to have their respect, didn't you? So you throw them a man's life as if you were throwing offal to a pack of ravenous dogs! You're humanitarians at other people's expense – on someone else's blood!

ZAKHAR. What's she talking about, for God's sake?

KLEOPATRA. The truth!

YAKOV (*to* TATIANA). I don't much care for this.

YAKOV *exits.*

PAULINA. Madam, we're decent, respectable people, and we will not allow ourselves to be shouted at by a woman with your reputation . . .

ZAKHAR (*alarmed*). Be quiet, Paulina, for God's sake!

KLEOPATRA. What's decent about you? Decent because you chatter about politics? And about the sufferings of the people? And about progress and humanitarianism? Is that it?

TATIANA. Kleopatra Petrovna, that's enough!

KLEOPATRA. I'm not talking to you! You don't belong here. It's none of your business. My husband was an honest man . . . straightforward and honest. He knew the people better than you ever will. But he didn't babble about them the way you do. And you, with your idiotic ideas, betrayed him. Killed him.

TATIANA (*to* PAULINA *and* ZAKHAR). Why don't you go?

KLEOPATRA. I'm going myself. You're loathsome to me . . . loathsome, all of you!

KLEOPATRA *exits.*

ZAKHAR. Did you ever see such a crazy female?

PAULINA (*crying*). We must give up the whole thing . . . we must go away! Insulting people like that . . . !

ZAKHAR. But why is she behaving like this? If she'd loved her husband, lived in peace with him . . . but she changes lovers twice a year. . . . And now, all this screaming . . .

PAULINA. We'll have to sell the factory!

ZAKHAR (*with distaste*). Give up? Sell? That's no way to talk, that's not it. No. We must think it out. Think the whole thing out. I've just been talking to Nikolai Vassilich – that female came rushing in and interrupted us.

PAULINA. He hates us, Nikolai Vassilich. He's full of malice.

ZAKHAR (*growing calmer*). He's embittered, and he's had a terrible shock. But he's a clever man. He's got no reason to hate us. And now, with Mikhail gone, there are so many practical considerations to bind us together. So many.

PAULINA. I don't trust him. I'm afraid of him. He'll cheat you.

ZAKHAR. Oh, Paulina, that's nonsense, you know. He has very sound judgement. He says that every hill commands a strictly limited horizon. Hm – yes. That's quite true, you know. And that if I try to see more than is physically possible from my hill, I'm bound to fall, and look ridiculous. And there's some truth in that, too. The fact is I've chosen a rather shaky position in my relationship with the workers, I have to admit that. This evening, when I was talking to them. . . . Oh, Paulina, they're so hostile, these people, they look at everything so – so suspiciously!

PAULINA. I told you. They're always enemies.

> TATIANA *laughs quietly and walks away,* PAULINA *looks after her, and continues deliberately in a louder voice.*

They're all enemies, all of them full of envy, that's why they attack us!

> ZAKHAR *paces quickly up and down.*

ZAKHAR. Well, yes, that's partly true, certainly. Nikolai Vassilich says it's not a class struggle but a race struggle – the white and the black. That's a crude way of putting it, certainly, it's stretching a point. . . . But . . . when you come to think of it . . . it's *us*, the people of culture, who created the sciences and the arts and so on and so forth. . . . Hm . . . equality . . . physiological equality . . . hm, well, maybe. . . . But first of all, become human, acquire some culture . . . then perhaps we can talk about equality.

PAULINA (*listening attentively*). I don't entirely understand what you're saying. You haven't spoken like that before.

ZAKHAR. It's all very sketchy, not thought out. But it's the way my ideas seem to be heading. There's something in it. One must understand oneself, that's the thing.

PAULINA (*taking his arm*). You're too gentle, my friend! That's why it's all so hard for you.

ZAKHAR. We know so little, so we often get a surprise. Sintsov, for instance – he surprised me. I'd got to like him for his simplicity, his clear logic. Now it turns out he's a socialist – that's where he gets his simplicity and his logic from!

PAULINA. Yes, he's very noticeable – such an unpleasant face! My dear, you ought to get some rest. Come along.

ZAKHAR (*following her*). And there's another worker. Grekov. Thinks the world of himself. Nikolai Vassilich and I were talking about his speech just now. . . . Only a boy, but the way he talked . . . such arrogance . . . !

> They exit. Voices are heard singing in the distance. Then, approaching, hushed voices. YAGODIN, LEVSHIN and RYABTSOV, a young boy, enter. RYABTSOV keeps shaking his head. He has a round, amiable face. The three of them stop under the trees.

LEVSHIN (*softly, mysteriously*). It's all to do with the business of being a comrade, Pashok.

RYABTSOV. I know.

LEVSHIN. It's a common, human business, this, every man's business. Every good man is valuable now, brother. Folk are raising their heads, opening their minds, they're listening, reading, thinking. And any one who's understood something, is valuable.

YAGODIN. It's true, Pashok.

RYABTSOV. I know. Why all the fuss? I'll go.

LEVSHIN. Ay. But you mustn't do anything without knowing what it means. Without understanding. [You're young. This'll mean hard labour for you . . .

RYABTSOV. I'll run away.

YAGODIN. Mebbe it won't be hard labour. You're not of an age for hard labour, Pashok.

LEVSHIN. We'll think on't as hard labour. In this sort of business, it's best to expect worst. If a lad's not afraid of hard labour, you know his mind's made up.]

RYABTSOV. My mind is made up, Efimich.

YAGODIN. Don't hurry it. Think it over.

RYABTSOV. What's to think over? There's been a killing. Some-one has to pay for it.

LEVSHIN. That's it. Someone has to. We play fair – one of theirs has gone down, we'll pay with one of ours. For if one doesn't go, they'll get after several, they'll get after the best, and our cause will pay dearer, Pashok, than it'll pay with you.

RYABTSOV. [I'm not arguing, am I? I may be young, but I under-stand well enough. We've got to hold fast to one another, like a chain.

LEVSHIN (sighs). That's it. Without that, we're alone.

YAGODIN (smiling). We'll make a chain, surround them, pull tight, and that's it.]

RYABTSOV. Fine. I've been through all that. I'm single, so I should be the one to go. Only, it does make me sick to have to pay for *that* blood.

LEVSHIN. It's for our comrades, brother, not for the blood.

RYABTSOV. I mean, such rotten blood. He was a vicious man.

LEVSHIN. It's the vicious has to be killed. The good ones are no hindrance, they'll die of themselves.

RYABTSOV. [Is that all, then?

YAGODIN. That's all, Pashok. So you'll tell them tomorrow morning?

RYABTSOV. Why put it off? I'll tell them now.

LEVSHIN. No. Tomorrow's better. Night's a kind counsellor.

RYABTSOV. All right.] I'll go now then, shall I?

LEVSHIN. God be with you.

YAGODIN. Go on then, brother, Walk bold.

> RYABTSOV *goes off without hurrying.* YAGODIN *twirls a stick in his hand, staring at it intently.* LEVSHIN *gazes up at the sky.*

LEVSHIN (*quietly*). There's some fine young folk growing up now, Timofey.

YAGODIN. Good weather, good crops.

LEVSHIN. If it goes on like this, we'll make it yet.

YAGODIN (*sadly*). Pity for the lad.

LEVSHIN. Ay, pity it is. I feel it. He's a good dear soul, and there he's away to prison, and over a bad business at that. There's the one comfort for him, though – it's all done for his comrades.

YAGODIN. Ay. Pity, though.

LEVSHIN. Leave off, will you? [Ah, but why did Yakimov have to go and pull that trigger? Where does a killing get you? Nowhere at all. You kill one cur, the owner buys another, that's all about it.

YAGODIN (*sadly*). So many brothers going down.]

LEVSHIN [Come on, sentry. We're supposed to be guarding the boss's goods and chattels.] (*They start off.*) Ah, dear Lord!

YAGODIN. What?

LEVSHIN. It's a mess. Why can't we hurry up and get things straight!

CURTAIN

Act Three

A large room in the Bardin's house.* In the rear wall are four windows and a door, leading on to the verandah. Through the windows can be seen SOLDIERS, POLICEMEN *and a* GROUP OF WORKERS, *among them* LEVSHIN *and* GREKOV. *The room does not look lived in: the furniture is sparse, old and of different styles; the wallpaper is peeling. A large table is placed along the right-hand wall.* KON *is angrily moving chairs about, placing them around the table.* AGRAFENA *is sweeping the floor. To the right and the left are large double doors.*

AGRAFENA. There's no call to be angry with me.

KON. I'm not angry. They can all go to hell. I'll be dead soon, thank God. My heart's on the blink already.

AGRAFENA. Everybody's going to be dead. It's nought to be proud about.

KON. It's enough. Everything's gone to rot. At sixty-five, dirty tricks are like nuts: I've not got the teeth for them. . . . They've picked up all those people: now they leave them to soak in the rain.

Enter, through the door on the left, BOBOYEDOV *and* NIKOLAI.

BOBOYEDOV (*cheerfully*). Aha, so this is the courtroom! Beautiful! Well, then, here you are engaged in the execution of your official duties, eh?

NIKOLAI. Yes, yes. Kon, call the corporal.

BOBOYEDOV. We'll serve up our dish like this: in the middle, that – what's his name?

NIKOLAI. Sintsov.

---

* In the RSC production this set was a disused billiard room.

BOBOYEDOV. Sintsov. Very touching! And round Sintsov, the workers of the world, eh? That's it! Ah, it warms your heart! ... The owner, here, now, he's a nice man, really nice. Not so well thought of by our people, though. No. I know his sister-in-law, she played in Voronezh – a superb actress, I must say, superb.

KVACH *comes in from the terrace.*

Well, Kvach?

KVACH. They've all been searched, sir.

BOBOYEDOV. They have? Well?

KVACH. Some cases positive, sir, some cases negative: evidence hidden. Wish to report, sir: District Police Inspector in a great hurry, sir, works carelessly.

BOBOYEDOV. Of course! They're always like that. Anything in the prisoners' rooms?

KVACH. Evidence hidden behind ikons belonging to prisoner Levshin, sir.

BOBOYEDOV. Well, take it all to my room.

KVACH. Yes, sir. [The young recruit, sir, recent transfer ...

BOBOYEDOV. What about him?

KVACH. Also careless in his work.

BOBOYEDOV. Oh, deal with him yourself, man! Go on!]

Exit KVACH.

You know, he's quite a sharp one, that Kvach. Doesn't look up to much, in fact he looks a fool, but he's got a nose on him like a dog!

NIKOLAI. You ought to do something with that clerk ...

BOBOYEDOV. Oh, certainly, certainly. We'll squeeze him dry.

NIKOLAI. No, I mean Pologgy, not Sintsov. I feel we could use him.

BOBOYEDOV. Oh yes, that one, the one we were talking to. Yes, yes, we'll bring him into it.

NIKOLAI *goes over to the table and carefully lays out some papers.* KLEOPATRA *appears in the doorway, right.*

KLEOPATRA (*from the doorway*). Captain – would you care for some more tea?

BOBOYEDOV. Thank you, thank you, I'd love some! [It's beautiful here, really. A lovely place. By the way, I know Madam Lugovaya, you know! Yes indeed! Didn't she play in Voronezh?

KLEOPATRA. Possibly ...] Well, how did your search go? Did you find anything?

BOBOYEDOV (*amiably*). Oh, we found everything, everything! We find things, all right, don't you worry. Even when there's nothing there, we find something.

KLEOPATRA. [I'm very glad. Very. My late husband took all these leaflets much too lightly, he said that paper never made a revolution.

BOBOYEDOV. Hm. Not quite correct, that, you know.

KLEOPATRA. ... and he used to call those leaflets, 'instructions to fools issued by the central committee of lunatics.'

BOBOYEDOV (*laughing*). Oh yes, very nicely put, but not quite correct either, I'm afraid.]

KLEOPATRA. But now they've moved on ... from words to violence.

BOBOYEDOV. Rest assured they'll be receiving a most severe penalty. Most severe.

KLEOPATRA. That's a great comfort to me. Your being here, Captain, made me feel easier at once. ... More free, somehow.

BOBOYEDOV. It's our duty to keep society in good heart.

KLEOPATRA. And it's so refreshing to meet someone who's contented and healthy. They're such a rarity.

BOBOYEDOV. Oh, we in the Security Corps, you know, we're all hand-picked men!

KLEOPATRA. Shall we go to the dining-room?

BOBOYEDOV (*as they leave*). With pleasure. Tell me, where is Madam Lugovaya going to be playing this season . . . ?

KLEOPATRA (*dismissively*). I've really no idea.

> *They exit.*
> *After a moment,* TATIANA *and* NADYA *enter from the verandah.*

NADYA. Did you notice the look old Levshin gave us?

TATIANA. I noticed.

NADYA. It's all so beastly. And – shameful. Nikolai Vassilich – *why*? What have they been arrested *for*?

NIKOLAI (*coldly*). Don't worry, there are quite sufficient grounds for their arrest. And I must ask you not to use the verandah while there are . . . those . . .

NADYA. We won't, we won't.

TATIANA (*looking at* NIKOLAI). Has Sintsov been arrested too?

NIKOLAI. Mister Sintsov is under arrest, yes.

NADYA (*walking about*). Seventeen people! And over by the gate there's their wives, crying. . . . The soldiers push them about, and laugh at them – can't you tell them to behave decently?

NIKOLAI. They're nothing to do with me. Lieutenant Strepetov's in charge of them.

NADYA. I shall go and ask him myself.

> NADYA *exits through the door on the right.* TATIANA, *smiling, walks over to the table.*

TATIANA. Listen, you [sarcophagus] (tombstone) of the Law, as the General calls you . . .

NIKOLAI. The General is not a strikingly witty man. I wouldn't repeat his little jokes, if I were you.

TATIANA. [No, I got it wrong. The Law's tombstone, that's what he calls you. Does that annoy you?

NIKOLAI. I'm in no mood for jokes at the moment.]

TATIANA. Are you really such a serious man?

NIKOLAI. May I remind you that my brother was killed yesterday?

TATIANA. What's that to you?

NIKOLAI. I beg your pardon?

TATIANA. Come on, don't pretend. You don't have any real
feelings about your brother. [Give me your arm – there – now
let's walk . . . like this. No, you've no real feelings for anybody,
no more than I have. Death – or, rather, the suddenness of
death, has a bad effect on everybody, but I can assure you
that not for a single moment did you feel for your brother with
a true, human feeling . . . You just don't have it.] (You don't
have any real feelings for anyone – no more than I have.)

NIKOLAI (strained). That's all very interesting. What do you
want from me?

TATIANA. Haven't you noticed that you and I are kindred spirits?
No? You should have done! I'm an actress, a cold person,
wanting only one thing – a good role to play. You also want to
play a good role, and like me you're a heartless, soulless
creature. Tell me – wouldn't you like to be public prosecutor,
instead of just assistant prosecutor?

NIKOLAI (softly). What I would like – is for you to stop this . . .

TATIANA (after a moment's silence, laughing). No. I'm hopeless at
diplomacy. I came to you with the intention . . . I was determined to be nice to you, to be utterly enchanting. . . . But as
soon as I saw you I started to be rude. You always make me
want to – shower you with insults, whether you're walking,
sitting, talking or – silently condemning people. But . . . I
wanted to ask you . . .

NIKOLAI (smiling). I can guess.

TATIANA. Perhaps you can. But now it's no use, is that it?

NIKOLAI. Now, or earlier. It would make no difference. Mister
Sintsov is very deeply compromised.

TATIANA. You rather enjoyed telling me that, didn't you?

NIKOLAI. I won't deny . . .

TATIANA (with a sigh). There you are – you see how alike we are?

I'm petty and vicious myself. Tell me – is Sintsov completely
in your hands – I mean, actually in *yours*?

NIKOLAI. Of course.

TATIANA. And if I ask you to release him . . . ?

NIKOLAI. It will have no effect.

TATIANA. Even if I beg you?

NIKOLAI. It would make no difference. . . . I'm amazed at you.

TATIANA. Really? Why?

NIKOLAI. You're a beautiful woman – certainly an original one.
Clearly you have a lot of character. [You've had every opportunity to arrange your life elegantly – sumptuously, even] and
yet you go and get yourself involved with this nonentity. . . .
Eccentricity is a disease. Any civilized person must be shocked
by your behaviour. Nobody who admires women, who loves
beauty, could forgive that kind of escapade.

TATIANA (*looking at him with interest*). So I'm condemned? Alas!
Is Sintsov, too?

NIKOLAI. That gentleman will go to prison this evening.

TATIANA. Is that settled?

NIKOLAI. Yes.

TATIANA. Not even a concession in the name of gallantry? I can't
believe it! If I wanted it – wanted it badly enough – you'd
release Sintsov.

NIKOLAI (*thickly*). Try – try wanting it badly. Try.

TATIANA. I can't. I can't bring myself to. Still, tell me the truth –
it wouldn't hurt just for once – if I did, would you release
him?

NIKOLAI (*after a moment*). I don't know.

TATIANA. I do. (*She's silent for a moment; then sighs.*) What
swine we are, the pair of us.

NIKOLAI. You know, there are some things that even a woman
can't do with impunity.

TATIANA. Oh, rubbish! We're alone, nobody can hear us. Surely
I'm entitled to say to you, and to myself, that we're both . . .

NIKOLAI. Please! I won't listen to any more!

ACT THREE 499

TATIANA (*with calm insistence*). All the same, it seems you value those principles of yours less highly than a woman's kiss.

NIKOLAI. I've already told you I won't listen to you.

TATIANA. Go away then. I'm not keeping you, am I?

He walks out quickly. TATIANA *wraps her shawl about her, stands in the middle of the room and looks out on to the verandah.* [*Enter through door on right* NADYA *and the* LIEUTENANT.

LIEUTENANT. A soldier would never hurt a woman. Never. I give you my word on that. A woman to him is – something sacred!

NADYA. Come and see for yourself.

LIEUTENANT. It's quite impossible. The army is the last bastion of chivalry towards women . . .

They exit again quickly through the door on the left.] *Enter* PAULINA, ZAKHAR *and* YAKOV

ZAKHAR. You see, Yakov . . .

PAULINA. But, think now, how else would you have handled it?

ZAKHAR. It's a question of facing facts . . . necessities.

TATIANA. What is?

YAKOV. They've got my head over a block.

PAULINA. All this extraordinary cruelty! Everyone's attacking us – even Yakov Ivanich, who's always so gentle. . . . We didn't send for the troops, did we? And certainly nobody invited the Security Corps – they always turn up of their own accord.

ZAKHAR. Blaming me for these arrests . . .

YAKOV. I'm not blaming . . .

ZAKHAR. You don't come straight out with it, but I can sense it.

YAKOV [(*to* TATIANA). There was I, just . . . sitting, and up he comes and says, 'Well, brother?' and I say, 'Foul, brother!' And that was all.

ZAKHAR. But you've got to understand that it's impossible, it just couldn't be allowed anywhere, to have the sort of socialist propaganda we've been getting here.

PAULINA. Take an interest in politics, certainly everyone should, but what's socialism got to do with that? That's what Zakhar says, and he's right.

YAKOV (*sullenly*). What kind of a socialist is old Levshin? He's just worked himself to a standstill, and now he's delirious with exhaustion.

ZAKHAR. They're all delirious!

PAULINA. You must have pity on us, my friends, we're absolutely worn out.

ZAKHAR. Do you think I enjoy having my house turned into a law court? But it was all Nikolai Vassilich's doing – how could I argue with him, after such a tragedy?]

KLEOPATRA (*entering quickly*). Have you heard? The murderer's been found, they're going to bring him in here.

YAKOV (*muttering*). Here we go . . .

TATIANA. Who is it?

KLEOPATRA. Some *boy*. I'm glad – it may be wrong of me from an humanitarian point of view, but I'm glad! And since he's only a boy, I'd have him whipped every day until the trial. (YAKOV, *grimacing, exits left*.) Where's Nikolai Vassilich? Have you seen him?

> *She goes towards the door, right, [as the* GENERAL *enters through it]. Laughter, and the tinkling of glasses, can be heard while the door is open.*

GENERAL [(*gloomily*). So there you are. All standing round like a bunch of wet hens.

ZAKHAR. It's a disagreeable situation, uncle.

GENERAL. What? All these security fellers? Yes. Can't trust 'em like real soldiers. That Captain's a thorough oaf. I'd like to play a trick or two on him – are they staying the night?

PAULINA. I don't suppose so – why?

GENERAL. Pity. We could have dumped a bucket of cold water over him when he goes to bed. I had them doing that with chicken-livered cadets in my academy days. Awfully funny, y'know, watching some naked feller leaping around and yelling, dripping wet!

KLEOPATRA (*from the doorway*). God knows what you're saying, General. Or why. That Captain's an excellent man, amazingly efficient. He rounded them all up almost as soon as he arrived. I think that deserves some appreciation.]

KLEOPATRA *exits*.

GENERAL. [Hm. In her book, any feller with long whiskers is 'an excellent man'. Everybody needs to know his own place, that's the point. Decency lies precisely in that. (*He goes towards the door on left.*) Each person keeping firmly in his own place. (*Shouts through door.*) Hey, Kon! It's you I'm after! There's a hole in the tent! (*Exits*)].

PAULINA (*quietly*). She really feels she's mistress here. Look how she behaves! Ill-bred, rude . . .

ZAKHAR. The sooner all this is over the better. How one longs for peace and quiet – a normal life!

NADYA (*running in*). Aunt Tanya, he's just a fool, that Lieutenant! I'm sure he beats the soldiers, too. He shouts, and makes fierce faces . . . Uncle, those wives *must* be allowed in to see the prisoners. Five of those men are married. Go on, please, tell that Captain, he seems to be in charge of everything.

ZAKHAR. [Look, Nadya . . .

NADYA. I'm looking, and you're not moving! Go on, please, go and tell him! They're *crying* out there! Oh, do *go*!]

ZAKHAR (*going out*). I don't think it'll do any good.

PAULINA. Nadya, you're always making trouble for everybody.

NADYA. It's you who's always making trouble.

PAULINA. We? What are you saying?

NADYA (*excited*). All of us – you, and me, and Uncle Zakhar – we make trouble for everybody. We don't *do* anything, but it's *because* of us . . . the soldiers . . . the police . . . the Security people . . . everything! And these arrests, too . . . and the women crying. . . . It's all because of *us*!

TATIANA. Nadya, come over here.

NADYA (*going up to* TATIANA). Well, here I am. What is it?

TATIANA. Sit by me and calm down. You don't understand any of it. There isn't anything you can do.

NADYA. And there isn't anything you can say. I don't want to calm down. I don't want to.

PAULINA. Your poor mother was right about you – you have an impossible character.

NADYA. Yes, she was right. *And* she worked, *and* she ate her own bread. But you – what do you do? Whose bread do you eat?

PAULINA. There she goes again. Nadiezhda, will you kindly stop talking like that! How dare you shout at your elders!

NADYA. What sort of elders are you? Why do you say 'elders'? You're just old.

PAULINA. These are your ideas, really, Tanya. You should tell her she's just a silly little girl.

TATIANA. Did you hear? You're just a silly little girl.

NADYA. There you are. That's all you can say. You can't even defend yourselves. Extraordinary people – there's really no place for you, even here, somehow, in your own home. Unnecessary people!

PAULINA (*severely*). You don't know what you're saying.

NADYA. Your house is full of soldiers, secret police, little fools with whiskers, all throwing their weight about, rattling their sabres, clanking their spurs, drinking tea, bellowing with laughter ... and arresting people, shouting at them, threatening them ... making their women cry. .... And look at you. What are you doing? You've been pushed off into a corner.

PAULINA. Can't you see you're talking nonsense? These people are here to protect us.

NADYA (*with distress*). Oh, Aunt Paulina! Soldiers can't protect anybody from stupidity! How could they!

PAULINA (*indignantly*). Wha-a-at?

NADYA (*stretching her arms towards her*). Oh, don't be angry, please! I mean, everybody!

PAULINA *walks out quickly*.

Now she's run away. She'll go and tell Uncle Zakhar that I'm a rude, obstinate girl . . . and he'll come and make a long speech . . . and all the flies will fall off the walls from boredom.

TATIANA. How are you going to live? That's what I can't see.

NADYA. Not like this – not for anything in the world! I don't know what I'm going to do, but it won't be anything like the things you do. I went past the verandah just now, with that stupid officer. Grekov was standing there, smoking. He looked at me – and his eyes were laughing! Yet he must know he's on his way to prison – Oh, don't you see, people like that who live as they want to aren't afraid of anything! They can afford to laugh! I'm ashamed to look at Levshin and Grekov – I don't know the others, but those two . . . I'll never forget them . . . . Here comes that fat fool with the whiskers. . . . Ooo-oo!

BOBOYEDOV (*entering*). Terrifying! Who are you trying to scare?

NADYA. It's me that's afraid of you. You will let the women through to see their husbands, won't you?

BOBOYEDOV. No, I won't. I'm wicked.

NADYA. Of course. You're in the Security Corps, aren't you? Why won't you?

BOBOYEDOV (*amiably*). It's not possible at the moment. But later on, when the men are being taken away, I'll give permission for them to say goodbye.

NADYA. But *why* is it impossible? It depends on you, doesn't it?

BOBOYEDOV. On me, yes. . . . That is, on the law.

NADYA. What's the law got to do with it? Let them through, please!

BOBOYEDOV. What do you mean, what's the law got to do with it! Are you another one who doesn't acknowledge the law? Tut tut tut!

NADYA. Don't talk to me like that! I'm not a child!

BOBOYEDOV. Are you sure? It's only children and revolutionaries who refuse to acknowledge the law!

NADYA. Well, then, I'm a revolutionary.

BOBOYEDOV. Dear me. Well in that case I'm afraid we'll have to send you to gaol. Arrest you, and straight off to gaol with you!

NADYA (*unhappily*). Oh, do stop joking! Let those poor women through!

BOBOYEDOV. I can't! The law!

NADYA. The law's stupid.

BOBOYEDOV (*seriously*). Hm ... You mustn't say that, you know. If you're not a child, as you say, then you must know that the law is established by the authorities and that the state cannot exist without it.

NADYA (*heatedly*). Law, authority, state ... [Oh, my God. But aren't they all supposed to be for the sake of *people*?

BOBOYEDOV. Hm, well, first and foremost, I think, for the sake of order.

NADYA. Well order's rotten too if it makes people cry. All your authorities and states ... none of it's any good if people cry. The state –] what nonsense! What good is it to me? (*She goes towards the door.*) The state! You don't understand a thing, you just go on talking.

> NADYA *exits.* BOBOYEDOV *is rather at a loss.*

BOBOYEDOV (*to* TATIANA). Quite a character, the young lady! But she's heading in a dangerous direction. Her uncle, I believe, is a man of liberal views, isn't he?

TATIANA. You should know. I don't even know what a liberal is.

BOBOYEDOV. Of course you do! Everybody does! Lack of respect for authority – that's what liberalism is. But I wanted to tell you, Madame Lugovaya, I saw you in Voronezh! I did indeed! I did so appreciate your acting – so subtle, so extraordinarily subtle! Perhaps you noticed me. I always sat next to the vice-governor's seat. I was an adjutant at the time, in the administration.

TATIANA. I don't remember. Perhaps. There are Security officers in every town, aren't there?

BOBOYEDOV. Oh, indeed there are, absolutely, in every town. And let me say, it's we in the provincial administration who are the true connoisseurs of art. [Possibly a few of the merchant class as well. For instance – take a presentation to a favourite actor at his benefit performance, you'll always find the names of all the officers of the local Security Corps on the subscription list.] It is, you might say, quite a tradition with us. . . . Where will you be playing next season?

TATIANA. I haven't decided yet. But of course it will have to be in a town where there are true connoisseurs of art – that can't be avoided, can it?

BOBOYEDOV (*missing the point*). Oh, of course. They're in every town, absolutely. You know, people *are* becoming more cultured . . . little by little.

KVACH (*speaking from the verandah*). Sir! They're bringing him in now, sir. The man who fired. Where do we put him?

BOBOYEDOV. In here. Bring them all in here. And call the assistant prosecutor. (*To* TATIANA.) Will you excuse me? [I must busy myself with a little work now.] (I must call the assistant prosecutor.)

TATIANA. [Will you be interrogating them?

BOBOYEDOV (*amiably*). Just a little, just scratching the surface, making their acquaintance, you know. Call it a quick roll-call!

TATIANA. May I listen?

BOBOYEDOV. Hm . . . Generally speaking it's not allowed – not in political cases. Ah, but this is a criminal case, isn't it? And we're not in a courthouse, are we? I would like to offer you some . . . ah . . . pleasure . . .

TATIANA. I'll be invisible. I'll watch from here.

BOBOYEDOV. Splendid! I'm delighted to be able to make even some small repayment for all the pleasure I've had from watching you on the stage . . . I just have to collect a few papers . . .]

BOBOYEDOV *exits. From the verandah* TWO ELDERLY WORKERS *come in, leading* RYABTSOV. KON *walks alongside,*

staring at his face. Behind them come LEVSHIN, YAGODIN,
GREKOV, *and a few other* WORKERS, *followed by* KVACH *and
some* SECURITY POLICE.

RYABTSOV (*angrily*). Why've you tied my hands? Untie me!

LEVSHIN. Go on, brothers, untie him. No need to insult a person.

YAGODIN. He won't run away.

FIRST WORKER. That's the way it's done. It's the law.

RYABTSOV. I don't want it. Take it off!

SECOND WORKER (*to* KVACH). Can we, sir? He's a quiet lad.
We can't understand . . . how he could have done it.

KVACH. All right. Untie him. It's not important.

KON (*suddenly*). There's no sense arresting that one. When the
shooting was going on, he was out on the river. I saw him. So
did the General. (*To* RYABTSOV.) Why don't you say something, you fool? Tell them it wasn't you! Why don't you? . . .

RYABTSOV (*firmly*). No, it was me.

LEVSHIN. He should know, soldier.

RYABTSOV. It was me.

KON (*shouting*). You're lying, you bastard! . . . (BOBOYEDOV *and*
NIKOLAI *enter.*) You were out on the river in a boat when they
did it. Singing songs, you were! Weren't you, eh?

RYABTSOV (*calmly*). That was after.

BOBOYEDOV. Which is the murderer? This one?

KVACH. Yes, sir.

KON. No he's not.

BOBOYEDOV. What's that? [Kvach, take the old man out. What's
he doing here, anyway?

KVACH. In service with the general, sir.]

NIKOLAI (*looking intently at* RYABTSOV.) Allow me, Bogdan
Denisich . . . [Leave him alone, Kvach!

KON. Keep your hands off me! I'm a soldier myself!

BOBOYEDOV. Wait, Kvach.]

NIKOLAI (*to* RYABSTOV). Was it you who killed my brother?

RYABTSOV. It was.

NIKOLAI. Why?

RYABTSOV. He gave us hell.

NIKOLAI. What's your name?

RYABTSOV. Pavel Ryabtsov.

NIKOLAI. I see. Now, Kon – what was it you were saying?

KON (*excited*). He didn't kill him! He was down on the river when Mr Skrobotov was shot. I'll take my oath on that! [Me and the General both saw him – the General even said, wouldn't it be good sport to upset his boat for him and make him take a bath. It's true!] What's this, then, boy? What are you up to?

NIKOLAI. Kon, what makes you so certain he was on the river at the actual moment of the murder?

KON. *Why, sir, the General and me came back to the house not five minutes after Mr Skrobotov had been shot and we'd just seen this boy sitting in his boat, singing. Anyway, you don't sing if you've just killed someone.

NIKOLAI (*to* RYABTSOV). Do you know that there are severe punishments laid down for anyone who makes false statements, or tries to shield a criminal? Did you know that?

RYABTSOV. That's naught to me.

NIKOLAI. All right. So you killed Mr Skrobotov?

RYABTSOV. Yes.

BOBOYEDOV. [You young animal!]

KON. He's lying.

LEVSHIN. Hey, soldier, it's none of your business, this.

NIKOLAI. What's that?

---

* In the 1906 text this speech of Kon's reads: 'It's two hours' walk from the factory to the place where he was . . .' For the 1933 production Gorky had altered this to: 'You couldn't get from the factory to the spot he was in even in an hour.' But even this reduction fails to make sense of the movements of characters in Act One, in which the General returns from the river, and Mikhail from the factory, only minutes after leaving the stage. In the RSC production it was imagined that the river was just at the bottom of the garden, and the factory gates not far beyond the trees that enclose the garden.

LEVSHIN. I say, the old soldier don't belong here, he's got no business interfering.

NIKOLAI. And do you have 'business interfering'? You're connected with this murder, are you?

LEVSHIN. (*laughing*). Me? I once killed a rabbit with a stick, mister, and it grieved my soul all summer.

NICOLAI. Well then, hold your tongue. (*to* RYABTSOV.) Where's the revolver you used?

RYABTSOV. I threw it in the river.

NIKOLAI. What was it like? Describe it to me.

RYABTSOV (*at a loss*). What was it like? Why, what they're like, you know, an iron thing . . .

KON (*joyfully*). Ah, backside of a bitch, he's never even seen a revolver!

NIKOLAI. What size was it? (*He measures about fourteen inches with his hands.*) This big? Well?

RYABTSOV. Yes. Well – a bit smaller, p'raps.

NIKOLAI. Bogdan Denisich, would you come here a moment?

> NIKOLAI *takes* BOBOYEDOV *to one side and talks in a low voice.*

There's something going on behind all this. That boy must be given some tougher treatment. Let's leave him for the moment.

BOBOYEDOV. But he's confessed! What more do you want?

NIKOLAI (*impressively*). But you and I suspect that this boy is not the real criminal but a substitute, do we not?

> Through the door where TATIANA *stands*, YAKOV *enters, cautiously. He stares in silence, sometimes closing his eyes. Now and again his head drops forward, as if he is dozing, then he jerks it up again and glances round in alarm.*

BOBOYEDOV [(*uncomprehending*). Aha, I see, yes, yes. Fancy that!

NIKOLAI. It's a plot – a collective crime. I'm going to make him pay for this!

BOBOYEDOV. What a villain, eh?]

NIKOLAI. For the moment, have the Corporal take him away, keep him in complete isolation. Complete! [I must go out for a minute –] (I have some further enquiries to make –) Kon! Kindly come with me. Where's the General?

KON. Digging for worms.

NIKOLAI *and* KON *exit.*

BOBOYEDOV. Kvach! Take this one away. And keep a close watch on him, right? Not a soul to speak to him, understand?

KVACH. Very good, sir. Come on, son.

LEVSHIN (*affectionately*). Goodbye, Pashok. Goodbye, friend.

YAGODIN (*grimly*). Goodbye, Pavlukha.

RYABTSOV. Goodbye. Don't worry.

KVACH *leads* RYABTSOV *out.*

BOBOYEDOV (*to* LEVSHIN). Old man – do you know that one?

LEVSHIN. Know him? Course I know him! We work together, don't we?

BOBOYEDOV. What's your name?

LEVSHIN. Efim Efimovich Levshin.

BOBOYEDOV [(*aside to* TATIANA). You just watch this.] (*To* LEVSHIN.) Now, Levshin, you tell me the truth. You're a sensible old man, I'm sure, and you know you must only tell the truth to the authorities, eh?

LEVSHIN. Why lie?

BOBOYEDOV (*with delight*). Splendid. Well then, tell me honestly – what's hidden behind the ikons in your room? Tell me the truth, now.

LEVSHIN (*calmly*). There's nothing there.

BOBOYEDOV. Is that the truth?

LEVSHIN. Ay, it is so.

BOBOYEDOV. Ah, Levshin, you should be ashamed of yourself. [There you are, bald and grey, and lying like a little boy! Now the authorities not only know what you do, they know what you think as well! This is a bad business, Levshin.] What's this I'm holding?

LEVSHIN. Can't quite make out . . . my old eyes are going.

BOBOYEDOV. I'll tell you. These are books, books forbidden by the government because they call on people to rise against the Tsar. They were taken from behind your ikons. Well?

LEVSHIN (*calmly*). So.

BOBOYEDOV. Do you admit that they're yours?

LEVSHIN. Maybe they are. One book looks much like another.

BOBOYEDOV. Then how could you lie like that, an old man like you?

LEVSHIN. I spoke naught but the truth. You asked me what was behind my ikons, and you wouldn't be asking that if everything hadn't been took out. So I knew there was nothing there so I said there's nothing there. Why try to shame an old man? I've not deserved that.

BOBOYEDOV (*at a loss*). So that's it. Well, let's have a bit less of your talk now, It doesn't do to joke with me. Who gave you these books?

LEVSHIN. You don't need to know that. That I'll not tell. I've forgotten. Don't you worry yourself about it.

BOBOYEDOV. Aha. Yes. Right. Alexi Grekov? Which of you is Grekov?

GREKOV. I am.

BOBOYEDOV. Were you the subject of an investigation, in Smolensk, into a case of revolutionary propaganda among the workers? Mm?

GREKOV. I was.

BOBOYEDOV. So young, and yet so gifted? A pleasure to make your acquaintance! All right, take them all out on to the verandah, it's getting stuffy in here. . . . Vyripaev, Yakov? Aha . . . Svistov, Andrey . . . ?

He follows the SECURITY POLICE *and* WORKERS *out on to the verandah, checking their names against the list in his hand.*

YAKOV (*softly*). I like those people.

TATIANA. Yes. But why are they so simple? Why do they speak so simply, look at things so simply ... and suffer? Why? Do they have no passion in them, no heroism?

YAKOV. They have a calm belief in their own truth.

TATIANA. [They must *have* passion. They must *be* heroes. But in here – didn't you feel it? – they just despise everyone!

YAKOV. Old Levshin's a good man. His eyes have such a look of understanding it all – they touch everything, so sadly and gently. He seems to be saying. Why go through all this, why don't you just move aside?]

ZAKHAR (*from the doorway*). They're really quite amazingly stupid, these gentlemen of the law. They've set up their little courtroom here – and Nikolai Vassilich is going around like some kind of conquering hero.

YAKOV. Zakhar, all you object to is that this business is going on in front of your eyes.

ZAKHAR. Of course! They might have spared me the pleasure! [Nadya's worked herself into hysterics. ... She's been thoroughly rude to Paulina and myself, called Kleopatra a shark, and now she's lying on the divan howling her head off. God knows what's going on ...]

YAKOV. But, Zakhar, it's the *significance* of what's happening that seems more and more sickening to me.

ZAKHAR. Yes, I know what you mean. But what can one do? If one is attacked, one must defend oneself ... [I simply can't find a place to put myself in this house, it's as if it had been stood on its roof. ... It's damp today ... and cold ... all that rain! Autumn's come early.]

ZAKHAR *exits.*
Enter NIKOLAI *and* KLEOPATRA. *Both excited.*

NIKOLAI. I'm convinced now that [he was bribed.] (Ryabtsov is shielding someone.)

KLEOPATRA. They couldn't have thought that up for themselves.

(*Calls to the verandah.*) Captain Boboyedov! (*To* NIKOLAI.)
The man to look for is the cleverest one.

NIKOLAI. [You think it was] Sintsov?

KLEOPATRA. Who else? (*Calling.*) Captain Boboyedov!

BOBOYEDOV (*from the verandah*). At your service, Madame.

> NIKOLAI *and* KLEOPATRA *join* BOBOYEDOV *at the veran-
> dah door.*

NIKOLAI. I'm convinced, now, that the boy must have been
bribed ... (I think we should move Sintsov into town for
intensive questioning. I'm sure the socialists are behind all
this ...)

> *He talks quietly to* BOBOYEDOV.

BOBOYEDOV [(*in a low voice*). Oh? Mm ...

KLEOPATRA (*to* BOBOYEDOV). Do you understand?

BOBOYEDOV. Mm, yes ... the cunning devils, eh?]

> *Exit* NIKOLAI *and* BOBOYEDOV *talking excitedly.* KLEO-
> PATRA *glances round, sees* TATIANA.

KLEOPATRA. Ah, you're here, are you?

TATIANA. Has something happened?

KLEOPATRA. I hardly think it matters to you. Have you heard
about Sintsov?

> YAKOV *glances at* TATIANA, *exits quietly.*

TATIANA. I have.

KLEOPATRA (*challengingly*). Yes, he's been arrested! And for my
part I'm glad to see all these weeds being pulled up. Are you?

TATIANA. I hardly think it matters to you.

KLEOPATRA (*gloating*). You liked Sintsov, didn't you?

> *She looks at* TATIANA, *and her face becomes more gentle.*

How strange you're looking ... your face seems ... quite
ravaged. ... Why?

TATIANA. Probably the weather.

KLEOPATRA (*going up to* TATIANA). You know ... this may be stupid of me ... but I'm a very direct person ... I've lived through a lot, felt a lot of emotion – and a lot of bitterness! I know that only a woman can be a friend to another woman ...

TATIANA. Do you want to ask me something?

KLEOPATRA. Tell you something, not ask. I like you. You're so free, and always so well-dressed. And you handle men so well. I envy you – the way you talk, the way you walk. . . . But sometimes I don't like you at all – in fact, I hate you!

TATIANA. That's interesting. Why?

KLEOPATRA (*strangely*). Who are you?

TATIANA. What does that mean?

KLEOPATRA. I don't understand who you are. I like everybody to be well-defined, I like to know what a person's after. I think people who don't know exactly what they want are dangerous, not to be trusted.

TATIANA. What a terrible thing to say! Why should I have to hear your opinions?

KLEOPATRA (*heatedly, and with alarm*). People ought to live close to one another, as friends, so that we could all trust one another! Don't you see? They've started to kill us now, they want to plunder everything we've got! [didn't you notice what terrible faces those men had? – like criminals!] *They* know what they want – they know, all right. And they live like a family of friends, trusting each other ... I hate them, I'm afraid of them. And we – *we* live like enemies, believing in nothing, bound together by nothing, each for himself. . . . Look at us! We depend on soldiers and police and – and Security officers! – to protect us. They depend only on themselves. And yet they're stronger than us.

TATIANA. I want to ask you a question, too. Were you happy with your husband?

KLEOPATRA. Why do you want to know that?

TATIANA. I just do. Curiosity.

KLEOPATRA (*after a pause*). No. He was always too busy. And too handsome . . . You found him attractive, didn't you?

TATIANA. No.

KLEOPATRA. That's odd. It seemed to me all women found him attractive. There's not much joy in that for a wife.

PAULINA (*coming in*). Have you heard? That clerk, Sintsov, turns out to be a socialist! And Zakhar was always so open and frank with him – even wanted to make him assistant book-keeper! I know it's only a small thing, but it just shows how difficult life's becoming. Your sworn enemies are right beside you, and you can't recognize them.

TATIANA. Thank God I'm not rich.

PAULINA. Say that when you're old! (*Gently, to* KLEOPATRA.) Kleopatra Petrovna, they want you to try your frock on again. And the black crêpe has arrived . . .

KLEOPATRA. All right, I'll go. My heart's beating unevenly. . . . How I dislike being ill!

PAULINA. I can give you some drops for the palpitations. They do help.

KLEOPATRA (*leaving*). Thank you.

PAULINA. I'll come in a moment.

    KLEOPATRA *exits.*

One must be gentle with her – it calms her down. It's good that you had a talk with her. I do envy you, Tanya – you always manage to find a comfortable middle position . . . I'll go and give her those drops.

    Left alone TATIANA *looks out on to the verandah, where the* PRISONERS *are waiting under guard.* YAKOV *appears through a door.*

YAKOV (*grinning*). And there was I behind the door, listening.

TATIANA (*absently*). Eavesdropping's supposed not to be nice.

YAKOV. It's a bad thing altogether, listening to what other people

are saying. They just seem pathetic ... and boring. Listen,
Tanya – I'm going.

TATIANA. Where to?

YAKOV (*shrugging*). I don't know. Anywhere. Goodbye. And
forgive me.

TATIANA (*gently*). Yes. Goodbye. Write ...

YAKOV. It's pretty nasty here.

TATIANA. When are you going?

YAKOV (*with a strange smile*). Today. Why don't you go away too?
Mm?

TATIANA. Yes, I will. Why are you smiling?

YAKOV. I just am. ... You know, we may never see each other
again.

TATIANA. Rubbish.

YAKOV. Anyway, I'm sorry. Goodbye.

> TATIANA *kisses him on the forehead. He laughs quietly, pushing
> her away.*

You kissed me as you'd kiss a corpse.

> YAKOV *goes out slowly.* TATIANA *looks after him, makes as if
> to follow, then with a slight gesture, stops.*
> Enter NADYA, *carrying an umbrella.*

NADYA. Come out to the garden with me. Aunt Tanya, please.
I've got such a headache. I've been crying and crying like a
fool. I know I'll start up again if I go out alone.

TATIANA. What is there to cry about, my dear? Nothing.

NADYA. It's all so annoying. I can't understand anything. Who's
right? Uncle Zakhar says he is ... but I'm not sure. *Is* he kind,
Uncle Zakhar? I felt sure he was, but now ... I don't know.
When he's talking to me, I feel that I'm the one who's spiteful
and stupid. ... But afterwards, when I think about him, and
ask myself questions about the whole situation ... I don't
understand a thing.

TATIANA (*sadly*). If you're going to ask yourself questions, you'll end up a revolutionary. And founder in that hurricane, my darling.

NADYA. One must *be* something – one simply must!

TATIANA *laughs quietly.*

Why are you laughing? One simply must. One can't live one's life gaping at everything and not understanding anything.

TATIANA. I laughed because everybody's been saying that today – everybody, all of a sudden. Why?

They start towards the garden. The GENERAL and the LIEUTEN-ANT enter. The LIEUTENANT steps smartly aside to let them pass.

GENERAL. Permanent mobilization has always been necessary in Russia, Lieutenant. It serves a dual purpose – (*To* NADYA *and* TATIANA.) Where are you off to, eh?

TATIANA. For a walk.

GENERAL. If you meet that clerk – what's his name? Lieutenant, what was the name of that clerk feller we were talking to earlier?

LIEUTENANT. Pol - er - Ploddy, General.

GENERAL. Tell him to plod along to see me. I'll be in the dining room, drinking tea with brandy and the lieutenant . . . ho-ho-ho! (NADYA *and* TATIANA *exit on to the verandah.*) Thank you, Lieutenant. You've got a good memory, that's excellent. Every officer must be able to remember the names and faces of every man in his company. A recruit's a sly animal – sly, lazy and stupid. His officer has to get right inside his soul and arrange everything there the way he wants it, so that the animal becomes human, open to reason, and devoted to duty. . .

Enter ZAKHAR, *preoccupied.*

ZAKHAR. You haven't seen Yakov, Uncle, have you?

GENERAL. No, I haven't seen Yakov. Is there some tea going?

ZAKHAR. Yes, yes.

Exit GENERAL *and* LIEUTENANT. KON *enters from the verandah, looking angry and dishevelled.*

Have you seen my brother, Kon?

KON (*severely*). No. I'm finished with telling people things. If I do see a man, I'm not telling a soul about it. I'm done with that. I've said too much in my time . . .

Enter PAULINA.

PAULINA. There's some peasants outside. They're asking if they can postpone paying the rent again.

ZAKHAR. Oh, really! What a time to choose!

PAULINA. They're complaining about the poor harvest. They say they've no money to pay you with.

ZAKHAR. They're always complaining. . . . You didn't meet Yakov, did you?

PAULINA. No. What shall I tell them?

ZAKHAR. The peasants? Tell them to go to the office . . . I'm not going to talk to them.

PAULINA. But there's nobody there. You know perfectly well that the whole place is in chaos today. It's nearly lunchtime, and that Captain's still asking for tea, the samovar hasn't been out of the dining room all morning . . . in fact, it's just like living in a madhouse.

ZAKHAR. You know, Yakov has suddenly decided to take himself off somewhere. These neurotics!

PAULINA. I'm sorry, Zakhar, but honestly it would be better if he left.

ZAKHAR. Yes, of course. He's maddening, always talking nonsense. . . . Just now he was going on at me about my revolver, wanted to go shooting rooks or something. . . . He got quite rude. In the end he just walked off with it. He's always drunk. . .

Enter SINTSOV *from the verandah, with* TWO SOLDIERS *and* KVACH. PAULINA *looks at* SINTSOV *in silence through her lorgnettes, then goes out.* ZAKHAR *adjusts his spectacles in embarrassment, then moves aside.*

[(*Reproachfully.*) Well, Mr Sintsov, this is very sad. I'm extremely sorry for you. Extremely.

SINTSOV (*smiling*). Don't bother yourself. It's not worth it.

ZAKHAR. Indeed it is! People should always sympathize with each other. Even if a man I've trusted hasn't justified that trust, if I see him in adversity it's my duty to sympathize with him. Certainly.] Well – goodbye, Mr Sintsov.

SINTSOV. Goodbye.

ZAKHAR. [You've no complaints you want to make to me?

SINTSOV. Absolutely none.

ZAKHAR (*embarrassed*). Splendid! Well – er – goodbye. Your salary of course will be forwarded to you – Oh yes, certainly . . .] (*He goes towards the door.*) But this is impossible! My house has turned into a police headquarters! (*Exits.*)

SINTSOV *smiles.* KVACH *has been staring at him intently all this time, particularly at his hands.* SINTSOV *notices, and for some seconds stares into* KVACH'S *face.* KVACH *laughs.*

SINTSOV. Well? [What is it?] (What's amusing you?)

KVACH (*joyfully*). Nothing! Nothing!

BOBOYEDOV (*coming in*). Mr Sintsov, you'll be going into town now . . .

KVACH (*joyfully*). Sir, this is not Mr Sintsov! It's something else entirely!

BOBOYEDOV. What? Explain yourself!

KVACH. I know him, sir! He was at the Bryansk works, and his name there was Maxim Markov. We arrested him there two years ago, sir. This gentleman's no clerk, sir, he's just a metal worker, and he's got no nail on his left thumb. I know. He must have escaped from somewhere, if he's living on false papers!

BOBOYEDOV (*pleasantly surprised*). Is this true, Mr Sintsov?

KVACH. It's all true, sir.

BOBOYEDOV. Why don't you say something, eh? Let's see your hand. . . . Is there a nail on the thumb, Kvach?

KVACH. No, of course not!

BOBOYEDOV. What's your correct name, then?

SINTSOV (*calmly*). Whatever you like.

BOBOYEDOV. And so you're not Sintsov! Tut-tut-tut.

SINTSOV. Whoever I am, you're obliged to be civil to me. Remember that, please.

BOBOYEDOV. Oho! I can see from the start we're dealing with a serious character here! Kvach, [take him into town yourself –] (you wait here –) and watch him like a hawk!

KVACH. Sir!

BOBOYEDOV (*cheerfully*). [Well, now, Mr Sintsov, or whatever your name is, you're off to town. Kvach, you report to the chief, tell him everything you know about this character, and ask for the file on the earlier case to be sent for. . . . No, don't, I'll do that myself. Wait here, Kvach . . .]

   BOBOYEDOV *goes out quietly.*

KVACH (*amiably*). Well, we meet again.

SINTSOV (*smiling*). Are you pleased?

KVACH. Course I am. Meeting an old acquaintance . . .

SINTSOV (*with distaste*). It's time you gave up this business, you know. An old dog like you, with grey hairs, still hunting people down – don't you find it humiliating?

KVACH (*amiably*). Course not. I'm used to it. I been in the service twenty-three years. And I'm not a dog, neither. My superiors have a great respect for me. Oh yes. Promised me an order. Cross of St Anne. How about that? I'll get it now, too.

SINTSOV. Because of me?

KVACH. Yes. Because of you. Where did you escape from, then?

SINTSOV. You'll find out.

KVACH. Oh, we will, don't worry! Remember that dark fellow at Bryansk, with glasses? Savitsky? A teacher he was. Well, he

was recaptured too t'other day. Died in prison, though. Very
sick, he was. There's not many of you, is there?

SINTSOV (*thoughtfully*). There will be. Just wait.

KVACH. [Really? That's good. The more politicals there are, the
better for us.

SINTSOV. More ribbons, you mean?]

> *In the doorway appear* BOBOYEDOV, *the* GENERAL, *the*
> LIEUTENANT, KLEOPATRA *and* NIKOLAI.

NIKOLAI (*glancing at* SINTSOV). I had a feeling about him. (*He
leaves again.*)

GENERAL. A fine specimen!

KLEOPATRA. Now it's clear where it all started.

SINTSOV (*with irony*). Listen, Mister Captain of Security, aren't
you handling things rather stupidly?

BOBOYEDOV. Don't you try to teach me!

SINTSOV (*insistently*). Yes, I will teach you! [Put an end to this
ridiculous exhibition.]

GENERAL. Just listen to that!

BOBOYEDOV (*shouting*). Kvach! Take him away!

KVACH. Sir!

> KVACH *leads* SINTSOV *out*.

GENERAL. The man's a wild beast, eh? Did you hear that snarl,
eh?

KLEOPATRA. I'm convinced he's behind it all.

BOBOYEDOV. That's possible, very possible.

LIEUTENANT. He'll be tried, will he?

BOBOYEDOV (*with a laugh*). We eat them just as they come – we
don't need sauce on them!

GENERAL. [Jolly witty, eh? Like oysters, the villains! 'Schlop!!]

> *Enter* KON.

BOBOYEDOV. [Exactly. Now, sir, we'll soon sort the whales from
the minnows, and relieve you of the whole comedy.]

He goes towards the door as POLICE INSPECTOR* *appears on the verandah. He shouts through the door before disappearing through it.*

Nikolai Vassilyevich? [Where are you?] The Inspector's here.

All except KON *follow him through the door. The* POLICE INSPECTOR *comes on from the verandah.*

INSPECTOR (*to* KON). Will the interrogation be in here?
KON (*sullenly*). I don't know. I don't know anything.
INSPECTOR. Table, papers . . . must be here. (*He calls out to the verandah.*) All right, bring them all in here! (*To* KON.) The dead man made a mistake – he said it was a red-haired man who shot him, but in fact he turns out to have dark hair.
KON (*irritably*). Live men make mistakes, too.

The PRISONERS *are brought in again from the verandah.*

INSPECTOR. Let's have them here then, in a row. You – (*To* LEVSHIN.) – you stand at the end. Aren't you ashamed of yourself, you dirty old crook?
GREKOV. Do you have to be insulting?
LEVSHIN. Never mind, Alyosha. Leave him be.
INSPECTOR (*menacing*). I'll teach you to talk!
LEVSHIN. Leave him. That's his job – insulting people.

Enter BOBOYEDOV *and* NIKOLAI, *who seat themselves at the table. The* GENERAL *sits down in an armchair in the corner, with the* LIEUTENANT *behind him. In the doorway are* KLEO-PATRA *and* PAULINA, *with* TATIANA *and* NADYA *behind them. Over their shoulders* ZAKHAR *can be seen watching crossly.* POLOGGY *appears from somewhere at the side, bows*

---

* In the 1905 text a new character called the Police Commissary appeared at this point. In the 1933 text he had been combined with the Police Inspector from the end of Act One, an economy which this version also adopts.

*to the men who are seated, then stops, looking lost, in the middle
of the room. The* GENERAL *beckons to him, and he tiptoes over
and stands beside the* GENERAL's *chair.* RYABTSOV *is brought
in.*

NIKOLAI. All right, then. We'll begin. Pavel Ryabtsov.

RYABTSOV. Well?

BOBOYEDOV. Not *well*, you fool! *Here, your honour!*

NIKOLAI. So you insist you were the one who killed Mr Skrobotov?

RYABTSOV (*irritably*). I said so, didn't I? Why ask again?

NIKOLAI. Do you know Alexi Grekov?

RYABTSOV. How do you mean?

NIKOLAI. That one. Standing next to you.

RYABTSOV. He works with us, yes.

NIKOLAI. In other words, you do know him?

RYABTSOV. I know all of them.

NIKOLAI. Naturally. But you've been in this Grekov's house?
Gone for walks with him? In fact, you know him well, you're
very close, you're close friends?

RYABTSOV. I go for walks with everybody. We're all friends.

NIKOLAI. Are you? I think you're lying. Mr Pologgy, tell us –
what's the relationship between Ryabtsov and Grekov?

POLOGGY. A relationship, sir, of very close friendship. The face
of the matter is, there are two groups here – the younger lot led
by Grekov, a young man of amazing impertinence in his
behaviour to those in superior positions, and the older group,
sir, headed by Efim Levshin, an old fellow, sir, fantastical in
his speech, sir, and foxy in his actions.

NADYA (*quietly*). Oh, the disgusting creature!

POLOGGY *glances round at her and looks at* NIKOLAI
enquiringly. NIKOLAI *also throws a glance in* NADYA's
direction.

NIKOLAI. Well? Go on.

POLOGGY (*with a sigh*). These two groups, sir, are linked by Mr Sintsov, who's on good terms with everybody. This element, sir, is unlike an ordinary man with a normal mind. [He reads books. Various kinds of books. And has his own opinions – about *everything*.] In his residence, which is nearly opposite mine and consists of three separate rooms . . .

NIKOLAI. No need for all the detail.

POLOGGY. Excuse me, sir! Truth demands completeness of form.

NIKOLAI. Of course. But we don't have the time.

POLOGGY. His residence, sir, is frequented most frequently by a certain type of person, including a certain Grekov here present.

NIKOLAI. Is that true, Grekov?

GREKOV (*calmly*). Don't ask me any questions. I shan't answer them.

NIKOLAI. That won't help you.

NADYA (*loudly*). Good, good!

KLEOPATRA. What's this performance for?

ZAKHAR. Nadya, my dear . . .

BOBOYEDOV. Sh-sh-sh!

There is a noise on the verandah.

NIKOLAI. I consider the presence of people who've no business here wholly undesirable.

GENERAL. Hm? Who has no business here?

BOBOYEDOV. Kvach, go and see what that noise is.

KVACH. There's a man trying to force his way in, Sir. Shoving at the door and cursing, sir.

NIKOLAI. What does he want? Who is he?

BOBOYEDOV. Ask him, Kvach.

POLOGGY. Do you wish me to continue, Excellency?

NADYA. Oh, the little swine!

NIKOLAI. No, wait. May I ask everybody with no business here to leave!

GENERAL. Excuse me, but how is one to understand that?

NADYA (*shouting boldly*). You're the ones with no business here, not me! You've no business anywhere! I'm in my own home, and I'm the one who can tell people to leave!

ZAKHAR (*agitated, to* NADYA). That's enough. You'd better go. At once. Go on, leave the room.

NADYA. I see. It's like that, is it? In other words, I'm the real outsider here, am I? All right, I'll go, but let me tell you . . .

PAULINA. Stop her, Zakhar! She'll say something appalling!

NIKOLAI (*to* BOBOYEDOV). Tell your men to close all the doors.

NADYA. You haven't a scrap of conscience between you! You're just heartless, pathetic, miserable creatures!

KVACH re-enters joyfully.

KVACH. Sir! Here's another one shown up!

BOBOYEDOV. What?

KVACH. Another murderer's shown up, sir!

Enter YAKIMOV, *a young red-haired man. He approaches the table.* NIKOLAI *stands up involuntarily.*

NIKOLAI. What do you want?

YAKIMOV. It was me killed the managing director.

NIKOLAI. You?

YAKIMOV. Me.

KLEOPATRA (*quietly*). Aha, you monster! So you've got a conscience, have you?

PAULINA. My God, what terrible people.

TATIANA (*calmly*). They'll win, you know.

YAKIMOV (*grimly*). Well, what next? Here I am. Eat me, then.

General confusion. NIKOLAI *whispers something quickly to the* INSPECTOR. BOBOYEDOV *smiles in bewilderment. The* GROUP OF PRISONERS *is silent, standing motionless. In the doorway* NADYA *is looking at* YAKIMOV *and weeping.* PAULINA *and* ZAKHAR *whisper together. In the silence* TATIANA's *voice can be heard distinctly.*

TATIANA (*to* NADYA). Don't cry. These people are going to win.

NIKOLAI. Well, now, Mr Ryabtsov. Where does this leave you?

RYABTSOV (*at a loss*). Er – don't rightly know.

YAKIMOV. Quiet, Pasha. Say nothing.

LEVSHIN (*joyfully*). Ah, my good brothers!

NIKOLAI (*banging his fist on the table*). Be quiet, will you!

The SOLDIERS *start to close in on the* GROUP OF WORKERS.

YAKIMOV (*calmly*). No need to shout, mister. We're not shouting.

LEVSHIN (*to* YAKIMOV). *Well, go on then, lad. Tell 'em what really happened. Tell 'em how he was poking at you with his gun and* . . .

BOBOYEDOV. *Did you hear what the old liar* . . .

LEVSHIN. *Don't call me a liar, mister.*

BOBOYEDOV. *Throw him out, Corporal.*

LEVSHIN. *There's no throwing. You can't throw us all out. You'll never do that.*

KVACH *closes in on* LEVSHIN. *The* SOLDIERS *start pushing the growling* WORKERS *towards the doors, pulling bags over their heads to silence them.* LEVSHIN *struggles with* KVACH.

GREKOV (*quietly*). No. You can't throw us all out.

LEVSHIN. *There'll be no more of that. No more darkness. No more* . . .*

NADYA (*suddenly, to* YAKIMOV). [Listen! you didn't kill him! It was them! They kill everyone, they kill off everything with their greed and their cowardice . . . (*To the others, as* YAKIMOV

---

* The lines in italics have been adapted from the rewritten ending in the 1933 text. In the RSC production the play ended when this line of Levshin's was cut off by his having a bag pulled over his head by Kvach, followed immediately by the shot, which froze the action. The shot itself is not mentioned in Gorky's stage directions, but it is perfectly well justified by the text.

is pushed back through the door.) It's you – you – you're the criminals!

LEVSHIN (*warmly*). Ay, lass. The killer's not the one who fires bullets, but the one who plants bitterness. True, my dear.]

General struggle and noise. Offstage, a shot. Silence.

CURTAIN